Designing Effective Web Surveys

Designing Effective Web Surveys is a practical guide to designing Web surveys, based on empirical evidence and grounded in scientific research and theory. It is designed to guide survey practitioners in the art and science of developing and deploying successful Web surveys. It is not intended as a "cookbook"; rather it is meant to get the reader to think about why we need to pay attention to design. It is intended for academic, government, and market researchers who design and conduct Web surveys.

Mick P. Couper is a Research Professor in the Survey Research Center, Institute for Social Research, at the University of Michigan, and in the Joint Program in Survey Methodology. He has been engaged in the practice and science of survey research for more than twenty years. He is a leading international expert on the design and implementation of Internet surveys and regularly teaches short courses, consults, and presents findings of research on Web survey design.

Designing Effective Web Surveys

Mick P. Couper

University of Michigan

CAMBRIDGE UNIVERSITY PRESS
Cambridge, New York, Melbourne, Madrid, Cape Town, Singapore, São Paulo, Delhi

Cambridge University Press
32 Avenue of the Americas, New York, NY 10013-2473, USA

www.cambridge.org
Information on this title: www.cambridge.org/9780521717946

First published 2008

Printed in the United States of America

A catalog record for this publication is available from the British Library.

Library of Congress Cataloging in Publication Data

Couper, Mick.
Designing effective Web surveys / Mick P. Couper.
  p. cm.
Includes bibliographical references and index.
ISBN 978-0-521-88945-2 – ISBN 978-0-521-71794-6 (pbk.)
1. Social surveys – Methodology. 2. Internet surveys.
3. Surveys – Methodology – Technological innovations. I. Title.
HM538.C78 2008
300.72′–dc22   2008021409

ISBN 978-0-521-88945-2 hardback
ISBN 978-0-521-71794-6 paperback

For Mary Beth

Contents

Acknowledgments

No man is an island, and no enterprise of this type is completed alone. First and foremost, I am deeply indebted to my colleagues and collaborators on many Web survey design experiments over the past several years: Roger Tourangeau, Fred Conrad, and Reg Baker. This collaboration has been both productive and fun, and I have learned much from them. This book is as much theirs as it is mine. Funding for this research has come from the National Science Foundation and from the National Institutes of Health. Without their financial support, we would know much less about how to design effective Web surveys. This research team has also included a group of very able current and former students at various times, including (in alphabetical, not chronological, order) Scott Crawford, Scott Fricker, Mirta Galesic, Courtney Kennedy, Mark Lamias, Andy Peytchev, Cleo Redline, Ting Yan, and Cong Ye.

I have greatly benefited from the opportunity to collaborate with a number of other researchers implementing Web surveys over the years. Their names can be found in the papers and presentation we have done together. Two groups deserve special mention: (1) Peter Ubel and his colleagues at the Center for Behavioral and Decision Sciences in Medicine (CBDSM) at the University of Michigan and (2) Wolfgang Bandilla, Michael Bosnjak (now at the Free University of Bozen-Bolzano), Lars Kaszmirek, and Wolfgang Neubarth at GESIS-ZUMA in Mannheim, Germany. I have had many fruitful discussions with both groups on a wide variety of design issues. In addition, GESIS-ZUMA has provided generous support over the years in my role as Senior Research Fellow. I also thank Gustav Haraldsen and colleagues at Statistics Norway and Lilli Japec, Lars Lyberg, and colleagues at Statistics Sweden, again for the chance to discuss a range of design issues over several visits. There are many others who shall remain nameless but whose contributions are no less important. It is not my intention to offend by leaving out names – the list would simply be enormous.

Significant feedback and ideas were received from students in many courses on Web survey design, through the Joint Program in Survey Methodology, the SRC Summer Institute, the Centre for Applied Social Surveys, Statistics Sweden, Statistics Norway, York University in Toronto, the Odum Institute at the University of North Carolina at Chapel Hill, Beijing University, the American Association for Public Opinion Research, the Joint Statistical Meetings, the Japanese Market Research Association, and many others. The participants in those courses were truly the guinea pigs for many of the ideas expressed in this book, and I continue to learn from them. The content should look quite familiar to those who have suffered through my long-winded diatribes on arcane design topics without the luxury of flipping through the pages to find the relevant information, as readers of this book can do. The participants asked good questions, provided many examples, challenged me on important issues, and generally tried to keep me honest.

I'm also grateful to those persons and organizations who were willing to share with me their examples of design – both good and bad. Many of these examples have become fodder for my critique, but I have also learned a great deal by seeing real examples of what Web survey designers are doing. Similarly, I appreciate those who've allowed me access to their instrument, in various states of readiness, in exchange for suggestions on design improvements. These include, but are not limited to, the Government Accountability Office, the Defense Manpower Data Center, the U.S. Census Bureau, Statistics Canada, Statistics Norway, and Statistics Sweden. I am certainly richer for the exchange.

Many of the examples I've seen and used were volunteered, and I am grateful to those who did so. Many other examples came from trolling the Web for material, joining a number of opt-in panels to see what others were doing, volunteering for banner-advertised surveys, and generally just vacuuming up whatever was out there. Over this time, I've become a true Web survey junkie. I have literally thousands of images captured from hundreds of different Web surveys. As of early 2008, my collection of the good, the bad, and the ugly of Web survey design approached 6,000 images, and I continue to collect examples of the best and the worst of what's out there. I have tried to anonymize most of the examples (where feasible) but have attempted to preserve the content of the original as closely as possible. Where the essence of an example cannot be presented without identifying the source, I have done so. But my goal is not to focus on particular researchers or companies or software products. We all make mistakes, and we can all learn from our mistakes.

I'd also like to thank the Survey Research Center for creating an atmosphere in which I can pursue topics such as this without anyone questioning my choice of research agenda. In particular, I am grateful to Bob Groves for his mentorship and encouragement over many years, which helped me believe that an endeavor such as this book was possible. Also, I am indebted to Eleanor Singer for her advice and support – she is an exemplary colleague.

Finally, but by no means any less importantly, my heartfelt thanks go to Mary Beth for her unfailing support and boundless patience.

Preface

One of the challenges of writing a book such as this is that the Web is changing rapidly. The World Wide Web of today is not the same as the Web of a few years ago. It certainly will not be the same as the Web (or its successor) of a few years hence. Much of the debate about general Web design (and it applies equally to Web survey design) is based on different assumptions about bandwidth, browser capacity, and so on. At one extreme, we're told to design for the lowest common denominator. In other words, design for what the Web *was*. This could result in boring, plain HTML, with no interactivity and few visual or other enhancements. At the other extreme there are those who argue one should design for what the Web *will be*, requiring the latest versions of browsers and plug-ins and the use of high-end systems to bring all the interactivity and enhanced features to the Web experience. Somehow, we have to strike a balance between these two extremes, designing instruments and developing design guidelines that are useful both now and in the future.

My effort to find a comfortable middle ground means that I am writing for today's dominant technologies but trying to focus on general principles rather than specific details, with the intention that they should apply to the future Web as much as to the present. There are some areas where this is obvious – good survey design is good survey design, no matter what the underlying platform or mode of delivery. However, there are other areas where it is less clear, for example, the use of client-side scripts, or applets, to deliver dynamic content versus restricting design to static HTML, with all activity being server-side. Whatever the tool that will be used for the former (JavaScript, DHTML, or whatever), the trend is clearly in the direction of greater interactivity, and I discuss the relevant design issues accordingly.

I will have failed in walking this tightrope of making the material relevant to both present and future design if readers dismiss my suggestions because the "flavor of the day" software or system has changed. I will have succeeded if the details are no longer applicable because of changing technology, but the general lessons learned about good Web survey design still apply. I will let you, dear reader, be the judge of that.

While I'm getting these issues off my chest, I should reveal other biases. I work primarily in the academic/government survey sector, and this book reflects that perspective. The goal of survey research in these sectors places relatively more emphasis on quality than on cost or speed of implementation. The latter goals might be more common in the market research sector. Thus, the rigor applied to a particular survey is valued on different dimensions in the two communities. In the market research sector, getting an estimate or result that is sufficiently accurate or reliable to make a business decision in a speedy and cost-conscious manner may be the overriding goal. In the academic and government sectors, the focus is more on "getting it right" or understanding the underlying phenomenon, with less regard for the cost side of the equation. Surveys in this sector are typically more complex and serve more varied purposes, resulting in a greater focus on overall quality. Both are legitimate approaches to the survey enterprise, but each leads to different design decisions and trade-offs where different aspects are emphasized.

The quality (or usefulness) of a survey is not an absolute, but must be evaluated relative to the stated aims of the survey and the claims made from the data. The quality of a survey can be thought of as the "fitness for [the intended] use" of the data it produces (Juran, 1979). Similarly, O'Muircheartaigh (1997, p. 1) defines error as "work purporting to do what it does not." One would not want to spend a million dollars on a survey estimate that is fleeting and used for media purposes only (e.g., a presidential approval rating at a particular moment in time). On the other hand, one would not want a government statistical agency to skimp on survey quality when it came to estimating such economic fundamentals as the unemployment rate or the consumer price index, nor would one want estimates of the prevalence and spread of disease, health coverage, or other public health issues to be done in a lackadaisical way. By now, it should be obvious to the reader where I come down. The focus of this book is intended to be squarely on high-quality surveys where the goal is not simply to entertain or to get a rough estimate but rather to produce statistically reliable and valid estimates of broad and lasting value to the research community, policy makers, and the public at large. That is, data that you can trust about things that are important to you.

Having said all of this, I believe that much of this book remains relevant to the broad range of survey endeavors from the frivolous to the deadly serious. Web survey design must be compatible with the goals of the survey and with the intended target audience. But, my core argument is that design has everything to do with quality in surveys. If one's goal is a high-quality survey yielding accurate and timely estimates, the design of the data collection process and instrument can and should be used to promote that goal. In other words, in the tradition of the Bauhaus movement in architecture, form follows function. Design is not an independent activity unrelated to the goals of the survey – rather, it is an integrated part of the process of achieving a particular goal.

Furthermore, design is not context-free. It would be a shame – for respondents and survey researchers alike – if Web survey design prescriptions resulted in cookie-cutter designs or one-size-fits-all approaches. It would be particularly disappointing if such were minimalist (black text on a white background; HTML 1.0) designs. The design of a survey should reflect the intended target audience, the survey organization conducting the study, the purpose of the survey, and the content of the instrument. Designing for the lowest common denominator, thereby avoiding any design enhancements, would lead to boring surveys and a lack of innovation. This book is not about stifling creative design but rather about designing surveys with care. The purpose of a survey is usually to gather data of high quality in a cost-effective manner. It is *not* to demonstrate the creativity or skill of the designer; there are plenty of other places for that. In other words, it's all about striking a balance, with a design that is visually pleasing but does not detract from the task at hand.

The designer of Web surveys can be creative but should do so in a way that enhances the experience for respondents and maximizes the quality of the data obtained. This means not only reaching the maximum number of potential respondents – that is, not excluding anyone from participating in the survey on grounds of browser incompatibility, failure to download the latest plug-in, lack of broadband access, or disability, whether it is vision, hearing, or some other physical impairment that makes it impossible for them to participate in the survey – but also encouraging them to provide the most accurate and honest responses that they can and supporting them in this task. Finally, the survey should leave them feeling good about the experience and likely to participate again, if called upon. Survey respondents are a precious commodity and should be treated as such.

Design should strike a balance. We should avoid the completely functional philosophy that led to Stalinist architecture. Aesthetics are certainly important (see Norman, 2004). But we should also avoid the other extreme of design for design's sake, without concern for usability. I am advocating for purpose-driven design, or respondent-focused design. In other words, form should closely follow function.

Finally, a brief word about my background. I should make it clear that I am not a programmer, nor am I an expert on technology of the Internet. I am a survey researcher, and what I do is design and implement surveys. More specifically, I'm a survey methodologist, and my time is spent doing research aimed at improving survey design. This is not a book for programmers but for survey researchers. My knowledge of HTML is limited to what I need to communicate with programmers on how to implement a certain design. My knowledge of CGI, CSS, Java, and the other esoterica of the Web is even more limited. This is a book *by* a survey researcher *for* survey researchers.

Over the past ten years or so, I have been involved in scores of Web survey design projects, whether as principal investigator, collaborator, consultant, or interested bystander. I continue to be amazed at the poor design of many Web surveys. I continue to hope that a book like this will soon be unnecessary, but the evidence suggests otherwise. The ultimate goal of this book is not to dictate but to get the designers of Web surveys to think.

Acronyms and Abbreviations

AJAX	Asynchronous JavaScript and XML
CAI	Computer assisted interviewing
CAPI	Computer assisted personal interviewing
CAPTCHA	Completely automated public Turing test to tell computers and humans apart
CASI	Computer assisted self-interviewing
CAT	Computerized adaptive testing
CATI	Computer assisted telephone interviewing
CGI	Common gateway interface
DOS	Disk operating system
DSL	Digital subscriber line
GUI	Graphical user interface
HTML	Hypertext markup language
HTTP	Hypertext transfer protocol
IP	Internet protocol
ISP	Internet service provider
IVR	Interactive voice response
RDD	Random digit dial
SMS	Short message service/system
SSL	Secure sockets layer
TLS	Transport layer security
URL	Uniform resource locator
XML	Extensible markup language

Chapter 1

The Importance of Design for Web Surveys

Design is choice
        Edward Tufte (2001, p. 191)

Why a book on the Web survey design? This question really has three parts: (1) why *Web*, (2) why *survey*, and (3) why *design*? I will try to address the three parts of this question in this chapter, but first I will briefly describe the major types of Internet and Web surveys prevalent today. This will set the stage for the discussion to follow.

1.1. Internet and Web Surveys

In the relatively short time that the Internet, and particularly the World Wide Web, has reached widespread penetration in the United States and elsewhere in the world, Internet or Web surveys have rapidly emerged as a major form of data collection. It's sometimes hard to imagine that Telnet was developed in 1987, and the first graphical browser (NCSA Mosaic) was released as recently as 1992 (see www.ncsa.uiuc.edu), given the attention that Web surveys are getting in the survey profession and research literature. The adoption of online surveys has spread faster than any other similar innovation, fueled in part by the dot-com frenzy of the late 1990s but also driven by the promise of faster and cheaper data collection. For example, according to ESOMAR's global research study conducted in 2001, an estimated 20% of the U.S. survey research market could be conducted online by 2002, reaching 35% by 2004 (see www.esomar.org). More recent data reveal that

U.S. online market research spending increased from $4 million in 1996 to over $1.6 billion in 2007 (Inside Research, 2007; see http://insideresearch.com/), with online research making up some 40% of all commercial research in the United States in 2006. While the rate of growth in online research appears to have slowed in recent years, the overall trajectory has still been nothing short of remarkable.

As is often the case in such innovations, the market research sector has rapidly embraced the new method of data collection, while government and academic survey enterprises have been somewhat slower to adopt Internet survey methods, using them more as supplements to rather than replacements for other modes of data collection. But this is changing too, and Internet surveys are an increasingly important component of all sectors of the survey world.

While Internet surveys show much promise, they also suffer from a number of potential limitations. Key among these is the likely coverage error arising from the fact that not everyone in the target population of interest may have access to the Internet. Furthermore, those who do have access appear to be different from those who do not on a variety of important measures of interest (e.g., Couper, Kapteyn, Schonlau, and Winter, 2007; Robinson, Neustadtl, and Kestnbaum, 2002; Schonlau et al., 2004). The Web also presents many challenges for generating probability samples of broad populations of interest, such as all Internet users. It is unlikely we will soon (if ever) see the development of random digit dial or RDD-like procedures for sampling Internet users, nor are lists of all Internet users and their e-mail addresses likely to be developed anytime soon. Nonresponse error is also a potential cause of concern in Internet surveys, as with all other modes of survey data collection. These sources of error are not the primary focus of this book and are reviewed elsewhere (see Couper, 2000; Fricker and Schonlau, 2002; Schonlau, Fricker, and Elliott, 2002). What *is* the focus of this book is measurement error and its reduction in Internet and, more specifically, Web surveys.

1.1.1. Different Types of Internet Surveys

Thus far, I have used the terms *Internet survey*, *Web survey*, and even *online survey* interchangeably. It's time to get a little more specific and narrow the focus to what this book will cover. Internet survey refers simply to any survey in which the data are collected via the Internet. The Internet can be used for survey data collection in several different ways. A distinction can be made between those surveys that execute on a respondent's machine (client-side) and those that execute on the survey organization's Web server (server-side).

Key client-side survey approaches include e-mail surveys and downloadable executables. In each of these cases, the instrument is transmitted to sample persons via the Internet. Respondents then answer the survey questions either by using the reply function in the e-mail software, by entering responses using a word processor, or by using software installed on their computers. Once complete, the answers are transmitted back to the survey organization. E-mail surveys (see, e.g., Couper, Blair, and Triplett, 1999; Schaefer and Dillman, 1998) have fallen out of favor, largely because of technical limitations and security concerns. As I note shortly, there are other types of client-side interactivity that can be active while a respondent is completing a Web survey online, but in the previous examples, the transmission of information back and forth to the server is not happening in real time.

Server-side systems typically involve the sample person completing the survey while connected to the Internet through a browser, with the answers being transmitted to the server on a flow basis as each *submit* or *next* button is pressed. Interactive features of the automated survey instrument are generated by scripts on the Web server. A key distinction between these two approaches is whether the Internet connection is *on* while the respondent is completing the survey. Web surveys are the prime example of the second type, and are by far the dominant form of Internet survey prevalent today. The focus of this book is on *Web surveys*.

In addition to different types of Internet surveys, there are also a variety of ways one can access the Internet. These range from "standard" graphical-based browsers on desktop computers, to WebTV and similar devices permitting access through the television, to an ever-expanding range of mobile or portable Internet devices such as WAP, or wireless application protocol on Internet-enabled mobile phones, and handheld wireless Internet devices such as Blackberries and the like. The focus of this book is on Internet access on standard devices, using one of the regular browsers (Internet Explorer, Mozilla Firefox, Safari, and so on) and based primarily on hypertext markup language, or HTML, the common language of the Web.

Even given these restrictions, Web surveys can be designed many different ways. For example, survey questions can be designed to be presented in a separate browser window (pop-up surveys) or the main browser. They can be designed to contain a single question (e.g., "question of the day" polls) or many questions. The questions can be included in a single HTML form or distributed across many forms. They can be more or less complex. And so on. I will primarily focus on longer rather than shorter surveys (i.e., ones with multiple questions) and surveys that are the main focus of the browser (i.e., not pop-ups). This is not to say that the design issues are not relevant for these other type of designs (they are), but simply that the context of the discussion in this chapter and throughout the book is on longer, more complex Web surveys.

Even within these limits of scope, there are variations that are likely to affect design. Two additional considerations are the target audience and whether the Web is the only mode of data collection or combined with one or more other modes. With respect to the target audience, or population of inference, Web surveys may be targeted to specialized groups or to broader targets, such as the general population. The likely experience with and knowledge of the Web is likely to vary, as is the type of equipment that respondents may possess. Similarly, Web surveys targeted at individual respondents answering on their own behalf have different design implications than those used in establishment or business surveys, where one or more respondents are answering on behalf of some larger entity. The nature of the task is likely to differ. Further, the design of a Web-only survey has different requirements than if the Web is only one part of a mixed-mode design. Ensuring comparability across the modes may place different constraints on the design. And this list can go on – there is an almost endless variety of Web surveys out there.

One particular design prescription is unlikely to be suitable for all of these. The design approach one adopts should be influenced by factors such as the target audience, the purpose of the survey, the content or topic of the questions, the importance of data quality, whether the Web is the sole medium of data collection, and so on. All these factors should be considered when choosing a particular design approach. In other words, there is no one type of Web survey, nor should there be one approach to the design of Web surveys.

1.1.2. How Web Surveys Work

Given that I have narrowed the focus to surveys consisting of several questions executed on a Web browser, we need a short aside on how the Web works – particularly with regard to HTML forms – to understand the limitation of the medium for designing and implementing surveys.

Figure 1.1 presents a rough schematic of how the Web works. The user – or respondent in our case – opens his or her Web browser by clicking on the link in the e-mail invitation or by typing in the uniform resource locator, or URL. This action sends a request via the Internet using hypertext transfer protocol (HTTP) to the Web server (i.e., the site identified by the URL) to deliver an HTML page to the respondent's browser (called the client). For most browsing activities on the

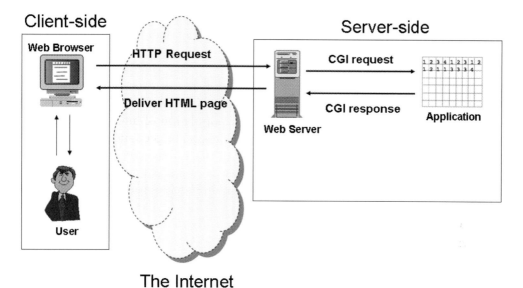

Figure 1.1 **A Web Survey Schematic.**

Web, this is basically the operation. Web surveys are a little more complex for two reasons: (1) data needs to be sent from the client to the server, and (2) the data need to be stored or processed in some way on the server.

For the first of these, HTML forms rather than pages are used. Forms are special types of Web pages that permit the input of information using a variety of form elements. We'll be looking at these in greater detail in Chapter 2.

To deal with the second issue, Common Gateway Interface (CGI) scripts are used. CGI is a standard for interfacing external applications with information servers, such as HTTP or Web servers. A plain HTML document that the Web server retrieves is static, which means it exists in a constant state: a text file that doesn't change. A CGI program, however, is executed in real time, so that it can output dynamic information. When the Web server receives the data from a form, it transfers this information to another application – for example, a database, a program, or a survey application – which acts on that information and sends a message back to the Web server regarding the next action to take.

A variety of different actions can occur, from simply storing the submitted information in a database, to processing complex algorithms to determine the completeness and consistency of responses, to generating new HTML forms dynamically based on the answers submitted. The CGI scripts and the survey application can also perform survey management functions such as controlling access to the survey, verifying that the survey has not already been completed by that respondent, permitting respondents to resume where they left off, generating automatic e-mail invitations and reminders, and so on. Much of the action in a Web survey is thus on the server-side.

Another implication of this brief description is that Web surveys are not made of HTML alone. Knowing how to create a home page and how to post information on the Web is not the same as knowing how to conduct a survey. The CGI scripts and the application used to run the survey on the server are critical elements. CGI scripts can be written in several different programming languages – Perl is a common scripting language, but ColdFusion, ASP, PHP, or customized survey packages can all serve this function.

1.2. Scrolling versus Paging Designs

For surveys longer than a single screen – that is, excluding pop-up or single-question surveys – there is a continuum of design choices, ranging from scrolling designs where the entire survey is a single HTML form, to paging designs where each question is presented on a separate HTML form. Before we discuss the variety of design approaches along this continuum of scrolling and paging designs, we need to clear up some terminology.

The terms *screen*, *page*, and *form* are often used interchangeably when discussing Web survey design, but they have different meanings. A *screen* is the physical device on which the browser and its contents are displayed. In computer-assisted interviewing (CAI) surveys, where the notion of one question per screen originated, the display was constrained to be identical for all interviewers. This was certainly true of DOS-based instruments where a screen meant the same number of displayable characters for all users (no more than eighty columns by forty rows). But even in graphical user interface (GUI) environments (such as Windows or Mac OS), where scrolling and resizable windows made the notion of screen less relevant, screen size is still largely constrained to present the information in exactly the same way for all interviewers (in computer-assisted telephone interviewing [CATI] or computer-assisted personal interviewing [CAPI]) or respondents (in computer-assisted self-interviewing, or CASI). Given user control over font size and browser window size, not to mention the variety of screen resolutions (e.g., 600×800, 1024×768) available, the notion of screen has even less precise meaning for Web surveys. However, we use it to refer specifically to the information that can (typically) be seen without the need for scrolling, given a typical or minimum set of browser settings. In other words, the term is used in terms of a design goal (visible without scrolling), even if not realized for every respondent and every browser setting. Couper, Traugott, and Lamias (2001), for example, use this notion of screen when talking about single-item versus multiple-item screens. Clark and Nyiri (2001) used the terms multiscreen and single-screen surveys to refer to paging versus scrolling designs, respectively. Dillman (2000) also uses the screen terminology.

The term *page* is used in two different ways in the survey design world. First, it is a holdover from the days of paper-based surveys and is used analogously to mean what can be seen on the screen at one time (in the same way that a single page of paper is visible at once). In the world of HTML, the word *page* is synonymous with document, and can be the size of a single screen or many screens. Most Web sites, for example, have a home page and many other pages or HTML documents that one can navigate to with the aid of hyperlinks.

In HTML, pages and *forms* are not exactly the same thing. A form is a specific type of page. While HTML pages are typically static, in that they are designed for the display of text and images, forms are interactive. Forms permit the submission of information *to* the Web server, as opposed to simply retrieving information *from* the server. Two features of HTML forms distinguish them from typical Web pages: (1) the fields or tools that permit the respondent to enter information or select responses and (2) the processing script that takes the information submitted and converts it into a usable format, that is, data. HTML forms are thus the principal tool for online surveys, which require a two-way flow of information between the respondent's browser and the Web server. E-commerce also makes widespread use of HTML forms – for most sites in which one has to submit some information (a name, address, credit card number, flight date and time, etc.) forms are most likely to be used. One way to distinguish a form from a page is that the former has one or more action buttons (*submit*, *reset*, *next*, etc.). Despite the difference between form and page, the terms are often used interchangeably. Thus, Lozar Manfreda and Vehovar (2002) use "page" to contrast one-page designs with multiple-page designs.

To summarize, I will attempt to limit the use of the term *screen* to what is visible within the browser window at any particular point, while using *page* and *form* to refer to different types of documents in HTML. While they have different meanings in HTML, I will use the terms synonymously.

In HTML terms, multiple-page designs are designed with a single question – or at most a small number of related questions – per form. More, specifically, part of the reason for such a design is to obviate the need for scrolling, and designers typically constrain the dimensions of the form such that it is visible in its entirety on the screen, under most common browser settings. In practice, depending on the length of a particular question and the number of response options, such survey designs may well require scrolling for some of the items.

Thus, a single-form or single-page survey is at the opposite end of the continuum to a single-question-per-form survey. The former has one submit button for the entire survey; the latter has one for every question in the survey. I will refer to single-form surveys as scrolling surveys and multiple-form surveys as paging surveys, to denote the primary actions respondents take to navigate through the instrument.

Web surveys can thus have any number of questions per form, ranging from only one to all of the survey items. Similarly, a Web survey can comprise any number of forms, from a single one for the entire survey to a separate form for each item. These define endpoints of a continuum, and there are many reasonable design alternatives along this continuum.

1.2.1. Scrolling Survey Design

In the prototypical version of this approach, the entire questionnaire is contained in a single HTML form, with one or more action buttons (e.g., submit, cancel) at the very end. This approach is most akin to a paper-based self-administered survey, where skips and routing are not automated, respondents can browse back and forth through the instrument, answering questions in any order, changing answers at will, and answering all or some of the questions before submitting the response. Dillman is an advocate of this approach, noting that "in general, I prefer questionnaires that scroll from beginning to end, a method that most closely resembles the general experience of using the Web" (Dillman, 2000, p. 395).

From a technical standpoint, the entire questionnaire is loaded into the respondent's browser (client) at the outset, and there is no further interaction with the survey organization's machine (server) until an explicit action is taken – *send*, *submit*, or whatever the button may be called. Clicking on a radio button or check box or entering text in a field communicates no information to the database running the survey. This information remains in the respondent's browser until explicitly transmitted to the server and then to the database for further processing.

If a respondent answers all questions but closes the browser before submitting the responses, or presses the *cancel* or *clear* button in the survey (if offered), no

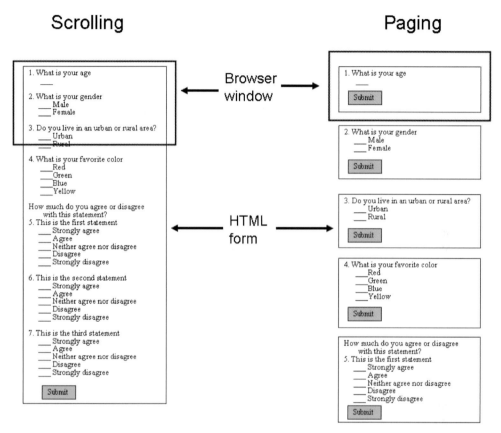

Figure 1.2 **Scrolling versus Paging Designs.**

information is transmitted to the server – in the same way as if a mail survey respondent were to complete the survey then fail to mail the questionnaire back to the survey organization.

There are several potential advantages of the scrolling approach to Web survey design. These include the following:

1. The design is similar to that of a paper survey, so it may be best for multimode studies in which one would want to minimize the possibility of differential measurement errors arising through mode differences.
2. Respondents can readily determine the length of the instrument and review forthcoming questions simply by scrolling to the end or noting the position and size of the scroll bar.

3. Similarly, respondents are free to move back and forth through the instrument and answer the questions in any order they prefer. This means they can back up and change answers to previous questions and can choose to omit questions if they so desire.

4. This approach is relatively easy to program. Further, given that standard or generic HTML is used throughout, this approach may be less susceptible to technical difficulties or browser compatibility problems.

5. Given that the instruments are simpler and no complex code is involved, the downloading of a static instrument may be marginally faster than a comparable interactive survey.

6. Given the above, there is less interaction with the server, reducing the likelihood of failures or errors during transmission.

However, there are also several potential disadvantages of using this design approach. Some of these are as follows:

1. The survey must be completed in a single sitting. One cannot do part of the survey, close the browser or disconnect from the Internet, and return to complete the rest later, unless additional programming has been done to accommodate this possibility.

2. All responses may be lost if the respondent fails to press the submit button after completing the survey.

3. Respondents see all questions, even those not yet answered and those that may not be relevant. This may lead respondents to choose the shortest path through the instrument as a way of satisficing (Krosnick, 1991). In other words, the respondent may be thinking, "If I answer 'yes' to this question, I have to answer the next 20 questions, but if I answer 'no' I get to skip ahead."

4. Skips and routing are not automated. As we know from research on paper surveys (Redline and Dillman, 2002), respondents are susceptible to both errors of omission and errors of commission when they have to make skip or flow decisions, and these are likely to occur in Web surveys too.

5. A variety of interactive design features are unavailable (unless embedded client-side scripts are used). This means that range checks, consistency checks, calculations, running totals, and other edits are not possible. Of course, these can be programmed to occur after submission of the form to the server, returning the results and accompanying messages to the respondent for follow-up. But it is usually best to provide this kind of feedback at

the time the respondent is answering the question. Other interactive design features that are difficult to implement in a scrolling design include dynamically generated fills, customized question text, randomization of questions or response options, and so on (see Chapter 5).

6. The order of responding cannot be controlled. While for some surveys it is desirable that respondents have access to surrounding questions to provide context, for certain types of questions (e.g., attitude measures or contingent questions), it may be important to control the order in which the questions are answered.

7. Scrolling may require greater dexterity and hand-eye coordination. This is especially true with longer surveys because the scroll bar will be shorter. Respondents must move back and forth between the response options (typically on the left) and the scroll bar (on the right). This may increase the likelihood of missed items.

The importance of each of these issues depends on the goals or features of the overall survey design. That is, what kinds of questions are to be asked; what expectations are there about the knowledge, experience, and motivation of the respondents; how long and/or complex the instrument is; and so on.

1.2.2. Paging Survey Design

In this type of design, the survey is chunked into several sets of HTML forms, each of which contains one or more questions. At the extreme, this may involve a single question per screen. This approach is the Web equivalent of CAI, with all the functionality that comes with such instruments (Couper and Nicholls, 1998). The instrument is often designed so that each form occupies a single screen, obviating the need for scrolling. The respondent answers one or more questions on that form and then presses a *submit* or *next* button. The answers are transmitted to the server, which processes the information and transmits the next form to the respondent's machine. The execution of instructions on the server uses CGI scripts written in a variety of programming languages or customized survey packages. Thus, these can be either generic software or proprietary systems. This approach permits customization of question text, randomization, automated skips, edits, and so on. In short, all the power and complexity we have come to expect from a computerized survey instrument (whether CATI, CAPI, or CASI).

The potential advantages of this approach look much like the disadvantages of the scrolling approach:

1. Minimal or no scrolling is necessary (but some scrolling is often used in practice).
2. Any data from partially completed surveys are retained. Respondents can complete the survey in multiple sessions, starting where they left off.
3. Skips and routing are automated. This permits complex skip patterns to be used, and the respondent does not need to be concerned about which questions to answer.
4. Immediate feedback can be provided for missing data, out-of-range responses, inconsistent answers, and so on.
5. Similarly, feedback can be used to provide help, motivate respondents to continue, or otherwise engage them in the task of completing the survey.

As should now be expected, the potential disadvantages of the paging approach map closely to the advantages of the scrolling approach. These are as follows:

1. Greater interaction with the server is required. This means that the survey may take longer to complete, and the likelihood of transmission failures is increased.
2. Respondents may have trouble knowing where they are in the instrument, which is similar to the problem of segmentation identified in early screen-by-screen CAI systems (House and Nicholls, 1988), in which the context of a particular question may be lost to the respondent.
3. Respondents have less control over the order in which they complete items. Of course, they could use the browser back button (if not disabled) or the survey's back button (if provided) to review and change answers to earlier questions, but this is less likely to be used than a scroll bar.
4. The paging approach is harder to program, typically requiring specialized survey software. Greater customization comes at a price. By way of analogy, contrast the effort of programming a CAI survey relative to an equivalent paper-and-pencil instrument.
5. The approach raises possible concerns about confidentiality. It is harder for respondents to change their mind about participation and be reassured that the answers already provided will indeed not be used by the survey organization. All answers already provided are captured by the system, even if the respondent decides to abandon the survey.

Given a paging design with more than one question per form, the questions or items can be grouped in different ways. For example, Norman, Friedman, Norman, and Stevenson (2001) refer to semantic chunking, that is, the grouping of sets of items that belong together thematically, versus paging or screen chunking, or the grouping of items to fit on one screen. The former may require scrolling, but the latter is designed to obviate the need for scrolling. The chunking or grouping of items can also be based on key server-side action, therefore logic-based chunking. In other words, break the survey at any point the server needs to do something, such as present a different set of items, validate a response, generate an error message, and so on. Logical and semantic chunking designs typically produce screens or pages with varying numbers of items, some of which may be single-item screens. My preference is for semantic or logic-based chunking (but see Section 1.2.4).

1.2.3. Research on Scrolling versus Paging Designs

Note that I say "potentially" when listing the relative advantages and disadvantages of each approach. This is for two reasons. First, the benefits of a particular design may only be realized under certain circumstances, when the particular features of that design are exploited fully in the survey. Second, to date, there have been relatively few empirical studies comparing the two design approaches. Furthermore, related to the first point, several of these studies compared relatively simple surveys without testing the limits of the different design approaches. For this reason, and because of relatively small sample sizes, the results from these studies have generally been inconclusive.

In one of the earliest studies to test the two design approaches, Vehovar, Lozar Manfreda, and Batagelj (1999) randomly assigned persons in the Research on Internet in Slovenia (RIS96) study either to what they called a flat instrument, or simple HTML form, or to an interactive, screen-by-screen instrument. With about 600 respondents per version, they found no significant differences in completion rates. The proportion completing the survey over those starting the survey was 85.4% for the scrolling version and 83.5% for the paging version. However, there was a significant difference in completion time, with the scrolling version taking an average of 368 seconds to complete, compared with 466 seconds for the paging version. Nineteen ninety-six is a lifetime ago in terms of bandwidth and transmission speed, and the same result is unlikely to hold today. Nonetheless, in the 1998 RIS study, in which only a paging version was used, a number of respondents (7%

of those who answered an open-ended question about the survey at the end) still complained of the slow download time.

Burris and colleagues (2001) reported on a faculty survey in which fifty-four respondents completed the scrolling version and fifty completed the paging version. They found no significant differences in completion time, although the average was 4.55 minutes for the scrolling version and 5.41 minutes for the paging version. With a larger sample size these differences may well have been significant. They also reported no differences in the rated ease of completion of the survey or in the distributions of responses to the survey questions. Forsman and Varedian (2002) compared scrolling and paging versions of a short (twenty-two question) survey among students and found no differences in completion rates or item missing data.

Clark and Nyiri (2001) presented the results of two surveys contrasting the two design approaches, one a survey of undergraduates and the other of graduate students. With somewhat larger samples sizes (about 70 per version for the first, and 140 per version for the second study), they also found no differences in item missing data, nor in the length of responses to open-ended questions. In a later study (Nyiri and Clark, 2003) of a sample of women in executive positions in the federal government, with 160 respondents completing the scrolling version and 121 the paging version, they again found no significant differences in item missing data rates or in the length of responses to open-ended questions. The scrolling version of the Clark and Nyiri survey of graduate students was actually broken into three pages. The first was a single screening question on eligibility, the second a set of four additional screening questions, and the third either twenty-two or twenty-seven questions, depending on the answers to the previous set of questions. This illustrates the hybrid nature of many of these designs. In other words, there may be few instances of a "pure" scrolling design, where all questions appear on the single HTML form, especially in the case of a long and complex survey. However, we may also find relatively few cases of surveys employing only one question per form.

Norman and colleagues (2001) conducted an experiment that compared different versions of a seventy-six-item Web questionnaire. The four versions were (1) a scrollable form, (2) a scrollable form with topical sections, (3) a paging form with screen-sized pages in topical sections, and (4) a paging form that presented each item one at a time on its own screen. The first and fourth versions represented the extremes of the scrolling and paging approaches. Approximately half of the participants received an index displayed on the left side of the screen that gave the section headings for the two versions that were organized topically and item numbers for the other two versions. The remaining respondents did not receive this index. Respondents had two tasks – (1) to complete the questionnaire and (2) to enter specific answers provided by the researchers to eight of the items. For completing the questionnaire, the scrollable format combined with the index (whether it displayed the numbers of individual questions or section headings) appeared to slow respondents down. For entering specific answers, on the other hand, the paging versions (with indices) appeared to be slowest. This suggests that a scrolling approach may be more suitable for survey tasks that require looking up information, a fairly common activity in establishment surveys.

In a more recent effort to explore the differences between these approaches in more depth, we embedded an experiment in a larger survey of undergraduate students (Peytchev, Couper, McCabe, and Crawford, 2006). Over 20,000 students at the University of Michigan were invited to complete the survey, with about 10% randomly assigned to the experimental scrolling version, which was divided or chunked into five topical sections. The balance was assigned to the standard paging version used in the previous round of the survey (McCabe et al., 2002). Response rates were no different between the two modes (just over 43% in each), as were break-off rates once the survey was started (around 6%). The paging version took significantly less time (22.93 minutes on average) than the scrolling version (23.53 minutes). This was particularly noticeable in one of the sections that contained a large number of questions that could be skipped. In the paging version, these skips were handled automatically, with respondents not even being aware of the questions not on the critical path. In the scrolling version, hyperlinks were used to facilitate skips, but all questions were visible to respondents. Section 3 contained 105 possible questions and three major skip points. The scrolling version took an average of 4.7 minutes for this section, compared with only 3.0 minutes for the paging version. Interestingly, relatively few of the respondents in the scrolling version made use of the hyperlinks to skip – about one in four respondents ever clicked on a hyperlink. But, when they did so, significant time savings were achieved, but still not reaching the same time as in the paging version. In addition to the reduction of errors of commission because of the automated skips in the paging version, there was also a significant reduction in the errors of omission. However, we found no interpretable differences in the distributions of substantive responses. In other words, the answers provided by respondents – and the conclusions we drew from the analysis – appear to be the same regardless of which version they completed.

In another recent study (Tourangeau, Couper, Galesic, and Givens, 2004), we looked at two different versions of a series of patient records to be completed by physicians or their staff. In contrast to the scrolling version, the paging version automated the skips and included other dynamic elements such as a look-up table for medications prescribed. The scrolling version of the patient record forms (PRFs) produced significantly higher levels of omission (1.13 per scrolling PRF versus 0.52 per paging PRF) and commission (0.36 per scrolling PRF and none in the paging version). However, the paging version took marginally longer than the scrolling version: 365 seconds per paging PRF versus 313 per scrolling PRF, a difference that is not statistically significant.

While there is clearly room for more research on this topic, one conclusion may be that the differences between the versions are not striking and may depend on other design features such as the complexity of the instrument, the need to consult records, and so on. Another is that the prototypical forms of these design types – one question per form or all questions on a single form – may be rare. Many, if not most, Web surveys I see these days involve some combination of approaches.

1.2.4. When to Use Scrolling or Paging Designs?

Which approach – scrolling or paging – should one use? The answer depends on both the goals and content of the survey one is conducting. There is no one approach suitable for all occasions (despite what some design guidelines may suggest). I use different approaches, depending on the particular survey I am designing. The choice depends on a variety of factors, such as the length and complexity of the survey, the threat of breakoffs or item missing data, the importance of contextual information, the target audience's experience with the Web, and their browsers' technical capacity. It may also depend on the Web survey software one has. Some software packages support scrolling design only, some paging designs only, and others both. Generally, the more expensive packages are page based, and the most expensive include client-side interactivity.

Given that there is still much research to be done on the optimal approach to design, and that the choice of approach should depend on other factors, I offer tentative guidance on when one approach may be more desirable than another. I recommend using a scrolling approach when:

1. The survey is relatively short.
2. The survey contains few or no skips or contingent question (i.e., everybody answers all questions).
3. Item missing data or breakoffs are not a major concern.

4. Providing context for later questions is desirable (i.e., respondents need to review answers to earlier questions).
5. The order of item completion is of little concern.
6. The Web survey is offered as an alternative to paper in a mixed-mode design.
7. Respondents need to print completed questionnaire for review or archiving (establishment surveys).

However, the paging approach may be more suitable when:

1. The survey is lengthy (permits respondent to complete in more than one session).
2. The survey contains skips, edits, fills, calculations, randomization, and so on.
3. The survey contains many graphics (these are only loaded when and if needed).
4. Respondents should answer questions in sequence.
5. The survey contains key screening items (if the respondent can see which path each choice may take, they may be less likely to answer honestly).
6. The Web survey is used in a mixed-mode design with CATI, interactive voice response, or other modes that tightly control sequence.

To reiterate, the choice of design approach should be guided by these and other considerations specific to the particular study at hand.

1.2.5. Client-Side Scripts

In the previous sections, I have described the prototypical designs using server-side scripts. In other words, all the action – whether skips, edit checks, error messages, or randomization – occurs on the Web server and not on the respondent's browser. This reflects one of the fundamental drawbacks of HTML for surveys and indeed for other Web applications requiring input from the user: HTML is a markup language designed initially for the presentation of information (mostly text, but also images, sound, and other media) in a standard format over the Internet, *not* as an interactive data collection or entry tool. As I've already noted, HTML forms offer one way around this limitation. Many of the dynamic or interactive features of Web surveys we see use sever-side programs or scripts to act on the information transmitted via the form.

An alternative is to build the dynamic elements directly into the Web form, using client-side scripts. Client-side scripts are generically known as dynamic HTML, or DHTML. The most common client-side scripting language in use is JavaScript, which is supported on most browsers. The use of client-side scripts permits interactive enhancements to either scrolling or paging Web surveys.

Scripts can be of two kinds. First, those that load automatically when the Web page is loaded can do a variety of tasks in the background, some very useful to the survey researcher. For example, many survey software systems run an automatic script when the respondent first enters the survey, to detect the capabilities of the respondent's browser. Client-side scripts can be embedded in survey forms to collect a variety of paradata – data about the process that can inform the design of future surveys – such as timing data, the order of clicks, and so on (see Couper, 2005; Heerwegh, 2003; see Section 6.7.2).

The second kind of script loads or executes in response to a user action. These can be of several different types, such as `onclick, onmouseover, onkey-press, onsububmit,` and so on. Both types of scripts produce a set of actions – which may or may not be visible to the respondent – without sending any information to the server. In browsers that do not have JavaScript activated, the script simply is not executed, and the rest of the HTML form is unaffected.

Scripts are not the only way one can add interactivity to a Web form. Java, developed by Sun Microsystems, is a full programming language that is embedded in a small applet in the HTML page. Flash, developed by Macromedia Inc., is increasingly being used for graphical interactivity, such as animations. In addition, as HTML evolves into extensible markup language (XML), the next generation markup language for the Web, we are likely to see greater interactivity possible in forms, with the introduction of XForms (see http://www.w3.org/MarkUp/Forms/). Audio and video can also be added with various plugins. The general term for these add-ons to basic HTML functionality is *active content*.

Given that client-side scripts, or applets, are quite widespread in e-commerce sites, why do we not see more use in Web surveys? There are several possible reasons for this. One is that not all browsers are equipped to handle client-side programming, and even if they are, some have chosen to disable these features in their browsers, whether as a matter of company policy or through personal preference.

Writing in 1998, DeVoto identified "gratuitous Javascript" as one of the "Seven Mortal Sins of Professional Web Designers" (http://www.jaedworks.com/shoebox/no-cookie/mortal-sins.html). She noted, "Safe use of Javascript (and other advanced technologies) relies on remembering that *not every visitor can interpret*

Javascript. Whether they use a browser that's not Javascript-aware, use one that includes a Javascript version that doesn't support your techniques, or simply leave it turned off out of concerns about stability or security . . . unless your site is about Javascript and nothing else, a fair proportion of interested visitors won't be able to use scripts" (DeVoto, 1998).

A number of different Web sites report browser statistics. Many of these are based on visitors to those sites, which may overstate the level of penetration of newer technology. Still, they can serve as a rough guide. For example, www.w3schools.com suggests that as of January 2007, about 94% of browsers have JavaScript enabled, somewhat up from 90% in October 2004 and 80% in October 2002. Another site, www.TheCounter.com, also reported 94% of browsers having JavaScript enabled in September 2007, up from 86% in October 2003. In any case, it's not the visitors to these web sites we're interested in, but the (potential) respondents to our Web surveys. For example, we routinely include such a detector in our Web surveys. In March 2003, using an opt-in sample provided by Survey Sampling International (SSI), 98.4% of those who logged in to the survey had JavaScript enabled, while 96.5% had Java enabled. In December 2003, we found only 1 respondent out of 3,195 without JavaScript enabled, and only 2.2% of respondents without Java enabled. These numbers have been relatively stable across subsequent studies. We used this information to direct respondents to an experiment that required Java – a test of visual analog scales or slider bars (see Couper, Singer, Tourangeau, and Conrad, 2006). However, of the respondents in this experimental condition who completed the survey, a further 4.3% failed to complete any of the eight slider bar items, which may suggest that the detection script slightly overestimates the Java capabilities of the browsers.

If you don't know whether a Web survey requires JavaScript or not, try it. Here's what I do: First, I disable JavaScript on my browser, then click on the link to the survey. In many cases, the JavaScript detect returns a "false" to the server, and I am simply rejected from the survey or prevented from going further. Some surveys at least note that JavaScript is required and provide information on how to enable scripts. Switching such features on and off in the browser is easy to do. With the increasing use of the Web for e-commerce, the technical limitations of browsers are likely to be less important, but respondent security concerns may remain a reason for active content not being universally accepted.

Another possible counter to the use of active content may be the added complexity that comes with embedding client-side scripts, or applets. Generally, more programming is needed – which also means more testing. For example, Schwarz and Reips (2001) conducted a Web-based experiment in Germany in which half the subjects were assigned to a JavaScript version and half to a standard CGI (server-based) version. The completion rates (completes among starts) were significantly different: 49.8% for the JavaScript version and 63.2% for the CGI version. While only a subset of the breakoffs could be attributed directly to non-JavaScript browsers, they note that the use of JavaScript "increases the likelihood of browser failures or system crashes through complex interactions with hardware and software systems over time" (Schwarz and Reips, 2001, pp. 88–89). It is particularly important to ensure that the scripts work the same way across multiple platforms and browsers. Despite the intention of being platform independent, there are variants of JavaScript that necessitate testing on different machines. Furthermore, one should also decide whether to offer an alternative for those with JavaScript or Java disabled or for those using assistive devices to access the Web. The question is then whether the added functionality is worth it. I address this in Chapter 3, when I look in more detail at some of the enhancements and tools that can be used with client-side scripts.

While it is tempting to add bells and whistles to one's Web survey, and many clients are tempted by such enhancements, I recommend using these tools only if necessary, and only if the target audience and survey content justify their use. Do *not* require active scripts as a routine price of admission to your survey, unless the design of the instrument and the goals of the measurement warrant this restriction.

1.2.6. Other Types of Designs

The scrolling versus paging approaches I have described are both on the continuum of sequentially designed surveys. There is another class of designs more common in establishment or business surveys than surveys of individuals or households. These can be called user-navigated, menu-driven, or tabbed designs. The basic idea is that there are a number of separate forms that can be completed in almost any order. Sometimes the order of completion is at the discretion of the respondent or respondents (for, in many establishment survey cases, different respondents may complete different sections). At other times, some modules of the survey may need to be completed before others can be accessed. This book does not focus on these types of designs – particularly the navigation and control aspects – although some of these issues will be touched on later. However, with regard to the individual forms and items, many of the issues discussed here are relevant to the design of these kinds of surveys. Furthermore, many designs are of a hybrid variety. For example, the Census Bureau's American Community Survey and 2010 Decennial Census design offer a tabbed or menu-based navigation. The basic approach is a page-based design, but respondents may answer questions in a different order or jump around the sections using the tabs.

1.3. Web Site Design versus Web Survey Design

Now that we've covered some of the background and terminology common to Web sites and Web surveys, we can turn to the second part of the question motivating this book: why a focus on Web *surveys*? Isn't there already a lot of material on Web design? A fundamental premise of this book is that, while Web surveys and Web sites have much in common, they are not the same. Let me elaborate.

Web sites have many different functions and a near-infinite range of designs. The original goal of the Web was to *present* or share information. There are still a large number of such sites around. Aside from some search and navigation tools, the focus of these sites is on the presentation of information. An increasingly large subset of the Web is devoted to activities in which the user is required to provide some information or select among options. These typically use Web forms to *collect* or gather information. E-commerce sites are the clearest example of these. But other examples may include online reservations, application forms, registrations, e-health applications, and so on. Web surveys also use HTML forms, but for a specific purpose. Thus, Web forms are a subset of all Web sites, and Web surveys are a subset of Web forms, as illustrated in Figure 1.3.

Many books are devoted to Web site design. Just two examples that I've found useful are Nielsen's (2000) *Designing Web Usability: The Practice of Simplicity* and Brinck, Gergle, and Woods' (2002) *Usability for the Web: Designing Web Sites That Work*. Interestingly, Nielsen's book does not mention the various types of input fields I discuss in Chapter 2. His book focuses on Web *page* or *site* design, rather than Web *form* design. In some of his Alertbox columns (see http://www.useit.com/alertbox/), he addresses issues related to form elements; for example, check boxes versus radio buttons in September 2004 and forms versus applications in September 2005. Similarly, the Brinck and colleagues book focuses primarily on Web site design but does mention forms.

Schober, Conrad, Ehlen, and Fricker (2003) have elucidated some of the differences between Web survey interfaces and more typical Web interactions using

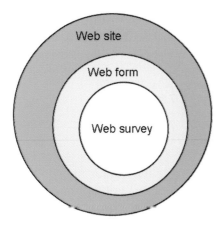

Figure 1.3 **Web Site, Web Form, and Web Survey.**

forms. In the latter, they note: (1) the user initiates the interaction, rather than being invited to participate; (2) the user requests information from the system, rather than being asked for information by the system; and (3) the system provides responses to the user, rather than the user providing responses to the system. They demonstrate this in an experimental study on users' requests for clarification between the different interfaces.

Thus, while the tools used by interactive Web sites and Web surveys may be similar (both use HTML forms and the same form elements discussed in the next chapter), the way they are used differs. This is relevant for the design of the interface for several reasons: (1) the kinds of information provided usually differ; (2) the motivation for completing the form differs; and (3) the importance of accuracy, or the consequences of inaccuracy, differs. For example, the consequences of selecting the wrong destination city (e.g., Portland, Oregon, rather than Portland, Maine) or dates in an airline reservation site are much different for the respondent than providing an incorrect birth date or place of birth in a typical Web survey.

Let's take one type of Web-based interaction from the world of e-commerce: flight reservations. Figures 1.4 and 1.5 show two examples of flight reservation pages, the first from America West and the second from Delta. The first thing we can note is how compact these forms are – everything one needs to be able to search for and select flights is presented in this area. The home page of each airline contains lots of additional information, but this is what they want the user to focus on. Given that all the information one needs to enter is in the same place,

Figure 1.4 **Flight Reservation from AmericaWest.com.**

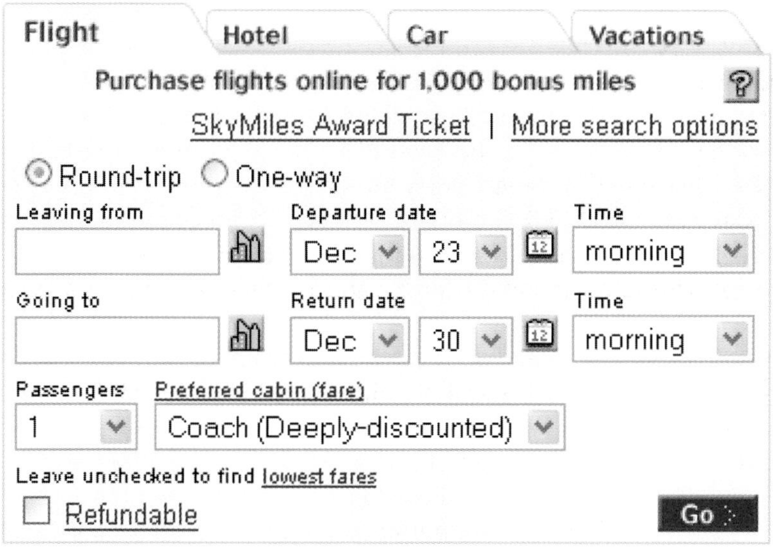

Figure 1.5 **Flight Reservations from Delta.com.**

one can enter it in any order before pressing the *search* or *go* button. In addition, both sites make judicious use of defaults – something to be guarded against in the survey world. For example, both sites have the round-trip option preselected, assuming this is the most common type of ticket. Both sites have a drop box for number of passengers, with "1" being the given choice. Hyperlinks are used for alternatives to the common options (multicity trips, award tickets, etc.).

But there are also several differences between the two sites. America West's hub (Phoenix) is listed first in the drop box, which contains a list of all airports – but only those airports – served by the airline. The dates also have starting values, beginning with the day on which the Web site was accessed (December 27) and with the return flight the following day. Delta's date default begins a week after the date the site was accessed (December 16) with the return flight being a week after that. Delta offers a text box for typing in the departure and destination cities but offers an icon to look up the airports in a list. One reason for the drop box on the America West site and a text box on Delta's may be that the latter serves many more destinations, making a drop box list unmanageably long. Many of these designs features are to be avoided when used in Web surveys, as I shall discuss in Chapter 2. But they work for the task at hand.

In fact, there is a great deal of similarity in the design of different airline Web sites, branding, color, and layout issues aside. This reflects the limited numbers of ways in which the same task (making an airline reservation) can be accomplished in optimal fashion. But there are also some distinct differences, reflecting the variation in services the airlines provide. Table 1.1 offers a summary of key features of these sites. Because these designs may be optimal for making flight reservations, does not mean that they should be used in Web surveys. Jakob Nielsen, in his Alertbox of September 26, 2005, recommends that designers should "pre-populate fields with the most common value" (http://www.useit.com/alertbox/defaults.html). Doing the same in a Web survey is not likely to optimize data quality, I would assert.

In summary, while much of what is known about Web site design may apply to surveys, we must always be cognizant of the particular application we are designing. Similarly, while there is much to learn about the appropriate use and design of forms and form elements such as radio buttons and check boxes. We must be mindful that surveys are different from other Web-based interfaces or interactions. Thus, for example, the discussion in Chapter 2 is very survey specific, whereas Chapter 4, which deals with more general layout and design issues, borrows heavily from the broader literature.

Table 1.1. Flight reservation web pages for selected airlines (December, 2005)

Airline	Airports	Dates and times	Number of passengers	Type of reservation
Alaska	Text boxes; hyperlink for city	Separate drop boxes for month, day, and time (default is today, 7 a.m. for both outbound and return); calendar icon	Drop box, separate for adults (default=1) and children (default=0)	Action buttons for one way and round-trip; hyperlink for multicity
America West	Drop boxes (default= Phoenix)	Separate drop boxes for month, day, and time (default is today, return is tomorrow)	Separate drop box for adults (default=1), children (default=0), seniors (default=0)	Preselected radio button for roundtrip; hyperlink for multicity
American	Text boxes; hyperlinks for city and airport code	Calendar icon first; separate drop boxes for month, day, and time of day (default is tomorrow, +3 days for return)	Separate drop box for adults (default=1), seniors (default=0)	Preselected radio button for round-trip; hyperlink for multicity
Continental	Text boxes	Text box (MMDDYYYY); calendar icon; default is +7 days, +14 days for return; drop box for time (default is anytime)	Drop box for adults (default=1)	Default is round-trip; hyperlinks for one way and reward travel
Delta	Text boxes; icon for city lookup	Drop box for day, month, and time (default is +7 days, +14 days for return, default time is morning); calendar icon	Drop box for number of passengers (default=1)	Preselected radio button for round-trip; hyperlinks for award ticket and more search options

(continued)

25

Table 1.1 (continued)

Airline	Airports	Dates and times	Number of passengers	Type of reservation
Independence	Drop boxes	Drop box for day first (default is today, return is today); then month/year; calendar icon;	Drop box for adults (default=1), children (default=0), and infants (default=0)	Preselected radio button for round-trip
Northwest	Text boxes	Drop boxes for month and day (default is +7 days; +14 days for return); drop box for time (default is anytime)	Drop box for number of adults (default=1)	Preselected radio button for round-trip; hyperlink for multicity
Southwest	Three separate scroll boxes (5 cities visible) for departure, arrival, and return cities	Scroll boxes (5 visible for month and day (default is +7 days, default return is none); radio buttons for time of day (preselected before 12 noon)	Drop box for number of passengers (default=1)	Hyperlink for award travel
United	Text boxes	Drop boxes for day, month, and time (default is +14 days, +21 days for return); calendar icon	Drop box for number of passengers (default=1)	Preselected radio button for round-trip; hyperlink for multicity
US Airways	Text boxes	Drop box for month, day and time (default is +21 days, +23 days for return)	Drop box for number of passengers (default=1)	

1.4. Why Is Design Important

Finally, to turn to the third part of the question asked at the outset of this chapter: why a book on Web survey *design*? Don't we have enough books on questionnaire design? What is so different about Web surveys that we need another book on survey design? To be clear, this book is *not* about question wording. Well-worded questions and well-crafted response options are necessary for all types of surveys. The question wording challenges are not unique to Web surveys, and there are already many good volumes on issues related to the appropriate wording of survey questions and the effect that wording may have on the answers to survey questions. This book is about those parts of a survey instrument that are typically not discussed in most of these texts.

1.4.1. Unique Aspects of Web Surveys

While Web surveys have much in common with other methods of survey data collection, in some respects, they are unique in the design challenges they present. What this means is that while there is much we may apply from other modes we also need to consider the unique features of Web surveys and the implications for design. The following combination of attributes is characteristic of Web surveys:

1. Web surveys are self-administered
2. Web surveys are computerized
3. Web surveys are interactive
4. Web surveys are distributed
5. Web surveys are rich visual (graphical and multimedia) tools

I elaborate on each of these attributes, and their implications for Web survey design, in Sections 1.4.1.1 to 1.4.1.5. In addition, these key attributes will serve as a backdrop for much of the discussion in the remaining chapters of this book.

1.4.1.1. Web Surveys Are Self-Administered

While it may be a truism to note this, it is worth remembering. In many respects, Web surveys should behave much like other forms of self-administered surveys, particularly mail questionnaires. The benefits of self-administration should also apply to the Web. These include the reduction of interviewer effects. There is a large body of literature on interviewer effects, focusing both on the attributes of interviewers (e.g., Hagenaars and Heinen, 1982; Kane and Macauley, 1993) and on their behavior (e.g., Brenner, 1982; Billiet and Loosveldt, 1988) in affecting survey responses. Removing the interviewer from the equation is likely to reduce these effects. For example, we should thus expect a reduction in socially desirable responding relative to interviewer administration (Tourangeau and Smith, 1996). However, interviewers do many things to reduce measurement errors in surveys – such as motivating respondents to provide complete and honest answers, clarifying questions, probing where necessary, and so on. With self-administration, there is no trained person to deliver the survey questions or assist the respondent, either with substantive issues or with technical difficulties.

With the interactivity that is possible in Web surveys (see Section 1.4.1.3), Web questionnaires may behave more like CASI instruments than mail surveys. Typically, with the latter, a trained interviewer is present to instruct and assist the respondent in the completion of the task. But with mail surveys, respondents are generally on their own. The interactive or dynamic nature of Web surveys (see Section 1.4.1.3 below) might allow us to compensate for some of the drawbacks of having no interviewer present to assist or prompt the respondent as and when needed.

There are other features of self-administration that are relevant to Web surveys. The elimination of the interviewer role means that such surveys are typically much cheaper than their interviewer-administered or interviewer-assisted counterparts. Further, like mail, Web surveys offer the respondent the convenience of completing the survey at a time (but not always place) of his or her own choosing, and often permit respondents to compete the survey over the course of several sessions, if so desired.

1.4.1.2. Web Surveys Are Computerized

This simply means that Web surveys potentially have all the power of modern CAI software. Of course, this depends on the software used by the designer and the particular design approach used (scrolling versus paging, static versus dynamic). The questionnaire can be as complex as the imagination of the survey designer and the capabilities of the software permit.

The following is a partial list of some of the features that can be built into a Web survey, given computerization:

1. Accommodation of a variety of questions types. These include single response, multiple response, numeric or text responses, "other, specify" answers, and so on.
2. Customized wording, or fills. These may be based either on preloaded responses about the respondent or on the respondent's answer to prior questions.
3. Skips, branching, or routing. This means the delivery of questions to a respondent based on answers given in a previous question. In some cases, as we have already seen, these are not automated.
4. Edit checks or data validation. These may be range checks, consistency checks, data completeness checks, logical/arithmetic tests, and so on, and include the presentation of customized error messages.
5. Dynamic rosters or loops. This refers to the ability to ask a series of questions about a number of entities in which the number of entities is unknown at the outset.
6. Randomization. The ability to randomize the order of questions, the response options, or any other features of the survey instrument.

The first set of features is discussed in Chapter 2, while the others are discussed in Chapter 5. This list is by no means complete. Some Web survey software can do only some of these, while others can do even more. For example, methods such as adaptive conjoint analysis (e.g., Curry, 2003) can only be done with computerization. Furthermore, these are features that focus particularly on instrument design – what the respondent sees and does – rather than on issues of program correctness, data storage and transmission, and handling irregular movement through the instrument.

The ability to randomize presents one of the great boons of Web surveys for research. As a result, the distinction between surveys and experiments is becoming blurred. It is a trivial matter to randomize the order of response options to minimize order effects. Randomizing the order of questions to measure or counter context effects is also easy. It is similarly easy to embed experiments in Web surveys at little additional cost. The exploitation of this powerful feature of Web surveys is certainly not limited to methodological inquiries. A variety of substantive questions can be explored by marrying the benefits of surveys and experiments (see, e.g., Piazza and Sniderman, 1998; Birnbaum, 2000a; Reips, 2001).

When all these features work correctly, the process of delivering a customized or tailored instrument to each respondent is fully automated. In the extreme, the series of questions that a particular respondent sees may be unique, with no two respondents seeing exactly the same instrument – what Sikkel (1998) calls the "individualized interview." Of course, if things do not work correctly, the experience may not be as smooth for the respondent.

This presents one of the trade-offs of complex survey instruments, whether on the Web or some other mode. The more one customizes the experience for the respondent, the more complexity one builds into the instrument, the greater the cost and effort required to program and test the survey, and the greater the likelihood that something might not work as intended.

Another potential risk of the computerization of survey – and particularly self-administered ones – is the danger of exerting too much control over the respondent. The computer can tightly control the sequence of questions presented to the respondent, can constrain the response options available, and can prevent certain actions. With a paper questionnaire, a respondent has the flexibility to add comments, choose multiple responses where only one is desired, or choose none. In short, the respondent can choose *how* to answer the survey, leaving it up to the researcher to deal with these issues after the fact. Much of this control is transferred to the instrument – and, by extension, the designer – in a Web survey (see Couper, 2007b). The designer must anticipate what the respondent might want to do and decide whether and how to accommodate the respondent's possible desires at the time of the design, rather than after the fact, during the editing or postprocessing stage.

This is another reason design is important. House and Nicholls (1988, p. 429) observed that while computerized control is one of CATI's greatest assets, it can also be its greatest weakness if "it strips the interviewer of the ability to improvise when unusual situations occur." The same is true for the respondent in a Web survey. In this respect, Web surveys have much in common with CAI.

I will return to design considerations when using these features later in the book (see Chapters 4 and 5).

1.4.1.3. Web Surveys Are Interactive

There are many definitions of interactivity (see, for example, Kiousis, 2002; Mc-Millan and Hwang, 2002). By interactive, I simply mean an instrument that is, to a greater or lesser extent, dynamic, responsive, active, or engaging. Interactivity is a feature of the combination of the self-administered and computerized nature of Web surveys. In other words, the Web survey instrument may take on some of the roles of an interviewer. In this respect, the Web is like neither paper nor CAI.

A paper questionnaire is static – every respondent gets the same thing. It is also passive – respondents can behave as they like in responding to a survey with no immediate consequences. For example, they can check both the "yes" and "no" boxes; write in a response, answer questions in any order, fail to answer questions, and either deliberately or by accident. This is partly the issue of control that I raised in the previous section.

In contrast, Web surveys can be much more dynamic. So far, we've only thought about the interactive nature of Web surveys as replicating the features of a computerized interview – skips, edits, randomization, and the like. However, the interactive aspects of the Web could potentially offer much more than this. Web surveys can potentially behave more like a conversation or dialogue – an interview, if you will, rather than a questionnaire (again, see Couper, 2007b).

The fact that the computer program or survey instrument can react to a respondent's input (or lack of input) permits us to replicate some of the things that interviewers may ordinarily do in interviewer-administered surveys. For example, the instrument could be designed to motivate respondents to continue completing the survey. This could be done either through periodic reminders at key points in the survey, or more tailored reminders customized to particular respondent behaviors that might indicate a high risk of breakoff, or at questions that are at risk of breakoff. Interactive elements could be used to reduce item missing data (e.g., deRouvray and Couper, 2002). They could be used to detect respondent difficulty with a concept or task and react accordingly (e.g., Conrad, Schober, and Coiner, 2007). They could also be used to motivate respondents to provide honest, complete, and accurate answers, either through periodic motivational messages given to all or messages tailored on particular respondent behaviors. For example, if a respondent generates repeated error messages as a result of trying to input the wrong information, this could trigger an open-ended field for them to explain their answer, or go from a "don't know" or "not ascertained" (DK/NA) response on income to unfolding measures. That is, instead of simply repeatedly generating generic error messages, give the respondent a chance to explain his or her answer or lack thereof.

While many of these potential enhancements are still speculative, we will see increasing efforts to exploit the power of the Internet in designing online surveys. Furthermore, interactivity is easier to implement in paging designs than scrolling ones and easier to do when the full range of client-side scripts or applets is available to the designer. But many examples of interactivity already exist in Web surveys. Several of these – running totals, interactive images and graphs, and slider bars – will be discussed in Chapter 3. Other examples of interactivity – error messages, progress indicators, and hyperlinks – will be examined in Chapter 5.

1.4.1.4. Web Surveys Are Distributed

One of the features of Web surveys that challenges designers is that the survey is completed using the respondent's own hardware, software, and communications. In this sense, the tools used to complete the survey are distributed.

Paper is truly WYSIWYG – what you see is what you get. It is standardized. Unless there are errors in the printing of the paper questionnaires, every respondent gets an identical instrument. Similarly, in computer-assisted interviewing (CATI and CAPI), the systems are generally under control of the survey organization. Even in CASI or audio-CASI, while self-administered, the look and feel of the instrument is identical for all respondents because the equipment is provided by the survey organization. This is not always so on the Web. Because the medium (the Internet) and the tools (computer and browser) to access and view the instrument are not under our direct control, we do not have the same ability to deliver standardized instruments on the Web as we do in other modes.

Here are some of the things that can vary, and hence directly or indirectly affect the look and feel of the survey instrument:

1. The browser used (e.g., Netscape versus Microsoft Internet Explorer versus Mozilla Firefox)
2. The browser version (e.g., Internet Explorer 7.0 versus 4.0)
3. The script the browser can read (e.g., HTML 4.0 versus HTML 1.0; Microsoft JavaScript is not identical to Netscape JavaScript)
4. The computer operating system (e.g., Windows XP versus Windows Vista versus Linux versus Mac OS)
5. The screen resolution (e.g., 1024 × 768 versus 800 × 600)
6. The size of the browser window (many users do not set their browsers to full-screen display)
7. The browser security settings (e.g., no cookies, no Java, no JavaScript, or prompt to accept/reject each cookie, script, or applet)
8. The connection type and speed (e.g., dial-up, DSL, cable modem)
9. The fonts available to the browser
10. The font size setting in the browser (e.g., small versus medium versus large)
11. Background color settings
12. The input devices used (e.g., keyboard versus, mouse, stylus, assistive device)

Many of these differences are features of the system being used; respondents may have more or less choice in these attributes or settings. Some users may not even know what these settings are, or know how to change them. For some respondents (e.g., those who use libraries, Internet cafes, or other public Internet access sites), these may vary from one browser session to the next. Others may reflect the personal tastes of the user.

Some may argue that these variations produce trivial differences in the look-and-feel of Web survey instruments. After all, the power of the Web is its universal nature. It is platform independent; regardless of the devices and settings above, everyone can access most of the content on the Web. But, as we shall see in this book, subtle differences in the online experience, while possibly having little effect on other types of online activities, may indeed affect the way people answers survey questions online.

The distributed and hence customizable nature of the Web can be both good and bad. It is good in that the instrument can adjust to a variety of user needs. For example, a person with poor eyesight can adjust the font size to make it easier to read. But it is bad to the extent that these variations change the experience for respondents in ways that may affect their answers to the survey questions.

Web surveys are still less distributed than CAPI, in the sense that each interviewer carries a laptop computer around with the survey application loaded on it. Updates to the instrument and the data collected in the interview are usually transmitted via modem or even mailing of CDs. But the look and feel of the instrument is standardized in CAPI, less so in Web surveys. In this respect, a correction to the Web survey instrument can be made once on the server, giving the designer more control over the server-side of the operations but less over the client-side.

1.4.1.5. Web Surveys Are Rich Visual Tools

One of the major potential benefits of the Web as a survey data collection tool is the ease with which rich visual information can be used. This ranges from the use of color and patterns in layout and design (see Chapter 4) to the inclusion of images such as drawings or photographs in the survey instrument (see Chapter 3). While the inclusion of graphical information has been possible in paper-based surveys, and a number of examples of their use exist, several factors mitigated against their widespread use in survey. These included (1) the cost of reproducing color images, (2) the difficulty of randomizing images or questions, and (3) the difficulty of controlling the sequence of display. These issues are trivial in surveys conducted via the Web. While images and videos are sometimes also used in CASI applications, such use has until recently been relatively rare. The Web is hastening the movement of survey instruments away from predominantly verbal media to both verbal and visual stimuli and, by extension as bandwidth increases, to full multimedia methods (see Couper, 2005).

I'll address the use of images in Web surveys in greater detail in Chapter 3, but the point here is that the ease with which such visual enhancements can be made to a survey instrument is one of the major distinguishing features of Web surveys. This presents both opportunities and challenges for Web survey design, as we shall see.

1.4.1.6. Summary

It is in the combination of these features that the Web is unique as a medium for survey data collection. In respect of any one of them, the Web has much in common with other modes. For example, in terms of computerization, these features are shared with computer-assisted surveys, whether interviewer-administered (CATI, CAPI) or self-administered (CASI). With respect to self-administration, it has much in common with mail or postal surveys. Indeed, some view Web surveys as the rendering of a mail survey on a computer screen and hence view the two modes as equivalent. One can certainly make a Web survey resemble a paper survey, but by doing so, one is eschewing the power of the Web, particularly with regard to the other elements such as the computerized, interactive, and visual nature of the Web. In other words, when the above features are considered together, it becomes apparent that the Web presents unique opportunities and challenges for survey design and implementation. It is these aspects that are the focus on this book.

1.5. The Importance of Design

A key assertion of this book is that design *is* important. Even if you are not yet convinced of this, by the time you get to the end, I hope to have made the case. Furthermore, design is holistic. Respondents don't care that one person wrote the questions, but another programmed the instrument, and a third designed the interface. They don't care that software limitations require you to use illogical or inappropriate designs. The instrument they see in the browser *is* the survey, and they will respond accordingly. As already noted, there is no interviewer to serve as go-between, to compensate for poor design, to explain what the designer *really* meant. Guidance on what to do and how to answer is derived directly

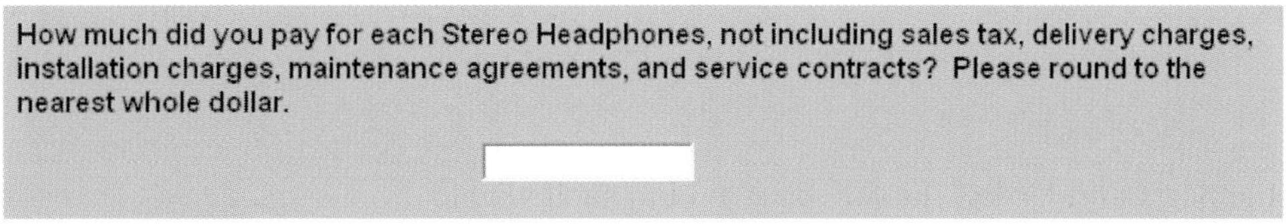

How much did you pay for each Stereo Headphones, not including sales tax, delivery charges, installation charges, maintenance agreements, and service contracts? Please round to the nearest whole dollar.

Figure 1.6 **Question on Purchase of Stereo Headphones.**

from the instrument itself, as with mail surveys. As Schwarz and his colleagues (e.g., Schwarz, 1996; Schwarz, Grayson, and Knäuper, 1998; Schwarz, Knäuper, Hippler, Noelle-Neumann, and Clark, 1991) have demonstrated, respondents use *all* available information to interpret the question and decide how to answer.

Let me give a few examples to illustrate why design may be important in Web surveys. Some time ago, I received a Web survey in which I was asked about a variety of household appliances I had purchased in the past three months. One of the choices was "stereo headphones," to which I responded in the affirmative, despite it not being a very salient purchase. The follow-up question is displayed in Figure 1.6.

And this is the exchange that followed, with *I* representing the Web instrument and *R* the respondent:

R: Can't remember
I: Invalid Characters: """"
R: 0
I: Invalid value. Valid range is "1/99999"
R: [A blank response]
I: Please enter your selection
R: 19.95
I: Invalid Characters: "_____"
R: [Closed browser]

All the error messages from the instrument appeared in boldface red type. I was trying to tell the survey that I could not remember how much I paid for the headphones. The only thing that the instrument was programmed to accept was a numerical response (whole numbers only). This illustrates two points: (1) that Web surveys can be much more of a dialogue than paper instruments and (2) problems can occur when the input requirements are too constrained. It seems that an answer in the prescribed format is more desirable than an accurate or honest answer. To the designer (or the client whose wishes the designer was following),

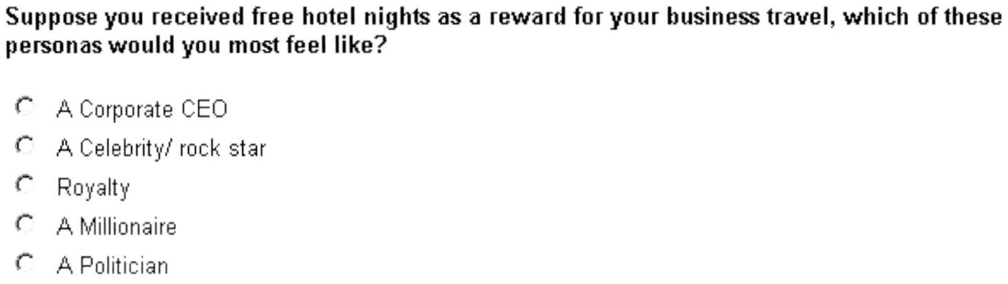

Suppose you received free hotel nights as a reward for your business travel, which of these personas would you most feel like?

    ◯   A Corporate CEO

    ◯   A Celebrity/ rock star

    ◯   Royalty

    ◯   A Millionaire

    ◯   A Politician

Figure 1.7 **Question on Hotel Rewards Program.**

it was inconceivable that someone would not be able to remember the exact price of a minor purchase made almost three months previously.

At times, it may be hard to distinguish between respondents who are satisficing (taking the easy way out; see Krosnick, 1991) and those who are trying their best to provide the right answer but are thwarted by the rigidity of the design. I would assert that the latter are more important to one's study and consequently the design should focus more on their needs. While designing more flexible instruments may mean more work for the designer and programmer, such effort may pay off in data of higher quality that better reflect the attitudes and intentions of the respondent.

This is not to beat up only on Web surveys – the above example on purchases is typical of the kind of item asked in the Bureau of Labor Statistics' quarterly Consumer Expenditure Survey, conducted by the Census Bureau. At least in the latter, one has an interviewer to which one can explain that the answer in unknown and provide a range or an approximation. Similarly, the interviewer is able to recognize when a respondent is unable to provide an answer and act accordingly. All one has on the Web is a dumb piece of software insisting on an answer that the respondent may be incapable of providing.

Another example comes from a survey I received from a different online panel vendor. The survey was about a proposed hotel affinity program, that is, points and rewards for frequent stays. One of the questions is reproduced in Figure 1.7.

Regardless of how one feels about the question itself, it may not seem irredeemable from a design perspective, until I point out that (1) no "none of the above" option was offered and (2) the option of simply skipping the question was not permitted. Attempting to proceed without answering produced a nasty error message demanding that all questions be answered. Clearly, the notion that *none* of the offered responses may apply was unthinkable to the designer. A more benign interpretation is that there was simply no communication between the client, the survey designer, and the programmer, with the latter simply applying the standard design approach for this survey vendor, namely, to require all items to be answered before proceeding.

These examples, and the many others like them one encounters in Web surveys, reflect not so much the limitations of the software but rather the lack of knowledge or concern on the designer's or programmer's part for the realities of the survey situation.

This is bad design, made worse by the unforgiving nature of computerized data collection instrument. One cannot simply write an explanation (unless space has been explicitly provided for this purpose). One cannot leave the field blank (unless the designer has allowed for this possibility). One cannot enter anything other than the allowable value predetermined by the person who developed the survey specifications or the programmer who implemented them. Computers can be much smarter and more forgiving than this, if we only build such flexibility into the systems.

Surveys have gone from being dialogues – albeit unbalanced and rule-based dialogues – to being interrogations. Charlie Cannell, who devoted much of his career to understanding the interaction between survey interviewers and respondents, would have been disappointed at the trend. And although this may sound like I'm railing against automation in surveys, and longing for the Luddite days of interviewers using paper instruments, this is certainly not my intent. I'm arguing against the mind-set that because computers make it easy for us to develop and deploy surveys, one does not need to think. Computers (and the Internet) are *tools* for the researcher to communicate with respondents, albeit in a structured way. Surveys are a way to elicit the information that the respondents possess, rather than a means to have them simply confirm (and conform to) our own view of the world. Computerized surveys (and particularly Web surveys) appear to be used as an instrument of the latter, rather than as a means to achieve the former.

All may not be as bad as it seems from the examples I show here and in the chapters to come. I have a plethora of examples of poorly designed Web surveys. But I have also seen many examples of well-designed and well-executed online surveys. Part of this may be a sampling or selection problem. The surveys that are readily accessible on the Web, for example, through a search on *Web survey*, are likely to be those that have no access restrictions and can be completed by anyone who wishes – and multiple times, if desired. Those designed by survey professionals are less likely to be encountered unless one is explicitly invited to participate in the survey. (As an aside, joining one or more opt-in panels is a good way to learn about Web survey design, both good and bad.) This observation may also explain why Bowker's (1999; cited in Dillman 2000) review identified many more Web surveys using scrolling designs than paging ones. The paging design tends to be used for more restricted surveys sent to specified persons, rather than those freely accessible on the Web. So, while the examples I choose may not be "representative" of the world of online research, there are still many examples of egregious design from commercial, government, and academic survey organizations alike, that a book such as this one still appears to be necessary.

The Web offers unique design challenges. While the importance of design is not new to Web surveys, the design tools and medium are. Each element of Web surveys has similarities with other methods (e.g., interactive Web surveys have something in common with interviewer-administered surveys), but it is in the combination of all these elements that Web surveys become unique. Similarly, Web surveys have much in common with Web design in general (e.g., issues of readability, layout, general use of tools, and design elements), but Web survey design is not the same as Web site design, as discussed in Section 1.3. We already know much about design that can be applied to Web survey design. But, we also have to recognize when these general design principles may not apply to Web surveys.

Much of what we have learned in designing paper-based surveys is relevant to Web survey design. But, I disagree with the view of some that Web survey design is an extension of design for paper-based surveys. The challenges are to recognize when and where the two media are different and to understand the implications of these differences for the design of surveys on the Web. Furthermore, to focus on the paper survey tradition may mean that the powerful interactive and graphical features of Web surveys remain largely unused. That is, the Web offers powerful design features that allow us to go beyond the limitations of traditional paper media.

Design is a balancing act. At one extreme, we can choose to design for the lowest common denominator, or least compliant browser, to use a Bowker and Dillman (2000) term. At the other extreme, we can build innumerable bells and whistles into our instrument, exploiting the technology to such an extent that few respondents are able to complete the survey. Design is not a goal in itself; that is the realm of art. The goal of design is to exploit the technology to the extent that it improves the process of providing accurate data in an efficient manner, while enjoying the experience of completing the survey.

Furthermore, design is not simply a matter of taste. Design can – and should – be evidence based. Design should be guided by theory and informed by practice. For example, Schneiderman (1992) discusses several measurable outcomes of usable designs. Similarly, the International Standards Organization (ISO) defines usability as "the extent to which a product can be used by specified users to achieve specified goals with effectiveness, efficiency and satisfaction in a specified context of use" (ISO 9241-11: Guidance on Usability, 1998). While user satisfaction is one component of usability, user performance (effectiveness and efficiency) are equally critical. While aesthetics should not be ignored (see Norman, 2004), the focus should be on design that facilitates the task of survey completion.

Good design thus serves several purposes:

1. It makes the task easier for the respondents; therefore, they may focus more on the primary task at hand (answering the questions) rather than on the secondary task (the procedures or mechanisms for doing so). In this way, good design should lead to more accurate data.
2. It makes the task more pleasant for the respondents; therefore, they may become more motivated to complete the survey or even to do a future survey.
3. It helps convey the importance and legitimacy of the survey; again this should lead to better quality data.

A poorly designed survey, conversely, suggests that you don't care much about the survey and, by extension, its outcome. Expecting that respondents will go to extra lengths to provide accurate and complete data when you weren't bothered to put together a decent survey is simply unrealistic. Put yourself in the respondents' position. This is the essence of user-centered design.

1.6. Focus of This Book

In this chapter, I've attempted to set the stage for what follows. I've alluded to several things I won't cover, but I've also already got into some of the specifics of design, such as the choice of scrolling or paging approaches. Let me wrap this up and move on to specifics in the remaining chapters. In summary, this book *is not* about:

1. Writing survey questions
2. Designing e-mail surveys, downloaded executables, or other types of Internet survey
3. Programming a Web survey
4. Setting up the hardware and systems to deploy a Web survey

Nor is the book about the very important survey issues of coverage, sampling, and nonresponse, that is, issues of sample representation. For those who want to read more about these issues, some sources include Couper (2000) and Schonlau, Fricker, and Elliott (2002), or visit www.websm.org for the latest papers on the topic. This book *is* about:

1. Designing effective Web surveys
2. Appropriate use of HTML and related tools for such design
3. Choosing the appropriate implementation strategies to maximize data quality or minimize survey errors

The Web is a powerful and easy-to-use survey design tool. This often creates the impression that anyone can do it. The message of this book is that the appropriate use of the tools to create a survey that maximizes data quality and minimizes error requires care. To return to Tufte's (2001, p. 191) quote, "Design is choice." This book is intended to guide the Web survey designer in making appropriate choices for a particular application.

Chapter 2

The Basic Building Blocks

The details are not the details. They make the design.
Charles Eames, American Designer (1907–1978)

In this chapter, I examine the basic tools available for constructing a survey question or, more specifically, for accepting the answer that respondents may provide. If we restrict ourselves to hypertext markup language (HTML) for now, there are only a limited set of input tool available to the designer. Despite this, I continue to be amazed at how often these tools are used with little apparent forethought. In the previous chapter, I noted that HTML forms are the dominant tools for delivering Web survey questions and alluded to some of the limitations of using HTML. Understanding each of the HTML form elements and how they are used is an important part of good Web survey design.

These input elements have both enabling and constraining functions. On the one hand, their shape and behavior suggest to the respondent the type of action that is permitted. If the input elements are used appropriately, and if respondents have any familiarity with completing forms on the Web, they will know what to do when presented with a certain type of input field.

On the other hand, the choice of input element often constrains Web respondents in ways not possible on paper. For example, a series of radio buttons allows a respondent to select one and only one of the available options. This is potentially both good and bad. It is good in the sense that a respondent is not able to violate the input requirements – in other words, you get the information you ask for. It is bad in the sense that it may make it difficult to accommodate unanticipated answers – the designer has to work harder to ensure that the answer the respondent wishes

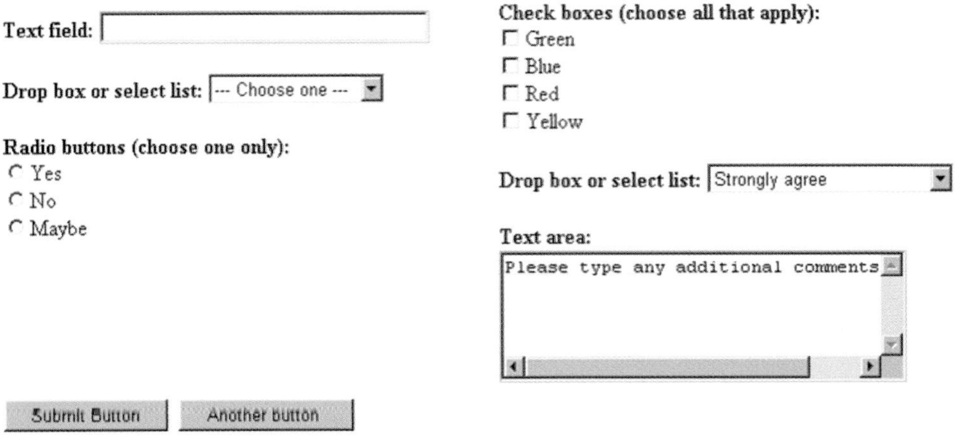

Text field: [   ]

Drop box or select list: [--- Choose one --- ▼]

Radio buttons (choose one only):
○ Yes
○ No
○ Maybe

Check boxes (choose all that apply):
☐ Green
☐ Blue
☐ Red
☐ Yellow

Drop box or select list: [Strongly agree   ▼]

Text area:
```
Please type any additional comments
```

[Submit Button] [Another button]

Figure 2.1 **Basic HTML Form Elements.**

to give can be accommodated (see also Section 5.5.6). Thus, while the wording of questions in Web surveys may appear similar to that for other modes of data collection, the way that responses are required to be input may have an effect on the responses obtained.

With this in mind, I begin this chapter with a review of the basic HTML input tools or form elements. The focus here is, first, on the choice of an input tool and, second, given that choice, the appropriate design of the tool. I then follow this in Chapter 3 with a discussion of a variety of other input tools that go beyond the basic toolkit.

2.1. Using the Appropriate Tool

As already noted, there are a limited number of form elements or widgets available in HTML forms. They go by various names, but generally include the following:

1. Radio buttons
2. Check boxes
3. Drop boxes or select lists
4. Text fields and text areas

These are illustrated in Figure 2.1. With this limited toolkit, the designer can represent virtually any type of question commonly asked on paper-based surveys.

HTML permits some degree of customization, but the underlying functions of these widgets remain unchanged. For example, one can rename the "Submit" button in whatever way one chooses, but the function – transmitting the contents of the form fields to the Web survey – is the same. Similarly, one has some control over the design of drop boxes, but the basic tool is quite limited, as we shall shortly see.

One of the class exercises I do, after introducing the form elements in Figure 2.1, is to ask participants to design on paper a simple Web survey instrument. Every time I do this, there is large variation in the tools used to represent the same question. For example, I get at least five different designs for a question on date of birth, not counting the variation in the order of month, day, and year. Among the more than 250 participants who have done this in many different settings, about 34% specify a single text box, while 11% specify separate text boxes for each field (see Figure 2.27), 22% use drop boxes, 29% use radio buttons (with or without other elements), and about 30% use check boxes. For a question on gender, most (88%) use radio buttons (64% aligning the two options vertically and 24% horizontally), but 7% use check boxes and 5% drop boxes. For a question on education level with more categories than the gender question, use of drop boxes increases to 28% and check boxes to 15%. The point is that the decisions about which HTML elements to use, and how to communicate this choice to the person programming the instrument, are not always obvious.

Despite – or maybe because of – the limited number of options, choosing the right tool for the right task is the critical issue. Why is this such a big deal? One of the most common mistakes I see in Web surveys is the use of a check box when a radio button is the appropriate tool. And this mistake is not only made by amateurs. Even one of the early texts on Web surveys fell into this trap, as do a number of Web surveys designed by university-based survey professionals. An example is shown In Figure 2.2. In spite of the verbal cue, one could select both "male" and "female," and one could select more than one age group.

Why are some Web surveys designed this way? There are several possible reasons. One suspicion I have is that it has to do with the separation between the designer of a survey (the person who crafts the questions) and the programmer (the person who implements it in the appropriate software language, whether directly in HTML or with software for designing Web forms or surveys). A box is a ubiquitous input tool in paper surveys, whether for single-choice or multiple-choice responses. Figure 2.3 shows an example from the National Ambulatory Medical Care Survey, using common paper survey formatting conventions. This is typical of many mail surveys too (see Dillman, 2000, for examples).

1. Gender (select one):
   □ Male
   □ Female

2. Age (select one):
   □ Under 30
   □ Between 30 and 60
   □ Over 60

3. Race (select all that apply):
   □ White
   □ Black or African American
   □ American Indian or Alaska Native
   □ Asian or Pacific Islander
   □ Other, please specify: [   ]

Figure 2.2 **Poor Use of Check Boxes.**

My guess is that designs such as in Figure 2.2 occur because the author or designer is prototyping in a paper paradigm, without great knowledge of the tools available on the Web. Or, the designer gives the programmer an existing paper instrument and asks for it to be replicated on the Web. The programmer is then implementing this design literally as specified. This gulf of communication – due in part to increased specialization and lack of knowledge of the tools being used – may be responsible for many of the more common errors we see in Web surveys.

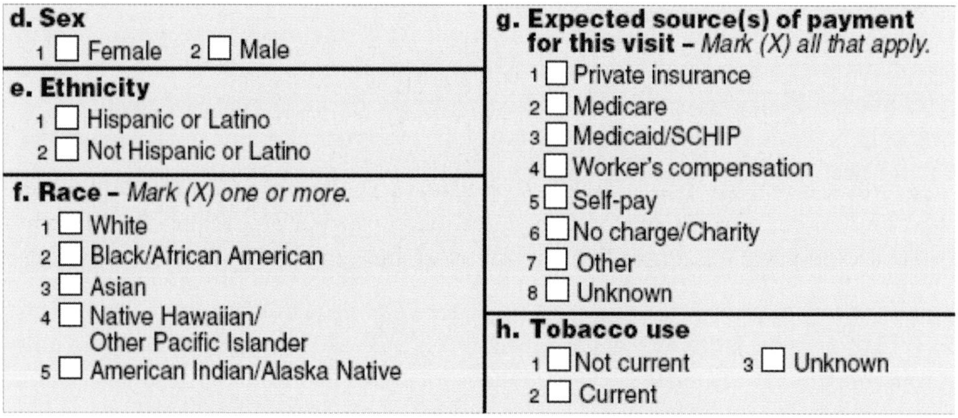

d. Sex
   1 □ Female   2 □ Male

e. Ethnicity
   1 □ Hispanic or Latino
   2 □ Not Hispanic or Latino

f. Race – *Mark (X) one or more.*
   1 □ White
   2 □ Black/African American
   3 □ Asian
   4 □ Native Hawaiian/
        Other Pacific Islander
   5 □ American Indian/Alaska Native

g. Expected source(s) of payment for this visit – *Mark (X) all that apply.*
   1 □ Private insurance
   2 □ Medicare
   3 □ Medicaid/SCHIP
   4 □ Worker's compensation
   5 □ Self-pay
   6 □ No charge/Charity
   7 □ Other
   8 □ Unknown

h. Tobacco use
   1 □ Not current   3 □ Unknown
   2 □ Current

Figure 2.3 **Example of Paper Questionnaire using Input Boxes for both Select One and Select Many Items.**

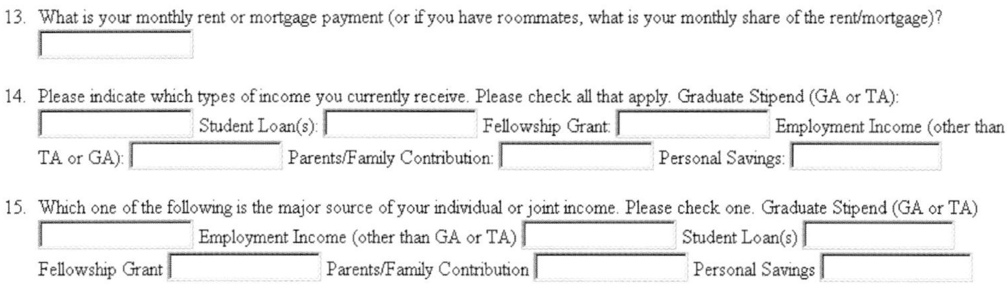

13. What is your monthly rent or mortgage payment (or if you have roommates, what is your monthly share of the rent/mortgage)?

14. Please indicate which types of income you currently receive. Please check all that apply. Graduate Stipend (GA or TA):
    Student Loan(s):   Fellowship Grant: Employment Income (other than
    TA or GA):   Parents/Family Contribution: Personal Savings:

15. Which one of the following is the major source of your individual or joint income. Please check one. Graduate Stipend (GA or TA)
    Employment Income (other than GA or TA)   Student Loan(s)
    Fellowship Grant   Parents/Family Contribution   Personal Savings

Figure 2.4 **Poor Use of Text Boxes.**

Alternatively, in the case of mixed-mode surveys, one could make arguments that the use of check boxes for both single-choice responses and check-all-that-apply responses most closely parallels the paper version. In the paper version there is nothing to constrain the respondents from selecting more than one response in a single choice question – leaving the researcher to clean up the variable during postsurvey processing. It could be argued that maximizing the equivalence of the paper and Web instruments requires "dumbing down" the Web survey to match the paper version. This is a dilemma faced in other combinations of survey modes too. For example, Groves (1989, Chapter 11) reviews some of the issues of comparability between face-to-face and telephone modes of data collection, and discusses the dilemma of optimizing for one versus the other. At least in the case of check boxes versus radio buttons, in my view, it makes more sense to use the tools appropriate for the mode (Web, in this case), and avail oneself of the opportunity to reduce errors of commission.

Figure 2.4 contains another example of a thoughtless replication of a single input tool (in this case a text box) for inputs of various types, some of which indeed require the entry of typed information (dollar amounts), but others appear to simply requires checking one response (see Question 15).

Another common design choice I encounter is the use of a drop box when a text field or set of radio buttons might be more appropriate. Figure 2.5 illustrates this based on real examples I've encountered, but suitably anonymized to protect

Figure 2.5 **Inappropriate Use of Drop Boxes.**

the perpetrator of this design faux pas. Imagine how much work it will take to answer these two questions. Even worse, the older one is – that is the poorer one's hand-eye coordination or sensorimotor abilities – the further one has to scroll to select one's age.

Why is this kind of design used? Two possible reasons for using a drop box are (1) to save space (relative to radio buttons) and (2) to control input (relative to text input). Neither of these arguments holds much water for many of the more egregious examples I have seen. There are many instances where drop boxes are an appropriate tool for a particular type of question, but they should not be used excessively in surveys. In addition, when choosing to use drop boxes, one needs to pay careful attention to design choices, as we shall see shortly.

These are but a few of the many examples of poor design I have collected over the past several years. They clearly indicate to me that people are either not aware of the effect of their design on the respondents' ability or indeed willingness to complete the survey, or know but don't care. Certainly, there are many good Web surveys out there today, and we have learned a lot about how to improve Web survey design. But the fact that I continue to encounter examples of thoughtless or careless design suggests that a book like this is still needed.

The point of these examples is that one should first choose the appropriate tool for the type of question one is designing and, second, one should then design the question consistent with the features and functions of the tools being used. With this in mind, let's examine each of the HTML input tools or form fields in more detail.

2.2. Radio Buttons

The radio button is a ubiquitous tool in Web forms in general, and in Web surveys in particular. However, it is important to understand the properties of this tool to ensure it is used appropriately. Radio buttons have several key features:

1. They come in a group or set, and operate dependently.
2. Once one button in the set has been selected, it cannot be turned off; one can only move the selection to another choice.
3. Radio buttons cannot be resized, regardless of the size of the surrounding text.

These features dictate how radio button items are designed and used. I will discuss each of the above points in turn.

2.2.1. Radio Buttons Come in a Group or Set

A defining feature of radio buttons is that the selections are mutually *exclusive*. When one item in a group is selected (turned on), any other item in the set that was previously selected is automatically deselected (turned off). This permits the selection of one and only one item in the set. Radio buttons are thus suitable for "Choose one" types of questions.

2.2.2. A Selection Cannot Easily be Canceled

Once one of the items in a set of radio buttons is selected, the selection cannot be canceled – it can only be moved to another item in the group. Why is this an issue? Well, without taking special effort to accommodate this situation, respondents may not have the opportunity to change their mind and decide not to answer that question. Of course, one could choose to ignore the problem, arguing that very few respondents are likely to want to cancel a choice (as opposed to moving it to a different response). This is in fact the approach many Web surveys take.

There may be some times where dealing with this issue is a requirement, for example, for questions of a very sensitive or threatening nature. In this case, there are several possible solutions, which include the following:

1. Use check boxes instead of radio buttons. Check boxes can easily be unchecked, leaving a question unanswered. However, as discussed elsewhere in this chapter, I don't view this as a desirable solution.
2. Offer a "Choose not to answer" response on every question. This will likely increase the number of people using this answer; see the literature on offering explicit "don't know" (DK) responses (e.g., Krosnick and Fabrigar, 1997; Schuman and Presser, 1981; see also Section 5.6). This is illustrated in Figure 2.6 below.
3. Have a preselected null response associated with the question. As the respondent selects a response, the radio button preceding the question is unselected (moved to the desired selection). As with the above option of offering a "rather not say" option, this may encourage "satisficing," as it is easy for respondents to simply leave the question unanswered. This approach is also illustrated in Figure 2.6.
4. Have a "clear" or "reset" button for each screen or form. This clears or empties the entire form, not just the item in question (unless there is only

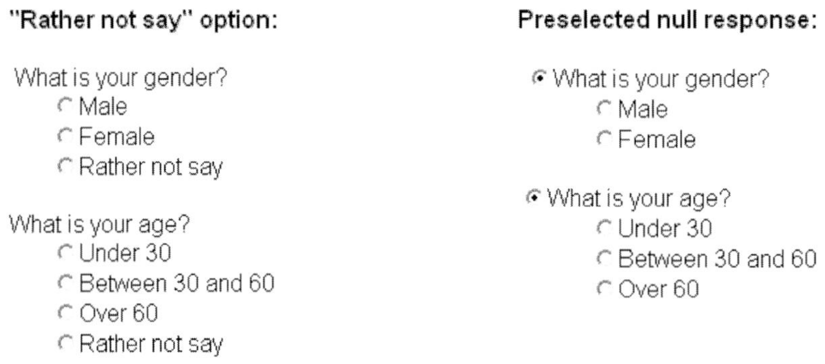

"Rather not say" option:

What is your gender?
- ◯ Male
- ◯ Female
- ◯ Rather not say

What is your age?
- ◯ Under 30
- ◯ Between 30 and 60
- ◯ Over 60
- ◯ Rather not say

Preselected null response:

◉ What is your gender?
- ◯ Male
- ◯ Female

◉ What is your age?
- ◯ Under 30
- ◯ Between 30 and 60
- ◯ Over 60

Figure 2.6 **Example of "Rather not say" Option and Preselected Null Response.**

one item on the form). As an aside, this is another argument for a paging design approach – the effect of a clear or reset action applies only to that form or screen, not to the entire instrument. I'll discuss this further in the context of action buttons (see Chapter 5).

5. Let the respondent use the "back" and "forward" buttons to reset the page. Again, this only works in paging designs – and then maybe not all designs, depending on how cache memory is used and whether pages are dynamically generated – and may interfere with the ability to go back and review previous answers.

When there are no design requirements that dictate the types of solutions illustrated in Figure 2.6, there are better ways to design questions to encourage respondents to choose one of the substantive responses. I will return to these designs later in Chapter 5 in the context of reducing item missing data.

The preselected null response in Figure 2.6 (right side) is different from that of offering the respondent an easy out and preselecting it (see Figure 2.7). This example is a combination of the two approaches illustrated in Figure 2.6 and is likely to encourage missing data.

Another example is shown in Figure 2.8. Unlike in Figure 2.7, the preselected "no response" options are more visually prominent, potentially legitimizing their use. Further, the approaches illustrated in Figures 2.7 and 2.8 make it hard analytically to distinguish between an item that was inadvertently skipped and one that a respondent deliberately chose not to answer. These examples illustrate the trade-offs that often occur, in that trying to solve one potential problem may exacerbate another.

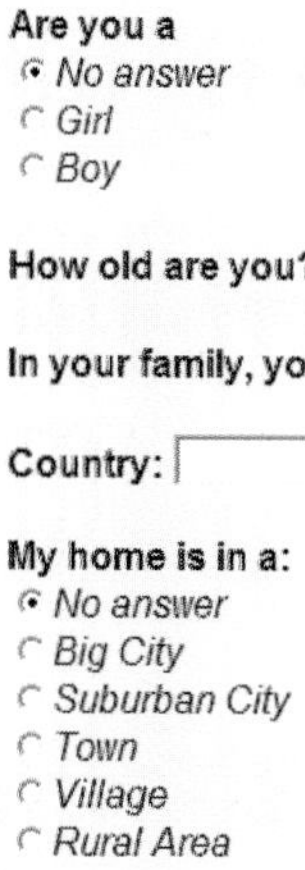

Are you a
- ⦿ *No answer*
- ○ *Girl*
- ○ *Boy*

How old are you? [*No answer* ▾]

In your family, you are the: [*No answer* ▾]

Country: [ ]

My home is in a:
- ⦿ *No answer*
- ○ *Big City*
- ○ *Suburban City*
- ○ *Town*
- ○ *Village*
- ○ *Rural Area*

Figure 2.7 **Example of a Preselected "No Response" Option.**

These approaches (Figures 2.7 and 2.8) are not the same as having one of the substantive options preselected (see Figure 2.15). The latter is unquestionably a bad idea for surveys. It may well make sense in e-commerce or other applications where default responses are provided, and users only need to modify or override a few selected items. In fact, Nielsen recommends doing so in an Alertbox (www. useit.com/alertbox/20040927.html): "Always offer a default selection for radio button lists." But in a survey setting, a respondent may simply skip over that item

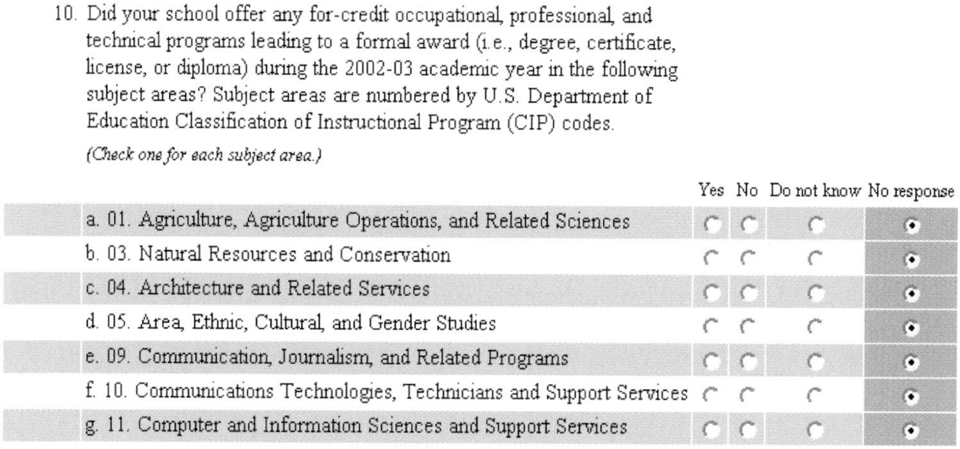

10. Did your school offer any for-credit occupational, professional, and technical programs leading to a formal award (i.e., degree, certificate, license, or diploma) during the 2002-03 academic year in the following subject areas? Subject areas are numbered by U.S. Department of Education Classification of Instructional Program (CIP) codes.

(Check one for each subject area.)

	Yes	No	Do not know	No response
a. 01. Agriculture, Agriculture Operations, and Related Sciences	○	○	○	⦿
b. 03. Natural Resources and Conservation	○	○	○	⦿
c. 04. Architecture and Related Services	○	○	○	⦿
d. 05. Area, Ethnic, Cultural, and Gender Studies	○	○	○	⦿
e. 09. Communication, Journalism, and Related Programs	○	○	○	⦿
f. 10. Communications Technologies, Technicians and Support Services	○	○	○	⦿
g. 11. Computer and Information Sciences and Support Services	○	○	○	⦿

Figure 2.8 **Example of a Preselected "No Response" Option.**

and it is not known whether the respondent intended to record that answer or simply missed the question. What may help a user in an information-seeking or e-commerce setting may inappropriately bias responses in a survey setting – another example of why Web surveys are not the same as Web sites. Unless of course one's perverse goal is to lead respondents to a particular answer – hardly the aim of a legitimate survey endeavor – my advice is simply never provide a preselected option to a survey question. What might be considered a misdemeanor offense in drop-box design – having the first option visibly displayed – is tantamount to a cardinal sin of survey design when using radio buttons.

2.2.3. Radio Buttons Cannot be Resized

Changing the size of the text associated with a radio button will not change the size of the button itself. No matter how large or small the font, the size of the radio button will remain unchanged in HTML. This is illustrated in Figure 2.9. Try this yourself: Change the font size in a Web form, and while the text should change size, the form field (radio button or check box) remains unchanged. Why should we be concerned about this?

The design of radio buttons means that they provide very small targets for selection. Unlike in Windows applications, HTML requires clicking on the radio button itself, rather than on the associated text, to activate the selection. Fitts' (1954) law, a widely used function in the field of human-computer interaction, suggests that the time to acquire a target is a function of the distance to and size of the target (see Schneiderman 1992, pp. 153–154). Mathematically, Fitts' law is stated as follows:

$$MT = C_1 + C_2 \log_2(2D/W)$$

Where MT is the movement time, C_1 and C_2 are constants that depend on the device being used, D is the distance to be moved from the start to the center of the target, and W is the width or size of the target. The precise predictions depend on the device being used (mouse, stylus, cursor keys, etc.). All other things being equal, this will mean that answering a Web survey should take more effort (time) on the part of the respondent than other forms of GUI survey instruments.

In more recent versions of HTML (4.01 and later), there is an attribute associated with a label that permits one to designate the entire text associated with a radio button (or other form elements, such as a check box) as a clickable area. This

○ Radio button with small font size

○ Radio button with medium font size

○ Radio button with large font size

Figure 2.9 **Effect of Font Size on Radio Buttons.**

is done using the instruction `label for="XXX,"` where XXX is the label to be associated with that response option. While this does not work in older versions of browsers (e.g., Netscape 4.7), including the attribute in the code will not affect those using such older browsers. Furthermore, browsers vary in the cues they provide that the text is clickable. For example, in some versions of Netscape, the browser does not render a box around the text when clicked, thereby providing no visual feedback of the selection. The examples in Figure 2.10 were generated in Internet Explorer 5.0, but later versions of Internet Explorer apparently also do not display the box around the text.

Figure 2.10 illustrates this feature. In the top example, only the radio button is an active area for clicking, as indicated by the box. In the lower version, generated in HTML 4.1 using the label instruction, clicking anywhere on the label text activates the corresponding radio button.

As an aside, this is a good example of how HTML is evolving, and focusing on a particular rendition of the language may quickly lead to outdated ideas. For this reason, standards and guidelines are not written in stone and will of necessity

a. In this example, one can click only on the radio button to activate the selection:

⊙ Yes, one can only click the radio button

○ No, one cannot click anywhere else

b. In this example, one can click anywhere on the label text to activate the selection:

⊙ Yes, one can click anywhere

○ No, one does not need to click on the radio button

Figure 2.10 **Selection Area in Older and Newer Versions of HTML.**

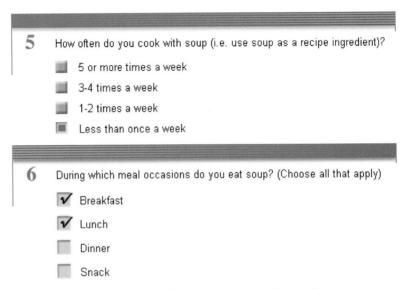

Figure 2.11 **Alternatives to HTML: Zoomerang.com Example.**

evolve. Focusing on the design principles or reasons behind a particular design choice is more important than the particular implementation of a design approach. It is also an example of how different browsers render things in slightly different ways and of the need for testing on multiple platforms and browsers. Still, the cue that the entire label is clickable may be subtle, and many users may be unaware of this ability, meaning that standard HTML radio buttons may still be less than desirable in terms of the sensorimotor effort required to select them.

Given this potential drawback with HTML radio buttons, a number of customized alternatives have been developed, using clickable images to replace the radio button widget. With this approach, anything can be used in place of the radio button (or check box, or any other HTML form element). The size and shape of the object is determined by the designer. A customized selection button could also be designed so that clicking a second time on the object deselects it, overcoming another drawback of radio buttons mentioned earlier.

Zoomerang.com, a widely used survey tool, uses this approach (see Figures 2.11 and 2.12), as do many other Web survey packages. This may require a little extra work in programming and more care in the design. In particular, one should ensure that the clickable image behaves in a way expected by the user and that the feedback provided (the changed image) makes sense to the user. For example, the early versions of the Zoomerang.com tool used a similar shape for radio buttons

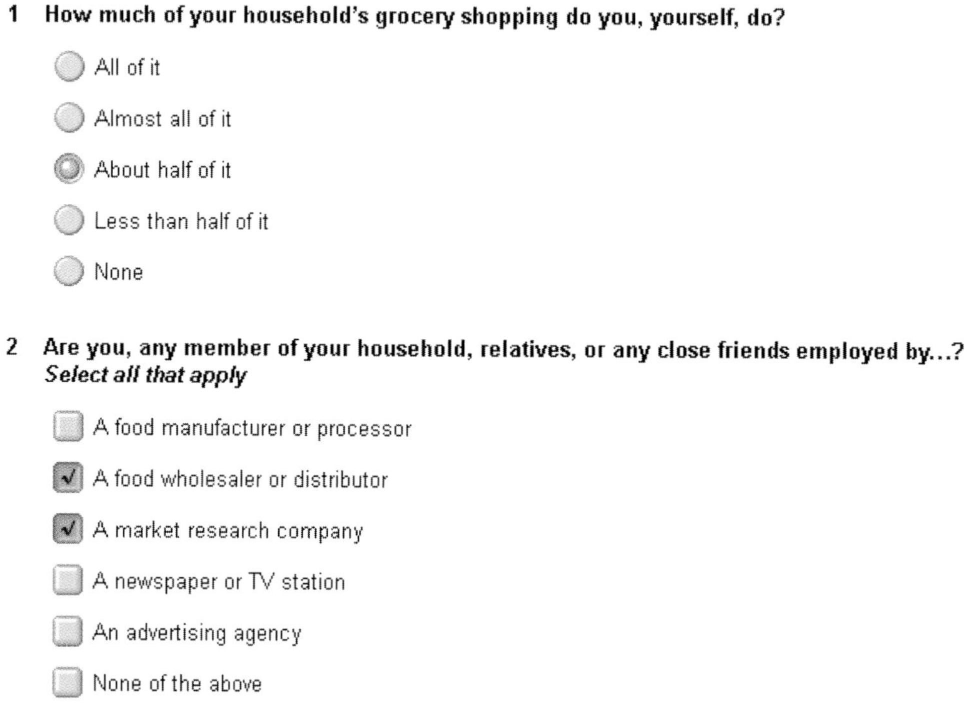

1 How much of your household's grocery shopping do you, yourself, do?

◯ All of it

◯ Almost all of it

◉ About half of it

◯ Less than half of it

◯ None

2 Are you, any member of your household, relatives, or any close friends employed by...?
Select all that apply

☐ A food manufacturer or processor

☑ A food wholesaler or distributor

☑ A market research company

☐ A newspaper or TV station

☐ An advertising agency

☐ None of the above

Figure 2.12 **Alternatives to HTML: Zoomerang.com Example.**

and check boxes, and only after clicking on each was the difference clear to respondents (see Figure 2.11). Alternative tools available on Zoomerang.com now permit a designer to use more familiar circles for single-selection item and squares for multiple-selection items, resembling the look and feel of the standard HTML tools (see Figure 2.12).

If such alternatives to radio buttons are so attractive, why are they not used more often? One reason is they may increase the download time of the page marginally. However, given the rise in bandwidth in recent years, and the rich graphics that many Web sites employ, this is hardly likely to be noticeable to most respondents. Another early objection raised was that the alternatives would not work in an identical manner across all platforms and browsers. Again, with the improvements in the most commonly used browsers, this concern has generally proved to be unfounded.

A more important concern relates to issues of accessibility. The alternative input tools may present problems for those using screen readers, depending on how the tools are implemented. One issue concerns labeling or describing the image for those who can't see it. For visually impaired users using screen readers, the designer must take extra care to provide a meaningful tag or label for the graphic image, to convey to the user that clicking on the image will have the effect described. However, a larger issue relates to the action taken by the system when the user clicks on the image. Clickable images where the action is to generate a new HTML page can be done in HTML, but if the form of the image changes when clicked (e.g., from an unselected to a selected state, as in the Zoomerang.com examples), client-side scripting is required. Thus, if JavaScript is not active, clicking on the buttons in a Zoomerang.com survey will have no effect – nothing will happen.

The more exotic the design of the widget used, the less likely it is to be familiar to the user. One principle of user-centered design is that the look and feel of tools should be consistent with user expectations (see Couper, 1999). Designing consistently with such expectations has the advantage of reducing errors and time, thereby also reducing respondent frustration.

To summarize, the standard HTML radio buttons have both benefits and drawbacks. The advantages of standard HTML radio buttons are as follows:

1. They are a standard feature of HTML forms, and thus work on all browsers.
2. Their operation is familiar to users.
3. No additional programming, design, or testing is needed to implement them.
4. They serve a useful forcing function, restricting the respondent to a single choice, when appropriate.

Their disadvantages are as follows:

1. They present a small target area for clicking and cannot be resized.
2. Once a respondent has selected an answer, it is harder to change his/her mind and not answer the question at all

Of course, this latter disadvantage could be viewed as an advantage, with the potential effect of reducing item missing data.

2.3. Check Boxes

Unlike radio buttons, check boxes operate independently. Each check box in a list or set of responses acts as a toggle – the setting is either on (checked) or off (blank).

A group of check boxes thus act as mutually *inclusive* toggles. One can check none, or one can check all; one can add selections or remove selections made earlier. Check boxes are thus appropriate for "choose all that apply" questions.

Some survey researchers hold strong views about the use of check-all-that apply questions. For example, in their classic text, *Asking Questions*, Sudman and Bradburn (1982) argue against the use of check-all-that-apply items. More recently, Dillman (2000, p. 399) notes, "I prefer to follow a more conservative approach and avoid the use of check-all-that-apply boxes," and recommends the use of a yes/no format for each item.

In one of the few empirical comparisons, Rasinski, Mingay, and Bradburn (1994) conducted an experiment using a paper self-administered questionnaire (SAQ). They found that fewer items were endorsed in the check-all version compared with the explicit yes/no version. They also found that items at the top of the list were more likely to be endorsed than those lower on the list. Their findings provide some support for Krosnick's (1991) argument that respondents tend to satisfice – that is, apply minimal effort – when completing survey questionnaires, and that a check-all-that-apply format may encourage such behavior.

Dillman, Smyth, Christian, and Stern (2003) tested the effect of check-all-that-apply versus forced-choice questions in a Web survey of college students (see also Smyth, Dillman, Christian, and Stern, 2005). They found that the forced-choice version consistently produced a greater number of items endorsed but caution that this could be a result of greater cognitive processing encouraged by the forced-choice, or increased acquiescence generated by the explicit yes/no format. However, they found similar order effects in the one question that explicitly tested this across formats, suggesting that order effects are not reduced in one format over the other. However, Smyth et al. (2005) found that respondents spent on average two-and-a-half times as much time on the forced-choice as on the check-all questions.

Given these arguments, should one avoid check-all-that-apply questions like the plague? They have a place in the survey researcher's toolkit but should be used judiciously. A long series of yes/no questions may get more complete responses (as the evidence above suggests), but possibly at the risk of increasing survey length that the risk of breakoffs increases. The choice of tool depends on the length of the list and the objectives, both of the survey overall, and of the particular question. Some questions can more readily be turned into yes/no questions, while others make less sense in that format.

Let's take an example. The following question (in Figure 2.13) is from a college student survey on drug and alcohol use (McCabe et al., 2002). This is *not* a core

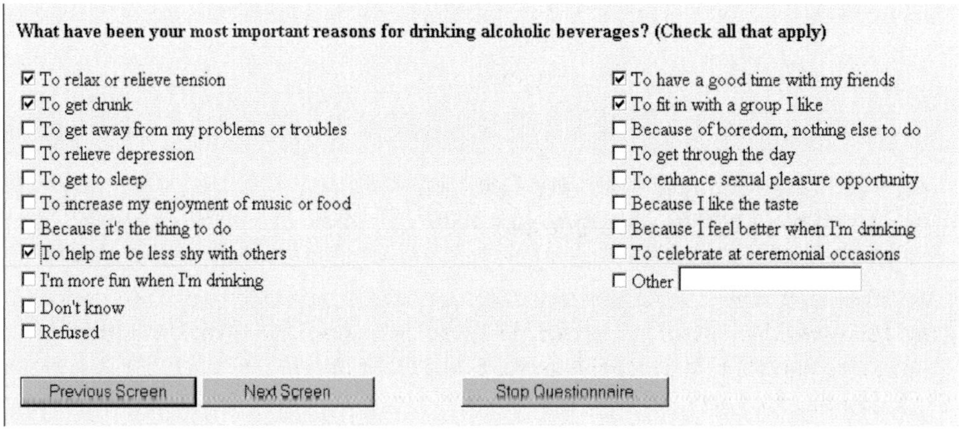

Figure 2.13 **Use of Check Boxes.**

question in the survey, and turning it into seventeen separate yes/no questions would add considerably to the length of the survey. However, given the choice of a response format such as this, care must be taken with the design of the response options. I'll return to this example later, in a discussion of layout issues (see Section 4.4.1.3). With regard to the classic primacy effect, that is the increased selection of items early on the list, Web surveys offer a potential solution. The response options can easily be randomized – much more so than in paper-based surveys. This means that the effect of the order of response options is reduced, as the effect is essentially distributed across all the response options on the list.

In addition to examples such as that in Figure 2.13, where the check box format may reduce respondent burden over a series of individual items, there are some commonly asked questions for which a check-all-that-apply format – and hence check boxes on the Web – is quite appropriate. Probably best-known among these is the multiple-response race question in the United States. The example in Figure 2.14 comes from the U.S. Decennial Census.

Aside from the issue of when it is appropriate to use check boxes, there are a couple of other design issues that are unique to check boxes on the Web. These are

1. How to deal with mutually exclusive options (e.g., selection and "none of the above").
2. How to restrict the number of options selected (e.g., select no more than 3 responses).

What is this person's race? Select one or more races.

☐ White or Caucasian

☐ Black or African American or Negro

☐ American Indian or Alaskan Native

☐ Asian

☐ Native Hawaiian or Other Pacific Islander

Figure 2.14 **Multiple Response Question.**

In both cases, scripts are required to resolve the inconsistency, and the decision is between whether this is a client-side script or a server-side script, or no script at all (i.e., accepting the inconsistency). The latter approach is essentially what is currently done in paper surveys.

Regarding the first of these issues, it may be visually appealing to have a radio button for the "none" response. If one or more check boxes were selected, the radio button would be deselected. If the radio button was clicked, all checked boxes would be cleared. However, this would take some client-side code to achieve, and may not be worth the effort, relative to a server-generated message regarding the inconsistency.

A final note on check boxes: like radio buttons, check boxes are usually presented in a set, even though they act independently. At the very minimum, a single check box could be used, not that this makes sense for most survey questions. A common practice on Web sites – presumably to "trap" unwary visitors into agreeing to be contacted – is to use a single check box, already prechecked (see Figure 2.15). I have not yet seen – and hope never to see – an egregious example like this in a real survey. However, I have been shown this as a "feature" in an unnamed Web survey software package, so at least somebody must think it is a good idea.

In some Web experiments, a single check box is used for consent to participate. Even for these uses, it is better to have two separate options (e.g., "yes" and "no") rather than a single check box option. If a single check box is used, under no circumstances should it be preselected as in the example in Figure 2.15.

Despite the obvious distinction between radio buttons and check boxes, as we have already seen, there continue to be examples where these two HTML form

☑Yes, please add me to your online panel. Please send me any information you may think is even remotely relevant to my interests, or which you think could squeeze another dime out of me. In fact, please feel free to sell my e-mail address to other marketers, spammers, or whatever you want to do with it.

Figure 2.15 **Use of Single Prechecked Check Box.**

elements are used inappropriately. In particular, because of the visual similarity of check boxes to standard selection objects in paper-based surveys, they are often mistakenly used for single-selection questions in Web surveys.

Some designers may want to use check boxes in mixed-mode surveys (paper and Web) to have the Web experience *exactly* resemble paper. In other words, in paper questionnaires, there is nothing to constrain a respondent from checking multiple boxes despite instruction to select only one. Doing the same on the Web seems to be importing some of the disadvantages of paper, even if the measurement experience differs across the two modes.

2.4. Drop Boxes

Drop boxes (also called select lists, select fields, or pulldown menus) are widely used in Web surveys and Web sites alike. Drop boxes in HTML share many similarities with their Windows counterparts such as list boxes or combo boxes. Probably for this reason, there are many – designers and users alike – who do not fully understand their behavior on the Web. There are several features or design choices for drop boxes in HTML we have to understand to use the tool appropriately. These features include:

1. The list is fixed; one cannot enter an item that is not on the list
2. There is more than one way to find and select items on the list
3. No data are transmitted to the server unless a selection is made
4. One can choose how many items to display initially
5. Drop boxes can be limited to a single selection or multiple selections

Let's deal with each of these in turn.

2.4.1. The Items on the List are Fixed

One limitation of HTML drop boxes is that the user can only pick items that are present on the list. In Windows-based applications, such as Visual Basic, there is a combo box, which combines a text box and a list. If the item is not available on the list, the user can still enter it using the text box. No such option exists in HTML. An HTML drop box behaves in the same way as a set of radio buttons – the selection of a response is limited to the options on the list.

One implication of this is that drop boxes are useful only for a closed list. In e-commerce they are often used for presenting dates, state names, products, and so on. That is, they are good for restricting the selection to only those options the designer wants to make available to the user. In Web surveys, if there is a possibility that the answer one wants from the respondent is not on the list, a two-step approach is needed to capture this response.

In radio button or check box questions, an "other, specify" response can be built into the response set. When using drop boxes, this must be done in two steps: (1) offer a "not on the list" or "other" response and (2) follow this with a text field to specify the additional response. That is, this approach requires a skip or conditional question.

2.4.2. There is More Than One Way to Find and Select Items

An HTML drop box is not a searchable list, it is a scrollable list. There are several ways to scroll through the list. One can use the mouse, either by clicking and dragging on the scroll bar, or by clicking in the box then using the scroll wheel on the mouse to move through the list. Alternatively, one can use the keyboard. But here is where the drop box behaves in ways often unexpected by users.

When using a keyboard, an HTML drop box permits first-letter lookup rather than a progressive search. Progressive search works in Windows-based applications, but not in a browser-based environment. In a progressive search, typing M-I-C will uniquely find Michigan in an alphabetical list of states. In a single-letter or first-letter search, typing M-I-C will take one successively to Maine (the first M state), then Idaho (the first I state), and then California (the first C state). To reach Michigan, one has to type M repeatedly (in this case four times). Similarly, in a first-letter search, M-M-M-M-M-M-M-M finds Maine then Maryland, Massachusetts, Michigan, Minnesota, Mississippi, Missouri, and finally Montana, whereas typing M-O will uniquely find Montana in a progressive search. This is probably not how users intuitively expect such lists to behave, and it is not how such lists behave in other Windows applications.

Snyder, formerly of the Nielsen Norman Group (NN/g, personal communication, January 16th, 2005) reported:

> In the NN/g e-commerce study conducted in January 2000 I watched 39 users from the state of New Hampshire fill out address forms. Most either used the mouse to select or tried to type NH for New Hampshire (which selected Hawaii instead on all the sites tested).

International Calculator

1. To which country are you mailing?

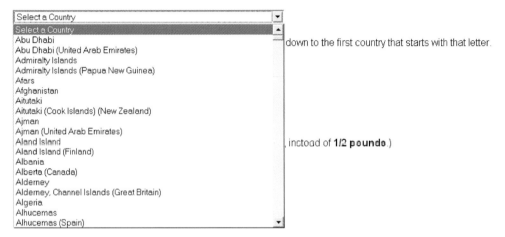

down to the first country that starts with that letter.

, instead of **1/2 pounds**.)

Figure 2.16 **USPS Example of Long Drop Box.**

> A few users complained about this and a couple even submitted the form with the wrong state. Only one user used the arrow keys to move down to New Hampshire after typing N. No one used the N key repeatedly. The users in this study had all shopped online before but we screened out anyone with software/Web development experience.

To use another example, if one was looking for "Congo" in a list of countries, and it was listed under Democratic Republic of the Congo (formerly Zaire), or Republic of the Congo (which is a different country, but whose former name was Congo), it would not be found where the user was looking. The work-around is to have several listings, one for each version of the country name. Interestingly, the CIA's World Factbook (https://www.cia.gov/library/publications/the-world-factbook/index.html) uses a drop box for a list of almost 300 countries and locations, and lists the two Congos under "Congo, Democratic Republic of the" and "Congo, Republic of the," not under "Democratic," or under "Republic." Another example is the U.S. Postal Service's international rate calculator (http://ircalc.usps.gov/) with almost 800 entries in the drop box (see Figure 2.16). In this example, there is at least text below the select list partially warning the user of the limitations of the tool: "**Tip:** Typing the first letter of the country you want will jump the list down to the first country that starts with that letter."

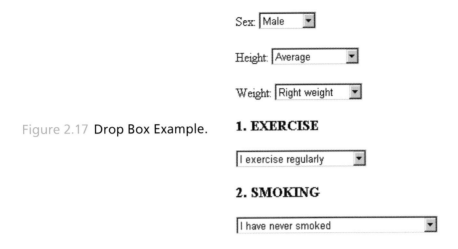

Figure 2.17 **Drop Box Example.**

This can seem even worse if numbers are used. For example, if I want to enter "59" using the keyboard method, I'd have to press the "5" key ten times. Don't tell me this is quicker than typing 59 in a text box. Many surveys use a drop list for age, often starting with the current year. The older one is, the further one has to scroll to find the right year. Add to this the fact that with a large number of responses, the scroll bar becomes very small, making those with the poorest sensorimotor ability do the most work.

As we shall see later (in Chapter 3), there are alternatives that act more like one would expect. However, they require JavaScript – an issue I've already discussed in Chapter 1, and will return to in Chapter 3 – and users may now be so inured to the way the standard HTML drop boxes work that they may not derive the benefits from any improvements.

2.4.3. The Data Field is Blank Until a Selection is Made

If the predisplayed selection is one that the user wants, he/she actually has to click on that selection to indicate the choice. Not doing anything will send a blank field when the form is submitted. In other words, an explicit action must be taken by the respondent to make a selection.

Take a look at the example in Figure 2.17. This was before the respondent had selected any of the responses. If the displayed options happened to match the respondent's answers, and one did nothing, the data fields would be empty when

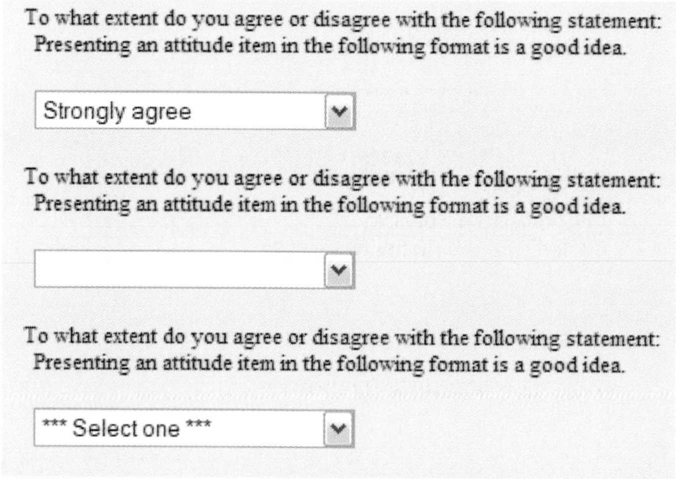

> To what extent do you agree or disagree with the following statement: Presenting an attitude item in the following format is a good idea.
>
> | Strongly agree | ⌄ |
>
> To what extent do you agree or disagree with the following statement: Presenting an attitude item in the following format is a good idea.
>
> | | ⌄ |
>
> To what extent do you agree or disagree with the following statement: Presenting an attitude item in the following format is a good idea.
>
> | *** Select one *** | ⌄ |

Figure 2.18 **Labeling of First Option in Drop Box.**

the form was submitted to the server. But the visual cue suggests that if that is the response one wants, one need do nothing.

The more typical approach is to have a "click here" or "select one" response be visible in the drop box, both to give respondents a visual cue as to what needs to be done, and to avoid leading them to a specific response. This is illustrated in Figure 2.18. The first example is similar to that in Figure 2.17. Not only does this approach suggest a desirable response, but it also provides no visual distinction between a question that has not yet been answered and one in which the displayed response was selected. The second example provides no clue to the respondent as to the format of the response options, or as to what needs to be done. The third example addresses some of these issues, and is the better approach to designing such questions – provided, of course, that a drop box is the way to go. In this particular example, there are better ways to design the question on the Web.

2.4.4. One Can Choose How Many Items to Display Initially

Another feature of drop boxes is that the designer has control over how many items to display initially in the drop box. This is done with the `size="n"` attribute, where n is the number of options visible. The vast majority of examples I have

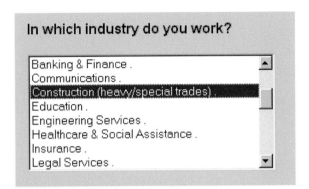

Figure 2.19 **Drop Box with Multiple Responses Displayed.**

seen display only one response in the field before it is clicked, the default setting for HTML. While this approach avoids the other problems discussed above – of leading the respondent to a particular response, or providing insufficient feedback that a response alternative has been picked – it still suffers from the drawback of giving the respondent little clue as to the available options. Figure 2.19 shows an example of a drop box set to display eight response options. This is closer in look and feel to a scroll box in a desktop application.

In designing a drop box or scroll box, it is important that the respondent be able to predict what the remaining responses are; in other words, they should be able to infer the invisible items from the visible ones. If not, they are disproportionately likely to miss the hidden options, as our research has demonstrated (Couper, Tourangeau, Conrad, and Crawford, 2004).

The display of response options helps reduce cognitive effort. For example, if you were asked how many times you'd been to the movies in the past twelve months, you could be embarked on a potentially lengthy enumeration and /or estimation process (see Tourangeau, Rips, and Rasinski, 2000). But, if before beginning to formulate your answer, it was made clear that the response options were a series of ranges (such as 0, 1–5, 6–10, etc.) or even a subjective estimation using vague quantifiers (never, seldom, often, etc.), the cognitive effort can quickly be short-circuited and the task becomes much simpler. I'm not saying that this is necessarily desirable from a question wording perspective, but that the design of the question *and* the presentation of the response options should match the task the respondent is expected to perform.

On the other hand, how would you like to wait until you have taken the time and effort to formulate what you consider to be an appropriate response, only then

Figure 2.20 **Drop Box with No Options Visible.**

to learn that the question was interested only in broad categories, rather than the precise value you had come up with? This is the effect of a drop box without the response options displayed. Take a look at the question in Figure 2.20 – only when the respondent clicks on the drop box does it become apparent that the question is about religiosity, with response options ranging from "extremely religious" to "extremely non religious."

2.4.5. Drop Boxes Permit Single or Multiple Selections

It is probably not widely known that drop boxes can also be designed to accept multiple responses. In other words, drop boxes can be designed to behave like a set of radio buttons (select one) or a set of check boxes (select many). To select multiple responses, the respondent must press "Ctrl" and click on each of the selections (much like doing a multiple selection in Windows). See the example in Figure 2.21.

But would one want to do this? Not only does this require a degree of dexterity and care to execute, but some of the selections may not be visible. Take a look at the examples in Figure 2.22. Both have four of eight response options displayed. There is nothing in the tool that suggests that one permits multiple selections while the other restricts the respondent to a single selection. In addition, it is not apparent which other options, if any, are selected in the example on the right.

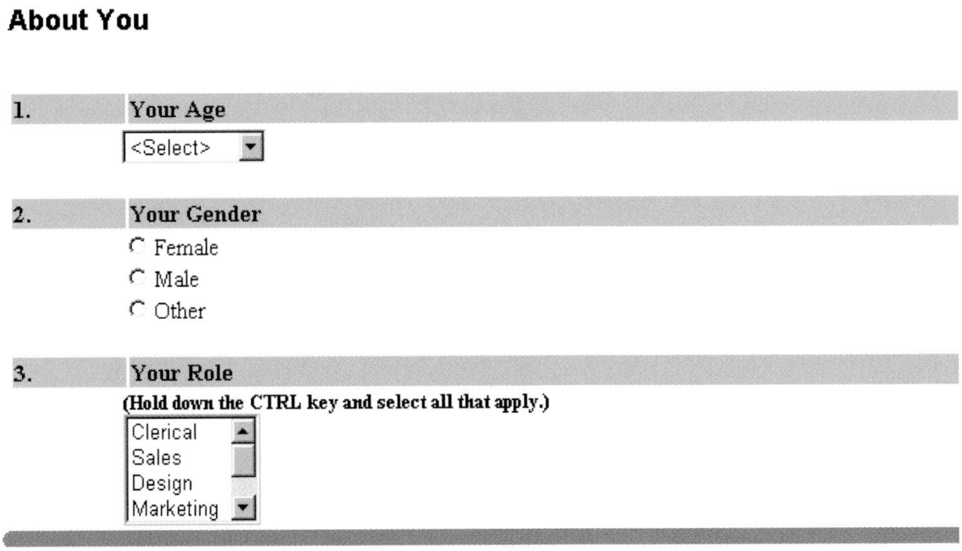

About You
1. Your Age
<Select>
2. Your Gender
Female
Male
Other
3. Your Role
(Hold down the CTRL key and select all that apply.)
Clerical
Sales
Design
Marketing

Figure 2.21 Multiple Response Drop Box.

In the example in Figure 2.21, it is apparent from the size of the scroll bar that there are only about six responses, of which four are shown. It would not take much additional space to show all the options.

Check boxes are a better tool for multiple selections. This does not address the issue of whether a "check all that apply" question is the optimal way to gather data of this type (see Section 2.3). In my view, there is no advantage – and many potential disadvantages – to using drop boxes for multiple selections. Mercifully, I have not seen too many such examples in Web surveys. But Figure 2.23 shows one such example, where a long list of options is provided, and it is likely that people will select several responses, making this a particularly onerous task, and one that

What is your favorite color?
Red
Green
Blue
Yellow
What are your favorite colors?
Green
Blue
Yellow
Orange

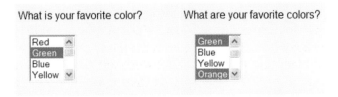

Figure 2.22 Drop Boxes with Single Selection and Multiple Selections.

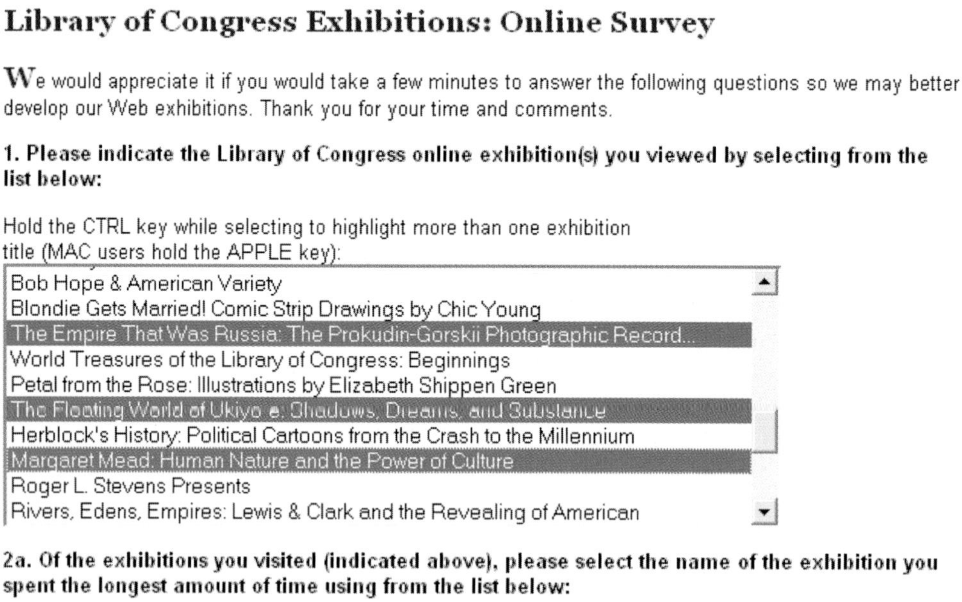

Library of Congress Exhibitions: Online Survey

We would appreciate it if you would take a few minutes to answer the following questions so we may better develop our Web exhibitions. Thank you for your time and comments.

1. Please indicate the Library of Congress online exhibition(s) you viewed by selecting from the list below:

Hold the CTRL key while selecting to highlight more than one exhibition title (MAC users hold the APPLE key):

```
Bob Hope & American Variety                                              ▲
Blondie Gets Married! Comic Strip Drawings by Chic Young
The Empire That Was Russia: The Prokudin-Gorskii Photographic Record...
World Treasures of the Library of Congress: Beginnings
Petal from the Rose: Illustrations by Elizabeth Shippen Green
The Floating World of Ukiyo e: Shadows, Dreams, and Substance
Herblock's History: Political Cartoons from the Crash to the Millennium
Margaret Mead: Human Nature and the Power of Culture
Roger L. Stevens Presents
Rivers, Edens, Empires: Lewis & Clark and the Revealing of American     ▼
```

2a. Of the exhibitions you visited (indicated above), please select the name of the exhibition you spent the longest amount of time using from the list below:

Figure 2.23 **Multiple-Selection Drop Box.**

requires manual dexterity and a good working memory. To make matters worse, the list of responses is not ordered in a recognizable way (e.g., alphabetically), creating further work for the respondent. Then in the follow-up question (2a), the respondent is required to select the one exhibition from among those selected in the earlier response. This task could be better accomplished using server-side scripts and a paging design, where the second question is conditional on the responses to the first (see Chapter 5).

2.4.6. When to Use Drop Boxes

Given all these issues and concerns with drop boxes, should one ever use this tool? If it is so bad, why is it so widely used in Web surveys? One reason may be a focus on the designer rather than the respondent. For example, using a drop box makes it easier to control the users' behavior by restricting their choices to only those response options that the designer decided to include, in the format that is predetermined.

Miller and Jarrett (2001) offer six questions – to which I could add two more – to help decide whether a drop box or an alternative form (radio button, check box, text field, etc.) should be used:

1. Is it more natural for the user to type the answer rather than select it?
   In many cases, typing the response may be faster than selecting the response from a long list. Examples include age or year of birth, or simple count variables. It is also easy to write scripts to ensure that such responses are in the required format within a limited range.

2. Are the answers easily mistyped?
   If the answer is yes, consider a drop box. Examples include names of medications, country names, or other lists where selecting from a list may be easier than typing. Here again, the focus is on making it easier for the respondent.

3. Does the user need to review the options to understand the question?
   This is particularly important in the survey world. If the respondent has the knowledge in their head (e.g., country of birth), finding that response in a well-ordered list may not be too difficult. But if the respondent needs to see the response options to determine how to answer the question, a drop box is probably not appropriate.

4. How many options are there?
   The larger the number of responses, the more preferable a drop box is over a long series of radio buttons. One rule of thumb is, if the number of response options exceeds what can reasonably be displayed in a browser window, use a drop box. Alternatively, one could also consider breaking the question into several parts or simply reducing the number of responses.

5. Is the user allowed to select more than one option?
   As I've already noted, steer clear of drop boxes for multiple response questions. Check boxes are a better tool if such questions are to be used.

6. Are the options visually distinctive?
   The more similar looking the response options, the greater the potential of confusion and error when selecting from a long list.

7. Is the list of options exhaustive?
   If the list does not include all the possible responses, an "other" or "not on the list" response will need to be added and a follow-up text box used to collect the additional information. This detracts from the utility of the drop box, as it may force the respondent to search the list before concluding that their chosen response does not appear.

8. Does the organization of the list fit the user's mental model? When presented with a long list, it must be clear to the respondent how the list is organized. Ordering states by their entry into the union or population size makes little sense. But what about year of birth? Ordering the list in reverse chronological order is quite common, but the oldest respondents – those with the poorest sensorimotor skills – will have to work the hardest to make their selection. Ordering the years chronologically means that the larger proportion of respondents – those who are younger, given the demographics of the Web – will have to scroll the furthest. In this case, typing in the year is likely to be faster than selecting from a list.

To summarize, drop boxes do have a use in Web surveys, but for specific types of questions. Most questions asked in Web surveys are better served by radio buttons or check boxes. Drop boxes are usually only appropriate when the list is closed and complete, when the user knows the response he/she is looking for, and when the list can be organized in a meaningful way to facilitate searching or browsing. This matches many of the tasks in e-commerce, which is why drop boxes are used routinely on online travel and shopping sites. But far fewer examples of appropriate questions occur in surveys, and so drop boxes should be seen much less frequently than is the case in Web surveys.

2.4.7. Summary on Drop Boxes

As I've noted previously, drop boxes tend to be overused in Web surveys, possibly because they are a popular tool on Web sites. So, here are some summary guidelines for the use of drop boxes:

1. Use sparingly and only where appropriate. The following conditions ought to be met to justify the use of drop boxes:
   • The list is too long to display on the page.
   • The answer is known to the respondent.
   • The list can be organized in a meaningful way.
   • Selecting the response would be more efficient than typing it in.
2. Do not make the first option visible in a drop box. Do not leave the initial response blank. Guide the respondent with a "Select one" instruction.
3. Avoid the use of multiple selections in drop boxes.

Figure 2.24 **Text Box and Text Area.**

We'll examine some of the research on drop boxes in Section 2.6, in the context of looking at research findings on the effect of alternative form fields on survey responses.

2.5. Text Fields

Text or numeric input is achieved through two tools: text boxes and text areas. While their purpose is similar – to permit typed entry of responses – these are really two separate tools. One is constrained to accept relatively short input such as a name, date, or telephone number. The other permits lengthy responses of any format, and is best suited to obtaining open-ended feedback. But there is often confusion between the two tools, and inappropriate use of one instead of the other. The two types are illustrated in Figure 2.24. I'll discuss each in turn.

2.5.1. Text Boxes

Text boxes are suitable for short, constrained input. They are best for one-word answers or for entry of a few numbers (e.g., age, date of birth, currency amount). Both the size of the displayed box and the maximum number of characters that can be input are under designer control. The HTML code for a text box looks like the following:

```
<input type="text" name="FullName" size="30" maxlength="30">
```

The `input type="text"` statement defines this as a text box, as opposed to other forms of input (radio button, check box, etc.). The `size="n"` defines the visible size of the field, with the default being 20 and the maximum 500. The

Name:	**Address:**
Mick P. Couper	P.O. Box 1248
Title:	**City:**
earch Professor	Ann Arbor
Department:	**State:**
ocial Research	MI
Business/Institution:	**Zip Code:**
sity of Michigan	48106

Figure 2.25 **Constrained Visible Area for Text Box.**

maxlength="n" part defines the maximum number of characters that can be entered. The visible size and the number of characters that can be input do not have to be the same. In the example in Figure 2.25, the visible size of the text box is smaller than the number of characters that can be entered in the field.

The example in Figure 2.25 is based on a real online order form I was asked to complete some years ago. While the equal-size text boxes may have made the form look elegant, the task was made harder, especially as one had to get the address right for mailing. In this case, the display size was set with size="12", while the length of the underlying input field was set to 30 characters with maxlength="30". In one of the worse examples I've seen of this design flaw, the task was to allocate 100 points across various attributes. However, the display width of the entry fields was only a single character, which meant that if one typed "20, "30," and "50," for example (and the helpful running total displayed "100"), the only thing visible in the fields would be three zeros. Similarly, setting maxlength less than size will mean that the respondent will be prevented from typing further, even though there appears to be more space for input. The visible field should convey to the respondent how much space is available, and should display all the information entered into the field.

At the other end of the spectrum, providing too much space may send a different message to respondents. Look at the example in Figure 2.26. What were they thinking? Every text box in this survey was exactly the same size, no doubt the result of a copy and paste operation. The size of the box should convey what kind of information, and how much, is desired. When a particular format is required, masks or templates can be used to guide the response (see Section 2.5.3).

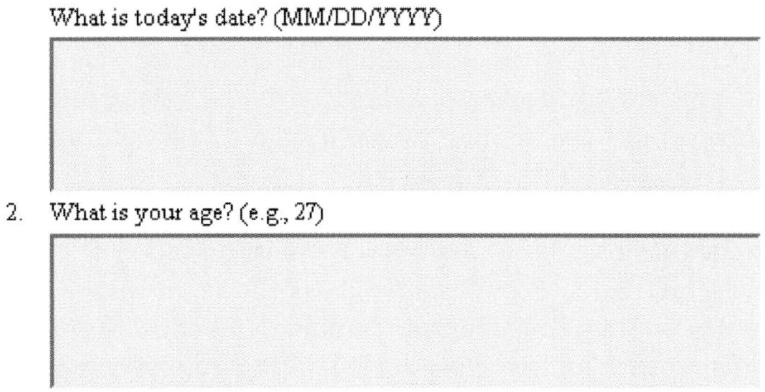

What is today's date? (MM/DD/YYYY)

2.   What is your age? (e.g., 27)

Figure 2.26 **Poor Use of Text Boxes.**

One final caution on this issue: the actual size of the displayed field may vary from browser to browser, and is derived from the default font, usually a proportionate font, in which "W" take up more space than "I." So, for example, I have found that setting `size="4"` for a year field and `size="2"` for a month field is insufficient on some browsers; so I usually use `size="6"` for year and `size="3"` for month, while keeping `maxlength="4"` and for year and `maxlength="2"` for month. This conveys the relative size of the two input fields while still serving to constrain input and make typed responses visible.

HTML text boxes have no client-side validation capacity. For example, one cannot restrict the input to numbers only, or prevent the entry of unwanted characters such as dollars signs, commas and periods for financial questions. This has to be accomplished with client-side or server-side scripts, along with other validations such as range checks and sums (see Section 3.8.1 on running totals).

2.5.2. Text Areas

In contrast to text boxes, text areas are useful for large amount of text, such as for narrative responses. Text areas can be as large as the HTML page, and will expand as needed, up to a limit of 32,700 characters. A text area is defined in HTML as follows:

```
<textarea name="Comments" rows="n" cols="n" >Please add any
additional comments here</textarea>
```

The number of rows and columns initially presented on the page is under designer control. The text "Please add any additional comments here" is optional, and appears inside the text area until the respondent starts typing. The `name="Comments"` tag defines the name of the data field transmitted to the server.

While text boxes are most suitable for constrained entry of open-ended responses, text areas are suitable for responses to questions such as "What is the biggest problem facing the country?" or "What is the main reason you chose that product?" or "Do you have any further comments to add?" In other words, text areas are the appropriate tool for questions requiring fully open-ended or narrative responses.

How well do open-ended questions like this work on the Web? Should one include them at all? There are several studies that suggest that the quantity and quality of responses to such questions on the Web are at least as good as, if not better, than those on paper surveys.

Ramirez, Sharp, and Foster (2000) looked at open-ended responses of employees who were given a choice of completing a Web or mail version of a survey. Across four questions seeking a narrative response, significantly more Web respondents availed themselves of the opportunity to enter a response for two of the questions, while there were no differences for the other two. The two that produced differences both solicited "negative" responses, leading Ramirez and colleagues to conclude that the Web "tends to increase item response when the question asks for potentially detailed or involved responses, often associated with questions asking for negative criticism" (p. 4). They also found that, among those who answered the open-ended questions, the length of the narrative provided was longer on the Web than on paper, significantly so for three of the four questions.

MacElroy, Mikucki, and McDowell (2002) conducted a mail and Web survey for organization members, with respondents given a choice of mode. The questionnaire had a final open-ended question for "Any final thoughts." Of the Web completes, 55% provided an answer to this question, compared with 39% of those who completed the paper version. In a random sample of fifty completes from each mode, the Web completes provided longer answers (an average of forty-eight words) than paper completes (thirty-two words on average). They also found that the Web responses had a higher number of "unique concepts" and were more sophisticated – higher reading levels and longer sentences – than the paper responses. One explanation for the longer Web responses may be that the text area provides essentially unlimited space, compared with the physical constraints of the paper form. But, as I discuss in Section 2.5.3, it may be the size of the visible space that is important in encouraging or limiting responses.

DeMay, Kurlander, Lundby, and Fenlason (2002) conducted a similar employee survey with respondents choosing Web or mail. They found that significantly more Web respondents provided comments than mail respondents (60.2% versus 47.5% in Study 1, and 43.6% versus 33.9% in Study 2), and that the comments were significantly longer in the Web than the mail version. They did not, however, find any differences in the quality of responses by mode.

Finally, Elig and Waller (2001) compared the use of open-ended questions among those who chose to complete a Web version of the survey versus a paper version. In the paper version, 50% of the last page was devoted to space for comments, while in the Web survey the text area occupied about 70% of an 800 × 600 screen. Web respondents entered an average of 337 characters, compared with 250 for the paper version; this translates to an average of seventeen words more for the Web than the paper.

An alternative explanation could be that those who chose to do the Web had more to say. However, all these findings corroborate earlier research from e-mail (Kiesler and Sproull, 1986; Mehta and Sivadas, 1995) and Web survey (Yost and Homer, 1998) experiments that Internet surveys yield responses to open-ended questions that are at least as long as those in paper surveys. So, it is fair to say that the length and quality of open-ended responses are not deprecated on the Web relative to mail.

While open-ended questions often get a bad rap in surveys because of the difficulties of transcribing and coding responses, one advantage of such questions on the Web is that they already come in electronic form, facilitating the use of qualitative analysis software for coding and classification of responses. But they may also serve a function for respondents – allowing them to elaborate on answers, vent about the survey, and the like. Given this, the inclusion of a limited number of narrative questions to elicit feedback seems like a good idea.

2.5.3. Design and Use of Text Fields

Most of this section will focus on text boxes because they are the most common form of typed input in Web surveys. But some of the design considerations should apply also to text areas, and so both HTML elements will be discussed here.

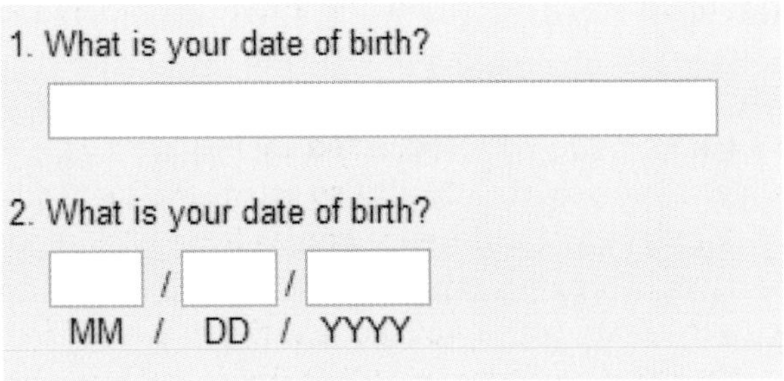

1. What is your date of birth?

[   ]

2. What is your date of birth?

[   ] / [   ] / [   ]
MM / DD / YYYY

Figure 2.27 **Two Approaches to Collecting Formatted Numeric Input.**

While the form element is called a "text" box, the most common use of these is for numeric input. Masks or templates are one way of constraining or guiding numeric input in text fields. There are two schools of thought on the collection of numeric strings such as dates, telephone numbers, and the like:

1. Provide a single input field, allowing the respondent to enter the information in any format.
2. Constrain input to a particular format by providing separate fields.

These two approaches are illustrated in Figure 2.27.

The first approach may make more sense when there are several different ways to provide the information, for example, international variation in telephone numbers or varying date formats. In fact, the Blaise computer-assisted interviewing software system adopts this approach, based on the argument that it gives respondents maximum flexibility in their responses (see Statistics Netherlands, 2002). But, in doing so, it is important to disambiguate the response. For example, 03-04-2007 could be March 4 or April 3. An unconstrained field such as this usually requires server-side validation of the response and verification with the respondent if necessary. If the survey is not designed for an international audience, the use of separate fields (such as shown in the second question in Figure 2.27) may provide respondents with more guidance. Another possible advantage (for respondents) of the second approach is that they may be permitted to provide a partial response (i.e., provide the year but not the day or month). In a single-field design, this may be harder to validate. At least in earlier versions of Blaise, for example (see Statistics Netherlands, 1996, p. 81), entering "1965" into a date field would return a value of 1-9-65 or January 9th, 1965.

In a series of experiments in Web surveys of college students, Christian, Dillman, and Smyth (2007) tested alternative formats of a month and year question ("When did you first begin your studies?"). They found that when the month and year text fields were of equal size 55% responded in the desired format (a two-digit month and four-digit year), while 63% did so when the month field was smaller than the year field. Much of this difference comes from 32% reporting a two-digit year in the former case, compared with 22% in the latter. I've already discussed the issue of using the visible display of the text field to provide visual guidance, and the Christian, Dillman, and Smyth (2007) finding reinforces the importance of doing so.

Of course, there are other ways to collect this kind of information. Drop boxes, for all their weaknesses discussed earlier, are often seen in Web surveys for some or all date information. Some sites even use a combination, such as drop boxes for month and day, and a text box for year. This requires the respondent to move back and forth between mouse and keyboard, slowing down the process.

While dates can be tricky, telephone numbers – at least in the United States – are more straightforward. In this case, a single field could be used, and the software could easily strip off the dashes, parentheses, or other special characters if a respondent does not follow the prescribed format. Thus, the software should be able to accept 123-456-7890, (123) 456–7890, 1234567890, and a variety of other types. Here the simplest form of validation is that the correct number of digits (ten) is entered and, if not, an appropriate error message is generated. So, while templates or masks may be more useful for some types of input (e.g., dates) than others (e.g., telephone numbers), it is best to be consistent in their use.

Masks or templates can also be useful in collecting information on dollar values, to lead respondents away from adding the currency sign or decimals, for example. Look at the two versions of the question in Figure 2.28. The first is from a real Web survey. The second shows how masks can be used to provide guidance to a respondent without the need for lengthy instructions.

We recently experimented with the two versions shown in Figure 2.28, for a question on medical expenditures (Couper, Tourangeau, and Conrad, 2007). The use of the mask significantly reduces the entry of unwanted characters such as dollar signs and decimals, from 20.1% in the version without masks to 5.4% with masks. Most of the mistakes were easily correctable – for example, 6.8% of respondents entered a dollar sign, and 4.1% a decimal point in the version without masks – but preventing errors in the first place reduces the necessity for error messages and complex code to clean up the entries.

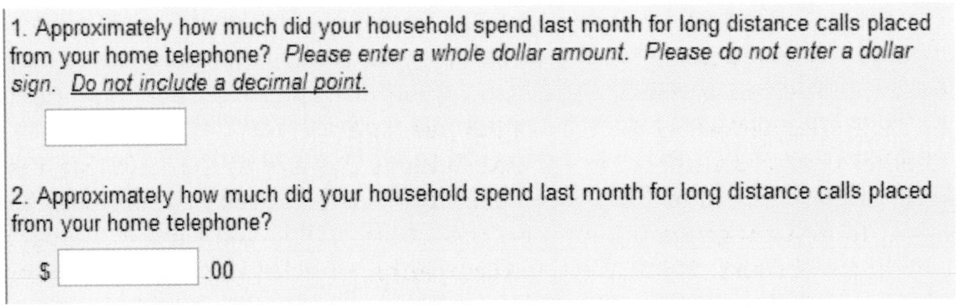

1. Approximately how much did your household spend last month for long distance calls placed from your home telephone? *Please enter a whole dollar amount. Please do not enter a dollar sign. Do not include a decimal point.*

2. Approximately how much did your household spend last month for long distance calls placed from your home telephone?

$ [   ] .00

Figure 2.28 **Text Boxes for Price Information.**

A server-side script can be used to evaluate the submitted string and send back an error message if the response is not in the desired format. In most cases in our experiment, the input can be made recognizable by simply stripping out extraneous characters such as dollar signs and decimals. Most survey software simply returns an error if any nonnumeric characters are input. Preventing errors by providing visual cues to the respondent as to what is desired is much preferred over having them try something several times until they got it right.

In the example in Figure 2.29, from the 2005 National Census Test, the intention is to have respondents enter as many different ancestries as are applicable. But the visual design, and limits of the text boxes (both `size` and `maxlenght` are set to nineteen characters) sends a strong signal to enter one (and only one ancestry) in each box. The design was intended to match the paper form, which has three lines for entering this information, but if several responses are expected in each box, it may make more sense to use a single text area, or to increase the length of each text box to encourage multiple entries. In fact, in later iterations of the design, this has been changed from three separate text boxes to a single text area. Now, a computer program – rather than the respondent – can do the work of parsing the responses and splitting them into separate fields. This can be done either during a postprocessing step, or by using a server-side script if the information is to be

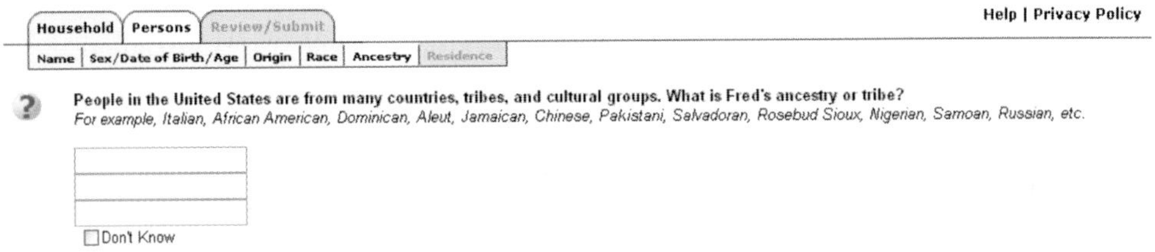

Figure 2.29 **Ancestry Question from 2005 Census Test.**

fed back to the respondent for confirmation or if the information will be used to generate a fill (see Section 5.3) or follow-up prompts. Such visual cues do not obviate the need for server-side validations, but they make them less necessary, reducing respondent effort and frustration (see Section 3.8.1).

Another design consideration for text fields is the size of the field. My first inkling of the effect of text box size came from an inadvertent experiment that resulted from a programming error in one of our early Web surveys (Couper, Traugott, and Lamias, 2001). We were comparing radio buttons with text boxes, but a random subset of the text box group got a longer input field (about twenty characters) than others who got the intended design (two characters). The task was a difficult one, with respondents expected to enter a number from 0 to 10, or a DK or NA, in each box. While about 11% of the responses in the short box version were outside this range of intended responses, this increased to 21% in the long box version, with many providing answers such as "about 3," "between 4 and 5," and so on. Presented with more space, respondents availed themselves of the opportunity to provide more information. As an aside, this is one of the potential negatives of highly structured automated surveys. Respondents are required to choose from a finite set of responses or enter information in a constrained field, often with little or no opportunity to elaborate, to qualify, or to explain their answers. We get our desired rectangular data set for analysis but may miss out on a wealth of information about the answer the respondent gave or about the question itself.

Later planned experiments confirmed this observation that providing more space encourages longer answers. Dennis, deRouvray, and Couper (2000) conducted an experiment in the Knowledge Networks panel in which respondents were randomly assigned to a large (n=164) or small (n=172) text box for each of three open-ended items:

1. Q0: Your Web TV can be used to surf the Web, chat with other viewers, program your VCR, e-mail your friends and family, and more. How do you use your Web TV?
2. Q4: In your opinion, what are the principal benefits, if any, of ordering goods on the Internet?
3. Q10: In your opinion, what role, if any, should the U.S. government play in overseeing Internet security and privacy?

We found that in each case the size of the box significantly affected the length of the response. Figure 2.30 shows the average length in characters of responses

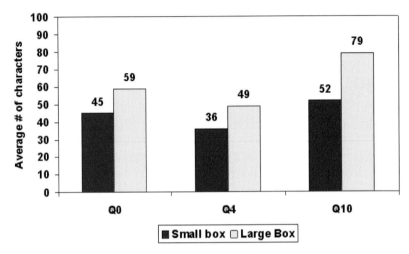

Figure 2.30 **Effect of Text Box Size on Length of Entries.**

to the three questions, by size of the text box. In this case, longer responses to open-ended questions were desirable.

Fuchs conducted a similar experiment in a study among German high school and vocational school students (see Fuchs, 2007; Fuchs and Couper, 2001). The experiment involved both Web and mail. In the Web version, the text boxes were fifteen and thirty characters long, with equivalent lengths for the paper version. He hypothesized that for questions to which respondents were likely to know the answer (e.g., "How many pupils are there in your class?"), respondents would be less affected by the size of the input field, but for questions to which they were unlikely to know the answer (e.g., "How much money do your parents make?" or "What is the population of your town?"), the size of the input field would matter more. He found some support for this, with longer fields resulting in more explicit estimates (e.g., "about 45"), more ranges (e.g., "between 10 and 20"), and more additional information (e.g., when asked about the length of the survey, one responded: "45 minutes, it was an awful long and boring questionnaire"). And, as expected, the effect of text box length depended on whether the answer might reasonably be known or estimated. The less sure respondents were about their answer, the more likely they were to qualify the response when presented with a longer text box. Interestingly, though, the results appeared to be stronger for the paper and pencil version than for the Web.

In a similar study, we varied the length of the input field for a question soliciting a frequency – the number of times the respondent had seen a doctor in the past two years (Couper, Tourangeau, and Conrad, 2007). The long input field (twenty characters) yielded significantly more ill-formed responses (words, ranges, quali-fied responses, etc.) than the short input field (four characters): 3.4% versus 0.7%, respectively.

Evidence for the effect of length on responses comes from other sources too. For example, Karlgren and Franzén (1997) varied the length of an online search field, actually using a text box versus a text area. The average query length was significantly higher in the long field entry condition (3.43 versus 2.81 words). While this doesn't seem like much, Jansen, Spink, and Saracevic (2000) found that the average query on Excite was 2.21 terms, and Silverstein, Marais, Henzinger, and Moricz (1999) reported that over 72% of AltaVista searches contained two or fewer terms.

So, when it comes to text fields, it is safe to conclude that the larger the field, the bigger will be the yield. This does not mean that bigger is necessarily better, as we have discovered. When short answers are desired, smaller text field yield answers that more closely match what is being sought. When narrative responses are desired, larger input fields encourage longer responses.

2.5.4. Summary on Text Fields

To summarize, here are some design guidelines for the use of text boxes and text areas:

1. Use the appropriate tool
    - Use text boxes for short constrained answers
    - Use text areas for long narrative answers
2. The visible size of the text field should reflect the information being collected
3. Match the displayed size to the size of the field in the database
4. Carefully label text box fields to convey the format and information being sought
    - Use input masks or templates to guide respondents
    - Split into several fields if necessary
    - Provide specific guidance if necessary (e.g., "Jan" versus "01" for month, "87" or "1987" for year)

The goal is to prevent errors and reduce the need for time-consuming respondent correction or costly programming to translate all possible responses provided into a common format for analysis.

2.6. Empirical Research on Alternatives

There are many prescriptions about the appropriate HTML tools for survey questions. For example, Magee, Straight, and Schwartz (2001) recommend avoiding the use of drop-down boxes whenever possible for "reasons of nonresponse," and note further that "some users are not yet comfortable with registering a response using drop-down boxes" (p. 4). Dillman (2000, p. 392) similarly advocates using drop-down boxes sparingly. My own views on drop boxes are clear from the earlier discussion. Yet, there is relatively little empirical research on the effect of alternative input options on Web survey responses. In fact, Reips (2002, p. 78) argued, "Surface characteristics of Web questionnaires like pop-up menus versus radio buttons and numerical labeling don't seem to have an influence on answering behavior of Web participants." Based on the evidence accumulated to date, the answer seems to be sometimes yes, sometimes no.

Couper et al. (2004) focused on response order effects in a comparison of radio button and drop box formats. We tested two different drop box formats, one where none of the responses were visible until the scroll bar was clicked, and the other where five of the ten substantive responses were visible, but respondents had to scroll to see the remaining five. We found strong effects of the order of response options in all versions, consistent with the literature on primacy effects (see Tourangeau, Rips, and Rasinski, 2000, Chapter 8). However, the effects were magnified in the condition with five options initially visible, with 68% choosing one of five breakfast cereal nutrients when they were initially visible, compared with 40% choosing one of the same five nutrients when they were not visible, a 28 percentage point difference. The equivalent effect of order was a difference of 11% for the radio button version and 6% for the drop box version with no options initially visible. We found similar but slightly less dramatic effects for a question on automobile features. Thus, in addition to order, the visibility of response options is a key factor in their selection. Interestingly, we found no differences in response time across the three versions.

Hogg and Masztal (2002; see also Baker-Prewitt, 2003) report on an experiment comparing drop boxes, radio buttons, and text boxes for a series of sixty-eight ratings on a five-point scale. They also varied the order of the scale, either starting with strongly agree or with strongly disagree. The sample consisted of members of an opt-in panel, with over 100 respondents completing each version. The radio button version had a thirty-second advantage over drop boxes for a task averaging round ten minutes, with average times of 9:55 for the radio buttons, 10:22 for drop boxes with descending options, 10:29 for drop boxes with ascending options, and 10:01 for text boxes. The distributions of the scores did not differ across versions, although the text box version produced a slightly flatter distribution, with fewer people selecting the "agree" response, and more selecting other responses. They found significantly less variation in individual scale usage among those using the radio button version, with 55% using the same scale point for at least 35 of the 66 positively worded items compared with 45% for the drop box version and 48% for the text box version, and conclude that the radio buttons may encourage respondents to select the response in the same column for several items.

Heerwegh and Loosveldt (2002b) report on a comparison of radio buttons and drop boxes. They note that drop boxes involve slightly less HTML code and hence take less time to download than corresponding radio buttons. In their case, a scrolling survey with drop boxes took about 59 seconds over a 28.8K modem compared with 118 seconds for the radio button version. They used two samples, one of third-year college students and the other from a public Internet database. They found no significant differences in completion rates in either sample. Controlling for download time (i.e., capturing actual completion time), the radio button version was completed significantly faster (an average of 801 seconds) than the drop box version (871 seconds) among students. However, no time differences were found in the general population sample (793 versus 792 seconds). Their conclusion – consistent with others – is that the results suggest that drop boxes are more difficult to use than radio buttons.

In later analyses of the same data, Heerwegh (2005a) found that respondents in the drop box conditions were also less likely to change their answers than those in the radio button condition. Such changes were detected using client-side paradata (Heerwegh, 2003). He uses this to bolster the argument that drop boxes are more difficult to use, discouraging respondents from changing their mind once a selection has been made. Whether such changes lead to better-quality data is a matter of speculation, but our own research (e.g., Couper et al., 2006) suggests that such changes are not infrequent. Heerwegh found between 3% and 8% of respondents changed their mind on any individual item.

In an experiment comparing a visual analog scale (a Java-based slider tool, see Section 3.8.2) with radio buttons and text boxes for a series of eight items on genetic versus environmental determinants of behavior, we found more missing data for the text box version (an average of 2.7% missing across the eight items) than for the radio button version (a missing rate of 1.0%). Average completion time for the eight items was 125 seconds for the radio button version and 158 for the text box version (Couper et al., 2006).

In an early experiment on a specific task of allocating ten friends, classmates, and acquaintances to different racial and ethnic groups, we found that radio buttons produced less missing data than text boxes (Couper, Traugott, and Lamias, 2001).

However, when respondents did enter a response, the text box entries were more likely to tally to 10 than the radio buttons. In this case, a large array of radio buttons did not support the task of constraining the sum to a fixed number.

Hennessy (2002) conducted a series of usability evaluations of alternative input formats. She found that respondents preferred radio buttons over drop boxes because they required fewer mouse clicks and all options were visible from the start.

Reja, Lozar Manfreda, Hlebec, and Vehovar (2002) compared three different formats to a question on "What is the most important problem the Internet is facing today?" An open-ended version of the question (using a text area) was contrasted with two closed-ended version, each with ten choices and an "other, specify" category, but with one restricting the respondent to a single choice (radio buttons) and the other permitting multiple selections (check boxes). The response options for the closed-ended versions were randomized. In addition to the distributions of responses differing significantly across versions, the open-ended version yielded multiple responses in 13% of the cases and uncodable responses in 12% of the cases. In contrast, 5% of the respondents in the single-choice and 8% in the multiple-choice versions entered something in the "other" category. A further 37% of the responses to the open-ended version did not fit within one of the ten precoded categories. Finally, respondents offers the check boxes selected an average of 3.8 responses, with a median of 3, in contrast to the mode of 1 for the radio button version. Their findings replicate the general findings on open versus closed questions (e.g., Schuman and Presser, 1979, 1981), and suggest that the choice of question format can have a large effect on answers to questions like this.

I'm aware of no other studies comparing radio buttons to check boxes. Some argue that the shape of the form field by itself does not provide sufficient cues that multiple responses are desired, or even permissible, or, by contrast, that a radio button restricts one to a single choice. I'll return to this issue in the context of providing instructions in Chapter 5.

2.7. Summary

In this chapter, we've looked at the basic tools to construct single questions for Web surveys. While the standard HTML tools cover most traditional ways of asking and answering survey questions, their behavior suggests careful choice of a tool for a particular question. In other words, particularly for those familiar with Web forms, the appropriate use of the form elements can serve as an affordance (see Norman, 1988), supporting the task at hand, and providing guidance as to the form of answer expected.

However, design goes beyond simply choosing the right tool for the job. There are many more design decisions to be made after one has selected a particular form element to use. These include layout (see Chapter 4), the use of tables or grids (see Section 4.4.3) and other issues to be discussed in later chapters. In the next chapter (Chapter 3), we turn to extensions of the basic HTML tools for constructing surveys questions, looking first at the use of images and second at the inclusion of active content to enhance interactivity in Web surveys.

Chapter 3

Going Beyond the Basics: Visual and Interactive Enhancements to Web Survey Instruments

---

Every Picture Tells a Story
Rod Stewart, 1971

In the previous chapter, I discussed the basic hypertext markup language (HTML) tools for constructing a Web questionnaire. In this chapter, I go beyond the basics in two ways. First, I look at extending basic Web survey design to include a variety of visual elements. While the presentation of images is a standard feature of HTML, the use of images in survey questionnaires has been relatively rare, so this can be viewed as extending the measurement capabilities of surveys on the Web. Second, I examine the many possible enhancements in HTML to facilitate a variety of survey measurement tasks. This includes a variety of interactive tools using client-side scripts and applets.

3.1. Images in Web Surveys

For many decades, the primary building blocks of surveys have been words, whether written on paper or spoken aloud by an interviewer. The advent of computer-assisted interviewing (CAI) did not change this primarily verbal focus, although the delivery methods were expanded from paper to computer screen, and from interviewer delivery to prerecorded delivery (audio-CASI). There have always been exceptions, but these were generally for specialized applications. Examples include smiley-face response options for low-literacy populations, show cards for words or pictures (pill cards, residential integration representations), ad testing and magazine readership surveys, feeling thermometers, visual analog scales, and the like (see Couper, 2005). But for mainstream surveys, the visual elements were generally limited to icons or symbols representing interviewer instructions, navigation, help, and so on – in other words, the auxiliary functions of surveys (see Redline and Dillman, 2002) rather than the core functions (questions and answers). The Web can and does change all that.

For the first several years of its existence, the Internet was a text-based system. With the advent of the first graphical browsers (Mosaic), in the early 1990s, the World Wide Web became what we know it today, primarily a visual medium. This is likely to change in the future, as the Web further develops and matures into a full multimedia system. For now, however, the predominant mode of interaction with the Web is by visual means. And, for most Web survey applications, this means textual presentation of information. What does that mean for Web survey design? There are three implications of the visual nature of the Web for the design of online surveys.

First, as I have already noted, the Web survey's closest relative is the paper-based self-administered survey. Whereas paper surveys were limited in the visual effects possible or affordable, the Web makes the addition of a variety of visual enhancements not only possible but also trivially easy to implement. Visual enhancements have long been used in paper surveys to aid respondent navigation, but these may be difficult to duplicate reliably on the Web. For example, arrows and boxes for skip patterns, while a trivial matter to draw (or produce using a word processor) and reproduce identically on thousands of questionnaires, must now be carefully tested to ensure they have the same effect across different browsers and platforms, or alternative techniques – such as hyperlinks – used to achieve the same effects. I'll return to this issue later in Chapter 5.

Again, this is all by way of saying the Web is *not* the same as paper. In some respects, it may be better, but in other respects, it may be worse. The point is that paper and Web are different media, and it is important to recognize this when designing surveys in each medium. Therein lies the rub. Because it is easy to include a variety of visual embellishments to a Web survey does not mean that they serve any useful purpose, such as reducing nonresponse rates or improving data quality. Indeed, many of the visual enhancements I have seen in Web surveys appear to have the primary purpose of showing off the designer's skill, rather than helping the respondents.

Second, and following from the first, we are seeing a move away from text-based surveys to those that make use of a variety of visual elements as stimulus material or as supplements to the verbal content (Couper, 2005). I'll discuss this point in greater detail in this chapter.

Third, literacy is, and will remain for some time, a key component of Web access. While there are certainly sites devoted to nonverbal content (and the music, photo, and video-sharing phenomenon has had a profound effect on the Web), and even survey organizations are adding voice (sound) to the visual content (in Web versions of audio-CASI, for example), the kind of people who have access to the Web and ability to make full use of it, are still those with relatively high levels of literacy. Witness the digital divide data by education for compelling evidence to this basic fact. For example, data from the Pew Internet and American Life Project from February to March 2007 reveal that only 40% of those who have not graduated from high school have Internet access, compared with 61% of those with a high school diploma and 91% of college graduates (see http://www.pewinternet.org/; see also Fox, 2005). While this issue largely affects coverage error rather than measurement error, it does mean that those with lower education, or with limited literacy levels, may be chronically underrepresented in Web surveys, and adding sound will likely not ameliorate this problem.

Thus, text-based questionnaires will likely dominate the Web survey world for some time to come. However, increasing use will be made of images for specific kinds of questions and to supplement the verbal content of other kinds. Graphical images are a powerful tool in the survey designer's toolkit, but one we need to learn to use appropriately and responsibly. Before I get into the design issues related to the use of images, a word or two on terminology is in order.

3.2. Visual Information

At its broadest, visual information can be thought of as everything one sees with the eye, as opposed to other senses, such as auditory, olfactory, or haptic senses. But typically in the visual design field, visual information refers to all the extra-text (nonverbal) information. It includes how the text is presented, but not the content of the text itself (the words). Thus, fonts, typefaces, color of text, and other typographical issues are often viewed as part of visual language. I will be returning to the issue of the visual presentation of textual material in the next chapter.

In the case of Web surveys, it is rare that a page will consist solely of visual material, with no accompanying verbal material. Thus, Horn's (1998, p. 8) definition

Figure 3.1 **Images Vary in the Amount of Information They Convey.**

of visual language as "the integration of words, images, and shapes into a single communication unit" is close to what I have in mind. Similarly, Ware (2000, p. 311) notes that most visualizations are not purely graphical but are composites, combining images with text or spoken language.

Visual elements can be of many different forms. For example, Horn distinguishes between images and shapes. The latter are close to what Dillman and colleagues (see Christian and Dillman, 2004; Redline and Dillman, 2002) refer to as "symbolic language," or the use of symbols such as arrows. Horn (2000, p.72) defines shapes as "abstract gestalts that stand out from the background as unities but that do not resemble objects in the real world" while images are defined as "visible shapes that resemble objects in the real world." The focus of this chapter is on the latter. But even so, "image" is still a very broad category.

Images come in many different forms, from simple line drawings to photographs, from icons to rich works of visual art. For example, Kostelnick and Roberts (1998) note that pictures can be realistic or abstract, visually dense or terse, highly informative or highly expressive. McCloud (1993) identifies several different dimensions along which images can vary: from simple to complex, from iconic to realistic, from subjective to objective, and from specific to universal. There are many different words to describe different types of images, for example, icon, line drawing, diagram, data display, map, pictograph, and photograph. Duchastel and Waller (1979) caution that any attempt to classify images based on their visual form is headed for trouble, so I will not attempt this here.

But let me just illustrate the point. Each of the images in Figure 3.1 represents a face, with varying levels of detail. The one on the left is nothing but three circles and a line, but we have no trouble recognizing it as a smiling face. But little else is conveyed. The middle clip-art graphic conveys more information. Not only is it a smiling face, but the gender of the person is now conveyed, as well as race and age. The photograph on the right, from one of our experiments on social presence in Web surveys (Tourangeau, Couper, and Steiger, 2003), is even richer in the amount of information it conveys. No longer are we just communicating a smiling face, but possible much more, depending on the cues to which the respondent attends. As Paivio (1979) has noted, image complexity depends on both the number and variety of components within the visual frame.

Another way to think about images is according to their function. For example, Duchastel (1978, 1980), writing in the context of instructional texts, identifies three categories of images, defined by their functional relationship to the verbal information. Images may be (1) motivational, (2) explicative, and (3) retentional. In other words, images can be used to interest and motivate the reader, to help explain a point made in the prose, or to enhance long-term recall of the prose. Kostelnick and Roberts (1998, p. 313) also note the emotional function of pictures; in their words, images can be used to "set the mood." Horn (1998, p. 225) echoes this: "Many images speak immediately, directly and emotionally – bypassing conscious evaluation.... Images have the power to evoke strong, immediate feelings as well as to subtly insinuate a background climate or overall mood."

Images can also be distinguished by their relationship to the verbal information. For example, van der Molen (2001) notes that the degree of text-picture correspondence can be coded as (1) direct, that is, semantically redundant, conveying the same basic propositional meaning, (2) indirect or only partially related, or (3) divergent (see Marsh and White, 2003, for a different taxonomy).

For our purposes, then, there are three elements or features of images we need to consider when examining their role in Web surveys:

1. The intended function or purpose of the image
2. The relationship of the image to the verbal elements
3. The form and content of the image

The first of these is known to the designer but may be inferred by the respondent from the latter two elements. Thus, what a designer may intend as being unrelated may be interpreted by the respondent as being relevant to the survey question.

The third feature of images includes both syntactic and semantic elements. The semantics of an image are the information that the image may convey to the respondent, that is, the content of the image. The syntax is how the image is presented, including features such as size, brightness, vividness, amount of detail, and type of image. These serve to draw the respondent's attention to the image and keep it there.

Regardless of their intended function and syntactic linkage to the question text, images have the ability to grab one's attention. Graber (1996), writing about the power of television images, writes "verbal stimuli are processed serially, one verbal unit at a time. By contrast, visual stimuli are processed simultaneously . . . . One quick glance at complex visual scenes suffices to identify situations that words would describe with far less fidelity in information transmission." McCloud (1993, p. 49) echoes this view: "Pictures are *received* information. We need no formal education to 'get the message.' The message is instantaneous . . . .Writing is *perceived* information. It takes time and specialized knowledge to decode the abstract symbols of language." Giner-Sorolla, Garcia, and Bargh (1999), among others, provide evidence that pictures are automatically evaluated. Given their ability to attract our attention, and the rich and varied content they convey, images are a powerful tool in the design of Web sites and surveys. For this reason, we must be particularly alert to the possibility of unintended inferences.

With this background in mind, let's turn to an examination of how images are being used in Web surveys, and how their use may enhance or interfere with the measurement process.

3.3. Functions of Images in Web Surveys

In terms of the purpose or function of the image, there are several possibilities in Web surveys:

1. Images *are* the question
2. Images supplement the survey question
3. Images are incidental to the question

One can think of these as a continuum of necessity of the image to the task at hand. In the first instance, the question would not work without the image, while in the last instance, removing the image would have little or no effect on the comprehension and completion of the question. The middle instance covers a broad range of possibilities, from images that are germane to the survey question to those that apparently add little to the question text. The best way to explore this continuum may be to look at some pictures.

Which of the following product names do you associate with the image below?

○ Allegra
○ Claritin
○ Reactine
○ Zyrtec

Next Question   Clear Answers

Figure 3.2 **Use of Image for Ad Recognition.**

3.3.1. Image as the Question

Here the image is necessary for comprehending and responding to the question – without the image, there is no question. Examples of this type include recall of advertising, brand recognition, scenic preference surveys, measures of attractiveness, and any other applications where the visual presentation of an image is the focus of the survey question. There is no question text at all, or the text is minimal. The image is the key stimulus presented to respondents. Let's look at a couple of examples.

Figure 3.2 shows a classic example of an image that is the core of a survey question. The purpose of the question could not be accomplished without the image. Such questions have often been used in paper-based and CATI or CAPI

Figure 3.3 **Use of Image in Scenic Preference Survey.**

surveys for advertising research, but the Web makes the delivery of a full-color image much more affordable. In addition, the Web permits randomization both of the sequence of images that may be presented and of the response options, a task that is harder to do on paper. In addition, though the collection of paradata (a concept I'll return to in Chapter 6, see Section 6.7.2), such as elapsed time from the delivery of the image to the selection of a response option, the researcher may gain more insight into the recognition process. It is these kinds of examples of image use that exploit the measurement potential of the Web.

The second example, in Figure 3.3, shows a question from a scenic preference survey (Wherrett, 1999, 2000). Full-color photographs are used to elicit reactions to

Have you seen the above banner ad?

   ○ Yes

   ○ No

   ○ Not sure

Figure 3.4 **Evaluation of Banner Ads on the Web.**

particular types of scenery. A verbal description of the same scene would contain less detail. With digital manipulation of images, it is possible to imagine varying features of the same scene to explore what it is about the scene that respondents find attractive.

Another example of this use of images comes from a study of mixed-race identity. In an innovative study exploring perceptions of persons of mixed race, Harris (2002) blended photographs of different people using morphing software to create images of composite mixed-race persons. These were then presented to respondents in random order as part of a Web survey. The images were not real people, but rather an artificial construction to elicit respondents' reactions. Again, this kind of study would be hard to imagine without the use of visual materials.

The next example of this type (see Figure 3.4) is similar to the first in that it shows how the Web can be used to evaluate ads, in this case banner ads on the Web. Again, the task is one of recognition. As is often done in these kinds of recognition studies, ads that were not published on the Web can be shown to evaluate the extent of false positives. With increased bandwidth, it is likely that in the future we will increasingly see examples such as these extended to include video (see Section 3.7). For now, most Web-based evaluations of TV commercials I have seen involve the presentation of a single image or set of storyboards presenting the full-motion commercial to the respondent in still images.

One final example will suffice. Figure 3.5 shows an example from the early days of the Web, in a survey to evaluate consumers' reaction to various logos for a new cellular phone service. I include this example for two reasons. First, it shows that images need not be full-color photographs and can range in complexity and detail.

12. Of all the logos presented, which one do you feel most effectively communicates the "Future Ready" concept as described above?

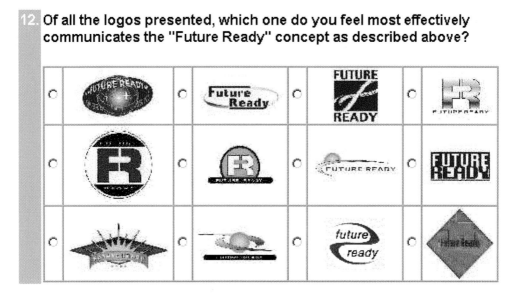

Figure 3.5 **Graphical Presentation of Logo Concepts.**

Second, it illustrates the dynamic nature of Web surveys relative to paper. This screen is made up of the subset of logos that were scored above a certain level in an earlier rating task. Thus, the screen is dynamically generated, not only in terms of which logos were included, but the logos were also randomized. This dynamic generation is extremely difficult to do on paper (I'll return to some of these issues in Chapter 5).

3.3.2. Supplemental Images

Further along the continuum are images that add something to the question. One example is an image illustrating a new brand or product, accompanied by a verbal description of the product. Another is an image used to describe a procedure, to provide clarification or assistance to the respondent regarding the subject of the question. Figure 3.6 is one such example of this, in a study providing people with decision aids to facilitate the choice between two alternative treatments for clogged arteries (the other being balloon angioplasty; Fagerlin, Wang, and Ubel, 2005). It could be argued that the sequence of drawings is not necessary, but they add clarity to the verbal description of the procedure.

If you have bypass surgery, a doctor will take a blood vessel from another part of your body and attach it above and below the clogged artery. This allows the blood to flow through the new passage rather than the clogged artery.

If successful, the procedure will relieve your chest pain.

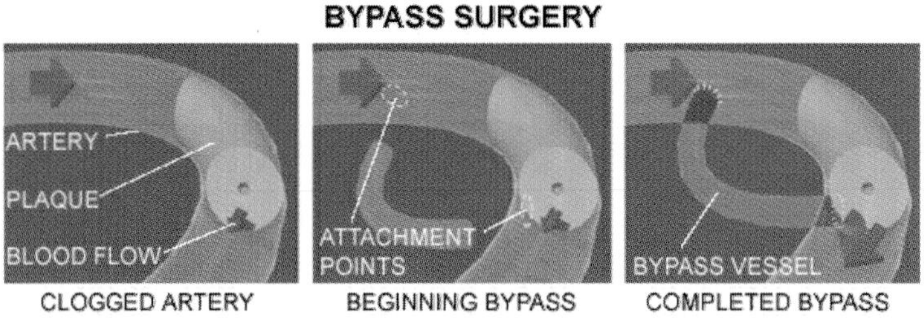

BYPASS SURGERY

CLOGGED ARTERY   BEGINNING BYPASS   COMPLETED BYPASS

Figure 3.6 **Use of Images to Describe a Procedure.**

Another example comes from a survey about drinking water (see Figure 3.7). The images – drawings in this case – are used to clarify the meaning of the different types of water filters asked about in this question. Given that respondents may not know the difference between a faucet-mounted filter and a countertop filter, say, the illustrations may improve the quality of responses.

In both these examples, the images are supplemental to the question text or written descriptions. In other words, the question could stand alone, without the accompanying image. But the images illustrate what is being described, in the first example a procedure (bypass surgery), and in the second a series of objects (water filters). For procedural instructions, a series of illustrations may be needed, much like a comic strip (see McCloud, 1999). One could go further and create an animated sequence (for example, using Flash) to convey the message more effectively.

A final example comes from the commercial side of the industry (see Figure 3.8). Without the make or model of the phone identified, the image serves a more important function. But other key information – size and weight, both difficult to convey in illustrations – is presented verbally. I include this example because it also shows the addition of sound and interactivity (click to hear it ring), both hard to do on paper. There are many other examples like this in the market research world, where new products or concepts are described and illustrated with an accompanying picture or drawing.

In cases where images are used to supplement the question text, a key issue is the degree of correspondence between the two; that is, how much does the visual message match with that contained in the verbal message. We'll return to this issue shortly.

Please check the box next to each of the water filter products that you are currently using throughout your house.

☐ 1. Carafe filter

☐ 2. Faucet-mounted filter

☐ 3. Counter-top filter

☐ 4. Under-sink filter

☐ 5. Reverse-osmosis system

☐ 6. Other

Figure 3.7 **Use of Images to Clarify Question Meaning.**

Shown below are pictures and descriptions of mobile phones. Click on a picture to see an enlarged image. Click on "Hear it ring" to listen to the ring quality of each phone.

PHONE 3		Hear it ring	Dimensions: 4.4 x 2.0 x 1.0 inches	Weight: 4.2 ounces
PHONE 4		Hear it ring	Dimensions: 4.6 x 2.2 x 0.9 inches	Weight: 4.4 ounces
PHONE 2		Hear it ring	Dimensions: 4.2 x 1.8 x 1.0 inches	Weight: 3.7 ounces
PHONE 1		Hear it ring	Dimensions: 3.4 x 1.8 x 1.1 inches	Weight: 2.9 ounces

Figure 3.8 **Use of Images to Supplement Verbal Descriptions.**

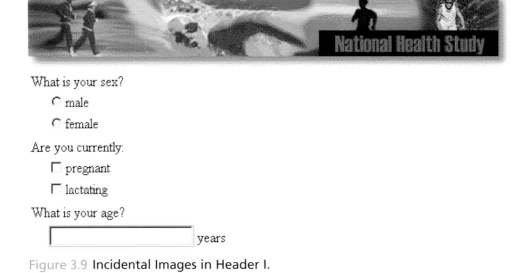

What is your sex?

  ○ male

  ○ female

Are you currently:

  ☐ pregnant

  ☐ lactating

What is your age?

  [   ] years

Figure 3.9 **Incidental Images in Header I.**

3.3.3. Incidental Images

Part of the distinction between supplemental and incidental images may lie in the syntactic connection between the image and the question text. Without knowing the intention of the designer, we must infer whether the picture is intended to be viewed as part of the question – a judgment that respondents may make on their own if the survey design does not communicate the linkage, or lack thereof, clearly.

Images in the banner, or header, area are probably not intended to be viewed as part of the survey question. They may serve branding purposes, or identify the survey itself, but not the question. Two examples are shown in Figure 3.9 and 3.10. Both are from health surveys, but they convey very different messages about what is meant by "health." To the extent that they activate a certain cognitive or emotional response in the respondent, they may affect the answers to survey questions. In this way, they contextualize the survey questions in ways that may not be intended by the designer.

Another example comes from a survey delivered on the Web site of the Southeast Michigan Council of Governments (see Figure 3.11). The image in the header is part of the site, not of the survey. But given that the survey is about issues related to urban sprawl and public transport, the fact that the image shows low-density

1) **What is your sex?**

☐ Male ☐ Female ☐ Abstain

2) **What is your marital status?**

☐ Single - never married ☐ First marriage ☐ Remarried ☐ Separated but still legally married ☐ Divorced ☐ Widowed ☐ Abstain

3) **How many children do you have?**

☐ 0 ☐ 1 ☐ 2 ☐ 3 ☐ 4 ☐ More than four ☐ Abstain

4) **Please indicate the ages of the YOUNGEST child living at home with you.**

☐ No children under 1 ☐ 1 year ☐ 2 years ☐ 3 years ☐ 4 years ☐ 5 years ☐ 6 years ☐ 7 years ☐ 8 years ☐ 9 years ☐ 10 years ☐ 11 years ☐ 12 years ☐ 13 years ☐ 14 years ☐ 15 years ☐ 16 years ☐ 17 years ☐ 18 years ☐ 19 years ☐ Over 19 years ☐ No children ☐ Abstain

5) **What is your current employment?**

☐ Full-time ☐ Part-time ☐ Unemployed ☐ Retired ☐ Student ☐ Abstain

Figure 3.10 **Incidental Images in Header II.**

suburban housing may communicate a message to respondents. We return to this example again in Chapter 4.

If we knew what the designer's intentions were in each of these cases, we could maybe better distinguish between supplemental images and incidental images. But it is not so much the designer's intentions as the respondent's interpretation of those intentions that is important here. In other words, even if the designer thought that the picture should have nothing to do with the survey questions – and the designer of the survey may not be the same person as the designer of the Web site – if the respondent views the image as relevant to interpreting and answering the survey question, there may be consequences for survey measurement, as we shall see shortly.

3.4. Effect of Images on Survey Responses

Why make the distinctions between the different functions or purposes of images in Web surveys? These are relevant because it is not just the content of the image

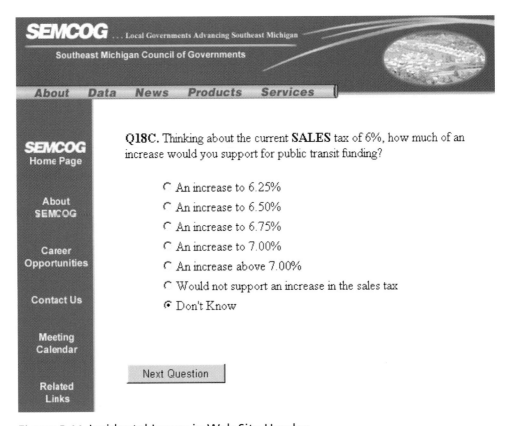

Figure 3.11 **Incidental Image in Web Site Header.**

that is important but also its relationship – both intended and perceived – to the survey task. Understanding this relationship may help us understand the effect that images may have on survey responses.

Three key elements of language – whether verbal or visual – can be identified. These are syntax, semantics, and pragmatics. I've already mentioned the first two, so a brief aside on pragmatics may be in order. Pragmatics refers to meaning in the context of the recipient. Pragmatics is the focus of much work on analyzing survey interactions (e.g., Maynard, Houtkoop-Steenstra, Schaeffer, and van der Zouwen, 2002). Thus, Grice (1967; see also Szabó, 2006) was the first to offer a systematic distinction between what is said and what is meant – or, in the visual context, what is presented and what is understood – with the former being the realm of semantics, and the latter, along with how the receiver understands the message, belonging to pragmatics. But, given that we need to know the speaker's/designer's intention and the listener's/viewer's interpretation in order to disentangle these differences, I will stick to the use of "semantics" here.

While the semantics of an image – the information contained therein – might be viewed as fixed, how that information is interpreted and what effect it might have on a respondent's answers depends in large part on the syntactic elements of the design. Syntax can refer to elements of the picture itself, such as color, shape size, and brightness (see Dondis, 1973, Chapter 2), and to the relationship between the image and the verbal elements – the survey questions in our case. Thus, Horn (1998, p. 51) talks about visual syntax as the combination and relationship of verbal and visual elements.

A key to the effectiveness of images when they are designed to supplement the text is their degree of congruence with the verbal message. In the field of multimedia learning, it has been demonstrated that learning outcomes (such as retention or recall) are improved when there is close correspondence between the pictures and prose (e.g., Carney and Levin, 2002; Moreno and Mayer, 1999; Nugent, 1992). Similar results are found in research on media and broadcasting (e.g., Brosius, Donsbach, and Birk, 1996; David, 1998; van der Molen, 2001).

Horn (1998) defines visual language as "the integration of words, images, and shapes into a single communication unit." Similarly, Ware (2000, p. 311) notes that most visualizations are not purely graphical but are composites, combining images with text or spoken language. The point is that images are usually not seen in isolation. When the visual and verbal elements are congruent, they can serve to reinforce each other. But, to quote Horn again,

> [What] happens to our thinking process when we place next to one another visual and verbal elements that are not obviously related or not related at all? Almost all of us will struggle valiantly to create meaning out of nothing, to understand the close juxtaposition of the idea conveyed by the visuals and the words . . . . We must be vigilant in visual language, perhaps more so than in prose, because readers will attempt to make meaning out of elements whose proximity may be accidental. (Horn, 1998, p. 111)

This discussion of the effect of images on responses to survey questions thus presupposes the presence of both visual and verbal elements. In other words, we're concerned with the second and third uses of images (supplemental and incidental) rather than the first (images instead of words) identified in Section 3.3. Let's look at a few examples before examining the research evidence.

In the first example (Figure 3.12), the visual syntax sends mixed messages. However, the image of the bank teller is not tightly coupled with the survey

TALKS

Do you currently use a bank
for your personal financial service needs?

☐ Yes
☐ No

Please make your selection ...

Figure 3.12 **Effect of Image on Survey Response.**

question on the left. In addition, its placement on the lower right of the screen suggests it is not of primary importance to the task. On the other hand, the size, color, and brightness of the image draw the eyes to it, making it hard to ignore. Given this, the picture is likely to be viewed by the respondent as pertinent to the question being asked. If so, the content of the image – the information it conveys – may affect the answer to that question – whether or not this is what the designer intended.

Incidentally, this example comes from a now-defunct dot-com enterprise, delivering speech-based online surveys. The idea was that a sound file of the question was played on each screen, much like audio-CASI in face-to-face surveys (see Turner et al., 1998). Why did this not work? My guess is it had less to do with bandwidth than with a sense that the audio did not add value to the written questions. Notwithstanding the rapid rise of music downloads, online games, and sharing of photographs, the Web remains primarily a text-based medium. The addition of audio, perhaps for those with low levels of literacy, is aimed at a group much less likely to use the Internet in the first place. This reiterates the point that the Web is primarily a visual medium, with words or text still the dominant core material (see Section 3.7).

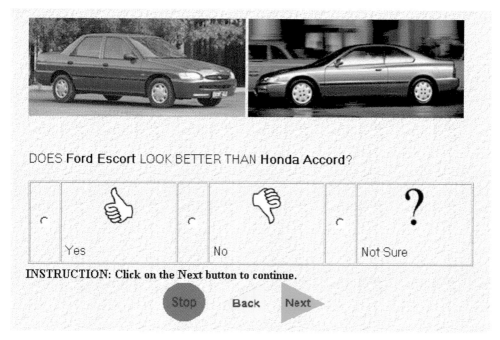

DOES **Ford Escort** LOOK BETTER THAN **Honda Accord**?

⌀ 👍 Yes	⌀ 👎 No	⌀ **?** Not Sure

INSTRUCTION: Click on the Next button to continue.

Stop   Back   Next ▶

Figure 3.13 **Effect of Images and Other Graphical Elements on Survey Responses.**

The next example (Figure 3.13) comes from a demonstration version of an online survey software system. This reminds me of those "spot the differences" games in the Sunday comics. While the intention appears to be to illustrate the words "Ford Escort" and "Honda Accord," there is much more information being conveyed by the pictures than by the words. For example:

- One car is red, the other silver
- One is in a rural setting, the other an urban environment
- One car has two doors, the other four
- The front grille is visible on one, not the other

And I could go on. The point is that each of these distinctions may convey different meanings to respondents. For instance, while the question intent may be to focus on make and model, a respondent might well be influenced by the color instead. This example illustrates the popular saying that a picture is worth one thousand – or even ten thousand in some versions – words. While intended to supplement the question text, the pictures may actually convey much more information than was intended by the designer.

The example in Figure 3.13 employs several other visual elements. In addition to the pictures, there are symbols or icons (the thumbs-up, thumbs-down, and question mark icons), colors and shapes (the red circle and green triangle for the stop and next buttons, respectively), and texture (the screen background pattern). As Blackwell (2001, p. 224), notes, "Just as there is a continuum between textual and visual languages . . . there is a continuum between visual languages that employ a great deal of pictorial representation, and those that employ very little." The example in Figure 3.13 represents a visually rich – although not necessarily effective – design.

For example, there is no clear connection between the two images and the corresponding text – is it clear that the Escort is on the left and the Accord on the right? The Gestalt laws of visual grouping (see Chapter 4, Section 4.4; Jenkins and Dillman, 1997) could be used to guide the design to create a closer linkage between these related elements. Similarly, the vertical lines break the association between the input field (radio buttons) and labels ("yes," "no"). One could question whether the use of the icons is appropriate. Does "thumbs-up" mean the same as "yes" – and does it mean the same thing across cultures? Finally, the size and brightness of the "stop" button may encourage its use relative to the other buttons, potentially leading to premature or unintended termination of the survey (see Chapter 5). However, the textured background does not appear to interfere with the task of answering the question (see Chapter 4, Section 4.3.2). Thus, aside from the poor use of images, there are many things that could be done to improve the design in this example.

The next example in Figure 3.14 is one of my favorite instances of gratuitous graphics – illustrations that appear to serve no useful purpose, other than demonstrating the designer's creative abilities. It is remotely possible that this graphic – and others in this university-based health survey – were included to keep respondents entertained and interested in completing the survey. But the consequence may have been to change or confuse the meaning of the survey question for respondents.

Let's look at the figure in more detail. The role of the image is quite ambiguous. What does the "amount shown above" refer to – the alcohol shown in the drawing or that entered by the respondent in the prior question? If the former, the image is a core part of the second question; if not, it is supplemental or incidental. The link between question and accompanying illustration is not very clear. This is an example of a weak syntactic link between verbal and visual elements. In addition,

Please add up your total weekly intake and enter it in the box

Do you think it is OK to drink in a week the amount shown above? Yes ⌒ No ⌒

Figure 3.14 **Example of Gratuitous Graphic.**

the content of the drawing may convey more than is implied by the question. Much more than simply the volume of alcohol is conveyed by the image – it implies both smoking and drinking, it suggests a mix of hard liquor (gin and vodka) and beer, and the crushed cans and overturned bottles suggest that this was some party!

The next example (see Figure 3.15) comes from a Swedish health survey (see Bälter and Bälter, 2005), designed to elicit how much time in a day is spent engaged in various levels of physical activity. Both iconic images and color are used to convey the notion of increasing levels of activity from sleep to vigorous physical exercise such as shoveling snow or mowing the lawn. But this example also illustrates the concreteness of images. Focusing just on the images gives the respondent a specific instance of a class of activities, whereas reading the accompanying text containing several examples that may better define the class of activities.

The example in Figure 3.16 is similar to that in Figure 3.15, in that it uses images to represent various classes of activities. But, in this case, the images are used in the place of words. In other words, there is no accompanying text to disambiguate the meaning of the pictures. Take a look at the third picture, which is an image of trams. Is this meant to exclude buses, subway trains, and other forms of public transport? Or is this meant to illustrate the broad category of public transport? Given that mopeds and motorcycles are separate items, one might assume the former, but the balance of the list (not shown) does not include such other types of public transport. This leaves the respondent with the decision about what to include or exclude when responding to this item.

Hur fysiskt aktiv är Du ett vanligt vardagsdygn?

I tabellen nedan finns 9 nivåer (grader) av ansträngning. A innebär den lägsta och I den högsta graden av ansträngning. För att man ska förstå vad varje nivå innebär finns exempel på aktiviteter som är just så ansträngande. Försök att uppskatta hur många timmar, halvtimmar och kvartar du Du ägnar dig åt aktiviteter som är lika ansträngande som nivå A till I. Börja med nivå A och ange sedan tiden per nivå. Summan ska bli 24 timmar.

			tim	min
A		t ex. sova eller vila		
B		t ex sitta i badkaret, sitta och lyssna på musik eller titta på TV		
C		t ex kontorsarbete, att sticka, sy eller sitta i möte		
D		t ex bädda, stryka kläder eller diska för hand		
E		t ex bowling, verkstadsarbete, meka med bilen, köra buss, dansa vals eller foxtrot		
F		t ex gå i snabb takt, hästridning eller sopa gatan		
G		t ex att måla huset, bära och stapla ved, åka skidor eller slalom		
H		t ex vägarbete, att klippa gräset med handgräsklippare eller skotta snö		
I		Hur lång tid av dygnets timmar ägnar du åt sådant som är mer ansträngande än nivå H?		

Summering av tiden

Figure 3.15 **Use of Color and Icons to Convey Meaning.**

Finally, look back at the header or banner images in Figures 3.9, 3.10, and 3.11. While these may be intended by the design as style elements (see Section 4.1 in the next chapter), they may be viewed as relevant to the survey by the respondent and may – whether consciously or not – affect their answers to the questions. Given that images are powerful attention-getting devices, they are likely to be perceived if

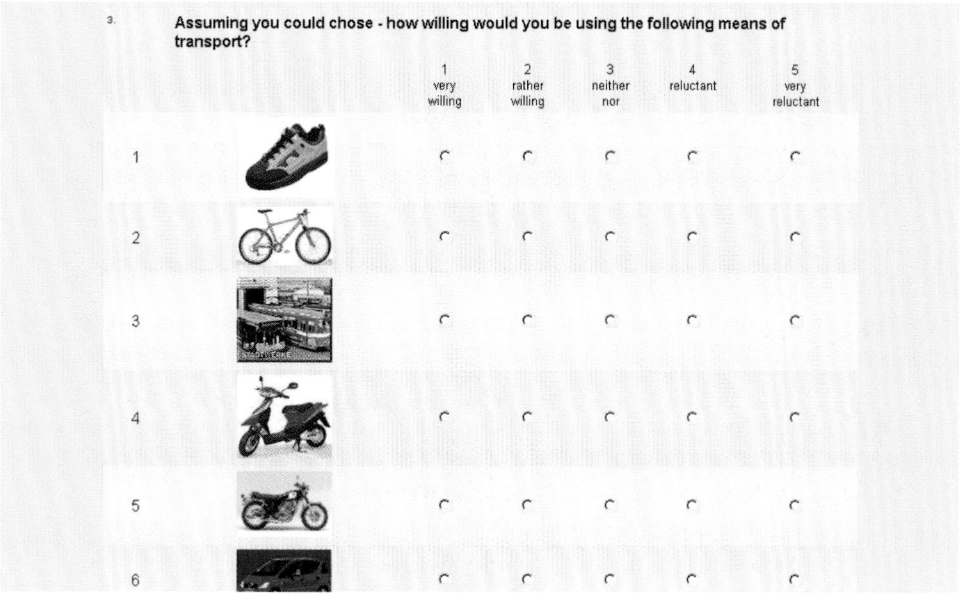

Figure 3.16 **Use of Images in Place of Words.**

they appear on the Web page. If not, why put them there? If so, they may influence a respondent's answer in ways possibly unintended by the designer. What then is the research evidence of the effect of images on survey responses?

3.5. Research on Images in Web Surveys

Research on images is mostly found in the world of multimedia instruction or media studies (newspapers and TV), and in advertising research. But relatively little research has been done on the role of images in Web surveys, or in surveys in general, which (with some notable exceptions) tend to rely on verbal descriptions. So, this section is as much a review of the issues and the outline of a research agenda than a definite set of findings that would guide decisions on the use of images.

Images have several properties that may affect the answers to an accompanying question:

1. They attract attention.
2. They tend to be more concrete than abstract.

3. They are a visually rich and complex information source, often open to several possible interpretations.

With regard to the latter, different respondents may see or react to different elements of the image, as I have illustrated with the examples. In other words, the image may bring to mind things that the question designer had not intended. The richer the content of the image (that is, the more information it conveys), the more likely this may be to occur. This is why we need to be particularly vigilant in the use of images.

Images could affect responses to survey questions in many different ways. For example:

- They may affect category membership; using images as exemplars, the range of objects or activities implied by the question covered may be changed.
- They may affect context, producing contrast or assimilation effects.
- They may affect mood or emotion.
- They may make vague ideas concrete.
- They may clarify or obfuscate the meaning of a question or key term.

These effects may be potentially good or bad, depending on the purpose of the question and the use of the images. Let's look at some research evidence on these issues.

One of our experiments looked at the effect of images on behavioral frequency reports, using images as exemplars (Couper, Kenyon, and Tourangeau, 2004). The pictures accompanying the survey question represented low-frequency or high-frequency instances of the behavior in question (shopping, travel, eating out). For example, when shown a picture of a couple dining in a fine restaurant, respondents reported significantly fewer events (eating out in the past month) on average than when they were shown a high-frequency instance of the behavior (a person eating fast food in a car). The average number of episodes per month was 11.8 in the first instance and 16.2 in the second. Furthermore, those exposed to the fine restaurant image reported significantly higher levels of enjoyment, and a significantly higher price paid for the last meal eaten out. Similarly, respondents exposed to a picture of grocery shopping reported more shopping trips in the past month than those exposed to a picture of clothes shopping. Similar effects were found for several other behaviors. We argued that the images served as cues for the retrieval of relevant incidents from memory, hence affecting the frequency reports. In a partial replication in Germany, Hemsing and Hellwig (2006) found similar effects.

In a subsequent set of studies (Couper, Conrad, and Tourangeau, 2007), we explored the role of images in changing the context of the survey question. Respondents saw a picture of a fit woman jogging or a sick woman in a hospital bed (or no picture, in some cases) while providing an overall rating of their health. Consistent with the context effects literature, we found a significant contrast effect, with those seeing the sick woman reporting significant higher levels of health than those seeing the fit woman. Again, these effects were substantial: 43% of respondents reported themselves to be in very good health (8–10 on a 10-point scale) when exposed to the picture of the fit woman, but 58% did so when shown the sick woman. When the pictures were put in the banner of the Web page, the effect was smaller than when the pictures appeared alongside the question, or appeared on a prior introductory screen, producing some support for the banner blindness hypothesis that material in banners is likely to be ignored (Benway, 1998; Benway and Lane, 1998). But the effects did not disappear, suggesting as noted earlier that even pictures that do not appear to be explicitly linked to the survey question may nonetheless influence the answers to that question.

Witte, Pargas, Mobley, and Hawdon (2004) conducted an experiment in a Web survey, in which some respondents were shown pictures (and others not) of animals on the threatened and endangered species list. Those exposed to the pictures were significantly more likely to support protection for the species. Their study also has some suggestive data on the effect of photo quality. The study included two species of fish, and inclusion of the photograph increased strong support for protection from 24% to 48% in the case of the Spotfin chub, but only from 46% to 48% in the case of the Arkansas shiner. One explanation they offer for this difference is the fact that the Spotfin chub stood out more sharply against the background, whereas the Arkansas shiner blended into the similarly colored background (Witte et al., 2004, p. 366).

In terms of images affecting mood, we conducted a study in which respondents were asked a series of depression and mental health items from the RAND SF-36 instrument (Couper, Conrad, and Tourangeau, 2003). For some respondents, the questions were accompanied by an image of bright sunlight; for others, an image of stormy weather was presented, and still others saw no picture. While the effects were generally modest, they were in the expected direction, with sunshine elevating respondents' reported mood and rain lowering it. The mood activation appears to have the biggest effect when it is occurs prior to answering the survey questions. For example, in response to the question, "During the past 4 weeks, how often have you felt downhearted and blue," 15.1% of respondent said "never" in the stormy condition, and 22.6% said "never" in the sunny condition when the images were shown on a lead-in screen prior to the battery of items. When the images appeared alongside the questions, these were 13.8% and 15.3%, respectively. This suggests that momentary changes in mood can be achieved by the simple expedient of the choice of image shown to respondents.

Not every study on images has yielded significant effects on survey responses. In an early test of the effect of images (Kenyon, Couper, and Tourangeau, 2001), we conducted a study among Knowledge Networks panel members around the American Music Awards (the Grammy Awards), with various images of nominated artists. We found no effects of any of several image manipulations. One possible explanation was the generally low level of interest in, and knowledge of, the Grammy-nominated artists among the panel members. If you have no idea who an artist is, showing a picture may not help. However, in a survey on political knowledge, also using the Knowledge Networks panel, Prior (2002) found that adding photographs of political figures significantly improved performance on political knowledge tests. Thus, for example, asking people if they knew what political office Dick Cheney held produced fewer correct answers than when the question was accompanied by a picture of Dick Cheney. When Cheney was shown alongside President Bush in a picture, the proportion correctly identifying his office increased further.

What have we learned from the few studies that have been conducted so far? First, it is clear that images *do* indeed affect the answer to survey questions, although not always. Second, these studies suggest the potential *risks* of including images, but no studies have yet demonstrated the *value* of including images. And third, studying image effects is complex – it depends both on the visual semantics and on the visual syntax. Clearly, there is much more work to be done in this area, especially in terms of finding ways that the inclusion of images may improve survey measurement or facilitate the task of answering the questions. For many of the effects demonstrated in the research reviewed here, we do not know which of the answers is the "correct" one or if, indeed, there is one correct answer. We know that images change responses but we do not yet know if or how they may improve the reliability or validity of responses.

Aside from the effect of images on measurement error, do they affect nonresponse or breakoff rates? The presumption is that the inclusion of images makes the survey more interesting and appealing, thereby encouraging completion. But is there any research evidence to support this?

Guéguen and Jacob (2002a) included a digital photograph of a male or female requester in an HTML e-mail invitation to a Web survey sent to students at a French university. When a photograph was included, subjects were more likely to comply with the request (84%) than when no photograph was included (58%). Furthermore, the female requester was helped more of the time than the male requester when a photograph was included, but there was no difference when no photograph was included. I'll return to the issue of survey invitations in Chapter 6.

In an experiment conducted as part of a Web survey on a highly sensitive topic among women (Reed, Crawford, Couper, Cave, and Haefner, 2004), different photographs of the principal investigator were used to suggest either a medical setting (using a white coat and stethoscope) or a regular academic setting (using a regular business suit). Respondents were only exposed to the photographs after they received the e-mail invitation and clicked on the URL to start the survey. No differences were found in overall survey completion. In addition, no differences were found in the distribution of responses to sensitive questions in the survey, by the framing suggested by the photographs and accompanying text.

In our experiments on the use of images described above, we have found no discernible effects on breakoffs. In other words, exposure to the pictures does not increase completion relative to those who saw no pictures. In the Grammy Awards study (Kenyon, Couper, and Tourangeau, 2001), respondents were exposed to up to six different image manipulations. We created an index from 0 to 6 for the number of pictures seen, and examined the relationship with debriefing questions at the end of the survey. The correlation with picture exposure and satisfaction with the survey was a mere 0.023 ($p = .29$, n.s.), while the correlation with subjective survey length was 0.057 ($p \leq .01$). Thus, while the inclusion of pictures appeared to have no impact on the subjective enjoyment of the survey, there was a modest positive association with perceived length.

But these studies (except Guéguen and Jacob, 2002a) were based on existing panels of Web users, whether opt-in or prerecruited. Their decision to start a survey, or to continue once begun, may be based on factors other than the visual appeal of the survey derived from the inclusion of images. In other words, these studies weren't designed to test the effect of images on breakoffs and may thus be an unfair test of that relationship.

To summarize the research, there is much we still don't know about how the inclusion of images may affect survey measurement error and nonresponse error. We have much to learn about when to use images and how best to do so. As researchers learn how best to exploit the visual power to the Web to improve the quality of answers obtained, and to improve the survey experience for respondents, we are likely to see a rise in the use of images in Web surveys. I can't wait to see what develops.

3.6. Summary on Images

The choices we make when adding rich visual material to Web surveys are consequential. We should carefully consider not only the content of the image, but also its function and relevance to the task at hand, as well as its syntactic relationship with the verbal materials comprising the Web survey. Images open up many possibilities for extending survey measurement beyond what can be conveyed through words alone. But, for all the reasons cited above, images should be used with caution – only when their purpose is clear, their content is unambiguous, and their link to the survey question or task is apparent to the respondent.

In addition to the substantive cautions about the interpretation of images and their effect on responses, there are a few technical issues to consider too. One is that images require vision, and that those using screen readers will not be able to "see" the image, but will require a description of the image (using the `alt` tag in HTML). This may not be much of a concern in the world of market or advertising research, but for government surveys, this may raise issues around accessibility and Section 508 compliance (see Coon, 2002; Horton, 2006; Rossett, 2006).

A second concern is that the inclusion of images may slow download time. In the early days of the Web, DeVoto (1998) stated this quite forcefully:

> Look. There are people out there who don't load images. There are people out there who *can't* load images. There are people out there paying for every second they spend online, and they're not gonna want to spend their pin money downloading a company logo and a bunch of themed section graphics, no matter *how* pretty they are. OK?

While concerns about download time are much less of an issue today, and while almost every Web site is graphic-rich, the careless use of images could slow things down for respondents.

In addition, images are of fixed size, whereas text on the Web can wrap according to browser dimensions, the font size can be changed, and so on. Careful control of the placement of the image in relation to the text is important to avoid oddly juxtaposed elements on the screen. This is an amateur mistake, but it happens enough in Web surveys I've seen that it is worth the caution. Be careful to test the spatial association of the images and accompanying text under different browser and user settings.

I'm reminded of those car commercials on television, in which the fine print cautions, "Professional driver on a closed course. Do not attempt this at home." A similar admonition might apply to using images in Web surveys. They may be easy to add to a Web survey, and it might be tempting to do so, but their appropriate use requires both design and technical skills. While images are potentially valuable design elements for surveys, don't be overly reliant on them if other alternatives exist.

3.7. Multimedia

So far, I have discussed static images. There are many ways in which the visual communication can be made richer still. One is to add animation, a technique increasingly seen on Web sites, using Macromedia Flash and other Web-based animation tools. The next level of fidelity is streaming video. Much of what I have written about images applies to video and sound. As the experience is enriched, what a survey question is and what it means to respondents may change.

Multimedia may offer a lot of promise for extending traditional survey measurement. For example, the promise of being able to show a TV commercial to a large sample of respondents in a self-administered setting offers much appeal to researchers. However, the current reality is still quite limited. The biggest drawbacks to the more widespread use of multimedia are bandwidth and media compatibility.

The dream of full-screen, high-resolution streaming video may still be some way off, although recent improvements in bandwidth and compression methods are making this more of a possibility. Multimedia generally requires a great deal of bandwidth. Not all respondents are capable of viewing streaming video. They may be connected to the Internet via modem, rather than broadband. Whereas digital subscriber lines (DSL) or cable modems can download files at almost 2 megabytes per minute, a 56K modem can only handle about 190,000 bytes per minute. The penetration of broadband is increasing rapidly in the United States, but it is still far from universal and – as with Internet coverage in general – is uneven. For example, the Pew Internet and American Life Project (see Horrigan, 2006) reported a 40% leap in the number of Americans who have broadband at home between March 2005 and March 2006, with an estimated 42% of American adults with a high-speed Internet connection at home in 2006. This has increased to 47% in early 2007 (www.pewinternet.org; Horrigan and Smith, 2007). This means that more than half of homes still have dial-up Internet connections. Those living in rural areas, older people, and those with lower income are all more likely to be dial-up users.

Even if they had broadband, respondents may not have the requisite media player and may be reluctant to download and install it to continue with the survey. Additionally, they may be in a setting (e.g., workplace or library) where the playing of multimedia may be restricted or unwanted. For certain types of research, and for certain groups of Web users, these may not be problems, but the broader the reach of the survey, the more likely one is to encounter problems when using multimedia.

To play sound or video requires a plugin or add-on media player. There are a variety of plugins available, compatible with several different formats, such as QuickTime, Windows Media Player, and Real Audio or Video. Not only does the respondent have to have a plugin installed in order to play multimedia from within the browser but also the appropriate medium must be downloaded, or the system must detect what the client is capable of playing and deliver the appropriate file to the browser. Castro (2003) discussed some of the technical complexities of delivering multimedia.

Figure 3.17 shows an example of what happens if the browser doesn't have the appropriate plugin. One of my favorite early examples was a Web survey that instructed the respondent on how to download the video player before continuing. The survey admonished, "PLEASE DO NOT CLOSE YOUR BROWSER TO THIS SURVEY WINDOW." The only problem was that the media player instructed the user to close all programs and restart the computer to activate the program. Doing so meant that access to the survey was lost, which meant that only those who had the media player preinstalled could complete the survey. Problems like this are not uncommon.

There have been several false starts in the effort to offer multimedia content as part of Web surveys. In one such example, a company called TalksAudio.com added sound to Web surveys (see Figure 3.12). Our own research on audio-CASI suggests that – particularly for those who are literate – and this includes most, if not all, of those currently completing Web surveys – the audio of the questions being read does not appear to offer any additional benefits over simply reading the questions on the screen (Couper and Tourangeau, 2006). For whatever reason, this company no longer exists, and I have seen no other such examples of this type of application.

Despite the difficulties of delivering streaming video, many have tried it with varying success, and many Internet research companies boast multimedia delivery as part of their portfolio. Others are using storyboards – essentially a series of still images – to represent multimedia content. A variety of other strategies have been tried. For example, when all of Knowledge Networks' (see http://www.knowledgenetworks.com/) panel members were provided with WebTV units, the system downloaded video files to the hard drive at a time when the system was not in use, permitting playback on the TV set without delay at the

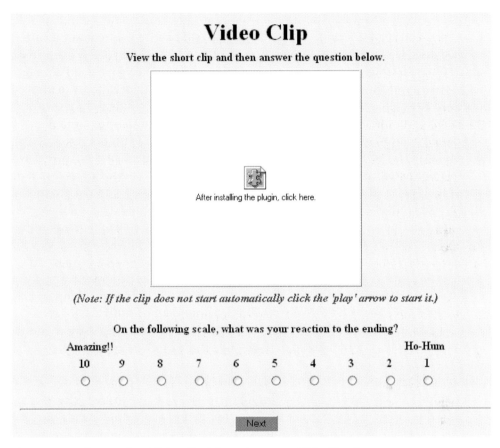

Figure 3.17 **Streaming Video Problem: Incompatible Plugin.**

appropriate point in the survey. Others are using Macromedia's Flash to present moving images, but Flash is not without compatibility issues.

Even when the technical issues are overcome – and I have no doubt they will be, given the direction of development on the Internet – questions still remain about if and when multimedia presentations are appropriate for survey measurement. While there are certainly some applications for which Web-based multimedia presentations are ideal (ad testing being one of them), it is not clear that rich media are appropriate for all survey settings. Many of these issues are discussed in Schober and Conrad's edited volume (2007), *Envisioning Survey Interviews of the Future.* My own view on the issue closely parallels that regarding images. While there are many potentially exciting research opportunities, one must always evaluate the benefits relative to the goals of the survey, and in terms of the quality of the resultant data. In many cases, the additional channels of communication may not improve survey measurement, and in some cases may even lower data quality. As with images, gratuitous motion is distracting, and Nielsen and Loranger (2005) recommend using multimedia for Web sites only when it helps to convey information. For us, it makes sense to use multimedia methods only when they add value to the survey, not simply for the sake of doing so.

Another concern is that as richer media are added to the Web survey experience, the issue of social presence becomes salient. One of the advantages of Web-based survey administration is the elimination of interviewer effects. But as we start adding pictures, video and sound to Web surveys, we may end up reintroducing some of these effects. The research of Nass and his colleagues suggests that even small cues can engender presence effects such as socially desirable responding (e.g., Nass, Moon, and Carney, 1999; Nass, Robles, Bienenstock, Treinen, and Heenan, 2003) or even gender and race effects (e.g., Nass, Moon, and Green, 1997; Nass, Isbister, and Lee, 2001). Our own research using interactive voice response, or IVR (e.g., Couper, Singer, and Tourangeau, 2004; Tourangeau, Couper, and Steiger, 2003), pictures on the Web (e.g., Krysan and Couper, 2005), and videos in CASI (Krysan and Couper, 2003) suggests that these effects are modest at best in surveys. Nonetheless, it remains an issue to watch as we move to richer multimedia experiences on the Web.

Despite all the concerns I have raised, there are research topics for which the presentation of multimedia material online is ideal. For these cases, the technical limitations may be worth the gain from delivering such stimuli cheaply and quickly to a large number of respondents online. We are likely to see a great deal of work in this area over the next several years. A more detailed discussion of multimedia in Web surveys at this time is likely to become quickly outdated. I look forward to seeing what develops. But for now, caution may prevail.

3.8. Interactive Elements

Together the visual and verbal elements comprise what the respondent *sees* or perceives. Another set of elements pertain to what the respondent *does*, and these are the interactive elements of a Web survey. When the respondent takes some action, these elements produce a change, whether simply changing from an unselected to a selected state in the case of a radio button, or submitting the responses to the server and delivering the next question, in the case of an action button.

These are the most basic forms of interaction – either a state change of an HTML element, or a server-side response to a respondent's input. In the second part of this chapter, our attention turns to the inclusion of client-side interactivity in Web surveys. In other words, we're going beyond the basic tools offered by HTML and server-side scripts.

In Chapter 1, I raised some of the concerns about using active content in Web surveys – in brief, these relate to capacity, accessibility, and security. Here, I want to focus on some of the potential advantages of doing so but also review the arguments against the use of active content, and review the research evidence on whether including active content improves survey measurement. Active content involves the use of plugins or scripts added to standard HTML to achieve client-side interactivity. The most common forms of active scripts are JavaScript and Flash, with Java further increasing the range of functions possible.

As with images, one can imagine a continuum of interactivity. At one end of the continuum is what can be achieved using HTML. Clicking on a radio button turns it "on," clicking in a check box puts a check mark in the box, and so on. As we have already discussed, HTML is very limited, essentially restricted to providing visual feedback for a user action, but not capable of taking action on its own. Client-side interactivity or dynamic HTML goes further. This can range from simple enhancements or improvements to the standard HTML tools (see Section 3.8.1) to the creation of new question types and ways of responding. This is clearly the area of fastest growth on the Web, with new tools and methods continually under development, with the latest of these – AJAX or asynchronous JavaScript and XML – referred to by Cisco CEO John Chambers as the "interactions Web" revolution (*USA Today*, October 26, 2005). My goal here is to offer a few examples of how some of these tools can be used in surveys, and what we know about how – and how well – these tools work.

Before I get into this, I will briefly review some of the programming tools to achieve such interactivity on the Web. Two commonly used tools are JavaScript and Java. JavaScript, initially developed by Netscape, is a scripting or programming language that is embedded in an HTML document. JavaScript code is typically embedded directly in the HTML code. So one way to see if a survey is using JavaScript is to view the source, and see what the JavaScript – and HTML for that matter – is doing. Both are rendered in plain text, so the commands can be easily followed. But the JavaScript could also be in a different file, whose location is referenced in the HTML code. There are other scripting languages (VBScript is another), but JavaScript is the most common and most modern browsers are capable of recognizing and acting upon JavaScript code.

Trigger	Event triggered
OnClick	User clicks on a check box or radio button
OnSelect	User selects text in an INPUT or TEXTAREA form field
OnMouseover	User moves mouse over a designated area
OnChange	User changes a form field
OnFocus	User enters a form field
OnBlur	User leaves a form field

Figure 3.18 **Examples of Common JavaScript Triggers.**

JavaScript achieves its interactivity by acting on user actions. Remember that in HTML, clicking a radio button does nothing other than change the state of the field from "not selected" to "selected." Only when the submit button is pressed can any action be taken based on the information transmitted to the server. JavaScript, by way of contrast, has several functions that can trigger predetermined actions. Some of these are shown in Figure 3.18.

These can be used to trigger a variety of actions. For example, with `OnClick`, a skip or edit check could be triggered when the respondent clicks on a radio button or check box. Similarly, `OnChange` could be used to validate the information in a form field as soon as the field is changed. This could verify that the string entered into a text box is numeric, and of the required length (e.g., for a zip code). `OnBlur` could be used, for example, to generate an error message if the user leaves a field without entering any information. We have used `OnMouseOver` to present definitions of key terms when the respondent moves the mouse over the term (Conrad, Couper, Tourangeau, and Peytchev, 2006). In general, while the appearance of the page can be altered and input fields can be enabled or disabled, not much can be done with the content or structure of the Web page itself. We'll return to this issue shortly.

Despite the similar names, Java is not the same as JavaScript. Java is a full-featured programming language developed by Sun Microsystems. Java was originally designed to be platform independent but because of disagreements between Microsoft and Sun on the development of the language, different versions of Java were developed at the height of the browser wars. The differences between these versions appear to be diminishing, but it remains important to test whether a Java applet executes in the same way (if at all) on different browsers and operating system platforms. Unlike JavaScript, which resembles HTML is the sense of being a scripting language, Java executes client-side by activating applets, small programs that run over the Internet. In fact, a JavaScript action is involved with the `script` tag in HTML, while Java is activated with the `applet` tag. A drawback of Java is that the applet needs to be downloaded to the browser before being executed.

A more recent development, and increasingly popular for the development of dynamic Web content, is known as AJAX, one element of what is being known as "Web 2.0" (see Couper, 2007a). AJAX stands for Asynchronous JavaScript and XML. The term "asynchronous" is a bit misleading, in that all Internet communication is asynchronous. However, in standard HTTP (hypertext transfer protocol) interaction, the user completes the form on the client-side before submitting the request to the server, which then processes the information on the form before responding. In AJAX, the interaction with the server is done without waiting for the user to finish what they are doing. In other words, the user may still be in the process of entering information or making choices on the page, while the Web form is interacting with the server in the background. Several popular Web sites already include AJAX, including Google Suggest (http://labs.google.com/suggest/), which uses a dynamic drop-down to offer suggestions in real time as one enters a request in the search field. Other examples include www.paguna.com and www.flickr.com.

Google Maps is another application that makes use of AJAX, and this feature has been used in a recent survey to provide interactive maps to respondents on which they could mark places where they consumed alcohol (Sinibaldi, Crawford, Saltz, and Showen, 2006). Essentially the technology behind AJAX blurs the distinction between client-side and server-side actions, permitting faster and smoother interactions. While the applications still reside on the server, Web pages get updated rather than entirely refreshed. As Garrett (2005), who first defined the term AJAX, noted, "Any response to a user action that doesn't require a trip back to the server – such as simple data validation, editing data in memory, and even some navigation – the engine handles on its own. If the engine needs something from the server in order to respond – if it's submitting data for processing, loading additional interface code, or retrieving new data – the engine makes those requests asynchronously, usually using XML, without stalling a user's interaction with the application." We're likely to see greater use of AJAX applications in Web surveys in the future to increase survey interactivity while reducing transmission time to and from the server.

With that background out of the way, let's look at some examples of what can be achieved with client-side interactivity. I'll group these into two broad but overlapping types: (1) adding client-side interactivity to HTML form elements and (2) creating new form or survey elements or tools.

3.8.1. Adding Client-Side Interactivity to HTML Form Elements

An increasingly common use of JavaScript in Web surveys is to add features to existing form elements, or enhance the utility of HTML tools. A few examples include managing skips in scrolling surveys, providing feedback to respondents in the form of running tallies and extending drop boxes to facilitate database lookup.

With regard to the first of these, I've already mentioned in Chapter 1 that one limitation of the scrolling design approach is that skips or branching cannot be automated. While the wording and order of questions cannot be changed on the fly in such designs, it is possible to use active scripts to control the input elements and hence guide respondents down certain paths. Figure 3.19 illustrates this. In this example, the items in the second question that are relevant for the respondent, based on the answers to the first question, are left visible, while those that are not appropriate are grayed out. This is accomplished using JavaScript, triggered by the click of the mouse buttons in Question 1.

An alternative approach that would not require client-side scripts would break this into two pages, with only the relevant items in Question 2 being displayed to the respondent. I'll return to this in Chapter 5, in the context of discussing skips or routing. But for now, this shows what can be done to add some interactivity to HTML form elements.

A second example takes us back to the dreaded drop box. As I noted in Chapter 2, drop boxes have a number of limitations, one of which was the difficulty of finding and selecting items in very long lists. An HTML drop box does not have a search capability; it is basically a scrolling list with first-letter lookup. Here again, JavaScript could be used to overcome this limitation. This is illustrated in Figure 3.20. While it is difficult to illustrate the dynamic features of the Web using the static medium of paper, I'll attempt to describe what happens.

The upper part of Figure 3.20 shows the standard HTML tool (see Section 2.4.2). Typing "M' will take one to the first "M" state on the list, Maine. But then typing "I" will not take one to Michigan (if that were the target), but to Idaho, the first "I" state.

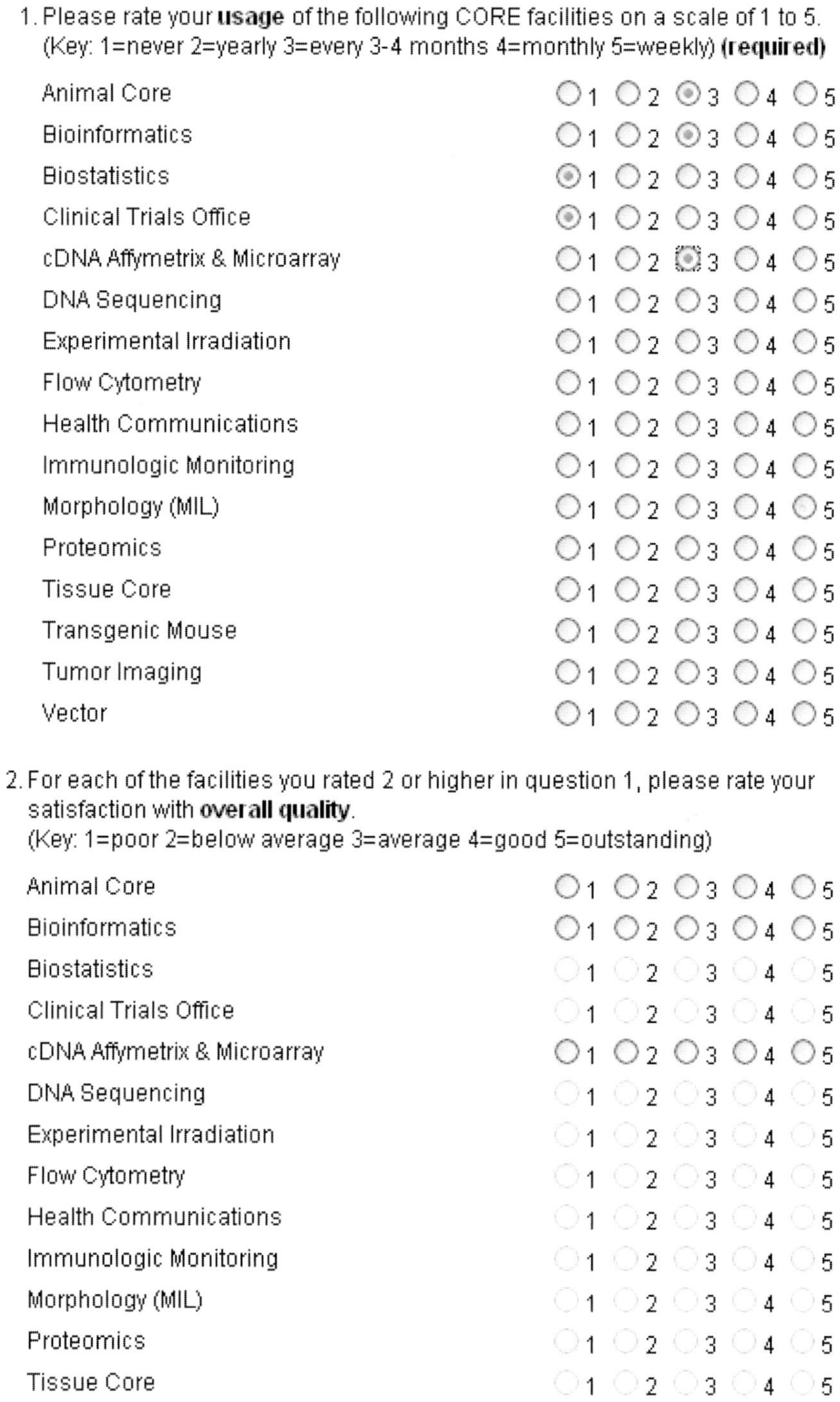

1. Please rate your **usage** of the following CORE facilities on a scale of 1 to 5.
   (Key: 1=never 2=yearly 3=every 3-4 months 4=monthly 5=weekly) **(required)**

Animal Core	○1 ○2 ◉3 ○4 ○5
Bioinformatics	○1 ○2 ◉3 ○4 ○5
Biostatistics	◉1 ○2 ○3 ○4 ○5
Clinical Trials Office	◉1 ○2 ○3 ○4 ○5
cDNA Affymetrix & Microarray	○1 ○2 ◉3 ○4 ○5
DNA Sequencing	○1 ○2 ○3 ○4 ○5
Experimental Irradiation	○1 ○2 ○3 ○4 ○5
Flow Cytometry	○1 ○2 ○3 ○4 ○5
Health Communications	○1 ○2 ○3 ○4 ○5
Immunologic Monitoring	○1 ○2 ○3 ○4 ○5
Morphology (MIL)	○1 ○2 ○3 ○4 ○5
Proteomics	○1 ○2 ○3 ○4 ○5
Tissue Core	○1 ○2 ○3 ○4 ○5
Transgenic Mouse	○1 ○2 ○3 ○4 ○5
Tumor Imaging	○1 ○2 ○3 ○4 ○5
Vector	○1 ○2 ○3 ○4 ○5

2. For each of the facilities you rated 2 or higher in question 1, please rate your
   satisfaction with **overall quality**.
   (Key: 1=poor 2=below average 3=average 4=good 5=outstanding)

Animal Core	○1 ○2 ○3 ○4 ○5
Bioinformatics	○1 ○2 ○3 ○4 ○5
Biostatistics	○1 ○2 ○3 ○4 ○5
Clinical Trials Office	○1 ○2 ○3 ○4 ○5
cDNA Affymetrix & Microarray	○1 ○2 ○3 ○4 ○5
DNA Sequencing	○1 ○2 ○3 ○4 ○5
Experimental Irradiation	○1 ○2 ○3 ○4 ○5
Flow Cytometry	○1 ○2 ○3 ○4 ○5
Health Communications	○1 ○2 ○3 ○4 ○5
Immunologic Monitoring	○1 ○2 ○3 ○4 ○5
Morphology (MIL)	○1 ○2 ○3 ○4 ○5
Proteomics	○1 ○2 ○3 ○4 ○5
Tissue Core	○1 ○2 ○3 ○4 ○5

Figure 3.19 **Use of JavaScript to Control Conditional Questions.**

HTML Version:

In what state were you born? (Type the first letter to find your state)

JavaScript Version:

In what state were you born? (Please enter the first few letters of the state)

Figure 3.20 **HTML versus JavaScript for Database Lookup.**

The lower part of Figure 3.20 shows a JavaScript alternative. This is what is called a "combo box" in Java (see http://java.sun.com/products/jlf/ed2/book/index.html). Such combo boxes can be noneditable or editable. Noneditable combo boxes (also called "list boxes" or "pop-up menus") allow users to select one item from the available set. Editable combo boxes provide users the additional option of entering a response that may or may not be on the list. Microsoft's "Visual" environments (Visual Studio, Visual C++, etc.) have similar features, in which a list box is noneditable and a combo box is editable. In other words, incremental search is a feature of many applications, yet requires special effort on the Web.

Has the Web convention become so ingrained that users do not think of using progressive or incremental search typing? I hope not! But, to be sure this does not cause confusion, one could use a slightly different design in the JavaScript version (as done in Figure 3.20) to convey to the respondent that it is a different tool. This illustrates the inevitable trade-off of respondent convenience (for the majority of respondents) versus extra programming effort (to detect and redirect those with JavaScript disabled). It also raises potential concerns about different formats yielding different responses and about respondent knowledge of and familiarity with the tool. Many of these dimensions are changing on an ongoing basis, making Web survey design both challenging and interesting. This is again why I believe design prescriptions are to be avoided.

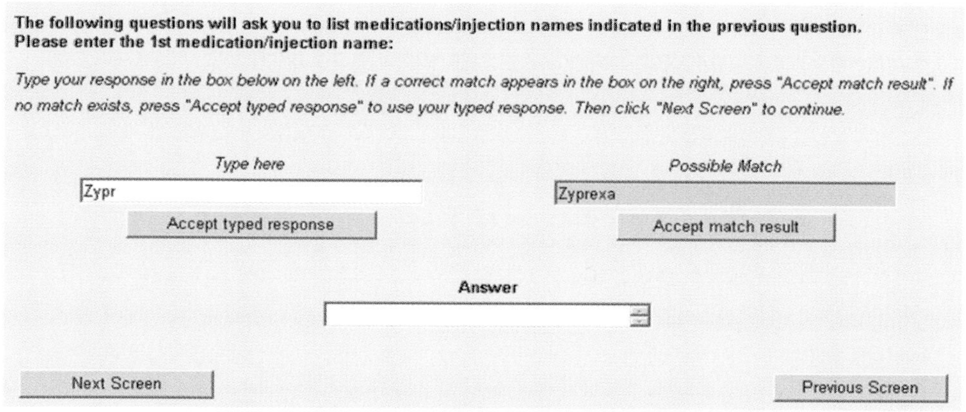

Figure 3.21 **Example of Dynamic Lookup Using JavaScript.**

We have used the editable feature to permit respondents to select from a very large database (see Tourangeau, Couper, Galesic, and Givens, 2004). As part of the National Ambulatory Medical Care Survey, physicians or their assistants complete a series of patient record forms (PRFs) for a sample of their patients. They then write on the paper questionnaire the medications/injections provided or prescribed. This information is then subjected to a coding operation, to match the written descriptions to the National Drug Code Directory (www.fda.gov/CDER/NDC). In a test of a Web-based alternative, we made the full ICD-10 database directly available to respondents. Given that new medications are constantly appearing on the market, the lookup tool needed to have an option to enter a medication not yet in the database, hence the use of an editable combo box. This is shown in Figure 3.21.

We compared this version to a static instrument, which required typing of up to six medications or injections for each patient in text fields, with later coding. About one-fifth of the medicines listed in the static version had to be corrected before coding, but over 90% matched medications in the database, compared with 100% (by definition) in the case of the dynamic version. When the database is of a size and complexity that the lookup task is more efficient and more accurate than paper, these tools are likely to be helpful on the Web. Funke and Reips (2007) also experimented with dynamic text fields but did not find any advantage over text boxes for short lists of items (e.g., the sixteen German "lande").

Another common and useful addition to HTML is the running tally or constant sum. Running tallies are good for two reasons: (1) helping respondents avoid

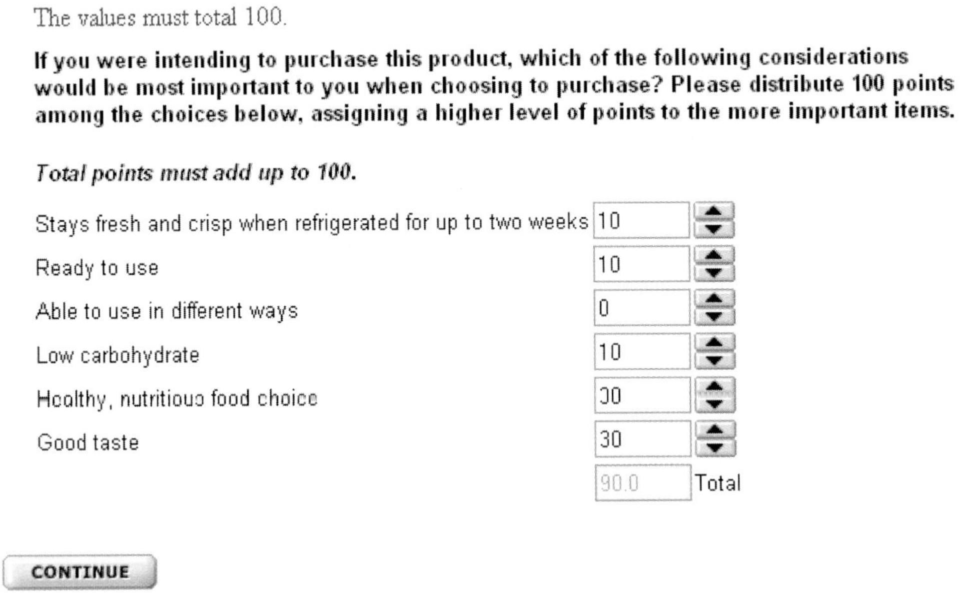

The values must total 100.

If you were intending to purchase this product, which of the following considerations would be most important to you when choosing to purchase? Please distribute 100 points among the choices below, assigning a higher level of points to the more important items.

Total points must add up to 100.

Stays fresh and crisp when refrigerated for up to two weeks 10

Ready to use 10

Able to use in different ways 0

Low carbohydrate 10

Healthy, nutritious food choice 30

Good taste 30

90.0 Total

CONTINUE

Figure 3.22 **Running Tally Example.**

an error is preferable to having them correct the error and (2) computers are generally better at math than people. In other words, it makes sense to let the computer take care of things that computers are good at, such as calculations and logic. Running tallies can be used for allocation of known amounts (e.g., 100%, 24 hours) or to report on information provided earlier, using fills (e.g., "Of the 12 trips you reported taking last year, how many were trips abroad?"). Peytchev and Crawford (2005) refer to the former as fixed summation validations, and the latter as respondent behavior validations, in their discussion of real-time validations in Web surveys.

Figure 3.22 shows an example of a survey question with a running total. This example has both client-side feedback (the 90.0 in the total box) and server-side feedback (the error message generated if the respondent pressed "Continue" with the total not equal to 100). As I'll discuss, if the respondent's browser does not permit active scripts, the client-side feedback will not appear, but the server-side message will. As an aside, this example includes another type of enhancement to HTML – JavaScript is used to render the spinner boxes, allowing respondents to increment or decrement values by clicking on the up or down arrows, as an alternative to typing the numbers directly into each box.

Our research on running tallies suggests that they improve the quality of the data collected with these types of questions (Conrad, Couper, Tourangeau, and Galesic, 2005). With accuracy measured as the number of tallies that equaled the constant sum (100% in our case), accuracy was 84.8% for a version without any feedback, compared with 93.1% for a version with server-side (delayed) feedback only, and 96.5% for client-side (concurrent) feedback. There was also an advantage of concurrent over delayed feedback in terms of the proportion of respondents entering an accurate response at the outset – that is, on the first try. Response times were also faster for the version with the running tally.

We have also done research on enhancing the design of grids (see Section 4.4.3) using dynamic elements (Galesic, Tourangeau, Couper, and Conrad, 2007). As items were answered in the grid, the row background changed from white to gray, or the font changed from black to gray. Both change versions had significantly less missing data than the no-change control. Drop-out rates were also slightly, but not significantly, lower while completion times were slightly higher. Our results suggest that dynamically changing the grid may help respondents with completion of these often-problematic survey elements.

3.8.2. Creating New Form or Survey Elements

In addition to these active content enhancements to standard Web survey tools, the dynamic and graphical nature of the Web is leading to the creation of a wide range of measurement tools that previously could not be done on paper, or required special tools or procedures. A few examples of such tools include slider bars or visual analog scales, card sort tasks, ranking tools, and interactive maps.

Visual analog scale or slider bars are popular tools in Web surveys. While the visual analog scale (VAS) and graphic rating scale (GRS) have been around a long time (e.g., Hayes and Patterson, 1921; Freyd, 1923), they take extra effort to code and key when administered on paper, and the Web offers direct capture of a respondent's input with great accuracy. An example of a VAS or slider bar is illustrated in Figure 3.23. The respondent clicks on the line to activate the slider and can then move the slider using the mouse until the desired position is reached.

Visual analog scales have been implemented using Java (e.g., Bayer and Thomas, 2004; Brophy et al., 2004; Couper et al., 2006), JavaScript (e.g., Funke, 2005; Lenert, Sturley, and Watson, 2002; Reips and Funke, in press), and Flash (Athale, Sturley, Skoczen, Kavanaugh, and Lenert, 2004). While the large literature on VAS implies the superiority of such online measurement tools, our own research

For the aspects of a grocery store listed below, how important would each be in determining at which grocery store you would shop?

Please click on the point of the line below to indicate how important you consider it.

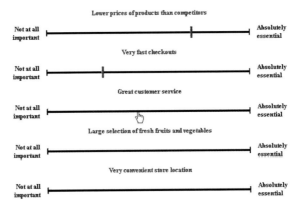

Figure 3.23 **Visual Analog Scale or Slider Bar.**

suggests that the results attained using a slider bar are quite similar to those from a discrete scale using a series of radio buttons (Couper et al., 2006; see also Bayer and Thomas, 2004; Cook, Heath, and Thompson, 2001; Thomas and Couper, 2007). Furthermore, our research found that the VAS produced higher rates of breakoffs and missing data, and took longer to complete than radio button or numeric input alternatives (Couper et al., 2006). While more research on the design and effectiveness of the VAS is needed, the early returns suggest that we are not gaining much by using such interactive tools. Nonetheless, slider bars are part of many Web survey vendors' suite of tools. A variety of related graphic input tools are being developed and tested (see, e.g., Lütters, Westphal, and Heublein, 2007; Stanley and Jenkins, 2007).

Similarly, online card sort tasks can be implemented using active scripting. A respondent drags a card with a visual or verbal description from the pack and drops it into one of several piles or buckets (see, e.g., Thomas, Bayer, Johnson, and Behnke, 2005). Figure 3.24 is an example from Greenfield Online's Web site (www.greenfield.com/rcdemocenter.htm).

Ranking tasks are also making their way into the Web survey toolkit (e.g., Neubarth, 2006). These involve a similar drag and drop action to card sort tasks. An even more sophisticated example that is increasingly popular in market research is the interactive grocery shelf, in which consumers can select items from a virtual shelf and place them in a shopping cart (e.g., Gadeib and Kunath, 2006;

How likely would you be to purchase each of the following types of cookies?

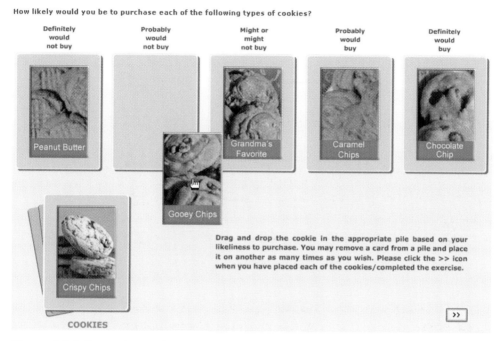

Figure 3.24 **Example Card Sort Task.**

www.greenfield.com/rcdemocenter.htm). Other examples of the use of graphical and interactive elements can be found in Dahan and Hauser (2002) and Dahan and Srinivasan (2000). But many of these interactive tools have yet to be rigorously tested, not only in terms of the quality of the data they yield, but also in terms of the effort to develop and implement them, and in terms of respondents' ability and willingness to use them. For example, Neubarth (2006) compared ranking and rating tasks in a Web survey and found the ranking task to take longer, have higher dropout rates and greater technical difficulties, and lead to lower respondent satisfaction than the rating task.

One final set of tools to mention here relate to the use of image maps. While clickable images are a standard feature in HTML, I mention them briefly here because of the visual elements used, the fact that they offer a more interactive alternative to the standard pick list, and that they are hard to implement on paper.

Figure 3.25 shows an example of a clickable image. Each of the German states ("Bundeslande") is defined as a separate region on the HTML page. In this example,

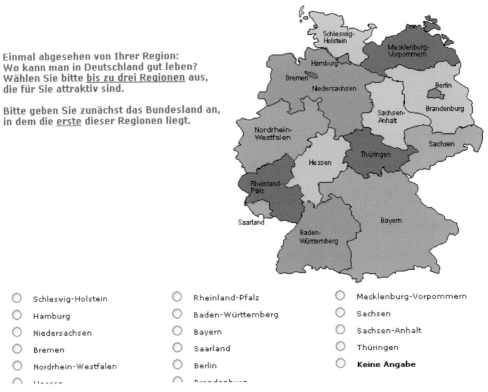

Einmal abgesehen von Ihrer Region:
Wo kann man in Deutschland gut leben?
Wählen Sie bitte bis zu drei Regionen aus,
die für Sie attraktiv sind.

Bitte geben Sie zunächst das Bundesland an,
in dem die erste dieser Regionen liegt.

○ Schleswig-Holstein   ○ Rheinland-Pfalz   ○ Mecklenburg-Vorpommern
○ Hamburg   ○ Baden-Württemberg   ○ Sachsen
○ Niedersachsen   ○ Bayern   ○ Sachsen-Anhalt
○ Bremen   ○ Saarland   ○ Thüringen
○ Nordrhein-Westfalen   ○ Berlin   ○ **Keine Angabe**

Figure 3.25 **Example of Clickable Image Map.**

the respondent can select a state either by clicking directly on the map or by clicking on the corresponding radio button. Image "maps" need not be maps at all – they are simply predefined regions of an image that return a particular value when clicked. For example, Athale et al. (2004) have used the method to display body image maps. Images can also be used more dynamically.

Figure 3.26 shows an example of a life calendar or event history calendar implemented in a Web survey (see Hoogendoorn, 2004; Hoogendoorn and Sikkel, 2002). As the respondent enters information about important life events, this information is presented graphically on the calendar. While in this example the generation of the calendar is done on the server and the graphic is a static display, it is possible to update the information using active scripting, and to make the calendar more interactive. For example, clicking one of the icons could display the details about the event entered by the respondent. In addition, it could be possible to drag the

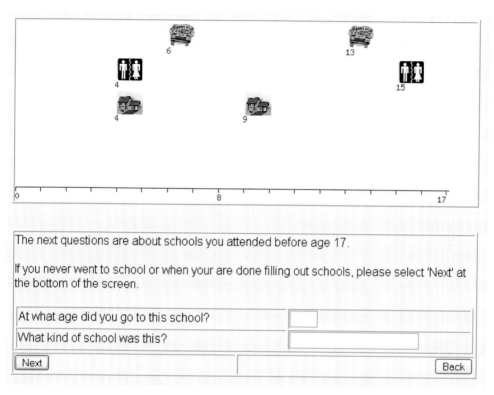

The next questions are about schools you attended before age 17.

If you never went to school or when your are done filling out schools, please select 'Next' at the bottom of the screen.

At what age did you go to this school?	
What kind of school was this?	

[Next]   [Back]

Figure 3.26 **Example of Online Life Calendar.**

icons to change the timing of events. Such actions would require client-side script-ing. The ability to zoom in or out of such displays could also be accomplished with active scripting.

Sinibaldi et al. (2006) have used interactive maps and AJAX to allow respon-dents to move around a map of their town, zoom in or out or scroll in various directions, and designate certain points on the map. Details of these map spots (e.g., address, latitude, and longitude) can then be recorded by the system. With AJAX, all this can be accomplished without waiting for the server to regenerate the map after each respondent action.

In this section, I've mentioned but a few examples of the many new measurement tools being developed and evaluated for use in Web surveys. To the extent they give us better-quality data or answers to questions we could not easily ask using standard survey approaches, we are likely to see more widespread use of these tools.

3.8.3. Capturing User Metrics or Client-Side Paradata

As an aside, many researchers (me included) are using JavaScript for another purpose, largely invisible to the respondents. At the start of a Web survey, it is common to include JavaScript code to capture various characteristics of the respondent's browser, with the goal of optimizing the survey experience. Examples of variables typically captured include browser type (e.g., Internet Explorer, Firefox), screen and browser dimensions (width and height), whether various plugins are enabled, and the like. This allows one to detect at the outset whether the respondent's browser is capable of rendering JavaScript, for example, and routing them to the appropriate version of the instrument.

Active content can also be used throughout the survey to collect paradata (see Couper and Lyberg, 2005) on the process of responding to the survey. Any action taken by the respondent can be used to trigger a JavaScript (see Figure 3.18) to capture information about the event. In this way, detailed time stamps – at the level of individual mouse clicks or keystrokes – can be recorded, as can the various selections a respondent may make as they answer the question. We can use this information to examine the order in which respondents answer a series of items on the same page, to learn when and why they may change their mind (e.g., make one selection then another before submitting the page), examine what information they type into a text field before a client-side or server-side error message clears the response and instructs them to enter a "valid" response, and so on. Heerwegh (2003) has some examples of how such client-side scripting can be used, along with the JavaScript code for doing so. In our research, we use such paradata extensively to learn how respondents answer Web survey questions. I return briefly to the discussion of paradata in Chapter 6.

3.8.4. Design Considerations for Interactive Elements

Given the promise of client-side interactivity for new and improved survey measurement, why are these tools not used more? In the early days of the Web, technical limitations of browsers prevented or discouraged many from using these advanced features. Nowadays, the challenge is not so much one of technical capability – most modern browsers are capable of handling active scripts – but rather issues of security and accessibility. For security reasons, some users choose to disable active content. In fact, the default setting on some browsers (e.g., Internet

Explorer 6.0 and later) is to block active content, or at least to warn users and give them a chance to override the security settings. Some organizations have a policy of blocking active content to avoid malicious damage to systems.

With regard to accessibility, screen readers and other assistive devices do not do as well with active content as with standard HTML. As Horton (2006, p. 175) notes, "Many of the accessibility features that are built into HTML are not available in other formats." I would add "yet" to this statement as this is likely to change, but for now it remains a concern. In fact, many of the federal statistical agencies in the United States have interpreted Section 508 of the Rehabilitation Act (see www.section508.gov; see also Coon, 2002; Rossett, 2006) to mean that *no* active content or client-side scripts can be included in their Web surveys.

At the other extreme, most commercial Web sites have embraced active content. In fact, it is almost impossible to conduct most e-commerce transactions using plain HTML. Most e-commerce sites require active content, and both JavaScript and cookies are an increasingly accepted element of Web use. Social networking sites such as YouTube and MySpace require active content to work. Media sites have similar requirements. Thus, the more actively the user engages with the Web, the more likely they are to enable such features or install plugins to permit their use. While e-commerce sites may be more willing to ignore a small number of (potential) customers in order to enhance the experience for others, survey designers are – or should be – more attuned to issues of representation.

Further, not all active scripting is equal. Most current browsers support JavaScript natively, whereas other add-on software such as Flash and Java require a plugin. To quote Horton (2006, p. 175) again, "Requiring a plugin for site access is risky, since many users will not have a plugin, and may not be able, or will choose not, to install it."

How big a problem is this for survey designers? In a study of over 13,000 applicants to the University of Mannheim in late 2005 to early 2006, Kaczmirek and Thiele (2006) used JavaScript to detect browser capabilities. While almost all applicants (99.7%) had JavaScript enabled, only 94.9% had Java enabled and 93.9% had Flash enabled. Even lower proportions had the required plugins when considering multimedia: while 92.9% had Microsoft's Media Player installed (this comes preinstalled on Windows-based PCs), only 50.7% had QuickTime and 40.1% had RealPlayer. In one of our recent studies, conducted in early 2006 using members of an opt-in panel, only 0.9% did not have JavaScript enabled, and an additional 1.3% did not have Java enabled. But this may underestimate the problem – in our test of visual analog scales we found that significantly more

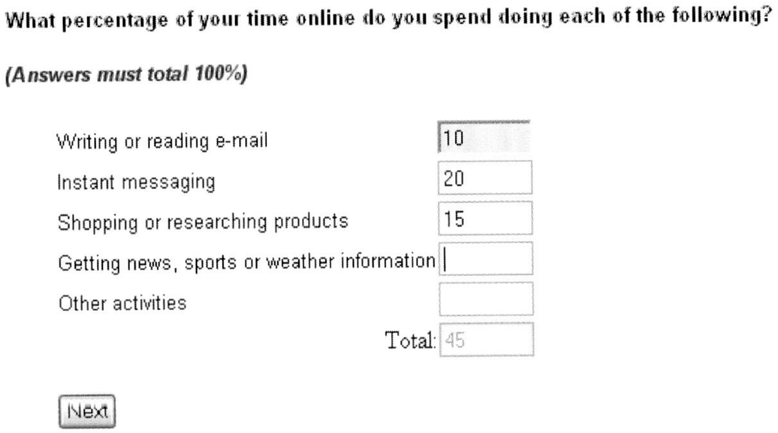

What percentage of your time online do you spend doing each of the following?

(Answers must total 100%)

Writing or reading e-mail	10
Instant messaging	20
Shopping or researching products	15
Getting news, sports or weather information	
Other activities	
Total:	45

Next

Figure 3.27 **Active Content Example I.**

respondents broke off or did not answer any of the Java-based scales than did on the corresponding radio button items (Couper et al., 2006).

What effect might this have on Web surveys – that is, what happens when a user does not have active scripts enabled? Figures 3.27 and 3.28 show examples of a running total question using JavaScript with the default preferences warning the user of active content in Internet Explorer. The first example (Figure 3.27) shows the warning generated by Internet Explorer on encountering a page with active content. The second example (Figure 3.28) shows the confirmation prompt when the user elects to permit active content. The respondent can enter numbers

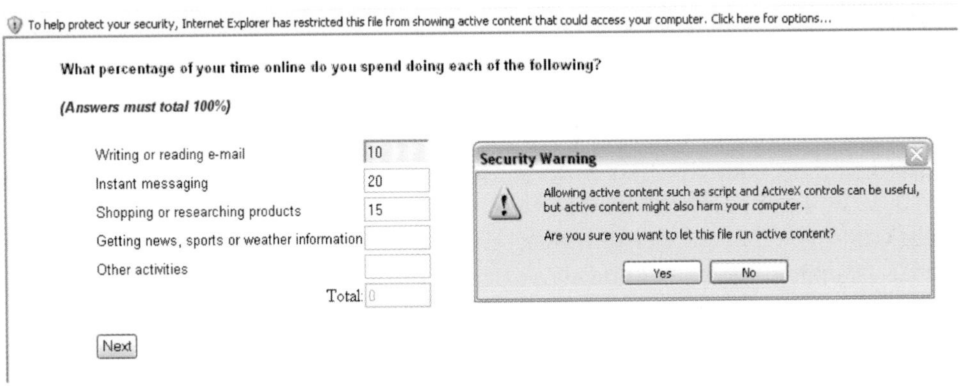

To help protect your security, Internet Explorer has restricted this file from showing active content that could access your computer. Click here for options…

What percentage of your time online do you spend doing each of the following?

(Answers must total 100%)

Writing or reading e-mail	10
Instant messaging	20
Shopping or researching products	15
Getting news, sports or weather information	
Other activities	
Total:	0

Security Warning

Allowing active content such as script and ActiveX controls can be useful, but active content might also harm your computer.

Are you sure you want to let this file run active content?

Yes   No

Next

Figure 3.28 **Active Content Example II.**

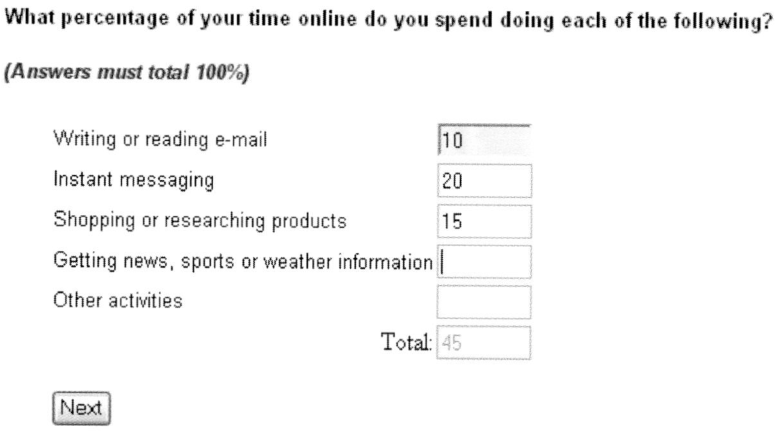

What percentage of your time online do you spend doing each of the following?

(Answers must total 100%)

Writing or reading e-mail	10
Instant messaging	20
Shopping or researching products	15
Getting news, sports or weather information	
Other activities	
Total:	45

Next

Figure 3.29 **Active Content Example III.**

in the fields without active content enabled, but the "0" in the total field does not increment (as it would with active content enabled). Figure 3.29 shows how it would look for those with JavaScript enabled. Those without JavaScript would still be able to answer the question, but without the benefit of the concurrent feedback.

Given all this, what should we as designers do? Some argue for designing for the lowest common denominator or least compliant browser. Others say one should exploit the interactive features of the Web to make the experience both more pleasant and easier for respondents. My view tends toward the latter position, but on two conditions. First, these tools should be used only insofar as the enhanced features are shown to improve data quality and/or enhance the user experience. Second, an alternative should exist for those who do not have active content enabled. This includes those using assistive devices. In some cases, the survey will still work, simply without the interactive feature enabled. For example, if JavaScript is used to enhance HTML functionality – such as dynamic shading, running totals, and the like – those completing the survey without JavaScript enabled will not enjoy the benefit of the enhancement, but can still complete the question (as in the above example). In other cases (e.g., a visual analog scale or card sort task using Java), one can route respondents to an alternative version that uses plain HTML. This can be readily achieved with JavaScript code to detect whether Java, Flash, or other active content is enabled. We used this approach in our test of visual analog scales (Couper et al., 2006), routing those who did not have JavaScript enabled to a radio button version of the items. Whether this is worth it depends on the advantages of the enhanced tool, the number of respondents affected, and the effort needed to create an alternative version in plain HTML.

In my view, the degree to which one uses these visual and interactive enhancements may well depend on the target audience. While the limitations are becoming less of a problem for most Internet users, they may remain a concern for certain key subgroups. For Web surveys of frequent e-commerce users, active content may not be much of a problem. Similarly, for surveys among those who are Web savvy and comfortable installing plugins and changing default browser settings, this may not be an issue. However, for surveys of more general populations and those aimed at specific groups with known limitations – whether for accessibility or security reasons – plain HTML may be best. Some organizations conducting Web surveys have little or no choice on the issue, being bound by policy or regulations. For other organizations, there is a choice. We need more research to tell us whether these enhancements are worth it. For some design elements (e.g., running tallies, dynamic look-up, dynamic grids), we have evidence that the tools improve data quality. For others (e.g., visual analog scales or sliders), the advantages don't seem to be there, or don't seem to be sufficiently large to warrant the use of active content. For yet others (e.g., ranking tools, card sort), the benefits may depend on the particular things being measured, and more work is needed to know under what conditions they work best.

3.9. Summary

It is with respect to the topics discussed in this chapter that we are likely to see the greatest changes over the next several years. The Internet is rapidly evolving. What was originally a text-based information medium is rapidly changing into a multimedia, multipurpose tool, serving information, communication, entertainment, and a variety of other needs (see Couper, 2007a). As the tools to deliver this richer content and interactivity become more commonplace, and as the bandwidth increases, the potential for transforming surveys on the Web increases. While these tools show great promise, I caution against the use of rich content or interactivity merely for the sake of doing so. These tools should be used only where it is appropriate to do so, and only when there are demonstrated advantages in terms of data quality or the user experience in completing the survey. I expect to see much research on these topics in coming years, with the potential for transforming the survey measurement process on the Web.

As we continue to learn what works and what doesn't work in Web survey – or under which circumstances certain tools work best – we will see such surveys increasingly diverge from traditional paper-based approaches. However, a competing pressure comes from mixed-mode designs where Web surveys are expected to produce measures comparable to mail, telephone, or other modes (see, e.g., Dillman and Christian, 2005; de Leeuw, 2005; see also Section 6.7.4). But in Web-only surveys, the medium can be fully exploited to produce new and better ways of asking and answering survey questions. This tension – between comparable measurements across modes versus optimizing the design of one mode – is a common one in the survey world. Both approaches will continue to coexist, but we will increasingly see Web surveys that exploit the visual and interactive qualities of the Internet – which itself is being transformed to do things that were difficult if not impossible to do before. These are truly exciting times for Web survey researchers.

Chapter 4

General Layout and Design

Beauty is in the eye of the beholder

Once could think of the computer screen or Web browser as an artist's canvas – the choices one can make in arranging the various elements on the screen, the colors and fonts one uses to represent them, the choice of background color or image, and so on, are virtually limitless. Unlike the artist, though, the goal of a survey designer is not to create a work of art but rather to facilitate the task for which the instrument was designed. Furthermore, unlike the artist's canvas which, once completed remains relatively fixed and permanent – the artist has full control over the expression of his or her ideas – the design of a Web survey on a computer screen, as rendered by a browser, is subject to variations that are often not under the full control of the designer. Therefore, the survey designer does not have the free reign of expression open to the artist.

In addition, whereas the artist may not care that some people do not like their creation, and people may see the same piece of art in many different ways, the survey designer must of necessity care that the information content is viewed and interpreted the same way by a variety of different respondents.

Despite these and other differences between the two genres, it is surprising how many examples of Web surveys can be seen in which the designer's creative juices have apparently been given free reign. The focus in such cases is – inappropriately, in my view – on the creator rather than the user.

Design has a specific function – that of facilitating the task. It is not a goal in itself. This is not to imply that Web surveys ought to be so plain that they are boring. Norman's (2004) book on *Emotional Design* is testament to the fact that emotionally or aesthetically pleasing design is valued. Focusing on the task simply means that, while design aesthetics are important, they should not interfere with the user's ability to complete the task accurately and efficiently, while still enjoying a pleasant experience.

In the preceding two chapters, I discussed the various elements that comprise an online survey instrument, with a focus on the input of responses. In this chapter, I turn to a different basic design focus – the canvas on which these questions and response formats are rendered.

4.1. The Elements of a Web Questionnaire

A Web survey comprises different elements. How, and how well, these elements fit together plays a role in how successful the respondent is at performing the various tasks that are required, from reading and comprehending the survey questions to providing an appropriate answer, navigating through the survey, seeking and obtaining assistance where needed, and so on. To guide the discussion on the design aspects covered in this chapter, it is useful to think of the different elements of a Web survey. In Chapter 3, I discussed the visual elements of a Web survey, focusing on the use of images. In this chapter, I expand the notion of visual information to talk more broadly about design elements.

Here, as in Chapter 3, I make a distinction between the visual elements and the verbal elements of a Web survey. The verbal elements are the words that make up the question text, response options, instruction, and so on. The visual elements are just about everything else. These range from the more obvious visual features such as the layout or spatial arrangement of the page, the use of background color or patterns, and the use of shapes, diagrams, images, and so on, to the less obvious visual features of the verbal elements – how the words are presented, including color, typeface, and use of emphasis. In other words, verbal elements can communicate in two ways – via their content or the meaning of the words, and via their design.

Dillman and his colleagues (see Christian and Dillman, 2004; Redline and Dillman, 2002) make a finer distinction. They identify numerical language – the use of numbers on a questionnaire – as separate from verbal language. They also identify symbolic language – the use of symbols such as arrows – as distinct from graphical language, which includes features such as size, brightness, and color, shape, location, and spatial arrangement of elements. For our purposes, I will treat numeric language as part of the verbal elements of design, and graphical and symbolic language as comprising the visual elements. Chapter 3 focused on images as part of the visual language. In this chapter, the focus turns more to the graphical elements in relation to the verbal elements and the spatial arrangements of the various elements of a Web survey.

A further distinction can be made between the design elements related to the task and the broader style elements. The task elements are those parts of the survey instrument that are directly related to the task of completing the survey. These include the survey questions, the response options, and the buttons used to move through the survey. Web surveys also contain style elements. These are the parts of the instrument that are orthogonal or incidental to the task itself, and may include the overall design of the site (e.g., the color scheme, typography, etc.), branding elements (logos, contact information) and auxiliary functions such as help, progress indicators, and so on. Another way to think of some of these elements is to identify primary task and secondary tasks:

- Primary tasks: survey questions and answers, "next question" button
- Secondary or supportive tasks: navigation, progress indicators, help, branding, etc.

The goal of design is to keep the respondent engaged in the primary task but have the secondary tasks available to them as and when needed. In successful design, the verbal and visual elements are in harmony, and are mutually supportive.

The various elements of a Web survey are illustrated in Figure 4.1. This example, from the Southeast Michigan Council of Governments (SEMCOG), is of a Web survey embedded in a Web site. The banner or header of the page pertains to the site rather than to the survey, as does the navigation pane on the left. But the use of color contrast serves to focus attention on the primary task, the survey question.

One of the key themes of this book is that Web surveys are not the same as Web sites. Many sites are designed to give the reader or user many alternatives, with lots of options on what to do next. In essence, the user is in complete control of the experience. In sites where a transaction occurs, once the user has decided on a course of action, the design of the site guides them carefully down a path until the transaction is complete or the purchase made. In Web surveys, we typically want the respondent to focus narrowly on a single task – that of completing the survey – without distraction or temptation to make side trips in cyberspace. Given this, the goal of visual design is to keep the respondent focused on the primary task of answering the questions while still making secondary tasks (navigation, help, review of progress, etc.) available if needed.

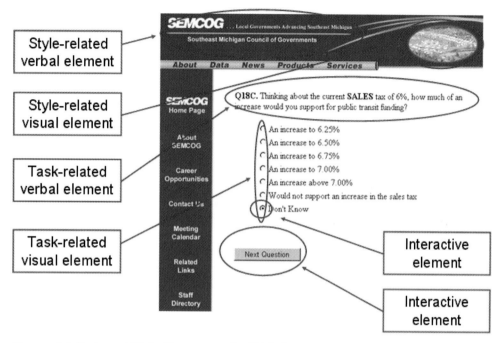

Figure 4.1 **Task and Style Elements of a Web Survey.**

Let's take a look at another example. Figure 4.2 shows a screenshot from the National Geographic Society's Survey 2001 (Witte et al., 2004). This example demonstrates that a survey does not need to be plain to be effective. The NGS survey contains a number of visual elements that support the primary and secondary tasks. Some of these are as follows:

- The header is visually separated from the question area. This contains branding and navigation/progress information.
- The color coding in the navigation bar is carried through to the main content – see the vertical "Internet" label in purple.
- The background pattern and color are visually interesting without affecting the reading of the questions.
- The secondary tasks are outside the main visual field – this includes the header content but also the confidentiality statement and "submit a comment" button. In other words, they are available if needed, but the design discourages their use.

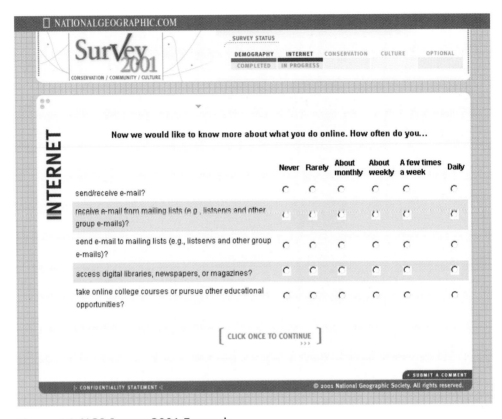

Figure 4.2 **NGS Survey 2001 Example.**

- While there are several items on the same screen, the use of color banding or shading is intended to help with visual separation of the items.
- While the "click once to continue" action button is a custom graphic rather than a standard HTML button, it is large and readily visible on the screen.

I'll return to several of these issues – such as progress indicators, multiple items on a screen, and action buttons – in later chapters. For now, we focus on the overall design.

To reiterate, the supportive elements of surveys (navigation, help, progress indicators, branding, instructions, etc.) should be visually accessible when needed, but should not dominate the main visual field. The only things that should

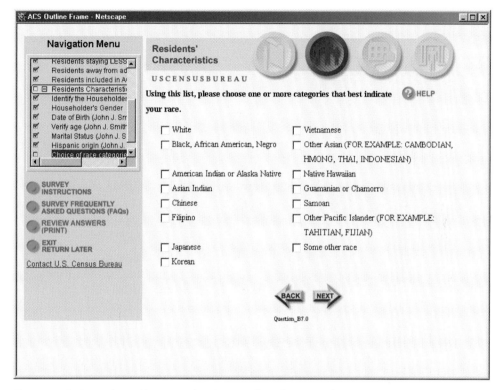

Figure 4.3 **American Community Survey (ACS) Example.**

occupy the main visual field should be those directly related to the task at hand – that of reading and understanding the question, formulating a response, and entering or selecting the appropriate answer. These elements include the question text, the response options, associated input fields and action buttons to proceed to the next question.

Both the SEMCOG and NGS surveys achieve this goal, but in different ways. Both pages contain a lot of information, not all of it related to the immediate task of answering the question(s) on the screen, but the pages are organized in such a way that the respondent's attention is focused on the important parts.

Let's look at another example, this time from the Census Bureau's American Community Survey (ACS; see Figure 4.3). This screen actually contains a single question but – in contrast to the NGS example – the navigational and help features dominate the display. Both the NGS and ACS examples are visually rich, but

Figure 4.4 **University of Michigan and Market Strategies Example.**

differ in how well the layout and design support the task of answering the survey questions.

All the above examples are fairly complex. Each has design elements that go beyond the question-and-answer process, such as navigation, menus, progress indicators, and so on. Many Web surveys are more straightforward than these examples. The example in Figure 4.4 comes from one of our experiments on Web survey design (e.g., Tourangeau, Couper, and Conrad, 2004). This still has some of the key elements of a Web survey, including branding (the UM logo is a style-related visual element) and contact information (verbal information related to secondary tasks) in the header. Even within the simplified design illustrated in Figure 4.4, there are a number of design decisions that need to be made, and these are the focus of the balance of this chapter. (As an aside, in all the above examples, the branding is an essential part of the overall design; therefore, I did not try to disguise the source.)

The overall design of the Web page or screen serves an important orienting function. The screen should orient the respondent both with respect to the location of key information and with respect to the tasks that are expected. As Lynch and Horton (2001, p. 81) note, "The primary task of graphic design is to create a strong, consistent visual hierarchy in which important elements are emphasized and content is organized logically and predictably."

Figure 4.5 is a rough schematic of the key parts of a Web page. This is simply to identify or label the regions of the page. Whether one uses each of these panes or areas and what one puts there are the focus of global design. If one is designing a Web survey for the first time, it may be useful to lay out the key elements schematically. This defines the style in terms of layout. Of course, many other elements of style, such as typeface choices and color schemes, remain to be decided,

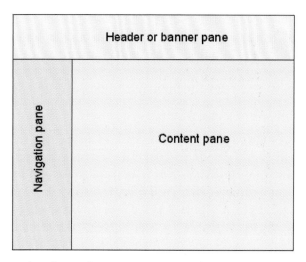

Figure 4.5 **Schematic of a Web Page.**

as I discuss in this chapter. Many Web software products offer a default style or layout, with varying ability to modify key elements. The more complex the survey interface, the greater the care that is needed in developing and testing the overall design.

Many Web surveys do not need or have a navigation pane as shown in Figure 4.5. Some do not use headers. That's OK, as long as the design makes sense from the respondents' perspective, and is consistent within the site, so that the same information is found in the same place on different pages. The SEMCOG design in Figure 4.1 is prototypical of Web sites, while our design in Figure 4.4 is found in many Web surveys.

On approaching a Web site for the first time, users – or respondents, in our case – initially take a global view. That is, they generally take in the whole screen at a glance, distinguishing key regions and elements, without attending to the detail. Then, they rapidly focus down on the relevant detail. This narrowing of focus is facilitated when the screen elements are in familiar places. Unexpected placement of elements or the use of jarring or strident graphical devices will distract the respondent and delay or even possibly interfere with the focus on the task.

Careful design and attention to the Web survey's style elements should speed up this process, helping respondents to find the relevant information and focus on the task. The global design or style elements are likely to be more important to the respondent at the beginning of the survey than later. As the respondent becomes increasingly familiar with and engaged in the task of completing the survey, the style elements should fade into the background. Similarly, the elements related to secondary tasks should not dominate the visual field, but should still be available if needed. Good design serves this function of guiding the respondent to the specific task they are being asked to perform and facilitating their completion of that task.

Consistent design within a Web survey should speed this task of familiarization. If the design elements do not change from screen to screen, respondents are likely to habituate to their presence. This can be used to help focus respondents' attention on the primary task. But, variation in design or layout could also be used to signal a new topic, a different task, or some other change that needs the respondent's attention. For example, in usability tests of interviewer-administered (CAPI) instruments, we observed a problem when a series of questions with similar format – that is, the same question stem and the same response options – is repeated on several successive screens (Hansen, Couper, and Fuchs, 1998). A common comment we heard from interviewers was, "Didn't I just ask this question?" as they tried to proceed without answering. Our diagnosis was that there were insufficient visual cues to indicate that the question had changed. Our solution in this case was to vary the vertical placement of the question from screen to screen to give a stronger cue that the content had changed. Being *too* consistent may blind respondents to important changes that we want them to notice.

For this reason, I do not advocate slavish adherence to design consistency. Two additional examples illustrate this point. In the NGS example (see Figure 4.2), the color of various style elements changes from section to section. All the elements in purple change to a different color depending on the section identified in the progress indicator. This serves as a subtle visual cue both of progress through the instrument, and of the topic of the questions. Similarly, one survey vendor places check boxes to the left of response options, but text boxes to the right. Given the visual similarity of a check box and a short text box, this change may help signal to the respondent that a different task is required, that of typing in a number rather than checking a box. So, while variety for variety's sake is not a good idea, change can at times be helpful. In other words, both consistency and change are design tools that can be used to good purpose (see Couper, 1994, 1999).

Once the respondent has focused more narrowly on the local level – the question and response options – information outside of the visual field is less likely to be noticed. The visual field is what one can reasonably see at any one time when focusing narrowly on a target. For example, Redline and Dillman (2002,

p. 183) notes that a person's vision is only sharp to approximately eight to twelve characters of 12-point text. Ware (2000, p. 157) takes a broader view, and prefers the term "useful field of view" (or UFOV), which defines the size of the region from which we can rapidly take in information. In other words, the UFOV may vary greatly, depending on the task and the information displayed. For example, when we are reading fine print, we can read the words only at the exact point of fixation; but we can take in the overall shape of a large pattern at a single glance. In other words, the greater the target density (e.g., the smaller the print), the smaller the UFOV. Knowledge of the field of view can be used in design to help focus the respondent's visual attention on the survey question without being distracted by secondary information or style elements. However, the design should also accommodate the respondent's need to zoom out if needed, and find secondary or supportive information as needed. That is, the design must work both at the global level and at the local level.

The phenomenon of "banner blindness" is an example of this narrowed field of view. Benway (1998) coined the term to refer to the fact that Web users often missed banner advertisements, despite their being bright and bold, and in some cases even animated (see Benway and Lane, 1998; Pagendarm and Schaumburg, 2001). Norman (1999; see also http://www.jnd.org/dn.mss/banner_blindness.html) offers the explanation that the reason people miss the banner is that they are looking for specific information, and expect to find it somewhere in the body of the Web page, not in the banner. Users have learned that banners typically contain advertising or other material that can be safely ignored. Norman concludes that the banner blindness findings "reaffirm the rule of consistency, coherence, and the following of established conventions." He adds, "If you want something to be salient, follow conventions."

Another reason for following conventional layout design is that it makes programming easier. The reason navigation information and links are put on the left, which is prime real estate in terms of how people read in the Western World, is because HTML facilitates such a design. The dimensions of a screen are defined from the top left corner. Wrapping occurs on the right, not on the left. This convention is so pervasive that even in countries where writing is not done from left to right, top to bottom, Web sites tend to hold to this convention. For example, traditional Japanese texts are printed from bottom to top and right to left. But Japanese Web sites tend to follow the Western convention, presenting text from left to right and top to bottom. For an example of this, look at the print and online versions of Asahi Shimbun, one of Japan's leading daily newspapers (e.g., www.asahi.com). Similar patterns can be found in Arabic, Hebrew, and Chinese Web sites.

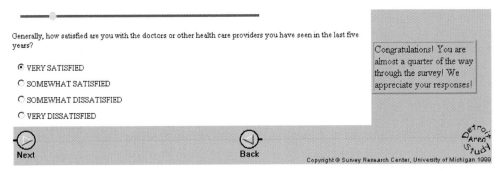

Figure 4.6 **Alternative Layout of Content and Branding Areas.**

Given that in the Western world we read from left to right, top to bottom, the top left part of the screen is likely to get the most attention initially, and the bottom right the least. If this is the case, why not put the navigation information on the right or on the bottom? An early test of this idea by Crawford (1999) is shown in Figure 4.6. This design was tested against a more traditional design with the branding information on the left. The two versions were tested in the context of a mixed-mode survey, using mail with a Web option. Unfortunately, too few people availed themselves of the opportunity to use the Web option to draw any conclusions about the differences between the two designs.

The structure of HTML makes the kind of design illustrated in Figure 4.6 hard to do. The dimensions of the browser display are defined from the top left corner. Wrapping occurs on the right, not the left. Scrolling goes in the same direction. Changing the size of the browser window or changing the font size may produce unexpected results for such a layout, making the task or ensuring the question area is visible across different browser settings a challenge. Given the strong conventions favoring the more traditional layout, and the way that HTML supports these conventions, there is little reason to deviate from the style used in most Web sites and Web surveys.

However, even within this broad orientation, there are still many possible layout variations. Some Web surveys center the questions and answers in the content area; some dispense with the navigation area. There is a great deal of variation in the placement of navigation buttons and, indeed, in which buttons are presented and how they are labeled (see Chapter 5, Section 5.5.2). As we shall see shortly, design elements such as typeface, color, and the like, are important parts of the overall design.

Thus, the designer still has many options at his or her disposal, or many design decisions to make to create the "look and feel" that uniquely identifies the survey organization and survey style while supporting the respondent's tasks related to survey completion.

How well these various elements are used will determine whether the survey design "works." Successful design uses these elements to focus the respondent's attention on the task. Thus, while the SEMCOG example in Figure 4.1 contains a lot of information extraneous to the survey task, the use of figure-ground contrast and the placement of these links in the expected location for support tasks, helps focus attention on the survey question. The NGS example in Figure 4.2 is visually rich, but once a respondent is oriented to the task, the secondary information in the headers, footers, and borders should fade into the background. By way of contrast, in the ACS example in Figure 4.3, the navigation area and headers visually dominate the screen, potentially making it harder for the respondent to stay focused on the survey question.

To quote Lynch and Horton again, "Graphic design is visual information management, using the tools of page layout, typography, and illustration to lead the reader's eye through the page. Readers first see pages as large masses of shape and color, with foreground elements contrasting against the background field. Secondarily they begin to pick out specific information, first from graphics if they are present, and only afterward do they start parsing the harder medium of text and begin to read individual words and phrases" (Lynch and Horton, 2001, pp. 81–82).

How we do this is the stuff of design. In the balance of this chapter, I review several of the design tools available to achieve a particular goal while trying to avoid imposing a design style.

To summarize, the visual presentation of a Web survey page can be seen as containing different elements:

- Verbal versus visual elements
  - Verbal: question wording, response options, instructions, etc.
  - Visual: layout, color, images, etc.
- Task versus style elements
  - Task: Parts of the instrument that are related to the task of completing the survey. Without the task elements, there is no survey.
  - Style: Parts of the instrument that are orthogonal or incidental to the task itself. The style elements can support the task of completing the survey or get in the way of doing so.

- Primary versus secondary elements or tasks
  - Primary: those pertaining to the tasks of reading, comprehending, and responding to the survey question and proceeding to the next question.
  - Secondary: those pertaining to activities that support the primary task and are only used when needed; secondary tasks include navigation, assistance, evaluating progress, and so on.

Design is the process of effectively presenting these different elements in the Web page to facilitate the task of completing the survey. Having done the broad view, let's narrow the focus to the individual elements of design.

4.2. Text and Typography

Let's first focus on the verbal elements of the Web survey, that is, the text used to present questions, response options, instructions, background information, branding, and the like. There are many issues to consider in making decisions about what typographic style to use for the various text elements. These relate to the legibility or readability of the text, variations across platforms and browser settings, distinguishing between different verbal elements on a screen, the message the typographic design or style may convey to respondents, and so on. We don't need to be experts in typography to produce effective Web surveys.[1] One can meet the key objective – enhancing the respondent experience – without delving too deep into the intricacies of typography. In this aspect of design – as in others – the more creative one tries to be, the greater the potential risk of unintended consequences of these design decisions. Following a few basic guidelines and understanding some of the basics will prevent many potential problems.

Typography matters more on the Web than on paper for several key reasons. One is that the resolution of the typical printed page (as rendered by a laser printer, for example) is around 1,200 dots per inch (dpi), whereas computer screens render at about 85 dpi (Lynch and Horton, 2001). This means that the crispness of text – and therefore its readability – may be deprecated online. A second reason is that the usable area of a computer screen is smaller than many printed pages, limiting the amount of information that can be presented without scrolling. This means real estate is more precious on screen than on paper. A third reason is that a printed

---

[1] For an accessible introduction to the complex world of typography, see Schriver's (1997) very useful book, *Dynamics in Document Design*. Chapter 5 of Lynch and Horton's (2001) *Web Style Guide* focuses on typography specific for the Web.

Times New Roman is a serif font

Arial is a sans serif font

Figure 4.7 **Example of Serif and Sans Serif Fonts.**

page is rendered in identical fashion for each reader by the printing process, whereas a Web page may vary from screen to screen because of the choice of browser used, the fonts installed, the screen resolution, the user's settings, and other such factors out of the control of the designer.

4.2.1. Typeface

Typeface is a more formal term for font, but I will use the two interchangeably. Two major typeface styles in use on the Web and paper today are *serif* and *sans serif*. Other typeface styles include script or cursive (which resembles handwriting), and typewriter or monospaced styles (e.g., Courier). Serifs are lines or curves that finish off the end of a letterform. A commonly used serif typeface in many computer applications such as word processors is Times New Roman. Sans serif fonts (such as Arial, Verdana, or Helvetica) are often used on Web sites. Figure 4.7 shows examples of serif and sans serif fonts.

Early versions of HTML did not permit the designer any control over the typeface or font. These were set by the browser, so pages were viewed in whatever font the user specified. More recent versions of HTML, implemented first in Netscape 3.0, gave the designer more control with the `<font>` specification, and cascading style sheets (CSS) have extended the range of design options and control over typography. But even with CSS, if the font is not installed on the user's machine, the browser will default to the nearest font available, in the same family. Users can also set their browser preferences to ignore font tags, retaining their chosen font for all pages.

So, while there are many common typefaces available to the Web designer, and countless others can be downloaded from the Web, not every browser will have every font installed. It is thus common when using CSS to specify alternative fonts. The generic form in CSS looks like this:

```
{font family: <ideal>, <alternative>, <common>, <generic>}
```

In other words, for a set of san serif fonts, this may look like the following:

```
{font family: Verdana, Arial, Helvetica, sans-serif}
```

Some fonts may not convey the
seriousness of the task

Avoid fonts that are difficult to read   Figure 4.8 **Typeface Examples.**

𝕬𝖛𝖔𝖎𝖉 𝖔𝖛𝖊𝖗𝖑𝖞-𝖊𝖑𝖆𝖇𝖔𝖗𝖆𝖙𝖊 𝖋𝖔𝖓𝖙𝖘

What this communicates to the browser is, if you have Verdana installed, render the text in that font. If not, use Arial, or Helvetica, or the generic sans serif font, in that order. Among these sans serif fonts, Verdana is designed specifically for screen display, while Arial and Helvetica are more generic fonts used for screen and print, and are likely to be available in most settings (see Gillespie's useful Web site, *Web Page Design for Designers*, www.wpdfd.com).

Now that there are many font options available, it might be tempting to get creative, and many Web sites do indeed do this. But this is not a good idea for Web surveys. One should use a font that is appropriate for the task. For example, a comic or script font may be appropriate for some Web sites (communicating fun), but not for a survey site. Similarly, a highly stylized font such as Old English may be used to convey a particular message, but again these are not likely to be used in Web surveys. In choosing a typeface, once should focus on (1) how common the typeface is to a variety of platforms and settings, (2) the readability or legibility of the typeface, and (3) the emotional meaning of typefaces.

Figure 4.8 shows some examples of typefaces unsuited for use in Web surveys.

The first font in Figure 4.8 is Dauphin, the second is Staccato, and the last is Old English. The latter is similar to that used for the *New York Times* logo (see www.nytimes.com), which serves an important branding function, but imagine the entire newspaper (print or online) produced using this font. Kostelnick and Roberts (1998) refer to these as noisy typefaces.

Related to the third point, the fonts in Figure 4.8 may not only be difficult to read, but they may also carry meaning beyond that of the words themselves. So far, I've been talking about the functional properties of typefaces – those that relate to readability. But typefaces also have semantic properties (see Childers and Jass, 2002; McCarthy and Mothersbaugh, 2002; Rowe, 1982). These affect a typeface's "apparent 'fitness' or 'suitability' for different functions, and … imbue it with the power to evoke in the perceiver certain emotional and cognitive responses" (Bartram, 1982, p. 38).

For example, Childers and Jass (2002) tested a variety of typefaces used in advertising. They found that typefaces significantly influenced consumer perceptions of brands and their memory of the brands. Novemsky, Dhar, Schwarz, and Simonson

10IIO	Arial
10IIO	Times New Roman
10lIO	Courier New

Figure 4.9 **Confusing Letters and Numbers.**

(2007) looked at the effect of font type on the expression of subjective preferences and in making choices. They demonstrated that fonts that are easier to read make it easier – both subjectively and objectively – for users to make choices between different objects.

In other words, in addition to affecting the readability of the text, the typeface itself conveys meaning and may affect behavior. Given this, one should select a typeface that matches the content and function of the survey. A typeface that may be appropriate for a survey focused on teenage leisure-time utilization might not be suitable for a survey of cancer survivors, for example. As Lynch and Horton (2001, p. 126) note, "each typeface has a unique tone that should produce a harmonious fit between the verbal and visual flow of your content."

Some typeface issues – like readability and tone – are common to both paper and Web. But a factor specific to screen-based fonts is whether they are aliased or anti-aliased. Aliasing describes the "staircase appearance ('jaggies') of curved edges of forms composed of pixels" (Staples, 2000, p. 26). This stairstepping is compounded in typefaces with serifs and in type rendered in small sizes, since fewer pixels are available to create each letter. Anti-aliasing solves this problem by blurring the edge of the letter into its background. Text rendered as graphics can use anti-aliasing (using Adobe Photoshop, for example), which means that smaller font sizes can be rendered more legible. This is useful for text included in artwork or graphic images. HTML text is aliased, and therefore one should avoid small font sizes in HTML.

One additional consideration in the choice of typefaces relates to potential confusion between similar-looking letters and numbers. Sans serif fonts may be particularly susceptible to this confusion. Figure 4.9 shows an example of this problem. From left to right, the respective characters are one, zero, lowercase el, capital eye, and capital oh. In the sans serif font, the lowercase "l" and uppercase "I" are indistinguishable, and in the other two fonts, the number 1 and letter "l" are virtually identical. Zero and the letter "o" can be similarly confused. In general, because of the potential for confusion illustrated above, it's not a good idea to mix letters and numbers or mix upper and lower case letters (for example in passwords, or e-mail addresses), but often this admonition is easier said than done.

In Chapter 6 (see Section 6.3), I show one consequence of using both numbers and letters for passwords.

So, which typeface should one use? It is fair to say that the research results are mixed, and depend on the medium (paper or screen), the type size, and whether the fonts are aliased or anti-aliased. It is argued (e.g., see Bernard and Mills, 2000) that serif fonts are easier to read on paper because the serifs help distinguish among individual letters. In contrast, the argument is that the quality of computer displays reduces the benefits of serifs and may make the letters harder to read, especially at smaller font sizes.

The evidence is by no means strong. Boyarski, Neuwirth, Forlizzi, and Regli (1998) found that serif typefaces were more pleasing and legible to the eye than sans serif typefaces on a computer interface. On the other hand, Bernard and Mills (2000) did a laboratory study to compare reading speed and accuracy, perceptions of legibility and sharpness, and general preference of several different typefaces on a computer screen. They found a slight advantage for the sans serif (Arial) font than the serif (Times New Roman). In a later study with twenty-two subjects and twelve different fonts, Bernard, Mills, Peterson, and Storrer (2001) found no significant differences in legibility between serif and sans serif fonts.

In general, most designers recommend sans serif fonts for Web sites. Schriver (1997, p. 508), for example, recommends sans serif for its "simple, highly legible, modern appearance." The Microsoft User Interface Guidelines (1997) similarly suggests avoiding serif fonts, as do the National Institutes of Health, in their guide, *Making Your Web Site Senior Friendly* (www.nlm.nih.gov/pubs/checklist.pdf). But Lynch and Horton (2001, p. 127) recommend a serif typeface such as Times New Roman for body text and sans serif face such as Verdana or Arial for headlines in Web pages. Mixing typefaces is also an effective way to distinguish between different survey elements (e.g., heading versus text, or questions versus instructions). But be careful of overdoing it – both Schriver (1997) and Lynch and Horton (2001) recommend using no more than two different typefaces.

There is also general agreement that at larger font sizes the choice of serif versus sans serif fonts makes little difference. But what is meant by a "larger" font size? This is a question I will take up next.

4.2.2. Font Size

"What font size should I use for my Web survey" is a question I'm often asked. To say at the outset, there is no direct answer to this question. To address the issue, we first need to talk about what "font size" means and how the concept differs between paper and Web. There are several reasons why talking about font size in Web surveys is not as straightforward as may seem:

- Font sizes on screen are different from front sizes on paper.
- Font sizes on some operating systems are different from font sizes on others.
- Font sizes can be specified in many different ways, some of which are absolute and some of which are relative.

On paper, the measures of font or type size we are familiar with refer to actual physical height of the letters. On paper, 72 points are approximately equal to 1 inch, and thus the commonly used 12-point font size is about 12/72 or one-sixth of an inch high. In contrast, computer screens are measured in pixels. For example, a 640 × 480 resolution monitor displays 307,200 pixels. Monitors with the same resolution can vary in size. The early Macintosh computers rendered 72 pixels to 72 points, which is where the notion of WYSIWYG (what you see is what you get) originated in the 1980s, with the display screen exactly representing the print version. By default, Windows-based PCs render 96 pixels to 72 points using regular font sizes, meaning that the same "font size" is almost 30% larger on a PC than on a Mac (see Zetie, 1995, pp. 192–195; http://www.wpdfd.com/wpdtypo.htm). In other words, while the Mac considers 72 pixels to be 1 inch, MS Windows considers 96 pixels to be an inch. If this all seems confusing, just remember that the same size font (e.g., 10-pt Times) will generally be smaller when viewed on a Mac screen than on a PC screen. A 9-point PC font is physically the same size as a 12-point Mac font measured on their screens. The point is that specifying fixed font sizes can be risky, given the different operating systems, monitor resolutions, and browser settings out there.

The language of font size specification in HTML reflects this difficulty. In earlier version of HTML (before 4.0), font size was specified with a number ranging from 1 to 7, with size 3 being the default font, roughly corresponding to a 12-point type. Font size could be specified in absolute terms (e.g., `<font size=3>`) which would override the user's settings, or in relative terms (e.g., `<font size=+1>`) which would adjust the font size relative to the user's settings (in this case, incrementing the size by 1). With the advent of cascading style sheets (CSS) in HTML 4.0 and higher, all that has changed. Now one can specify font size in many different ways. For example, one can set font size using points, pixels, inches, millimeters, x-height (the height of the font's lowercase letter x) or em (the height of the font) units as measurement (see, e.g., Castro, 2003, pp. 162–163). The latter two, along with the percentage setting, can set font size relative to the parent font. Unfortunately, not all browsers support all these options. The World Wide Web Consortium (W3C) that sets standards for HTML and its variants, recommends using the "em" unit to set font size relative to the base font chosen by the user in their browser (see Lynch and Horton, 2001; www.w3c.org).

In an online posting in 2001, Pemberton (chair of the W3C HTML and Forms Working Groups at the time) wrote, "The cure is to *never* use absolute font sizes. One thing that people often *do* seem to do is set their base font setting to something readable. Key off of that. The main text of a Web page should *always* be 100% of what the user has as their base font, and in general, headings should be something larger. You should probably never go lower than 70% of the base font for the fine print."

Some might believe that one way to standardize the Web survey instrument for all respondents is to use a fixed font size, thereby overriding the defaults users may have set on their browsers. In this way, it might be argued, a standard "look and feel" is presented to all respondents, and the designer has control over the spacing and layout of surveys questions and response options. After all, this is what we do on paper surveys. This is usually a bad idea. Why do I say this? It ignores one of the basic features of the Web from the user's perspective and that is customizability. Browsers permit users to specify the default font size, to vary the color settings, to alter the size of the browser window or pane, and to tweak a variety of other display settings. Users can and do make use of these features, whether as a matter of personal taste, or to enhance the readability of material. Why should we then override or ignore these preferences?

It's not just about user control or preferences. As a rapidly aging person, I'm keenly aware of the eye strain produced by small font sizes, whether on paper or online. As a designer, don't assume that the respondent's eyesight is as good, or even better than, yours. Also, don't assume that the size and resolution of the monitor the respondent is using to complete your survey is as large as yours. Respect the fact that the Web gives people control over the size of the text presented in the browser.

4.2.3. Other Aspects of Typography

Readability is affected not only by typeface and the size of text. Other factors include leading (the amount of space between lines of text), line length, justification, and case. I'll address the use of additional features of text – such as bold, italics, capitalization, color, and so on – for emphasis in the next section.

Leading is an important factor in the readability of text, whether on paper or online. Leading refers to the amount of vertical space between lines of type, and is also referred to as line spacing (in MS Word, for example) or line height (in CSS). Word processors set at single-spaced text typically add about 20% to the point size of the font, thus for a 10-point font size, the height from the bottom of one line of text to the bottom of the next is 12 points. In general, tightly cramped lines of type are hard to read, but too much leading makes it harder to locate the start of the next line. While this was hard to control in HTML, in CSS line height can be specified as a percentage of the font size.

Leading is related to line length. Longer lines of text require head movement or may strain eye muscles – the span of acute focus is about 3 inches wide at normal reading distances (Lynch and Horton, 2001, p. 123). Readers have greater difficulty finding the beginning of the next line after reaching the end of a long line of text. With greater leading (more space between lines), the negative effect of long lines of text is reduced somewhat. Schriver (1997) recommends line lengths of forty to seventy characters or about twelve words per line on paper, and less than that – between forty and sixty characters – online (see also Galitz, 1993; Grabinger and Osman-Jouchoux, 1996). Dyson (2004) provides a nice summary of the research literature on line length and related text layout issues.

How do we control line length on the Web while still respecting respondents' browser settings and preferences? One way is to put the text in a table with an invisible border, and define the table width relative to the width of the browser. I'll address this later (in Chapter 5) in the context of designing grid or matrix questions. When a navigation pane is used (see Figures 4.1 and 4.3), the screen width may be reduced sufficiently to eliminate this concern. But left unconstrained, the text may take up the full width of the browser window, which may impede the respondents' reading and comprehension of the survey question.

In terms of text justification, the recommendation is to use left-justified, ragged-right margins, rather than fully justified text. For example, Trollip and Sales (1986) found a 10% decrease in reading time with text that was fully justified compared with text that was left-justified only.

Most of the research on these factors affecting readability is based on reading of large bodies of text, with reading speed or accuracy often the dependent variable. It's not clear how much these apply to typical Web survey questions. However, where large bodies of text – such as instructions, informed consent statements, help or definitions, or lengthy questions – appear in a survey, these cautions might

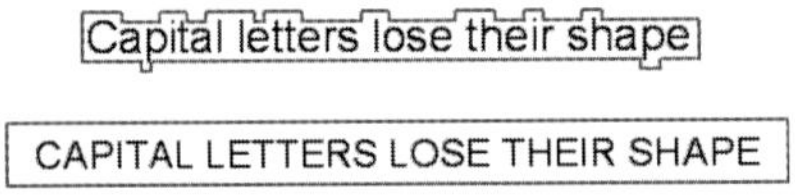

Capital letters lose their shape

CAPITAL LETTERS LOSE THEIR SHAPE

Figure 4.10 **Uppercase Text Slows Reading.**

well apply. I'll return to the issue of space later in this chapter, but for now it is worth making sure that readability of text is optimized, using combinations of typeface, font size, line length, leading, and justification.

A final topic is that of case or use of capital letters. In many cases, the use of capitalization is a throwback to the days of DOS-based systems where only a few options were available to differentiate certain text elements (e.g., question wording) from others (e.g., instructions). With regard to case, the literature is in agreement: mixed-case text – or what MS Word calls "sentence case" – is read at speeds significantly faster than text set in all uppercase (e.g., Galitz, 1993; Schriver, 1997).

The reason for this is that when words are capitalized, they lose the characteristic shapes provided by the ascenders and descenders. Uppercase letters are all the same height, whereas lowercase letters vary in height, aiding comprehension (see Figure 4.10). Furthermore, given that initial capitalization uses ascenders, and there are nine letters with ascenders (b, d, f, h, i, j, k, l, and t) and only five with descenders (g, j, p, q, y), the tops of letters are more important in aiding recognition of letter forms and thus comprehension of text (as illustrated in Figure 4.11). The examples in Figures 4.10 and 4.11 are based on those in Howlett (1996) and Lynch and Horton (2001).

Fortunately, the overuse of capitalization is relatively rare in Web surveys. Figures 4.12 and 4.13 include some exceptions, to show how capitalization may discourage respondents from reading the intended text. In addition to the difficulty of reading, capitalization is like shouting. It is better used for selective emphasis than for large chunks of text.

In the example in Figure 4.12, the caps and box around the instruction were probably intended to draw respondent's attention to the content. But it may well have the opposite effect, discouraging respondents from reading the text.

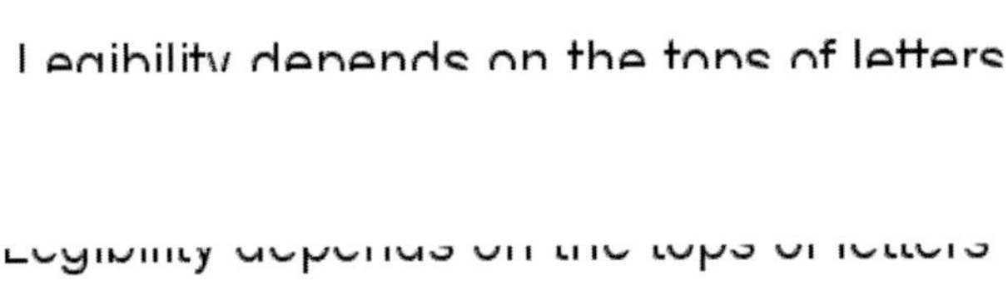

Legibility depends on the tops of letters

Legibility depends on the tops of letters

Figure 4.11 **Ascenders in Lowercase Letters Facilitate Reading.**

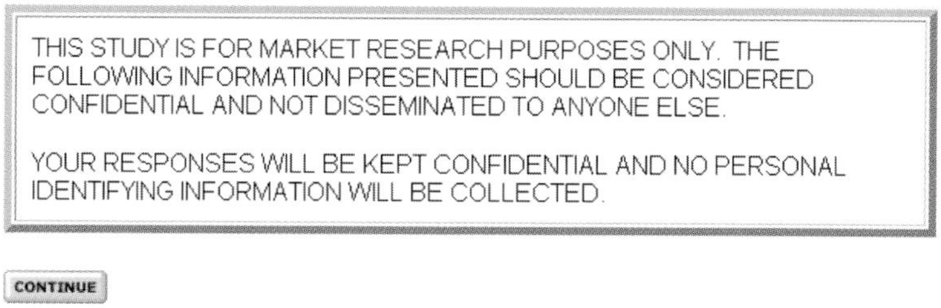

THIS STUDY IS FOR MARKET RESEARCH PURPOSES ONLY. THE
FOLLOWING INFORMATION PRESENTED SHOULD BE CONSIDERED
CONFIDENTIAL AND NOT DISSEMINATED TO ANYONE ELSE.

YOUR RESPONSES WILL BE KEPT CONFIDENTIAL AND NO PERSONAL
IDENTIFYING INFORMATION WILL BE COLLECTED.

CONTINUE

Figure 4.12 **Use of Capitalization for Instructions.**

The second example shows both capitalization and boldface used for question text. Regardless of how difficult the task illustrated in Figure 4.13 may actually be, a screen like this *looks* difficult, not only because of the emphasis of the question text, but also because of the use of drop boxes (see Chapter 2) and the relatively limited "white space" (the unused areas of the screen). Given the separation of questions and answers, other techniques (e.g., background color, typeface) could be used to distinguish questions from response options.

Another commonly encountered example of the overuse of capitalization is the end-user license agreements (EULAs) one encounters when downloading or installing software. These are presented as large blocks of compact text, often all capitalized, and typically in scrolling pop-up windows. The message they convey is one of discouraging reading, much like the legal fine print in many printed documents.

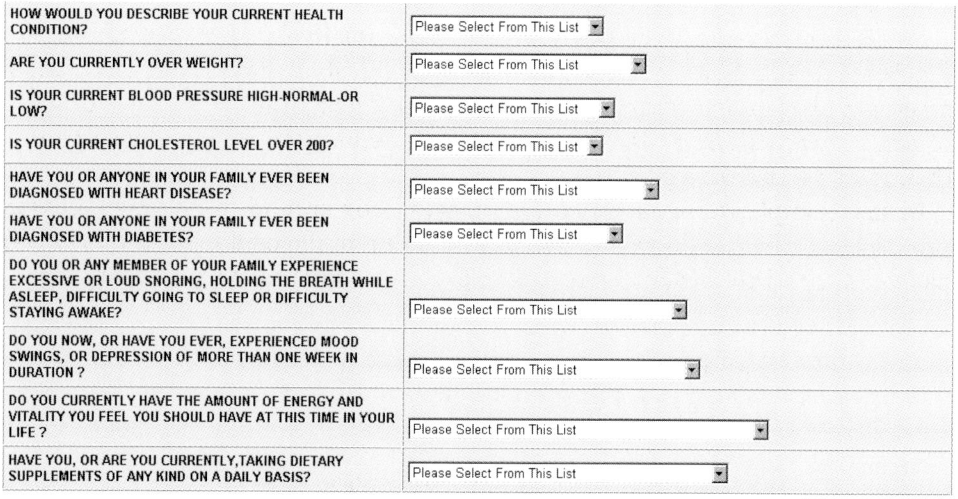

HOW WOULD YOU DESCRIBE YOUR CURRENT HEALTH CONDITION?	Please Select From This List
ARE YOU CURRENTLY OVER WEIGHT?	Please Select From This List
IS YOUR CURRENT BLOOD PRESSURE HIGH-NORMAL-OR LOW?	Please Select From This List
IS YOUR CURRENT CHOLESTEROL LEVEL OVER 200?	Please Select From This List
HAVE YOU OR ANYONE IN YOUR FAMILY EVER BEEN DIAGNOSED WITH HEART DISEASE?	Please Select From This List
HAVE YOU OR ANYONE IN YOUR FAMILY EVER BEEN DIAGNOSED WITH DIABETES?	Please Select From This List
DO YOU OR ANY MEMBER OF YOUR FAMILY EXPERIENCE EXCESSIVE OR LOUD SNORING, HOLDING THE BREATH WHILE ASLEEP, DIFFICULTY GOING TO SLEEP OR DIFFICULTY STAYING AWAKE?	Please Select From This List
DO YOU NOW, OR HAVE YOU EVER, EXPERIENCED MOOD SWINGS, OR DEPRESSION OF MORE THAN ONE WEEK IN DURATION ?	Please Select From This List
DO YOU CURRENTLY HAVE THE AMOUNT OF ENERGY AND VITALITY YOU FEEL YOU SHOULD HAVE AT THIS TIME IN YOUR LIFE ?	Please Select From This List
HAVE YOU, OR ARE YOU CURRENTLY,TAKING DIETARY SUPPLEMENTS OF ANY KIND ON A DAILY BASIS?	Please Select From This List

Figure 4.13 **Use of Capitalization and Boldface for Question Text.**

While there is agreement that capitalization is bad for large bodies of text, there is less consensus over the use of uppercase for emphasis. This brings us to the next topic.

4.2.4. Selective Emphasis

Having chosen a particular typeface and layout to maximize readability, there are still other decisions to be made with regard to typography. One of these is how to draw attention to selected parts of the text – in other words, the use of emphasis. The basic tools for doing this are italics, bold, underline, capitalization, and color. These could be used not only for emphasizing key words in the question, but also for distinguishing questions from response categories, or from instructions.

I've already said that using all capital letters is a bad idea. The same is true of all italics or all bold. But with regard to selective emphasis – focusing attention on particular words or phrases, the screen- and document-design literature is less clear. For example, Galitz (1993) notes that uppercase is suitable for headings, titles, and emphasis, because it aids search. Vartabedian (1971) found that screens with uppercase captions were searched faster than those using mixed case, and Williams (1988) found similar results with menu choice descriptions. However, in the Web survey setting, we don't want respondents to read only the emphasized word but rather to read the entire sentence while noticing the emphasized portions. Schriver (1997) suggests that when extra emphasis is needed, bold is a better cue than uppercase (see also Coles and Foster, 1975).

Italicized text is useful for selective emphasis. But again, one should avoid using italics for large blocks of text because the readability of italicized text, particularly at resolutions typical of computer screens, is much lower than in comparably sized roman text (Lynch and Horton, 2001, p. 132).

Underlined text is often used for emphasis in printed materials, including surveys. But doing so on the Web is not a good idea, because of the association of underlined text with hyperlinks. The same is true of color. The default setting for hyperlinks is blue and underlined, but the use of other colors, with and without underline, is also common. Thus, Neilsen notes in his Alertbox of November 1996, "On the Web blue text equals clickable text, so **never** make text blue if it is not clickable. It is also bad, though not quite as bad, to make text red or purple, since these two colors are often used to denote hypertext links that have already been visited" (see www.useit.com/alertbox/9611.html). He later writes (www.useit.com/alertbox/20040510.html), "To maximize the perceived affordance

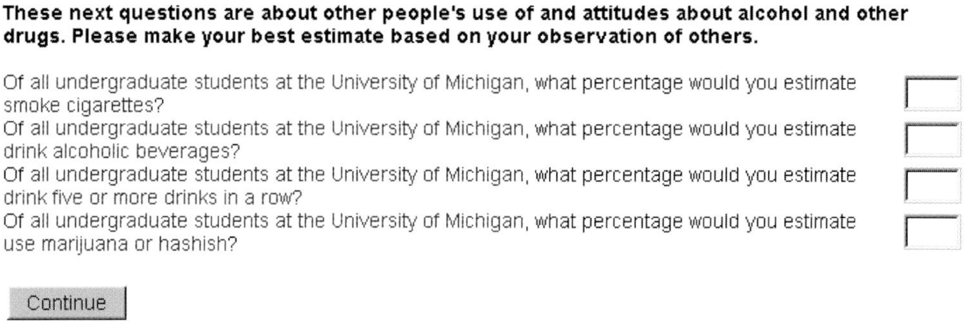

These next questions are about other people's use of and attitudes about alcohol and other drugs. Please make your best estimate based on your observation of others.

Of all undergraduate students at the University of Michigan, what percentage would you estimate smoke cigarettes?

Of all undergraduate students at the University of Michigan, what percentage would you estimate drink alcoholic beverages?

Of all undergraduate students at the University of Michigan, what percentage would you estimate drink five or more drinks in a row?

Of all undergraduate students at the University of Michigan, what percentage would you estimate use marijuana or hashish?

Continue

Figure 4.14 **Use of Blue for Emphasis Suggests Hyperlinks.**

of clickability, **color** and **underline** the link text." The blue underlined text is a hyperlink to a discussion of perceived affordances, while he used bold for emphasis. Nielsen goes on to say, "Don't underline any text that is not a link, even if your links aren't underlined. Reserve underlining for links. Because underline provides a strong perceived affordance of clickability, users will be confused and disappointed if underlined text doesn't have an actual affordance to match this perception." The National Cancer Institute's *Research-Based Web Design and Usability Guidelines* (www.usability.gov/guidelines; see also U.S. Department of Health and Human Services, 2006) similarly notes, "For text, users expect links to be blue and underlined." Another drawback of the use of color for emphasis is that color-blind users may not be able to distinguish it from regular text.

The example in Figure 4.14 illustrates the problem. Readers may be tempted to click on the phrase "all undergraduate students at the University of Michigan," for example, expecting a definition of the term. But this is not a hyperlink. It is simply emphasis, and way too much of it. Given how many words are emphasized, the key distinctions that the designer wanted the respondent to focus on – smoke cigarettes, drink alcoholic beverages, and so on – are lost in the sea of blue. A judicious rewrite of the question would help: Start with a lead-in containing the common text, and then follow this with each of the key behaviors.

I would recommend bold, italics, or uppercase, in that order, for emphasizing selected words or phrases. It is best to avoid underline and color, and particularly the combination of both. Furthermore, the key to effective use of various typographic devices for emphasis is *selective* use. Overuse of emphasis leads to what Lynch and Horton (1997) called "a 'clown's pants' effect where everything

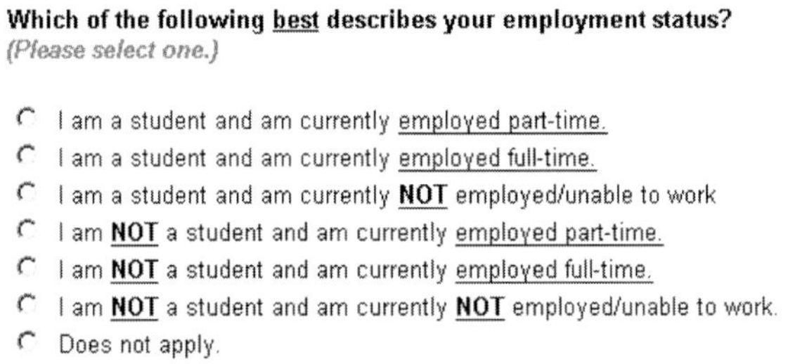

Which of the following best describes your employment status?
(Please select one.)

- ○ I am a student and am currently employed part-time.
- ○ I am a student and am currently employed full-time.
- ○ I am a student and am currently **NOT** employed/unable to work.
- ○ I am **NOT** a student and am currently employed part-time.
- ○ I am **NOT** a student and am currently employed full-time.
- ○ I am **NOT** a student and am currently **NOT** employed/unable to work.
- ○ Does not apply.

Figure 4.15 **Overuse of Emphasis.**

is garish and nothing is really emphasized." Figure 4.15 shows what can happen when emphasis is overdone.

While the emphasis in Figure 4.15 was intended to help the respondent, it is likely to have had the opposite effect. Part of the problem is that the designer is asking the question to do too much. One solution may be to ask two questions: (1) Are you a student? (2) Are you employed? Another is to use headings to separate the responses applicable to students and those not.

While it is tempting to use color for emphasis in Web surveys, color is actually not very good for this purpose. Aside from the association with hyperlinks, there are other reasons why the use of color – and especially blue – for emphasis may not be a great idea. As White (1990, p. 122) warns, "Do not fall in the trap of thinking that color is as strong as black because it looks brighter, more cheerful, more vibrant, and so more fun to look at. It is not. You have to compensate for its weakness, to make color as visible as black. There just has to be more of it, so you have to use fatter lines, bolder type, or larger type to overcome the problem."

Let's take blue as an example. Using blue for emphasis sends conflicting visual/verbal messages. Blue is a "lighter" color (i.e., has lower luminosity) than black; therefore, the visual effect is to make it stand out less, not more as intended. However, it may be argued that the change in color contrast from black to blue text is sufficient to draw attention to the emphasized words. Colored text can only be read when it is quite close to the eye's focal point, although color itself can be seen far from the focal point. In particular, some argue that because human eyes are not designed to see blue as well as other colors, it should not be used for anything that needs to be focused on, such as text (see Horton, 1991). As Grandjean (1987, pp. 30–31) notes, "If a reader is familiar with the significance of colors, then colors will help to locate the required information quickly, but the recognition of a word or symbol itself depends on the legibility of characters and not on their color." Following White (1990), one suggestion is if color is used for

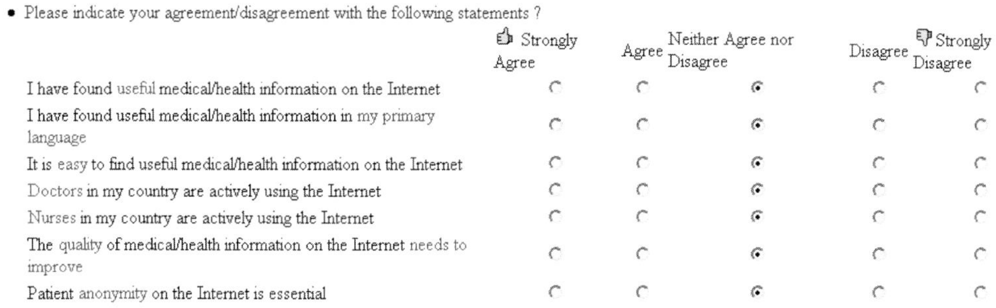

• Please indicate your agreement/disagreement with the following statements ?

	Strongly Agree	Agree	Neither Agree nor Disagree	Disagree	Strongly Disagree
I have found useful medical/health information on the Internet	○	○	◉	○	○
I have found useful medical/health information in my primary language	○	○	◉	○	○
It is easy to find useful medical/health information on the Internet	○	○	◉	○	○
Doctors in my country are actively using the Internet	○	○	◉	○	○
Nurses in my country are actively using the Internet	○	○	◉	○	○
The quality of medical/health information on the Internet needs to improve	○	○	◉	○	○
Patient anonymity on the Internet is essential	○	○	◉	○	○

Figure 4.16 **Use of Color for Emphasis and Question Text.**

emphasis, change other features too – that is, make the emphasized text bold, or increase the font size. As I discuss in the next section, using color redundantly with other cues makes it easier for color-blind respondents or those using monochrome monitors.

Finally, color conveys meaning, as we shall see later. For example, red should be reserved for error messages or warnings, rather than for emphasis. The example in Figure 4.16 not only uses red for emphasis but also uses blue to distinguish a question lead-in from individual items.

I'll return to the issue of color in the context of color contrast and choice of background colors. The choice of an appropriate color for emphasis should depend, of course, on the choice of background color for the Web survey.

4.2.5. Summary on Typography

With regard to issues of typography, here are some summary recommendations:

- Choose an appropriate typeface, and use it consistently; in many cases, these decisions have already been made for the parent site.
- Resist the urge to be creative in the use of typefaces.
- Do not specify absolute font sizes; allow respondents control over font size.
- If you specify relative fonts, do not go below the default settings on the respondent's browser; increase rather than decrease font size.
- Use a combination of line length and line spacing to enhance the readability of text.
- Use different typefaces and features consistently to differentiate different types of text (questions, response options, instructions, links, etc.).

- Don't mix different typographic devices; that is, don't use CAPS, **bold**, and underline, and certainly not **ALL TOGETHER**.
- Use emphasis selectively and sparingly.

This can all be summarized in the following admonition: Typography is a powerful tool – use it wisely.

4.3. Background Colors and Patterns

4.3.1. Color

Unlike paper surveys where, without going to great additional expense, most questionnaires are rendered with black text on white or single-colored paper, color choices become an important design decision for Web survey researchers.

As with typography, there is a big world of information on color, and great depths that can be explored. My goal here is again to try to touch lightly on the subject, enough to make a point that decisions about color – like those of many other design aspects – are important, even if one's focus is designing Web surveys to minimize measurement error rather than designing visually pleasing or aesthetically beautiful Web sites.

There are many excellent Web sites devoted to issues of color. Two that I find particularly useful are Morton's site *Color Matters* (http://www.colormatters.com/), and the Poynter Institute's Web site on *Color, Contrast, and Dimension in News Design* (http://poynterextra.org/cp/index.html). There are also a number of good books on the use of color in design, some focusing specifically on the Web. These include e-books by Morton (see www.colorvoodoo.com) and Weinman's volumes on *Designing Web Graphics* (see www.Lynda.com/products/books). A classic text on color is Itten's 1961 book, *The Art of Color*, republished as *The Elements of Color* in 2003.

There are also many prescriptions about color. Don't use this color, avoid that combination, and so on. But aside from some key pitfalls to avoid, the choice of color is more about aesthetics than many of the other issues I've discussed thus far. The point of this section is that we should be aware of the possible effects of color choices or decisions on respondents, but then be free to choose color combinations that result in visually pleasing design. But "beauty is in the eye of the beholder" and what may be aesthetically pleasing to one person may be less so to another. So here again moderation and careful design are the key to avoiding potentially jarring visual presentations.

Color is important for several reasons:

- Some people are color blind, and may not be able to distinguish among different colors.
- The choice of color may affect contrast and aspects of readability of the verbal information presented.
- Color conveys meaning and may affect the answers respondents give in direct or indirect ways.

I'll address each of these topics in turn. First, I'll take a brief detour to define some terms and clarify the meaning of color. Color can be defined in terms of three dimensions (Dondis, 1973; Horton, 1991), namely, hue, saturation, and brightness.[2] Briefly these are

- *Hue* (also sometimes called chroma) is what we commonly think of as color. Red, yellow, and blue are the three primary or elemental hues.
- *Saturation* is the degree of purity of a color. Colors can be diluted in different ways, by adding white, black, gray, or the complementary color. The more saturated a color, the less diluted it is. For example, red is more saturated than pink.
- *Brightness* or *lightness* (also called *luminosity*) is the amount of white or black in a color. Black, white, and gray are achromatic (they lack color) and therefore lack hue and saturation characteristics of color, varying only in brightness. The more white, the brighter the color; the more black, the darker the color.

One way to think of the difference between saturation and brightness is to imagine the dials on older television sets. Turning one dial would change the picture from color to black and white. The brightness of the display would not change, but the saturation would be reduced. However, turning the brightness dial would not remove the color but would make the picture more or less bright.

Early computer monitors represented each pixel with 8 bits of memory, producing a maximum of 256 different colors. Most systems today now use a 24-bit system, permitting the display of millions of unique colors. Eight bits of memory is dedicated to each of the three primary colors, with 256 values possible for each. Color is represented in HTML by specifying the hexadecimal value of the three

---

[2] Itten (2003) identifies four additional color contrasts, but these three are sufficient for our purposes.

primary colors: red, green, and blue, hence RGB values.[3] White is represented by #FFFFFF, which is the maximum value of each of the three colors, while black is #000000. A saturated primary color such as blue would thus be #0000FF. Hue is changed by mixing values of the different colors, while brightness or luminescence is changed by increasing or decreasing values of a color. With CSS, the mix of the RGB can now be specified directly in percentage terms; for example, `color: rgb(%73, 100%, 100%)` is a pale blue. Most Web development or design software, such as Macromedia's Dreamweaver or Adobe Photoshop, has palettes for the selection of colors, meaning one does not need to learn the hexadecimal or percentage values for colors.

Figure 4.17 shows an example from Adobe Photoshop's color picker (Microsoft's Paint looks similar). The color selected (see the circle in the large box) is #BBFFFF, corresponding to the pale blue identified earlier. The box contains various saturation and brightness levels for the same hue. As one moves from left to right, saturation increases. As one moves from top to bottom, brightness decreases.

Despite the nearly limitless range of colors available, in the early days of the Web, there was a legitimate concern that not all colors were rendered the same on all platforms. This led to the development of the "browser-safe color palette," a set of 216 colors that were identical across Macintosh and Microsoft operating systems and a variety of browsers. Given the widespread use of 24-bit systems, it is no longer imperative to stick to the 216 browser-safe colors.

Weinman is credited with first identifying the browser-safe colors in 1996, in her book, *Designing Web Graphics*. As she notes on her Web site (www.Lynda.com):

> Though this might seem blasphemous to older readers of my books, or loyal Web site visitors, I believe it's safe to design without the palette. I believe this because so few computer users view the Web in 256 colors anymore . . . . Conversely, there's no harm in using the browser-safe palette either. It simply limits your choices to 216 colors. Most people don't have a lot of color picking confidence, and working with limited color choices is easier. At this point, there's no right or wrong when it comes to which colors you pick, but more important to know how to combine colors in pleasing and effective ways.

---

[3] The RGB color system is an additive color system, where white is the additive combination of the three colors, while black is the absence of light. This book is printed using the CMYK system, for cyan, magenta, yellow, and key (black). CMYK is a subtractive system, where white is the natural color of the paper, and black is produced from a full combination of colored inks. Thus, colors rendered on the printed page may not exactly reproduce those on a computer screen.

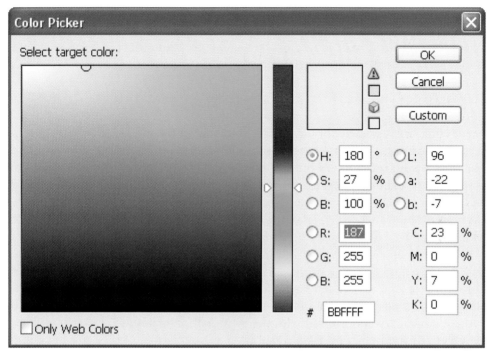

Figure 4.17 **Color Picker from Adobe Photoshop CS.**

With this background out of the way, let's proceed to discuss the three key reasons why the choice of color scheme for a Web survey must be done carefully.

4.3.1.1. Color Blindness

While this is a relatively rare phenomenon overall, color blindness differentially affects men and women. About 8% of men and 0.04% of women have some degree of color deficiency (Rigden, 1999). The most common form of color blindness involves the inability to distinguish between red and green. This concern leads to a common recommendation in the design literature on the use of color. As Rigden (1999) notes, "Color should never be the primary cue for information. The options should be clear without color, and the color is simply added as a means of emphasis." Both Schneiderman (1992, p. 326) and Galitz (1993, p. 434) recommend designing for monochrome first, in part because of the prevalence of monochrome displays at the time and because of concerns about color deficiencies.

While the former is no longer an issue, the concern about color blindness is still sufficient to suggest not relying solely on color to communicate essential meaning. One thing is clear: Don't use red text on a green background, or vice versa, even if you're doing a survey about Christmas.

4.3.1.2. Color Contrast

A more important reason for being concerned about the choice of color relates to the visual contrast of the verbal information presented on a colored background. The goal of the background should be to support the primary task, that is, to help focus visual attention on the survey question and response options without creating visual fatigue. The degree of contrast between the foreground (text) and background may affect the readability of the survey questions. This depends both on the color used for the text *and* that used for the background.

While light text on a dark background was the way text was presented on early DOS-based computers, this was because rendering the white letters took less computing power and consumed less energy than generating the white background on the screen, not because it made the text easier to read. Despite the change to white backgrounds that started with the introduction of graphical user interfaces, in which all the pixels on the screen are active, there are still some who cling to the old notions. Figure 4.18 shows an example of a survey with blue text and white response options on a dark background. Such designs may be appropriate for certain audiences (e.g., an alcohol-reduction Web site aimed at teenagers, acl.indepthlearning.org), but most sites now use dark text on a light background for ease of reading. In a recent experiment, Květon, Jelínek, Vobořil, and Klimusová (2007) found that inverse video (light stimuli on dark background) produced slower performance and more errors than dark stimuli on light background.

In addition to black or other dark colors, highly saturated colors should also be avoided for background use. A saturated color is one that is bright and doesn't have any other colors mixed with it. Green, blue, and red are all saturated colors. One of the biggest problems with saturated colors is that they lead to visual fatigue. Every saturated color has a different wavelength that needs to be focused at different depths behind the lens of the eye. It is also hard to perceive the depth of saturated colors – they have a tendency to appear as if they are floating either behind the computer screen or in front of it – a phenomenon known as chromostereopsis (e.g., Faubert, 1994).

Given this, it is best to use saturated colors sparingly, and for areas that are very important and require a user's attention immediately.

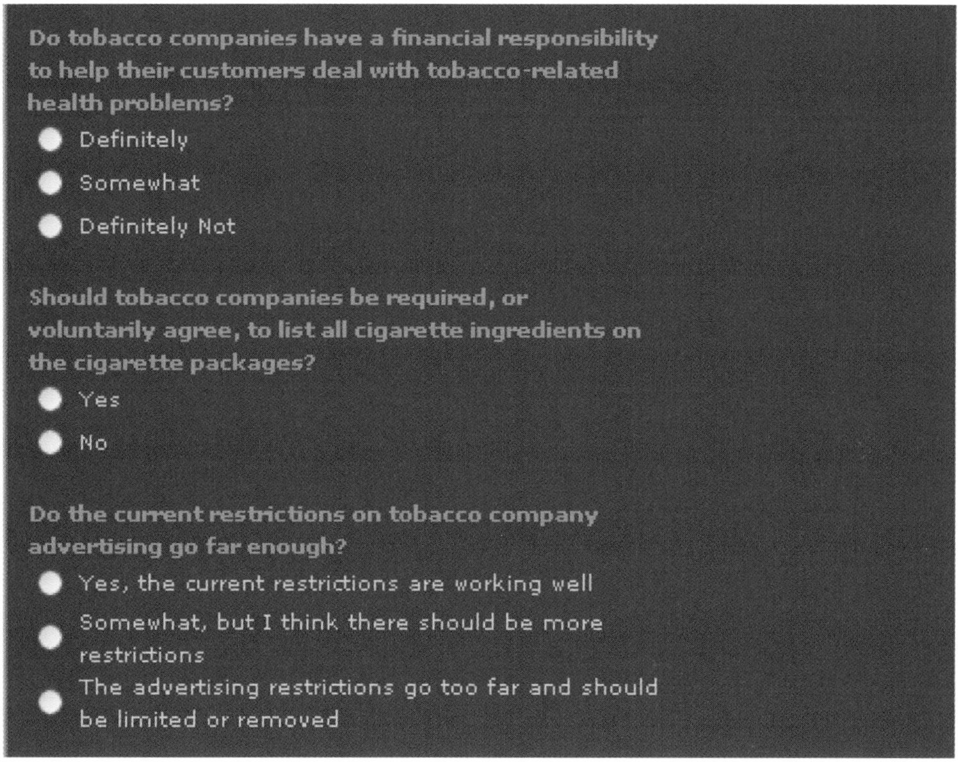

Figure 4.18 **Poor Color Contrast.**

Figure 4.19 shows examples of black text (#000000) on different color backgrounds. The top two on the left are both saturated colors. The hexadecimal RGB code for the red background in the top left of Figure 4.19 is #FF0000, which means maximum red, no green, and no blue. Similarly, the middle left background is #0000FF, or no red, no green, and maximum blue. In contrast, the bottom left background is #EEFFFF, which means that the red has been reduced slightly, while green and blue are still at their maximum. Remember that if red was also at the maximum value, the background would be white. The yellow background in the top right is created by maximizing red and green, and setting blue to zero, hence #FFFF00. Finally, the code for the right middle background is #00FF00 and that for the bottom right is #EEFFEE.

On an LCD monitor the background colors in the bottom row of Figure 4.19 are almost indistinguishable from white, while on a CRT monitor, they are,

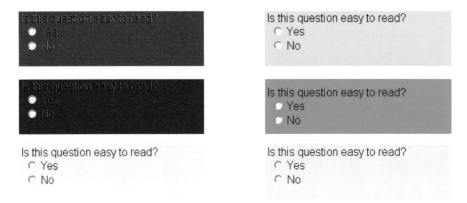

Figure 4.19 **Examples of Background Colors.**

respectively, pale blue and pale green. This suggests that colors still appear different in different environments (in this case, monitor types), indicating the need for careful testing under different settings.

Given the myriad choices available, how do we decide whether a particular choice has sufficient contrast to permit easy reading of the text? The W3C (see www.w3.org) offers two formulas, one for determining color brightness and the other for color difference, or the contrast between two colors.

The first formula is

$$((\text{Red value} \times 299) + (\text{Green value} \times 587) + (\text{Blue value} \times 114))/1000.$$

The difference between the back brightness and the foreground brightness should be greater than 125. Let's take a look at the two blue backgrounds on the left side of Figure 4.19. With the text being black (R=0, G=0, B=0), the foreground brightness is 0. The brightness for the dark blue background is

$$((0 \times 299) + (0 \times 587) + (255 \times 114))/1{,}000 = 29.07.$$

Thus, the difference between the foreground and background brightness is less than the minimum of 125. For the light blue background, the brightness is

$$((238 \times 299) + (128 \times 587) + (255 \times 114))/1000 = 251.68.$$

This is above the recommended minimum, indicating good contrast. The second formula suggested by W3C is

$$((\text{max}(\text{Red value 1, Red value 2}) - \text{min}(\text{Red value 1, Red value 2}))$$
$$+ ((\text{max}(\text{Green value 1, Green value 2}) - \text{min}(\text{Green value 1, Green value 2}))$$
$$+ ((\text{max}(\text{Blue value 1, Blue value 2}) - \text{min}(\text{Blue value 1, Blue value 2})).$$

In this case, the difference should be greater than 500. For the black text on the dark blue background, this is:

$$((0 - 0) + (0 - 0) + (255 - 0)) = 255.$$

This is again lower than the recommended contrast, while for the light blue background it is

$$((238 - 0) + (238 - 0) + (255 - 0)) = 731.$$

This is higher than the minimum of 500. Thus, both approaches suggest that the black text on dark blue background provides insufficient contrast, while the same text on the light blue background has sufficient contrast. For those not wanting to go through the trouble of calculating these formulas, there are several Web sites where this can be done directly (see www.juicystudio.com/services/colourcontrast.asp, for example). Tools for converting hexadecimal to decimal and vice versa can also be found on the Web (see, e.g., www.statman.info/conversions/hexadecimal.html).

As long as the contrast is sufficient to allow easy reading of the text, the choice of a particular color scheme may be largely one of aesthetics. Hall and Hanna (2004) note a consistent finding in the literature that people tend to find short wavelength colors (blues and greens) as more pleasant than long wavelength colors (reds and yellows). Based on their own research, they suggest that black text on a white background is best for retention and readability. However, chromatic or colored text/background combinations are more likely to be seen as visually pleasing and stimulating.

Similarly, in the early online version of their guide, Lynch and Horton (1997) suggested that "subtle pastel shades of colors typically found in nature make the best choices for background or minor elements." They continued, "Avoid bold, highly saturated primary colors except in regions of maximum emphasis, and even there use them cautiously" (Lynch and Horton, 1997). I prefer to use a light blue background, both for PowerPoint presentations and for Web pages because it is slightly less visually fatiguing than a pure white background. My preference is for something close to the bottom left example in Figure 4.19. The fact that blue is harder to focus on for text makes it ideal as a background color.

4.3.1.3. The Meaning of Color

In addition to the readability of text on different colored backgrounds, the color may directly communicate in other ways. Color has meaning, whether through cultural conventions or learned associations, or through the actions associated with color in the instrument itself.

Certain colors have well-defined meanings, although they are often situation specific. For example, red means "hot," especially when linked with blue for "cold." Red also means "stop," when linked with green for "go." Red is also commonly used to mean danger or warning. In other words, red has a number of strong associations and should be reserved for warnings or errors messages.

Remembering that we are taking about the *World Wide* Web, colors may have different associations in different cultures. For example, while red means danger in the Western world, in Chinese culture it is associated with life and good fortune, and while green is associated with life in Western culture, it is associated with death in Chinese culture (Ware, 2000, p. 135). Similarly, yellow often has a negative connotation in the West, suggesting cowardice, but is associated with nobility in Japan and happiness in the Arabic world (Kostelnick and Roberts, 1998, p. 340; Horton, 1991). These added design concerns apply to international research.

In addition to the global meanings, color can also take on local meaning in the context of the particular Web survey or site. Matching the background color of a Web survey to its parent site, for example, may help with branding. Color could be used to identify different tasks or different sections of the instrument (see the *National Geographic* example in Figure 4.2). In each of these cases, use color consistently, so once the meaning is understood it is supportive of the primary task of completing the questionnaire or the secondary tasks of finding additional information, tracking progress, and the like.

If different colors are used in a Web survey, respondents will assume that the colors have meaning. But as Brown (1988, p. 67) notes, "Because color changes are attention-getting, color variations that are not relevant to performance of the user's task are likely to be more distracting than helpful." Thus, it is best to use only a few colors, be consistent in their use, be redundant with other cues, and respect cultural conventions.

In addition to the meaning associated with colors, they can also affect respondents emotionally. Artists effectively use color to convey emotional meaning, as do advertisers. For example, blue hues have been show to elicit more relaxed feeling states than yellow, while red elicits more excitement (see Gorn, Chattopadhyay, Yi, and Dahl 1997; Gorn, Chattopadhyay, Sengupta, and Tripathi, 2004; Valdez and Mehrabian, 1994).

The effect can be even more subtle. Reber and Schwarz (1999) use the notion of "perceptual fluency," and suggest the ease with which words are read, depending on typography and color contrast, may affect their recognition. They found that statements presented in colors that were easier to read (e.g., dark blue or red on a white background) were more likely to be judged true than statements that were harder to reader (e.g., yellow or light blue text on a white background). They suggest that the easier the statements are to read and process, the more likely they are to be experienced as familiar, leading participants to feel that they have heard or seen the information before, suggesting it is probably true.

Gorn et al. (2004) examined how background color affected subjects in a Web download task, and found that screen color affected both the perceived quickness of a Web download and how long subjects were willing to wait before quitting the task.

Even closer to home in terms of survey design, Weller and Livingston (1988) found that questionnaires printed on a pink background produced less emotional responses than those printed on a blue background, in a study among students evaluating a jury vignette. Etter, Cucherat, and Perneger (2002), in a meta-analysis of several questionnaire color experiments, found that questionnaires printed on pink paper had higher response rates than those on white paper, while blue, yellow, and green questionnaires had no significant effect relative to white (see also Godar, 2000).

Turning to Web surveys, Pope and Baker (2005) varied the background color of a survey of college students, using a blue or pink background for a survey on alcohol-related issues. While the differences were not statistically significant, possibly due to small samples, the blue background took less time to complete (28.6 minutes on average) than the pink (29.6 minutes), and the perceived length of the survey was also shorter (25.2 minutes for the blue and 26.8 minutes for the pink background). Interestingly, the effect seemed to differ by gender, with the difference in actual and perceived times between the two colors being larger for men than for women. In other words, men were faster using the blue background than the pink (25.9 versus 30.1 minutes), while women were faster using the pink background than the blue (29.2 versus 31.0 minutes). While none of these differences are statistically significant they are nonetheless suggestive.

In a follow-up study, Baker and Couper (2007) contrasted a white background with blue (#99FFFF) and yellow (#FFFF99) ones in a survey among opt-in panel members. With 1,500 completes, we found that background color had no significant effect on actual completion time, estimated length of the survey, or other subjective ratings of the survey. However, breakoff rates were significantly ($p < .05$) higher for the yellow version (15.05) than for the blue version (10.8%), with the white background in the middle (13.7%).

These studies suggest that mundane decisions such as the choice of background color may have some effect on actual and subjective performance, although not in all cases and possibly not very large. However, in both the previous studies, the legibility of the text was equivalent across conditions, potentially mitigating the effects of color. As contrast changes affect readability or as the background color has some associated meaning related to the survey questions, as Bischoping and Schuman (1992) found with the color of pens used in a preelection poll, the effects may be more pronounced.

Figure 4.20 shows an example of background color that seems unrelated to the survey questions (focusing on the National Football League). While the question numbers are quite visible, the background/foreground contrast for the questions themselves is less supportive of the task.

Another example is shown in Figure 4.21. Here a number of different colors are used, one to differentiate the answer fields from the questions, another as backdrop to the questions themselves, and a third to separate the questions from each other. In addition, red is used for instructions – a color that is more appropriate for error messages or warnings. While the intention of the designer seems clear, the result – in my view – is a gaudy screen that has the potential to distract rather than support the respondent.

4.3.2. Patterns

Patterned or textured backgrounds – while easy to do on the Web – may be even more problematic for readability than solid colors. We've all seen Web sites that are so heavily patterned or textured that it is almost impossible to read the text. These are typically on personal Web pages or art sites where the goal is to demonstrate how facile the designer is or evoke an atmosphere, to the point of compromising

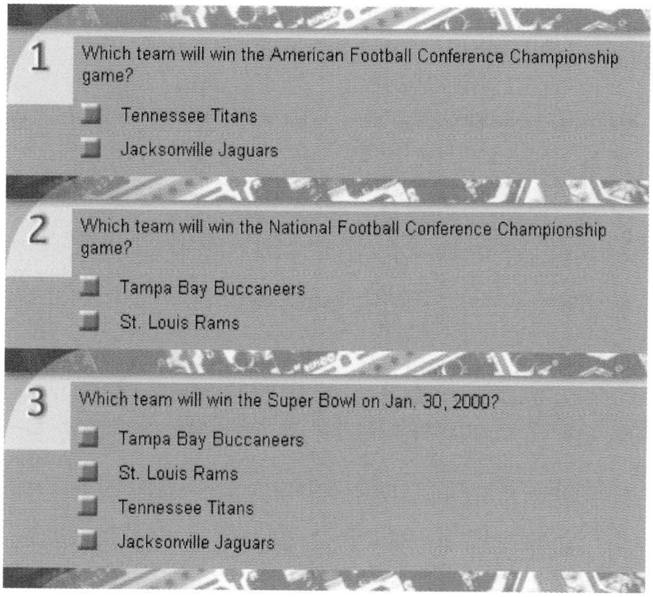

1 Which team will win the American Football Conference Championship game?
- Tennessee Titans
- Jacksonville Jaguars

2 Which team will win the National Football Conference Championship game?
- Tampa Bay Buccaneers
- St. Louis Rams

3 Which team will win the Super Bowl on Jan. 30, 2000?
- Tampa Bay Buccaneers
- St. Louis Rams
- Tennessee Titans
- Jacksonville Jaguars

Figure 4.20 Use of Color for Background.

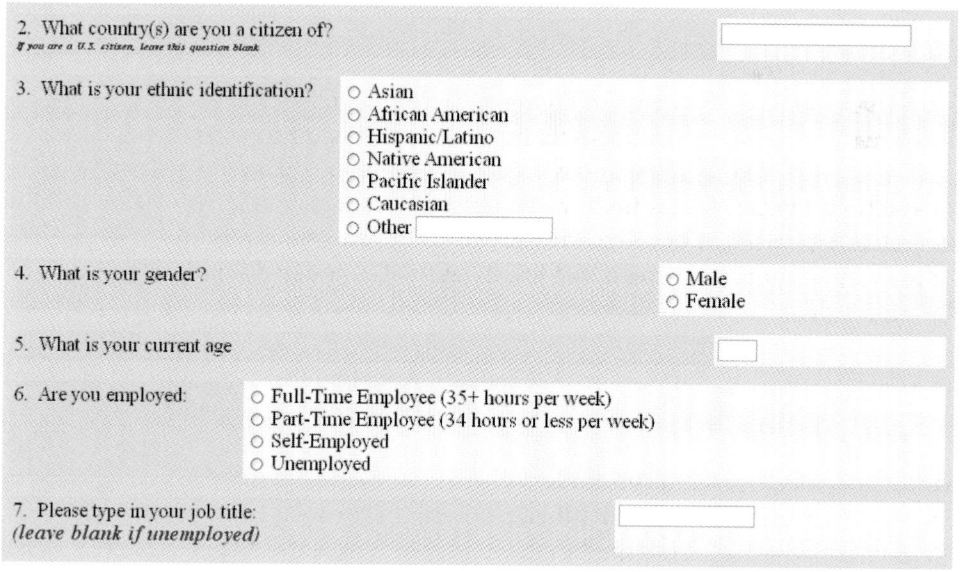

2. What country(s) are you a citizen of?
If you are a U.S. citizen, leave this question blank

3. What is your ethnic identification?
- Asian
- African American
- Hispanic/Latino
- Native American
- Pacific Islander
- Caucasian
- Other

4. What is your gender?
- Male
- Female

5. What is your current age

6. Are you employed:
- Full-Time Employee (35+ hours per week)
- Part-Time Employee (34 hours or less per week)
- Self-Employed
- Unemployed

7. Please type in your job title:
(leave blank if unemployed)

Figure 4.21 Use of Color for Background.

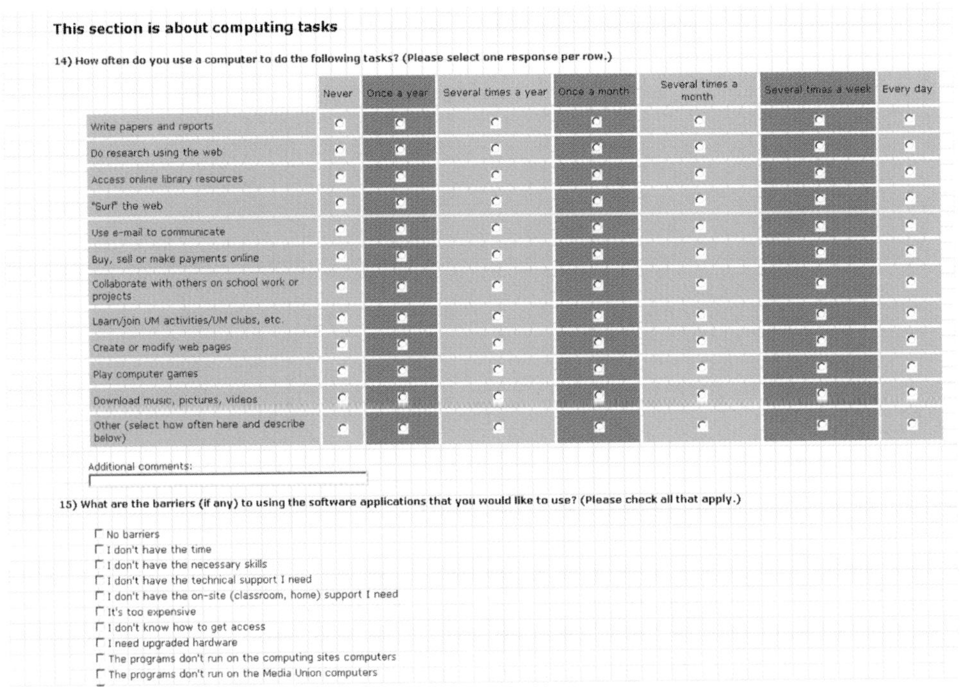

Figure 4.22 **A Background that May Interfere with the Task.**

legibility. Fortunately, this is relatively rare on the leading e-commerce sites and in Web surveys. Nonetheless, I have seen a number of examples where the background pattern of a Web survey may interfere with the task of survey completion – enough at least to warrant this discussion.

One such example is shown in Figure 4.22. The lines and shading, rather than the survey questions, dominate the page. Contrast this example with the *National Geographic* example earlier in this chapter (Figure 4.2). That survey uses a similar graph-paper pattern, but only in the border areas, thereby avoiding any interference with the task of reading and responding to the survey questions.

Kostelnick and Roberts call this "visual noise." As they note, "Web sites that use color are vulnerable to noise...In some Web pages that blend colors for text and background, the perceptual problems can be so severe that users can't read the text at all. Noise renders the site unusable" (Kostelnick and Roberts, 1998, p. 58). Although not unusable, the survey shown in Figure 4.22 may be visually fatiguing after several such pages. Another example of visual noise is shown in

Figure 4.23 **Background Image Interferes with Task.**

Figure 4.23. Here the background pattern makes it hard to see some of the response options.

As Lowney (1998) has noted, "Text is most legible when drawn against a plain background of a contrasting color. Text drawn over a varied background, such as a wash of colors, a bitmap image, or lines, may be illegible for many users because the image can distract from or blend with the edges of letters making them hard to recognize." There are ways that decoration – color and patterns – can be added to a Web survey without getting in the way of the primary task. Again, the *National Geographic* survey in Figure 4.2 is one such example. But if a patterned background serves no useful purpose other than decoration, one wonders if it is worth doing. Like other design elements discussed in this chapter, color, texture, and pattern are powerful design features that can enhance the survey experience if used appropriately.

4.4. Layout or Spatial Arrangement of Elements

I began this chapter talking about the global layout of the Web page. In this section, I take a more local view, focusing more narrowly on the layout of the survey questions. I've discussed how typography and the use of color can affect how the respondent perceives and executes the task. In the same way, the spatial

Principle or Law	Description
Proximity	Things that are close together are seen as belonging together
Similarity	Similar elements are seen as grouped together
Closure	A closed contour tends to be seen as an object; there is a tendency to complete an incomplete figure
Symmetry or balance	Symmetrical elements are seen as belonging together regardless of distance
Continuity	Visual elements that are smooth and continuous are seen as visual entities

Figure 4.24 **Some Gestalt Principles of Perception.**

arrangement or layout of the visual and verbal elements may facilitate or hinder the task of completing the questionnaire. Tufte (1990, p. 50) makes this point: "It is not how much space there is, but rather how it is used. It is not how much information there is, but rather how effectively it is organized."

That the spatial arrangement of elements can have an important effect on how objects are perceived has been known for a long time but was formalized in the well-known Gestalt principles or laws of perception (see Koffka, 1935; Wertheimer, 1938a, 1938b, 1958). While there appears to be no agreement on what constitutes the set of laws (Wertheimer called them "factors"), several authors have described or interpreted various Gestalt principles in the context of design (e.g., Kostelnick and Roberts, 1998; Jenkins and Dillman, 1997; Moore and Fitz, 1993a, 1993b; Schriver, 1997; Ware, 2000), so there is no need for me to go into detail here. Figure 4.24 briefly summarizes some of the more commonly attributed Gestalt perceptual laws.

In addition to those listed in Figure 4.24, there are a few higher-order laws that describe the process of visual perception. One of these is the Law of *Prägnanz*,[4] which states that of all possible perceptual experiences to which a particular stimulus could give rise, the one most closely fitting to the concept of a "good figure" would most likely be perceived, where "good" means simple, regular, and symmetrical. In other words, we tend to see the object or entity that requires the least amount of cognitive processing.

---

[4]   *Prägnanz* is a German word that has no direct English translation. Various synonyms, such as "precision," "goodness," or "simplicity," have been used.

Another principle derived from the Gestalt perspective is that of figure-ground separation or contrast. Figure-ground contrast refers to the ability to distinguish what stands in front (the figure) from what stands behind (the ground). As Ware (2000, p. 212) notes, all the Gestalt laws, along with other factors such as color and texture, contribute to achieving figure-ground segmentation.

How are these Gestalt perceptual principles relevant to design? Schriver (1997, p. 325) notes that they are important because "they can help us guide the reader's focus of attention, emphasize certain groupings, and organize sequences of the content. In effect, they can be employed rhetorically." The Gestalt psychologists focused primarily on the spatial arrangement of objects. In the previous chapter, I discussed the use of images in the context of visual rhetoric. In this chapter, I have also discussed color and texture, among other design tools. These can all be employed in achieving a desired design goal. The Gestalt principles help us understand *why* these layout and design devices may achieve a particular goal but don't tell us *how* to do so. We should remember, as Schriver (1997, p. 324) notes, "these principles are descriptive, not prescriptive."

There are various layout issues to address. I begin with the alignment of response options and the visual juxtaposition of input field and labels. Next, I turn to the vertical versus horizontal alignment of response options and the use of "banking" or columnar presentation. I then move to more complex layout issues involving the use of tables, matrixes, or grids. In other words, I deal with layout issues of increasing complexity, before ending with some general observations about complexity and overall design.

4.4.1. Alignment

I've already talked about the justification of text in Section 4.2.3. Here, I'm focusing on the alignment of response options and input fields. Several alignment decisions are needed in designing Web surveys, including the following:

- Should input fields be to the left or right of the labels or above or below the labels?
- Should response options be arranged horizontally or vertically?
- Should response options be split into several columns, and if so, how should this be done?

I'll address each of these questions in turn.

4.4.1.1. Alignment of Input Fields and Labels

Should radio buttons or check boxes be placed on the left or right of the response options? This issue has not received much research attention in paper-based surveys, but raises similar issues in that mode. In his 1978 book, Dillman recommended placing the input field to the left of the label. In the 2000 edition, he raises the possibility that doing so may cause difficulties in terms of skip instructions and suggests considering putting the input field on the right of the response options. The input field can then be followed by any skip instructions (see Redline and Dillman, 2002). Another reason the juxtaposition of the input field and response label matters on paper is that with the input field on the left, the label is obscured for right-handed persons.

The first of these issues may apply only to scrolling designs on the Web, where skips are not automated and hyperlinks or arrows are used to guide respondents to the next applicable question (see Section 5.1.1). In a paging survey with automated skips (see Section 1.2.2 and Section 5.1.3), placement of skip instructions or hyperlinks for navigation is not an issue. Furthermore, in either type of Web survey, the use of the mouse as input means that the input labels are not obscured by the hand when selecting an input field – although, of course, this may again be a concern in Web applications using a touchscreen or stylus.

The choice of layout should thus be based on other considerations. Research by Bowker and Dillman (2000) found no difference in respondent preference or performance with either left or right justification of response options, suggesting that the placement of the input fields relative to the labels should have little influence on responses. Hartley, Davies, and Burnhill (1977) experimented with different layouts of a paper survey, including the two versions shown in Figure 4.25. They administered the questionnaires to children in a school setting, and found no significant differences in completion time. But, they argued that placing the input fields on the left was quicker for the designer to type and therefore preferred. This latter point has its parallels in the Web world, where putting answer fields to the right may require the use of HTML tables, which likely adds to the design time.

Given this, the placement of the input fields to the left of the item label (as illustrated on the left of Figure 4.25) produces fewer formatting problems in HTML and should be preferred for this reason. The format on the right in Figure 4.25, while just as easy to script in HTML, makes it harder for respondents to find the input fields, and review the answers they have provided.

Figure 4.26 shows a different example of input fields on the right of the response options. In this example, an HTML table needs to be used to align the input fields.

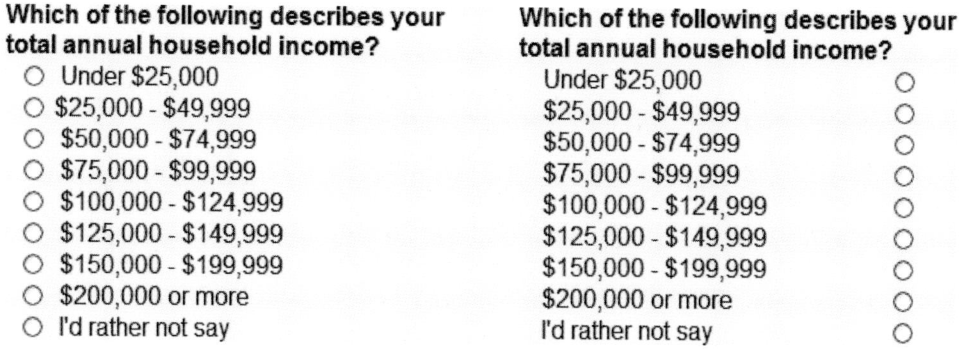

Which of the following describes your total annual household income?
- ○ Under $25,000
- ○ $25,000 - $49,999
- ○ $50,000 - $74,999
- ○ $75,000 - $99,999
- ○ $100,000 - $124,999
- ○ $125,000 - $149,999
- ○ $150,000 - $199,999
- ○ $200,000 or more
- ○ I'd rather not say

Which of the following describes your total annual household income?
- Under $25,000 ○
- $25,000 - $49,999 ○
- $50,000 - $74,999 ○
- $75,000 - $99,999 ○
- $100,000 - $124,999 ○
- $125,000 - $149,999 ○
- $150,000 - $199,999 ○
- $200,000 or more ○
- I'd rather not say ○

Figure 4.25 **Input Fields on Left versus Right of Response Options.**

The table has two columns, the first containing the left-justified response options, and the second containing the radio buttons. This approach not only necessitates the use of tables but also risks weakening the link between the response and the corresponding input field as the gap between the two increases. This could be countered by using dot leaders to connect the two or by right justifying the text within the left column, but both these solutions do not seem worth the effort.

While there is no strong empirical evidence supporting placing the input fields to the left or right of the response options in a vertically aligned response set, the example in Figure 4.27 should be avoided. Aside from the fact that this question

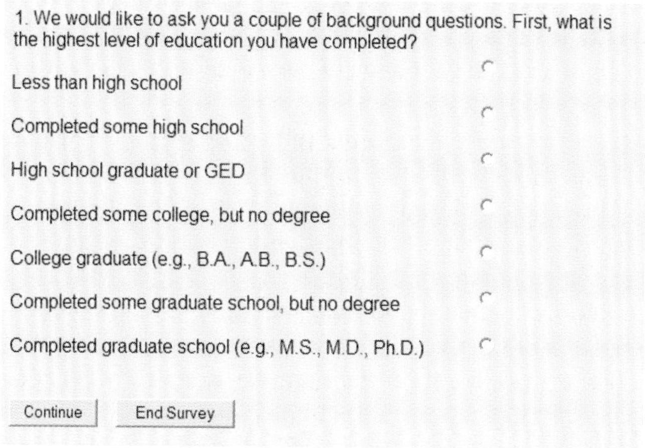

1. We would like to ask you a couple of background questions. First, what is the highest level of education you have completed?

Less than high school ○

Completed some high school ○

High school graduate or GED ○

Completed some college, but no degree ○

College graduate (e.g., B.A., A.B., B.S.) ○

Completed some graduate school, but no degree ○

Completed graduate school (e.g., M.S., M.D., Ph.D.) ○

Continue   End Survey

Figure 4.26 **Left-Justified Options and Right-Justified Input Fields.**

4) Please indicate the ages of the YOUNGEST child living at home with you.

☐ No children under 1 ☐ 1 year ☐ 2 years ☐ 3 years ☐ 4
years ☐ 5 years ☐ 6 years ☐ 7 years ☐ 8 years ☐ 9 years
☐ 10 years ☐ 11 years ☐ 12 years ☐ 13 years ☐ 14 years
☐ 15 years ☐ 16 years ☐ 17 years ☐ 18 years ☐ 19 years
☐ Over 19 years ☐ No children ☐ Abstain

Figure 4.27 **Unjustified Response Options.**

(from a real survey) offers confusing verbal and visual cues – the question reads "ages" and the check boxes reinforce the plural notion, but the question is intended to ascertain the single age of the youngest child only – the lack of alignment makes it difficult to associate a response with an answer category. Look at the "13 years" response, for example – should one check the box before or after it to select that response?

The only reason I can imagine for laying out the response options this way is to save space, but this argument has little merit on the Web. If one wanted to avoid scrolling to see all the response options, separating the responses into separate columns – also called banking, which I will discuss shortly – is preferable. I have seen no experimental research on this, but I am comfortable asserting that this design makes it harder for respondents to find the correct field to select. In addition, the custom-designed square boxes may suggest that multiple responses are permissible, but in fact they behave like radio buttons, permitting only a single selection.

The placement of the input field to the left of the response options in a vertical format is ubiquitous in Web surveys, so much so that it could be considered a *de facto* standard. However, I've seen sufficient exceptions like those illustrated in Figure 4.27 that it is worth emphasizing the point. Furthermore, it is a common practice to align scales horizontally (see Section 4.4.1.2). Also, it is common to depart from the standard when the form of the input changes. For example, matrix questions (see Section 4.4.3) usually place the response options to the right of the items. Finally, boxes that require numeric entry are also often seen on the right, especially when a series of numbers are to be entered.

With some exceptions, the placement of input fields – whether radio buttons or check boxes – to the left of their labels is easiest to accomplish in HTML, has the fewest formatting problems, and appears to have no negative consequences for

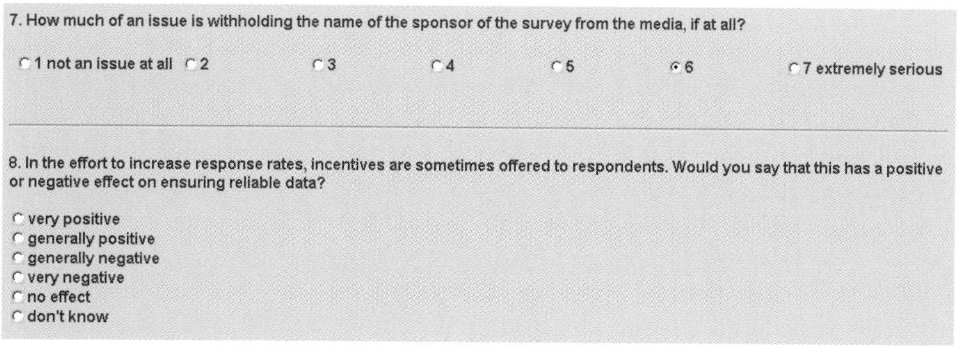

7. How much of an issue is withholding the name of the sponsor of the survey from the media, if at all?

◦ 1 not an issue at all ◦ 2	◦ 3	◦ 4	◦ 5	◦ 6	◦ 7 extremely serious

8. In the effort to increase response rates, incentives are sometimes offered to respondents. Would you say that this has a positive or negative effect on ensuring reliable data?

- ◦ very positive
- ◦ generally positive
- ◦ generally negative
- ◦ very negative
- ◦ no effect
- ◦ don't know

Figure 4.28 **Horizontal and Vertical Alignment.**

respondents. Decisions about departures from this design should be made with care. Whichever format is chosen, using the format consistently throughout the instrument will help respondents orient themselves to the task. Changes in the chosen layout should be made deliberately, for instance, when the goal is to signal a shift in the response task. Finally, the design should make the link between each input field and its associated label clear to the respondent.

4.4.1.2. Horizontal Versus Vertical Orientation

The growing convention with discrete choice (radio button) questions appears to be that, while most response options are aligned vertically on the screen, scales are aligned horizontally, as illustrated in Figure 4.28. Support for this convention comes from Jenkins and Dillman (1997, p. 179) who write, "Based on both the Gestalt Grouping Laws and the graphic language literature, one can make an argument for listing closed-ended answer categories vertically and scaling categories horizontally." They argue that grouping closed-ended categories vertically is a form of typographical cuing that should give respondents the correct impression that the categories are distinct entities. They continue, "On the other hand, grouping them horizontally might give the false impression that they are continuous, much the same way a sentence is a continuous thought that runs across the page horizontally. By the same token, the grouping of scaling answer categories vertically may give respondents the wrong impression that the categories are unassociated, when in fact they are continuous" (Jenkins and Dillman, 1997, p. 179).

Jenkins and Dillman cite a study by Gaskell, O'Muircheartaigh, and Wright (1994) in support of this view. Gaskell and colleagues' study manipulated the orientation of response scales on show cards in an interviewer-administered survey.

They found that the effect of response alternatives on answers were in turn affected by both the presence of priming questions and the orientation of the response scale but could not disentangle the main effect of orientation. Meadows, Greene, Foster, and Beer (2000) replicated the Gaskell et al. (1994) experiment in a self-administered survey and found no effect of vertical versus horizontal alignment on the distribution of responses.

We conducted an experiment on scale orientation in a Web survey (see Baker Couper, Conrad, and Tourangeau, 2004). In the context of exploring the separation of "don't know" responses from substantive scale values, we tested the horizontal versus vertical orientation of scales on both fully labeled and end-point-only labeled scales. We found no significant differences in the means or distributions of responses, nor did we find any differences in missing data rates or item completion times. At the same conference, Bayer and Thomas (2004) reported on an experiment with vertical and horizontal slider bars, and found that scale orientation had no effect on response distributions. Toepoel, Das, and van Soest (2006) found a slight shift to the right in the distributions of responses to vertically aligned scales relative to horizontally aligned ones, suggesting that the horizontal orientation may be less susceptible to primacy effects. However, consistent with other studies, they found no significant differences in mean scores.

Given the lack of strong evidence for one format over another, what should one do? This could be left to the designer's discretion, but as I shall discuss below (see Section 4.4.2), greater care must be taken when using a horizontal orientation for response options. For this reason, I lean toward the vertical orientation of response options, indented below the question text, and with the input fields to the left of the labels. Furthermore, one should be consistent in the use of a particular design approach. Look at the examples in Figure 4.29 and 4.30. These are both from the same survey. Not only does the orientation vary, but the notion of a scale is disturbed by the alignment of response options.

As I've already noted, once one has chosen a particular layout design, applying that design consistently throughout the survey should ease the respondent's task of survey completion. Conveying the sense of a scale continuum with careful and consistent design will help respondents make appropriate use of the scale points.

4.4.1.3. Columnar Format or Banking

Dillman popularized the term "banking" to refer to arranging response options in columns (see Dillman, 2000, p. 126). Banking is often used in paper questionnaires because of the value of real estate on the form. Response options are presented

4. Now we would like to ask about your attitudes regarding the environment.

Some people believe that pollution, population growth, resource depleteion, and other man-made problems have put us on the brink of an environmental crisis that will make it impossible for humans to continue to survive as we have in the past. Others believe that these fears are overstated and that we are not in a serious environmental crisis.

Using a scale where zero means that there is no real environmental threat to civilization, and ten means that human civilization is on the brink of collapse due to environmental threats, what do you think about the current environmental situation?

◌ 0 - **No real threat**	◌ 6
◌ 1	◌ 7
◌ 2	◌ 8
◌ 3	◌ 9
◌ 4	◌ 10 - **Brink of collapse**
◌ 5	

[Continue]   [End Survey]

Figure 4.29 **Vertical Scale Alignment over Two Columns.**

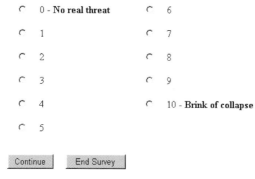

32. Below we list some of the arguments that are made against relying on residents' willingness to pay in donations or higher prices as a way to inform government decisions on issues like global climate change. Using a scale where 0 means "you **completely disagree** with the argument", and 10 means "you **completely agree** with it", please indicate your view of each argument:

a. Residents from poor households can afford to pay less, so their views have less weight than those from rich households.

completely disagree   ◌ 0 ◌ 1 ◌ 2 ◌ 3 ◌ 4

◌ 5 ◌ 6 ◌ 7 ◌ 8 ◌ 9 ◌ 10 **completely agree**

b. Government officials should rely on scientific expertise about global climate change, not on the preferences of ordinary residents.

completely disagree   ◌ 0 ◌ 1 ◌ 2 ◌ 3 ◌ 4

◌ 5 ◌ 6 ◌ 7 ◌ 8 ◌ 9 ◌ 10 **completely agree**

Figure 4.30 **Horizontal Scale Alignment over Two Rows.**

Gender		Age		Ethnic Background	
Male	○	Under 21	○	Caucasian	○
Female	○	21-30	○	African-American	○
		31-40	○	Asian	○
		41-50	○	American Indian	○
		51-60	○	Hispanic/Latin American	○
		Over 60	○	Other	○

Marital Status		Family Annual Income		Education	
Single	○	Under $20,000	○	Did not finish high school	○
Married	○	$20,000 to $40,000	○	Graduated high school	○
Divorced	○	$40,000 to $60,000	○	Graduated college	○
Other	○	$60,000 to $80,000	○	Graduate training	○
		Over $80,000	○		

Figure 4.31 **Example of Banking for Multiple Questions.**

in several columns to reduce the amount of vertical space used by a particular question. With space being costless on the Web, banking may be less necessary. However, there is still a trade-off between dividing a long list of response options into two or more columns so that all responses are visible on the screen, versus a single list that requires scrolling to see the later items. I'd assert here that horizontal scrolling should be avoided at all costs. Given this, the width of the columns may be more important than their length.

While banking is typically used for a single question with a number of response options, Figure 4.31 shows an example of banking for a set of different questions. In this case, there seems to be no benefit to arranging questions this way on the Web.

Christian (2003) tested several different versions of the same item in a Web survey completed by nearly 1,600 Washington State University students. Christian and Dillman (2004) conducted similar experiments on paper, with roughly equivalent results. An example of one of the questions from Christian (2003) is shown in Figure 4.32. While the addition of numbers did not change the distribution of responses (i.e., the two designs on the right of the figure did not differ significantly), the linear version differed significantly from the other versions. The mean rating of student life was significantly lower (2.16) in the linear version than in the triple horizontal (2.36), triple vertical (2.41), and triple vertical with numbers (2.36). In terms of individual responses, the biggest difference was for the "good" category, with 23% selecting that category in the horizontal version and

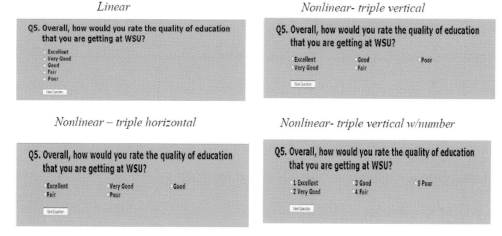

Figure 4.32 **Experimental Conditions from Christian (2003).**

33% in the vertical banked version. This suggests that respondents are reading horizontally rather than vertically. While the Gestalt grouping law of proximity may suggest that the two options in the first columns of the triple-banked version would be seen as belonging together, it appears that conventions of reading order led respondent to read the response options horizontally (from left to right) rather than vertically.

There are other examples where columnar presentation may affect the responses obtained, even in interviewer-administered surveys. In an early comparison of computer-assisted and paper-and-pencil telephone interviewing, Bergman, Kristiansson, Olofsson, and Säfström (1994) found significant differences by method in a question on attachment to the labor market. While the question wording was identical, the paper-and-pencil version grouped the response categories into two columns, the first indicating strong attachment, and the second weak attachment. In the computer-assisted (CATI) version, the response categories were placed in a single column. With external evidence suggesting that the paper-and-pencil version provided more reliable responses, the CATI version was changed to resemble the paper version, and the significant differences subsequently disappeared.

Given the effect that such banking may have on response distributions, there seems no reason to bank for questions with only a few response options, such as that in Figure 4.32. However, for longer lists, the trade-off may be one of grouping the items in several columns or providing a single long list that will necessitate scrolling. Of course, with questions such as this, the first thing one might want to

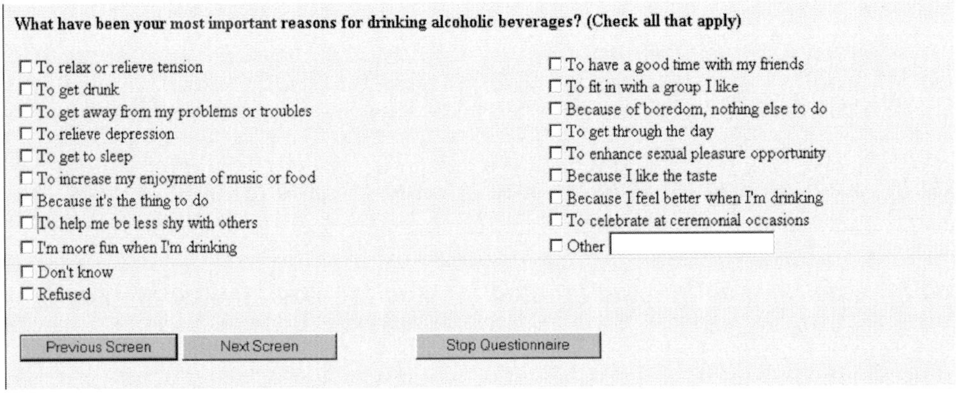

What have been your most important reasons for drinking alcoholic beverages? (Check all that apply)

☐ To relax or relieve tension
☐ To get drunk
☐ To get away from my problems or troubles
☐ To relieve depression
☐ To get to sleep
☐ To increase my enjoyment of music or food
☐ Because it's the thing to do
☐ To help me be less shy with others
☐ I'm more fun when I'm drinking
☐ Don't know
☐ Refused

☐ To have a good time with my friends
☐ To fit in with a group I like
☐ Because of boredom, nothing else to do
☐ To get through the day
☐ To enhance sexual pleasure opportunity
☐ Because I like the taste
☐ Because I feel better when I'm drinking
☐ To celebrate at ceremonial occasions
☐ Other [   ]

[Previous Screen] [Next Screen]   [Stop Questionnaire]

Figure 4.33 **Responses in Two Columns.**

ask is whether a list of responses of that length is necessary. The first – and often the best – thing to consider is whether the question might be split into two or more parts.

In Chapter 2, we saw an example of the use of check boxes, with the choices arranged in two columns. That was actually part of an experiment Baker and I conducted in a 1999 survey of University of Michigan students (for background on the survey, see McCabe et al., 2002). That version is reproduced here in Figure 4.33, along with the single-column version in Figure 4.34.

While we did not randomize the order of the responses, we interleaved them so that we could detect effects of presentation in one versus two columns. The literature on response order effects suggests we should get more items endorsed at the top of the list in the single column version – this is the classic "primacy effect" (see Krosnick and Alwin, 1987; Tourangeau, Rips, and Rasinski, 2000). For the two-column version, we expected fewer items to be endorsed in the right column, for two reasons: (1) regular reading order is column-by-column where there is sufficient visual separation, meaning that these are the last items to be read and (2) the spatial separation of the second column from the first may result in some respondents not even noticing that column. This is indeed what we found. With about 1,300 respondents in each group, we found that significantly more items were endorsed in the top half of the single-column version and in the left column of the two-column version. To examine a specific example, the item "To increase enjoyment of music or food" appears on the left in Figure 4.33 and in the lower half of Figure 4.34. This item was endorsed by 25.5% of respondents in the two-column version and 15.8% in the one-column version.

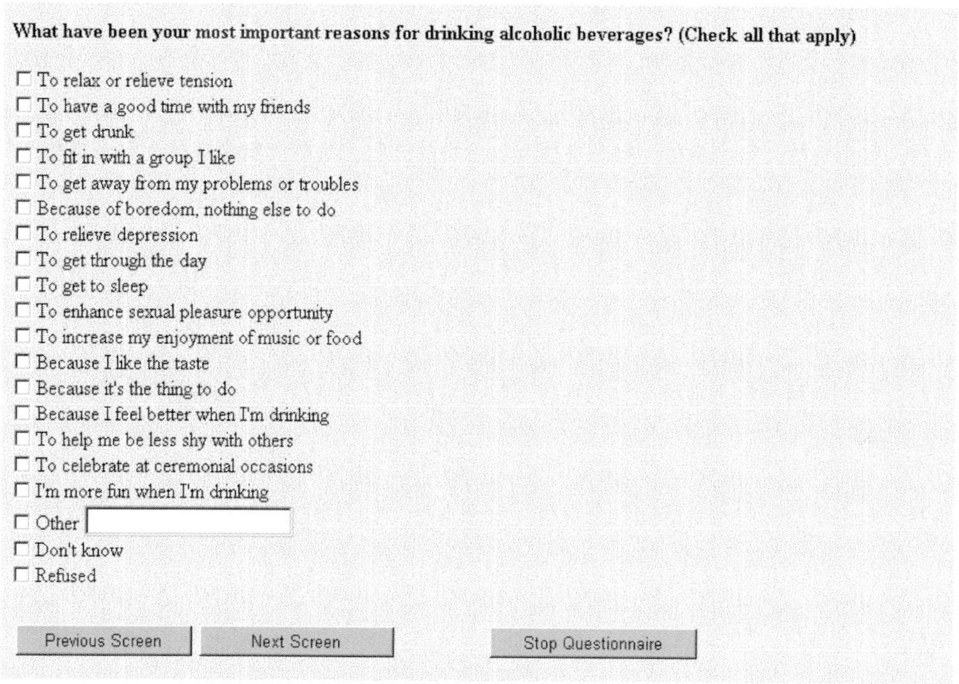

Figure 4.34 **Response Options in One Column.**

The grouping of items into separate columns may facilitate the completion task if the grouping makes conceptual sense. The example in Figure 4.35 is from the 2005 National Census Test (see Bentley and Tancreto, 2006). Here the response options are grouped into two columns, one for related individuals and the other for unrelated individual. Usability testing of this instrument (see Murphy and Ciochetto, 2006) suggested that while several respondents missed the "Related" and "Not related" heading in the dark blue header, they recognized that the two columns were conceptually different.

One should be careful that the grouping and related headings do not convey unintended information to the respondents. In a series of experiments on this issue, Smyth and colleagues (2004) explored the effect of different arrangements of response options on the choice of responses. In one version, breaking a list of six items into two groups by the addition of headings, increased the number of response chosen but largely because respondents were more likely to select one or more answers from each group (70% with headings versus 41% without). In a

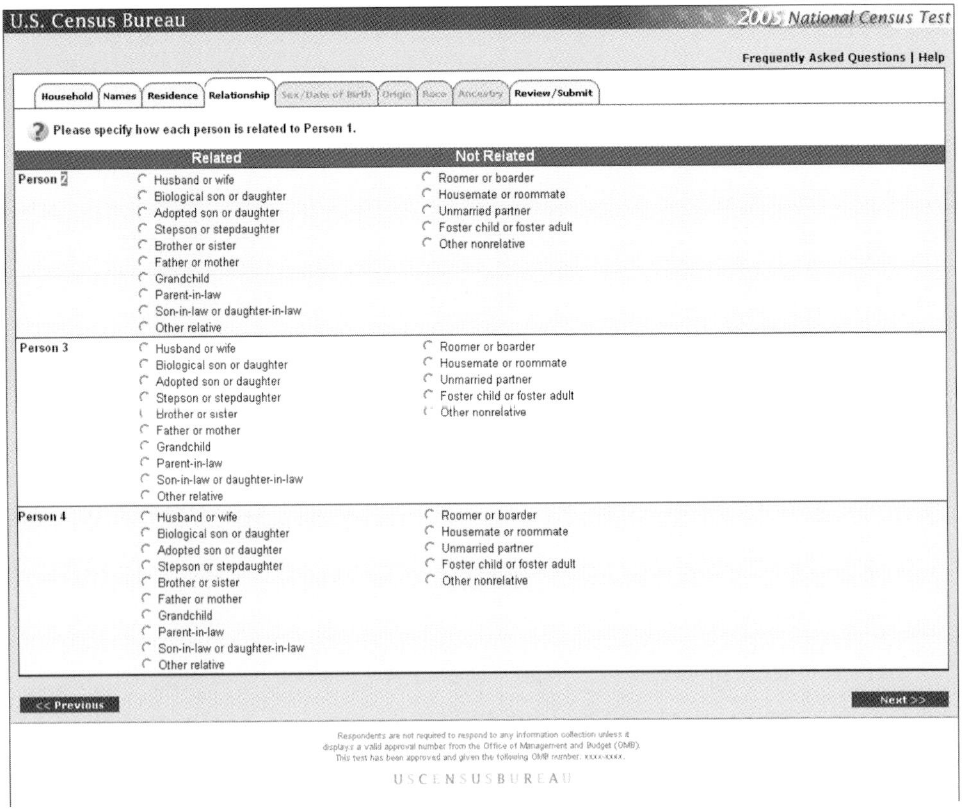

Figure 4.35 **Grouping of Items into Columns.**

second experiment, they found that the addition of headings made no difference to the selection of a set of responses organized in two columns (double-banked). Respondents were equally likely to endorse items in both columns when headers were present or absent. One possible explanation is that the set of items, on sources of financial support for students, listed financial aid in the first column and other sources (including parents and employment) in the second; more options in the second column were chosen than in the first. This suggests that putting the more common items in the second column may have helped to counteract the effect of banking.

A final consideration with columnar presentation of response options is to ensure that the input fields are clearly associated with the relevant labels. Take

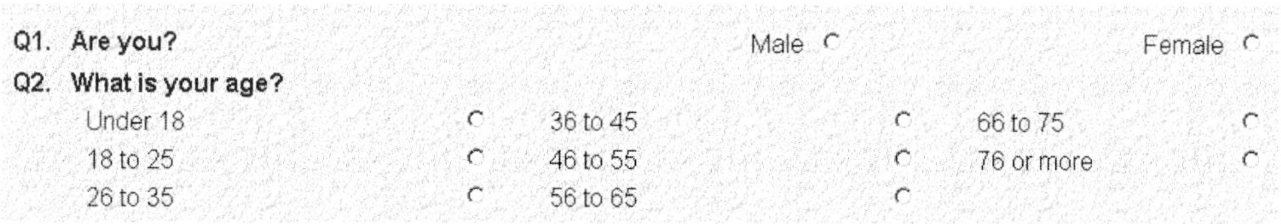

Q1.	Are you?			Male ○			Female ○
Q2.	What is your age?						
	Under 18	○	36 to 45		○	66 to 75	○
	18 to 25	○	46 to 55		○	76 or more	○
	26 to 35	○	56 to 65		○		

Figure 4.36 **Problems with Alignment of Radio Buttons and Labels.**

a look at the example in Figure 4.36. Not only do the widely spaced columns increase the likelihood of horizontal scrolling for those with small browser panes, but the link between the radio buttons and the corresponding labels is not clear. Applying Gestalt grouping principles would help here.

All the examples shown in this section make use of the table function in HTML to achieve the columnar presentation of questions or items, which bring us to the next topic.

4.4.2. Use of HTML Tables

Several times already in this chapter I've alluded to the need for tables to control layout in HTML.[5] In this section, I address this topic more explicitly. HTML tables are powerful design tools. However, we need to understand how tables – and particularly the default settings – work if we want to use them effectively. Tables can be used both for single-item layout (as I'll address here), and for multiple-item grids or matrixes (see Section 4.4.3). They are particularly useful for controlling alignment.

In the example in Figure 4.37, the structure of the HTML table is visible. Each of these questions is a table with one row and ten columns. In the first question (Q23) the labels are left justified within the cell, while in the second (Q24), they are right justified. While the tables are used to create a horizontal layout for the responses, the table lines make it hard to link the input fields (radio buttons) with their respective labels (response options). Tables are used to control layout in many of the other designs already shown (such as Figures 4.21 and 4.36).

---

[5] Increasingly, cascading style sheets (CSS) are being used to control layout; however, many of the same issues remain applicable.

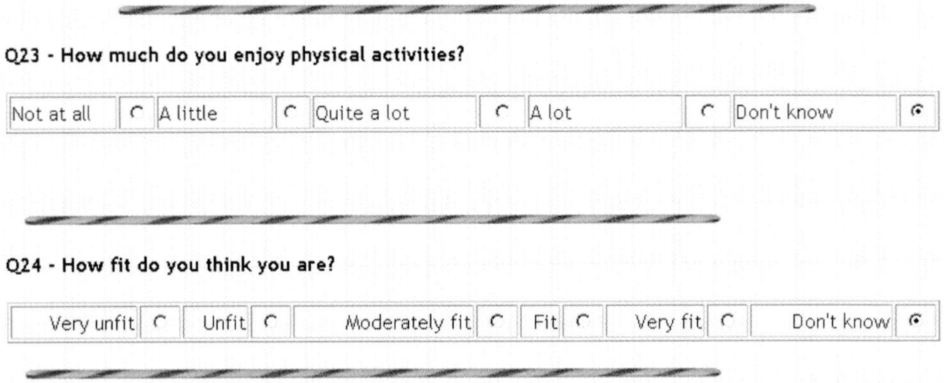

Q23 - How much do you enjoy physical activities?

| Not at all | ○ | A little | ○ | Quite a lot | ○ | A lot | ○ | Don't know | ● |

Q24 - How fit do you think you are?

| Very unfit | ○ | Unfit | ○ | Moderately fit | ○ | Fit | ○ | Very fit | ○ | Don't know | ● |

Figure 4.37 **Use of Tables with Visible Lines.**

When using tables (and we'll return to this when discussing grids), avoid overuse of the lines. Use lines (table and cell borders) judiciously to provide visual guidance to the respondent. In the previous example (as in several other examples we've already seen), the lines serve to break the link between label and corresponding input field, rather than making the association stronger. Putting the label in the same cell of the table as the radio button would solve this problem. Doing so has another advantage too – it makes it easier for people using screen readers because of vision problems (Coon, 2002).

There's a lot that can be done with tables to control layout in HTML. The example in Figure 4.38 makes use of a table even though this is not readily apparent. The table has three columns. The left column is divided into three rows, with the top and bottom rows containing the two end-point descriptions, using left-justified text. The middle column contains the radio buttons (center justified), and the background color of the cell is set to white to make the scale more visible. Finally, the right column contains the numbers and labels for the response options, again left justified. This shows that within table cells, background color, justification, and other font features can easily be varied.

The problem is that table lines are mostly an all-or-nothing affair. Figure 4.37 has tables lines "on" while Figure 4.38 has them off (the border is set to zero width). Figure 4.39 shows an example of a series of tables with different specifications of the `border` function in HTML. With `border=0` as in the first instance, no lines appear. In the subsequent examples, the width of the lines is increased to 1 and 3, respectively.

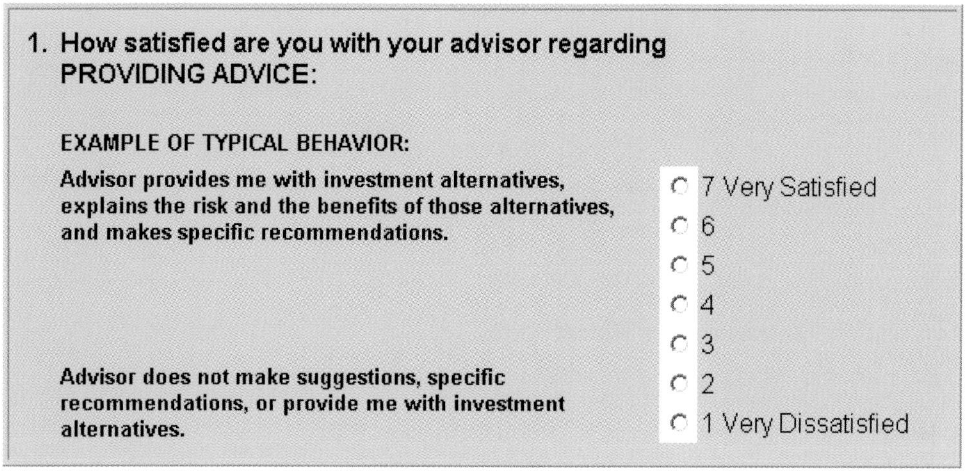

Figure 4.38 **Use of Tables to Control Layout.**

In HTML, one cannot set the borders of individual cells in the table, but this can be accomplished in two ways. One way, although not very efficient, is to embed tables within other tables and vary the border setting for each. Another way to control cell borders directly is with CSS, which gives one more control over layout settings than is possible with HTML tables. The drawback here is that not many survey software packages currently give the designer direct control over style sheets, so these must often be handcrafted. I'm sure this will change in the near future, and we will start to see more tables that look like those in Figure 4.40, or with even fewer lines.

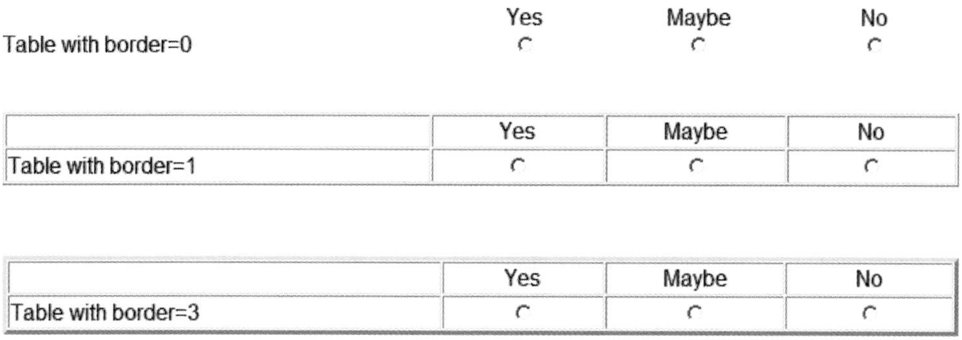

Figure 4.39 **Specification of Table Borders in HTML.**

How familiar are you with the following companies?

(Select one answer in each row.)

	Not at all familiar	Have only heard the name	Somewhat familiar	Very familiar	Not Sure
MasterCard International Incorporated	○	○	○	○	○
Visa International Incorporated	○	○	○	○	○
American Express Company	○	○	○	○	○

Figure 4.40 **Table with Customized Lines.**

4.4.3. Grids or Matrlxes

Thus far, we've talked about the use of HTML tables to control the horizontal spacing of response options and input for single questions. Now we turn to a discussion of matrix or grid questions. By these I mean a series of items where the rows are typically a set of items and the columns are usually the response options, with the respondent selecting one or more responses in each row. A prototypical grid question is shown in Figure 4.41.

Several Web survey researchers and practitioners have argued against the use of grids. In one of the first observational studies of Web response behavior, Jeavons (1998) observed that breakoffs were more likely on screens containing grids than

Frequently Asked Questions
Email us at life@msisurvey.com
Call toll free 1.866.674.3375

The next few questions ask about the style or manner you use when carrying out different mental tasks. Your answers to the questions should reflect the manner in which you TYPICALLY engage in each of the tasks mentioned. There are no right or wrong answers, we only ask that you provide honest and accurate answers.

	Strongly disagree	Moderately disagree	Neither agree nor disagree	Moderately agree	Strongly agree
I enjoy work that requires the use of words.	○	○	○	○	○
When listening to someone describing their experiences, I try to mentally picture what was happening.	○	○	○	○	○
I do a lot of reading.	○	○	○	○	○
I find it helps to think in terms of mental pictures when doing many things.	○	○	○	○	○
I enjoy learning new words.	○	○	○	○	○

Next Screen   Previous Screen

Figure 4.41 **Prototypical Grid Question with Shading of Rows.**

on other types of screens. This observation led several others to conclude that grids were a bad idea, and their use should be avoided. For example, both Poynter (2001) and Wojtowicz (2001) recommended that grids should be avoided. Dillman (2000, pp. 102–105) says one should minimize the use of matrices, arguing that they are difficult to comprehend, and "result in a loss of control over the basic navigational path." Similarly, Gräf (2002) argued that matrix questions in tabular forms should be avoided since respondents might possibly choose those answers that are easiest to reach with the mouse, rather than those that express their real opinions.[6]

Despite these cautions in the literature, in practice, grids are a widely used tool in Web surveys. I first review the research evidence on the benefits and drawback of grids before turning to issues of how to design grids, given their use.

4.4.3.1. Research on Grids

Given the strong views that are held about grids, research on the topic is surprisingly light. In an early experiment on grids, Couper, Traugott, and Lamias (2001) examined a five-item knowledge measure (with the items in a grid on a single page or on five separate pages) and an eleven-item attitude measure (with the items grouped on three pages with four, four, and three items, respectively, to avoid scrolling, or on eleven different pages). We found that the correlations were consistently higher among items appearing together on a page than items separated across several pages; however, the overall effect was not large, and none of the differences between each pair of correlations reached statistical significance. Factor analyses of the set of attitude items produced similar factor structures across the two versions. Thus, the grouping of items in grids appeared to have only a marginal effect on the responses.

We did find significantly lower rates of missing data (including use of a "don't know" response) in the grid versions. We also found that the grid version took significantly less time to complete. The five knowledge items took an average of 54.2 seconds when in a grid versus 65.9 second when presented on separate pages. Similarly, the attitude items took 113.6 seconds when in three separate grids versus 128.1 seconds when on eleven separate pages. This suggests that grids may increase efficiency without reducing data quality.

---

[6]   In a later paper, Gräf (2005) offers a more balanced view of grids, discussing both the advantages and disadvantages of their use.

Toepoel, Das, and van Soest (2005) compared four different versions of a forty-item scale with five agree-disagree response options, ranging from one item per page to all forty on one page. As with our study, they found modest increases in interitem correlations among items placed together on a page. However, they also found higher missing data rates with more items per page. Completion times increased with increasing number of items on the page, but were slowest for the forty-item per page version, probably because of the need to scroll to see the column labels. Subjective ratings favored the versions with four or ten items per page, with the forty-item and one-item versions least favored. Their results point to the danger of putting too many items in a grid.

In another of our experiments on grids, Tourangeau, Couper, and Conrad (2004) compared eight agree-disagree items (measured on a seven-point scale) about diet and eating habits, presented either on a single page, on two pages (four items and four items) or on eight separate pages. The interitem correlations replicated the earlier findings, with higher correlations among those items presented together. For example, when the items appeared in two grids of four items each, the median correlation for items in the same grid was 0.382, but the median correlations was only 0.351 for items in different grids.

While these results suggest that respondents view the items in a grid as belonging together – the "near means related heuristic" of Tourangeau, Couper, and Conrad (2004) – it does not mean the responses are necessarily more valid. One concern with grids is that of nondifferentiation (Krosnick, 1991), in which respondents give the same answer to all items. Respondents who got the items on a single page showed less differentiation than those who got them on two screens or on eight. In addition, for two of the items that were reverse-worded, respondents were less likely to notice the reverse wording when the items appeared in a single grid. Finally, respondents took significantly less time to complete the items when they were on one page (an average of 60.4 seconds) than when they were on two pages (65.4 seconds) or on eight pages (99.0 seconds). These results suggest that respondents use proximity of the items as a cue to their meaning, perhaps at the expense of reading each item carefully. Thus, the increased correlations could be a result of increased nondifferentiation and the increased speed could be an indicator of reduced attention. This view is supported by additional analyses carried out by Peytchev (2005, 2006) on these and other grid experiments we have conducted. Using structural equation modeling, Peytchev argues that while the correlations may increase, measurement error does too, when evaluating the prediction of a criterion measure using these items.

An alternative to the extremes of one item per page or grids is of course to present the items in sequence on the page but not in the form of a grid. Bell, Mangione, and Kahn (2001), tested an item-by-item (the "expanded" format) versus a grid version (the "matrix" format) of the SF-36 health questionnaire. They reported mean response times of 5.22 minutes for the expanded version and 5.07 minutes for the matrix version, but the difference was not significant. In addition, the Cronbach's alpha scores, based on item-total correlations, did not differ significantly by version. They conclude, "The expanded format was twice as long vertically, but did not distract users significantly as they considered and answered each question" (Bell, Mangione, and Kahn, 2001, p. 619).

Iglesias, Birks, and Torgerson (2001) conducted a similar experiment in a paper instrument (using the SF-12 short form health survey), among a sample of older persons. They report that Cronbach's alpha reliability scores were slightly higher for the item-by-item approach (0.94 versus 0.90 for physical health, and 0.91 versus 0.88 for mental health), while the item missing data rate was significantly lower for the item by item version than for the grid.

Yan (2005a, 2005b) reports the results of a comparison of three different versions of a set of six items:

- Each item on a separate page
- Item-by-item on the same page (Bell, Mangione, and Kahn's "expanded" version)
- All items together in a grid

She found that the highest interitem correlations were obtained in the grid condition, followed by the same page condition then the separate page condition. But in a follow-up question, she asked respondents how related they thought the items were and found no differences across the three conditions. She also found no significant differences in nondifferentiation by layout.

Aside from these comparisons of grids to other formats, I know of few studies on the *design* of grid or matrix questions, given their use. In one exception, Galesic, Tourangeau, Couper, and Conrad (2007) experimented with dynamic shading of grids as respondents completed items. We found that dynamic shading significantly reduced item missing data, relative to a version with no such feedback, and slightly (but not significantly) reduced breakoffs on the three grids tested. Much research remains to be done on how best to design grids, given their popularity in Web surveys. In the absence of such research, I offer my own opinions on effective grid design.

4.4.3.2. The Design of Grids

There are a number of strong voices against the inclusion of grid questions in Web surveys. I'm not convinced that grids are inherently bad. Consistent with the theme of this book, I believe it may depend much more on how grids are designed. I have seen many egregious examples of grid design, and believe that poor design – rather than the use of grids *per se* – may be the source of the negative findings. Thus, the jury is still out, and much more work is needed on this issue.

Grids require careful design. If designed correctly, they can facilitate the task of survey completion. If poorly designed, they can confuse or even overwhelm respondents, leading to satisficing behaviors such as nondifferentiation, item missing data, and even breakoffs. More than any other design feature, the careful design of matrix questions is critical. There are several design issues to consider in using grids. These include:

- Should grids be arranged horizontally (with items forming the rows and response options the columns) or vertically (with items forming the columns and response options the rows)?
- Should the response options follow or precede the items?
- What is the optimal or maximal number of rows (items)?
- What is the optimal or maximal number of columns (response options)?
- Should response options (column headings) be kept visible at all times?
- Should more than one response be allowed per item?
- Should the table size be fixed or vary with browser size?
- Should the column widths be equal or unequal?
- Should table lines, shading, and other visual cues be used?

Many of these issues are related; for example, the greater the number of items in the grid, the greater the need for visual cues. Similarly, the more response options there are, the bigger the concern about horizontal scrolling, fixed versus flexible table size, and the spacing of columns. We'll see several examples in this section as we work through this list, some of which exhibit multiple design problems.

In terms of orientation of items versus response options, the prototypical grid design arranges the items in row, and the response options in columns (as show in Figure 4.41). We tested a set of inversed grids in one study (see Galesic et al., 2007) and found that arranging the items in columns and response options in rows significantly increased completion times and missing data rates relative to the standard approach. While I know of no other research on this issue, the default

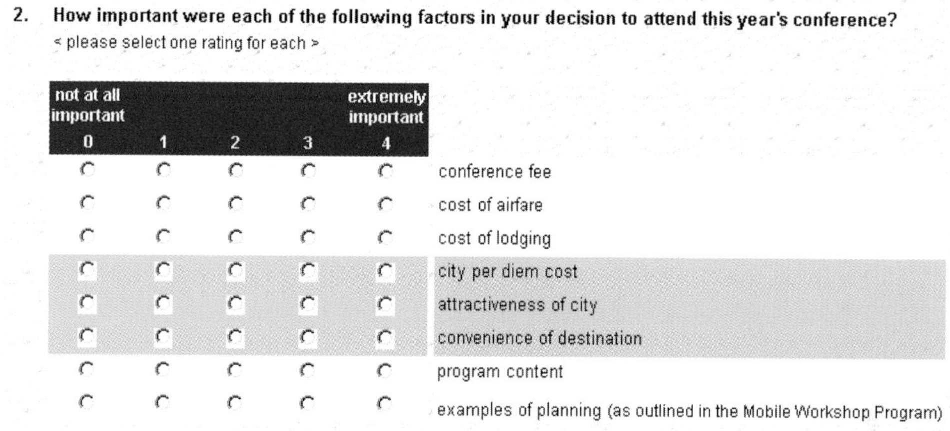

2. **How important were each of the following factors in your decision to attend this year's conference?**
< please select one rating for each >

not at all important				extremely important	
0	1	2	3	4	
○	○	○	○	○	conference fee
○	○	○	○	○	cost of airfare
○	○	○	○	○	cost of lodging
○	○	○	○	○	city per diem cost
○	○	○	○	○	attractiveness of city
○	○	○	○	○	convenience of destination
○	○	○	○	○	program content
○	○	○	○	○	examples of planning (as outlined in the Mobile Workshop Program)

Figure 4.42 **Response Options Preceding Items.**

orientation is well-enough entrenched that it may be risky to present items in columns, even though it may be tempting to do so if there are only a few items but many response options. If one chooses to break with convention, it becomes even more important to use visual and verbal cues to orient the respondent to the task, for example, to pick one response per column.

The second issue is whether response options should follow or precede the items. Again, the convention here is quite strong, with most designers presenting the items first followed by the response options. But take a look at Figure 4.42. Even though I argued in Section 4.4.1.2 that such a format was desirable for vertically oriented response options in a single question, it makes less sense when the items are in a grid. Note also the shading of the middle three items in the grid. Without the shading, respondents may have trouble figuring out which row of radio buttons belongs to which item. This alternate shading is a commonly employed strategy in grid design to help orient respondents, as seen in several other examples.

Turning to the issue of how many rows or columns should there be in a grid, one needs to think in both dimensions, that is, both horizontally and vertically. In general, vertical scrolling is a common occurrence on the Web, while horizontal scrolling is abhorred by Web designers. As Nielsen notes in his Alertbox of July 11, 2005 (http://www.useit.com/alertbox/20050711.html), "users hate horizontal scrolling," while they expect vertical scrolling. Requiring a respondent to scroll in both directions to see the full table is viewed as very poor design. In the example in Figure 4.43, the red box indicates approximately how much of the grid

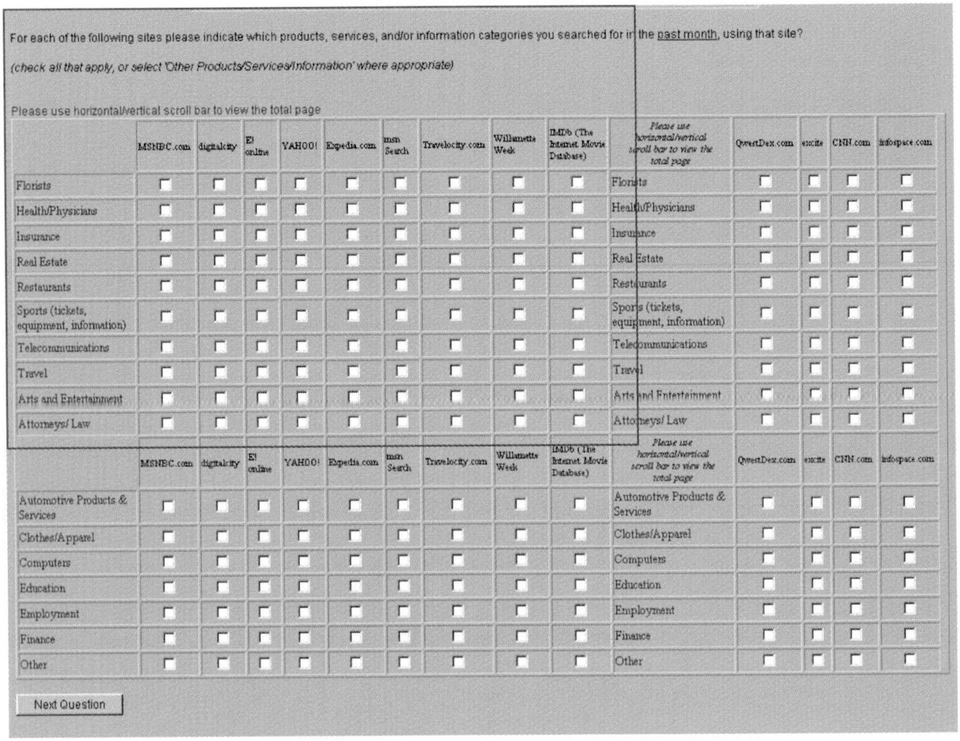

Figure 4.43 **Horizontal and Vertical Scrolling in Grid.**

would be seen if viewed on a 600 × 400 monitor. Thankfully, I've seen very few of these kinds of egregious designs in recent years. My guess is that designers got the message quickly when pages like this produced high rates of abandonment or missing data. But survey designers still try to squeeze too much into grids.

Even though we can probably all agree that the design in Figure 4.43 is not good, it still doesn't answer the question of how many rows or columns to include in a grid. This should be answered indirectly – there is no fixed maximum number of items or response options. The answer depends on the length of each item or label, and the complexity of the task. While it is important to avoid horizontal scrolling, doing so by squeezing too much onto the page is also not a good idea. For a long list of items, it may make sense to break the list into separate pages, but a modicum of vertical scrolling is generally not a problem. The important thing, as I discuss shortly, is to make sure that the grid scales well across different screen and browser dimensions.

39.	Making announcements on the website	(	(	(	(	(	(
40.	Seeing what's happened recently on the website	c	c	c	c	c	c
41.	Getting email when something new has been posted on the website	c	c	c	c	c	c
42.	Seeing a schedule of tasks and/or deadlines for a project	c	c	c	c	c	c
43.	Assigning tasks and tracking completion	c	c	c	c	c	c
44.	Allowing colleagues outside of the University of Michigan access to the website	c	c	c	c	c	c
45.	Taking a vote or a poll of colleagues online	c	c	c	c	c	c
46.	Saving bookmarks for other websites	c	c	c	c	c	c
47.	Giving presentations through the website	c	c	c	c	c	c
48.	Sharing your computer display with someone so you can both see and manipulate it	c	c	c	c	c	c
49.	Sharing a "whiteboard" with someone so you both can see, draw, and type on it	c	c	c	c	c	c
50.	Posting and playing digital audio and video	c	c	c	c	c	c
51.	Videoconferencing to participate in a meeting or observe an experiment	c	c	c	c	c	c
52.	Accessing an audio or video recording of a meeting or other session	c	c	c	c	c	c
53.	Hosting a database online that you can share with others	c	c	c	c	c	c
54.	Version control of documents for working drafts	c	c	c	c	c	c

Figure 4.44 **Part of a Long Scrolling Grid.**

The longer the list of items, the more important it is to ensure that the column headings remain visible to respondents. Figure 4.44 shows an example of a very long series of items, each measured on a six-point scale. Without the labels, the respondent is forced to remember the direction of the scale: low to high, or high to low. Some designers have used HTML frames to keep the labels visible, but frames are generally frowned on by the Web design community (e.g., Horton 2006, Chapter 7; Nielsen, 2000). Another solution is to repeat the headings, as done in Figure 4.43.

Whether more than one response should be allowed per item can be viewed in two ways. First, some grids involve check-all-that-apply responses (see Figure 4.45). Rather than processing each item (row) in turn using a scale that applies to all rows, the respondent must process each cell individually. This makes the task much more onerous (the example in Figure 4.43 has similar characteristics). The example in Figure 4.45 is part of a larger grid, containing about twice as many items as shown. Not only does the respondent have to process each row and column, but the headings are not repeated for the latter half of the list, forcing the

1. Below is a list of financial websites. We are interested in how familiar you are with each site. Please check the appropriate columns for each website. (Select as many as apply in each column.)

	I am **not aware** of this website.	I am **aware** of this website.	I have **seen online advertising** for this website.	I have **seen or heard traditional advertising** (e.g., newspaper, magazine, television, radio, other) for this website.	I have **visited** this website.	I have **recommended** this website to someone else.
QuoteStream.com	☐	☐	☐	☐	☐	☐
AmericanExpress.com	☐	☐	☐	☐	☐	☐
CNN.com	☐	☐	☐	☐	☐	☐
AmeriTrade.com	☐	☐	☐	☐	☐	☐
NYTimes.com	☐	☐	☐	☐	☐	☐
FoxNews.com	☐	☐	☐	☐	☐	☐
TheStreet.com	☐	☐	☐	☐	☐	☐
CapitalOne.com	☐	☐	☐	☐	☐	☐
ABCNews.com	☐	☐	☐	☐	☐	☐
CBS.MarketWatch.com	☐	☐	☐	☐	☐	☐
Citibank.com	☐	☐	☐	☐	☐	☐
CNBC.com	☐	☐	☐	☐	☐	☐
Bloomberg.com	☐	☐	☐	☐	☐	☐

Figure 4.45 **Long Scrolling Grid with Multiple Responses per Item.**

respondent to remember the column headings or scroll back and forth to see them (see also Figure 4.44). But, whereas in Figure 4.44, the respondent may remember the direction of the scale, trying to keep track of each column label in Figure 4.45 is a much harder task.

Second, a related problem is trying to do two or more tasks in the same grid. Look at the example in Figure 4.46 (and also Figure 4.56 later in this chapter). An obvious solution in this case would be to ask the importance question first, followed by the satisfaction items. A general solution to many Web survey design

2. In the table below, please rate the overall importance of each issue and your satisfaction with AMD's performance overall on that issue.

	Importance						Satisfaction					
	Very Important	Important	Neutral	Unimportant	Very Unimportant	N/A	Excellent	Very Good	Good	Fair	Poor	N/A
Products overall (features, effectiveness, quality)	○	○	○	○	○	○	○	○	○	○	○	○
Ease of doing business overall	○	○	○	○	○	○	○	○	○	○	○	○
Sales overall (quality and effectiveness)	○	○	○	○	○	○	○	○	○	○	○	○
Support overall (quality and effectiveness)	○	○	○	○	○	○	○	○	○	○	○	○
Pricing of products and services overall	○	○	○	○	○	○	○	○	○	○	○	○

Figure 4.46 **Two Tasks in One Grid.**

flaws, especially those involving grids, is to find ways to break the task into separate components. In my view, both of these types of designs – those illustrated in Figures 4.45 and 4.46 – are asking the respondent to do too much. It is designs like these that give grids a bad reputation.

The next issue to address relates to fixed versus variable grid dimensions. One of the design choices one has in HTML is whether to fix the table dimensions by allocating a fixed number of pixels to each column, or whether to allow the columns to vary in width according to the width of the browser window. This is achieved by defining the column width as a percent of the table width or of the browser width. The advantage of the former approach is that the grid is identical in appearance for all respondents,[7] no matter how wide their browser is set or what their screen dimension are. Of course, this may necessitate horizontal scrolling if the table dimensions exceed those of the browser. The variable approach adjusts to the browser width, wrapping the text in the columns of necessary to keep all columns visible within the browser pane. This adjustment is done automatically. Depending on the complexity of the table, this may take marginal additional time to recalculate and recalibrate the table. However, for most users this calibration time is hardly noticeable.

I return to the issue of screen size in Section 4.5, but for now, I'll focus on the design of fixed versus flexible tables. Figures 4.47 and 4.48 show examples of these two different approaches. There are three versions of the same HTML table in Figure 4.47. The first shows a table defined with fixed dimensions. The HTML code to do this is as follows:

```
<table border="1" width="800">
```

This specifies a table with a width of 800 pixels. Each of the columns is then similarly defined, with 300 pixels allocated to the first column, and 100 to each of the remaining columns. The second table in Figure 4.47 is a variable-width or relative-size table. Here the width of the table is defined as a percentage of the browser width, as follows:

```
<table border="1" width="90%">
```

The table is left aligned, and takes up 90% of the browser width. It could also be centered. In this second table, the width of the columns was not specified. As

---

[7] If respondents change the font size, the appearance of the grid will change. Further control could be achieved by specifying a fixed font size, but I've already argued that this is not a good idea.

Table with size defined in pixels (fixed)

	Strongly agree	Agree	Neither agree nor disagree	Disagree	Strongly disagree
1. This course is the best I have ever taken	○	○	○	○	○
2. This course is the worst I have ever taken	○	○	○	○	○

Table with size defined in percent (relative)

	Strongly agree	Agree	Neither agree nor disagree	Disagree	Strongly disagree
1. This course is the best I have ever taken	○	○	○	○	○
2. This course is the worst I have ever taken	○	○	○	○	○

Table with size defined in percent (relative): maintain column width

	Strongly agree	Agree	Neither agree nor disagree	Disagree	Strongly disagree
1. This course is the best I have ever taken	○	○	○	○	○
2. This course is the worst I have ever taken	○	○		○	○

Figure 4.47 **Fixed and Flexible Tables: Before.**

can be seen, the width is then derived from the amount of text in the column. In other words, the "neither agree nor disagree" column is wider than the "agree" column (I address this issue below). The final table in Figure 4.47 differs from the second in two respects. First, the width of the table is set to 100% of the browser width. Second, instead of deriving the width of columns from their content (the default in HTML), the width of the columns is specified, but still in relative terms. In other words, 25% of the table width is allocated to the first column, and 15% to each of the remaining columns.

In Figure 4.48 we see what happens to these three tables when the width of the browser is reduced. In the case of the fixed-width table, the rightmost response option is no longer visible, and the respondent needs to scroll horizontally to see it. On the other hand, the two flexible designs adjust to the width of the browser, keeping the same relationship between the column widths. In other words, all columns are reduced proportionately to fit within the browser, with the text wrapping as necessary to do so.

The argument in favor of fixing the table dimensions is that for those with very large (i.e., wide) screens and browsers maximized, the columns won't be excessively stretched out across the full width of the screen, making it harder to read the question text (see Section 4.2.3) and to align each item with the corresponding input fields. On the other hand, fixing the table width may cause problems for those with smaller screens, necessitating horizontal scrolling or even missing the

Table with size defined in pixels (fixed)

	Strongly agree	Agree	Neither agree nor disagree	Disagree	Strongl disagre
1. This course is the best I have ever taken	○	○	○	○	○
2. This course is the worst I have ever taken	○	○	○	○	○

Table with size defined in percent (relative)

	Strongly agree	Agree	Neither agree nor disagree	Disagree	Strongly disagree
1. This course is the best I have ever taken	○	○	○	○	○
2. This course is the worst I have ever taken	○	○	○	○	○

Table with size defined in percent (relative): maintain column width

	Strongly agree	Agree	Neither agree nor disagree	Disagree	Strongly disagree
1. This course is the best I have ever taken	○	○	○	○	○
2. This course is the worst I have ever taken	○	○		○	○

Figure 4.48 **Fixed and Flexible Tables: After.**

response options on the right of the grid. In my view, the latter concern is more important than the former, as those with wide screens can – and often do – set their browser width to be less than that of the full screen, whereas this recourse is not available to those with smaller screens. Put another way, it's impossible to make the browser any bigger than the screen, but it is certainly possible to make it smaller.

The next issue relates to the spacing of response options. This is not confined to grids, but applies to any horizontally aligned set of responses (see Section 4.4.1.2). Typically, HTML tables are used to control the layout of questions in such cases (see Section 4.4.2). As we have seen above, the default in HTML is to allocate space to columns according to the amount of text in that column, resulting in the uneven spacing of columns in the second table in Figure 4.48. Does this matter?

Our research suggests that it does. In our first experiment on the issue, we varied the spacing of a 9-point scale in a survey of University of Michigan students

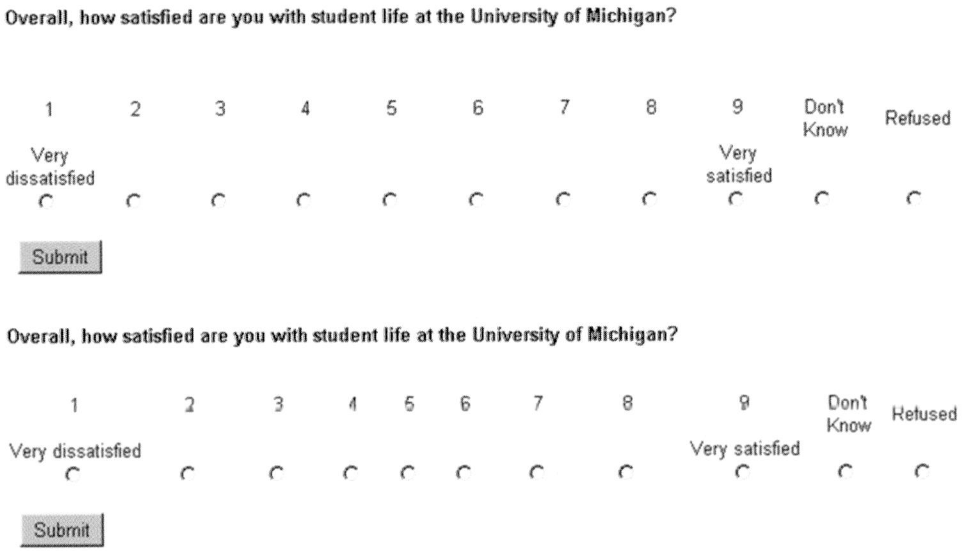

Overall, how satisfied are you with student life at the University of Michigan?

1	2	3	4	5	6	7	8	9	Don't Know	Refused
Very dissatisfied								Very satisfied		
○	○	○	○	○	○	○	○	○	○	○

Submit

Overall, how satisfied are you with student life at the University of Michigan?

1	2	3	4	5	6	7	8	9	Don't Know	Refused
Very dissatisfied								Very satisfied		
○	○	○	○ ○ ○			○	○	○	○	○

Submit

Figure 4.49 **Spacing of Response Options I.**

(McCabe et al., 2002). Three versions were compared. In the first, all response options were evenly spaced; in the second, the end points were further apart but the remaining options were equally spaced; and in the third, the spacing between the options increased incrementally from the midpoint. The first and third versions are illustrated in Figure 4.49. We found that increasing the size of the end points significantly increased the likelihood of their selection. That is, respondents were pulled to both extremes when they were made more visually prominent relative to the other options.

In a second study, we employed a different spacing manipulation to explore the "middle means typical" heuristic (Tourangeau, Couper, and Conrad, 2004). This argues that respondents tend to anchor and adjust their responses relative to the midpoint of the scale, and changing the visual midpoint may affect this process. The two versions we tested are shown in Figure 4.50. In the first, the conceptual midpoint ("even chance") appears in the middle of the scale (the visual midpoint). In the second version, the width of the response options increases from left to right, shifting the conceptual midpoint to the left of the visual midpoint. We found a significantly higher mean score to the second scale than the first in Figure 4.50, reflecting this shift. Furthermore, 58.3% of respondents chose an option to the right of the midpoint in the first version, while 63.4% did so in the second.

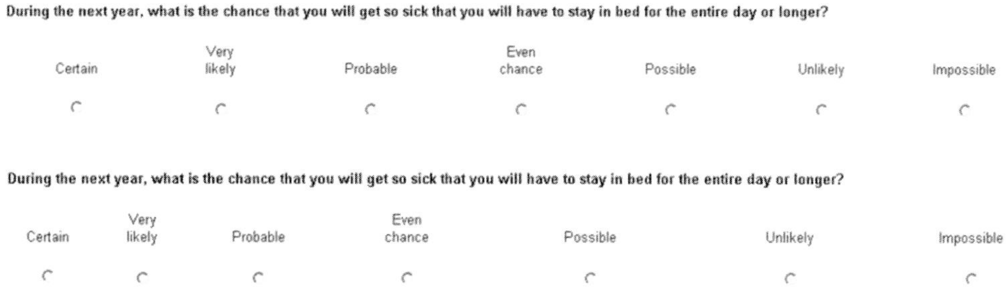

During the next year, what is the chance that you will get so sick that you will have to stay in bed for the entire day or longer?

Certain	Very likely	Probable	Even chance	Possible	Unlikely	Impossible
○	○	○	○	○	○	○

During the next year, what is the chance that you will get so sick that you will have to stay in bed for the entire day or longer?

Certain	Very likely	Probable	Even chance	Possible	Unlikely	Impossible
○	○	○	○	○	○	○

Figure 4.50 **Spacing of Response Options II.**

While neither of these examples used grids, there is no reason to believe the effect would not apply equally to grid questions. In other words, spacing matters, and the Web survey designer would be well-advised to override the HTML default for column width and allocate equal spacing to each response option to avoid inadvertent favoring of some options over others. This applies both to grids and to horizontally aligned response options using tables. Fortunately, this is easy to do, whether one used fixed or variable table widths.

The final topic to address with regard to the design of grids relates to the use of table lines, shading, and other devices to provide visual guidance. As I've already said in Section 4.4.2, I'm not a big fan of table lines, as they add to the visual clutter on the screen. However, without lines, the link between items and response options may not be as strong as desired to facilitate accurate completion of the task. Contrast the two examples in Figures 4.51 and 4.52.

The first example, in Figure 4.51, uses both table lines and shading. Compare this with the cleaner design using only shading in Figure 4.41. The use of both shading and lines seems like overkill. (As an aside, note the unclear instruction in Figure 4.51 – the task is to select one response *per row*.) While this may be too much, the example in Figure 4.52 may be too little. While this may look clean and uncluttered, the respondent may have a harder time associating the radio buttons with the correct response options. There is no device to lead the eye from the item to the response options. In my view, horizontal shading strikes a balance between too little guidance and too much clutter. Such shading not only helps with the link between items and response options but also serves as visual reinforcement that the task is a row-by-row rather than column-by-column one. Dynamic shading may provide additional visual guidance to aid respondent navigation in grids (see Galesic et al., 2007). Of course, shading is not the only visual tool; judicious spacing between items may achieve the same purpose. Figure 4.22 earlier in this

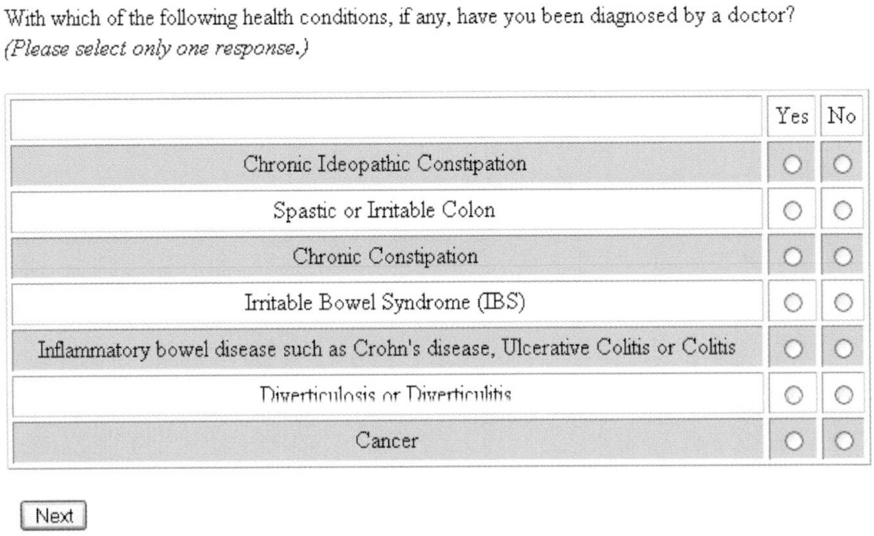

With which of the following health conditions, if any, have you been diagnosed by a doctor?
(Please select only one response.)

	Yes	No
Chronic Ideopathic Constipation	O	O
Spastic or Irritable Colon	O	O
Chronic Constipation	O	O
Irritable Bowel Syndrome (IBS)	O	O
Inflammatory bowel disease such as Crohn's disease, Ulcerative Colitis or Colitis	O	O
Diverticulosis or Diverticulitis	O	O
Cancer	O	O

Next

Figure 4.51 **Use of Table Lines and Shading for Visual Guidance.**

chapter shows an example of vertical shading that interferes with the task of answering row by row.

A final set of examples will suffice to illustrate the various design choices to facilitate visual orientation in grids. Figures 4.53 to 4.55 show the progression in the design of the instrument for the National Survey of Student Engagement (NSSE). To their credit, the NSSE staff at Indiana University has posted demonstration versions of each year's Web survey on their Web site at http://nsse.iub. edu/html/sample.cfm. This allows us to see how the design has changed from the first survey in 2000 to the present. Figure 4.53 shows the 2000 version of the NSSE.

The variety of colors produces the "clown's pants" effect (Lynch and Horton, 1997) alluded to in Section 4.2.4. While the horizontal color banding leads one from the items to the response options, the vertical banding serves to break this link.

The 2001 version of the same question is shown, in Figure 4.54. Note the left-justified text for each item, which makes it harder to align the item with the corresponding response options. While the spacing is sufficient to separate the items from each other, it may not be sufficient to also separate the sets of response options and link them with the items.

Are you CURRENTLY BEING TREATED for any of the following conditions? Select all that apply.

	Yes	No
Cardiovascular disease (such as angina, congestive heart failure, coronary heart disease, heart attack, or peripheral vascular disease)	○	○
Diabetes	○	○
Impaired glucose tolerance (pre-diabetes)	○	○
Diverticulitis	○	○
Gastroparesis	○	○
High blood pressure	○	○
Arthritis	○	○
Inflammatory Bowel Syndrome	○	○
Food allergies	○	○
Kidney problems or renal failure	○	○
	Yes	No
Ulcers	○	○
Stroke	○	○
High cholesterol	○	○
Osteoporosis	○	○

Figure 4.52 **Grid with No Table Lines or Shading.**

College Activities

In your experience at this institution during the current school year, about how often have you done each of the following?

	Very often	Often	Occasionally	Never
Asked questions in class or contributed to class discussions	○	○	○	○
Used e-mail to communicate with an instructor or other students	○	○	○	○
Made a class presentation	○	○	○	○
Rewrote a paper or assignment several times	○	○	○	○
Came to class **unprepared**	○	○	○	○

Figure 4.53 **2000 Version of NSSE.**

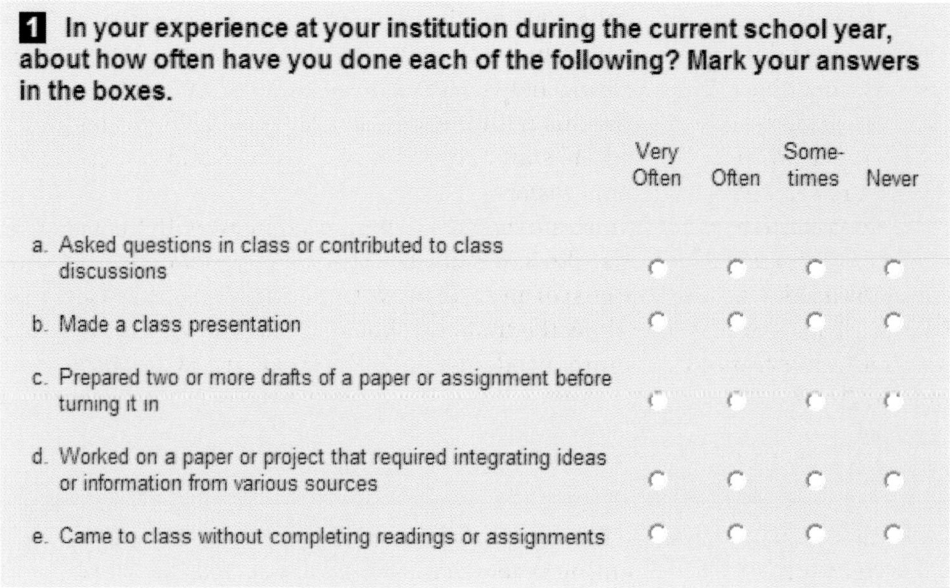

1 **In your experience at your institution during the current school year, about how often have you done each of the following? Mark your answers in the boxes.**

	Very Often	Often	Some-times	Never
a. Asked questions in class or contributed to class discussions	○	○	○	○
b. Made a class presentation	○	○	○	○
c. Prepared two or more drafts of a paper or assignment before turning it in	○	○	○	○
d. Worked on a paper or project that required integrating ideas or information from various sources	○	○	○	○
e. Came to class without completing readings or assignments	○	○	○	○

Figure 4.54 **2001 Version of NSSE.**

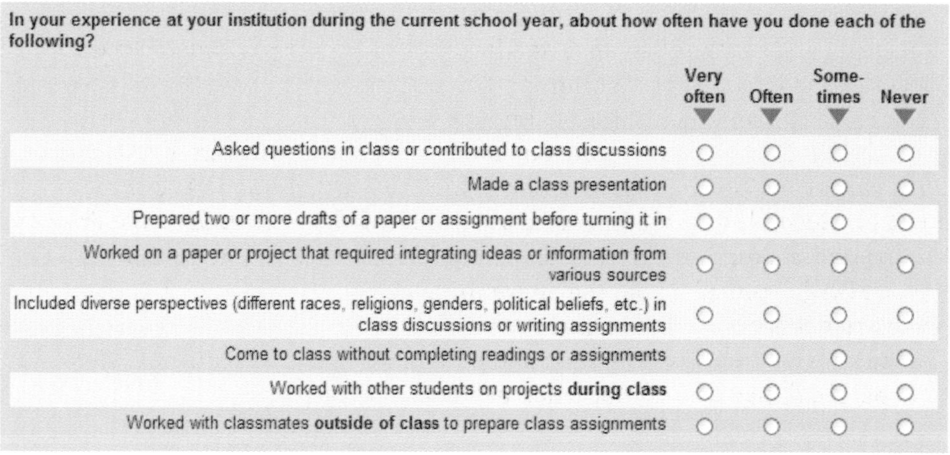

In your experience at your institution during the current school year, about how often have you done each of the following?

	Very often	Often	Some-times	Never
Asked questions in class or contributed to class discussions	○	○	○	○
Made a class presentation	○	○	○	○
Prepared two or more drafts of a paper or assignment before turning it in	○	○	○	○
Worked on a paper or project that required integrating ideas or information from various sources	○	○	○	○
Included diverse perspectives (different races, religions, genders, political beliefs, etc.) in class discussions or writing assignments	○	○	○	○
Come to class without completing readings or assignments	○	○	○	○
Worked with other students on projects **during class**	○	○	○	○
Worked with classmates **outside of class** to prepare class assignments	○	○	○	○

Figure 4.55 **2006 Version of NSSE.**

Finally, we jump ahead to the 2006 version of the NSSE (shown in Figure 4.55). The item descriptions are now right justified to bring them closer to the response options, and the use of banding helps align the items with the corresponding response options. But contrast this with the 2001 version – in 2006 the alignment makes it a little harder to find the start of each item, whereas the lettering and left justification in 2001 makes this easier.

These examples serve to illustrate the many options available to the Web survey designer with respect to grids. Devices such as lines, shading, color, and spacing can all be used to achieve the goal of an aesthetically pleasing design that facilitates the task. The examples also show the trade-offs that a designer faces – in achieving one goal, another may be compromised. The design of grids is not a task to be taken lightly.

4.4.3.3. Summary on Grids

Much more can be said about the design of grids. I've addressed several of the major issues that come up when putting several items together in a matrix. Each of these should not be viewed in isolation – effective grid design requires considering these issues in combination, and making trade-offs between competing survey goals and design recommendations. What we have seen in this section is that there are many more ways to mess up with grids or matrixes than with single-item questions. Poor design is compounded in such instances.

One last example will suffice to illustrate this point. Figure 4.56 is from a survey aimed at school-age children, who are likely not to be very familiar with completing Web questionnaires – although they may be quite savvy Web users in general. This question tries to do too much. First, note that columns 3–6 comprise the response options for one question, while the last column is a separate yes/no question. Second, the columns are not of equal width. Third, the table lines and background shading add visual clutter, as does the unnecessary numbering of items. Finally, note also that the "never or hardly ever" and "no" responses were preselected – not a good idea at all.

In summary, grids are complex, and should be designed with care. Here are a few specific things to consider when designing grids:

- Avoid horizontal scrolling; make sure that all columns (response options) are visible.
- Make sure that column headings are visible when scrolling vertically.

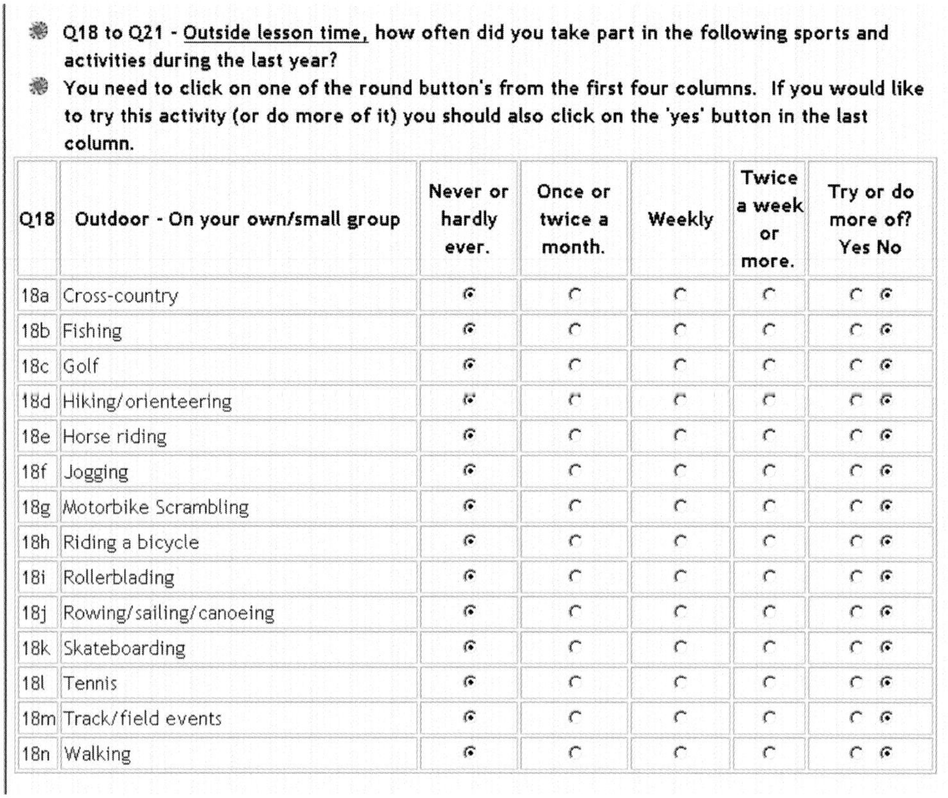

Q18 to Q21 - Outside lesson time, how often did you take part in the following sports and activities during the last year?

You need to click on one of the round button's from the first four columns. If you would like to try this activity (or do more of it) you should also click on the 'yes' button in the last column.

Q18	Outdoor - On your own/small group	Never or hardly ever.	Once or twice a month.	Weekly	Twice a week or more.	Try or do more of? Yes No
18a	Cross-country	◉	○	○	○	○ ◉
18b	Fishing	◉	○	○	○	○ ◉
18c	Golf	◉	○	○	○	○ ◉
18d	Hiking/orienteering	◉	○	○	○	○ ◉
18e	Horse riding	◉	○	○	○	○ ◉
18f	Jogging	◉	○	○	○	○ ◉
18g	Motorbike Scrambling	◉	○	○	○	○ ◉
18h	Riding a bicycle	◉	○	○	○	○ ◉
18i	Rollerblading	◉	○	○	○	○ ◉
18j	Rowing/sailing/canoeing	◉	○	○	○	○ ◉
18k	Skateboarding	◉	○	○	○	○ ◉
18l	Tennis	◉	○	○	○	○ ◉
18m	Track/field events	◉	○	○	○	○ ◉
18n	Walking	◉	○	○	○	○ ◉

Figure 4.56 Grid Design Example.

- Use fluid rather than fixed tables; allow the table to adjust to the size of the browser.
- Ensure that columns for scalar response options are of equal width.
- Use shading and spacing judiciously to guide the eyes and mouse to response options associated with each item.
- Avoid visual clutter; minimize the amount of extraneous information in the table.
- Consider breaking the grid into smaller pieces if it becomes too complex.

As a final note on grid design, for accessibility reasons (for those using screen readers), make sure that the tables linearize – screen readers will read rows then columns. When the reader is in a particular cell, it must be clear which column and which row that cell belongs to. If it's easy for a sighted reader to get lost in a grid, imagine how hard it may be for one relying on a screen reader.

4.4.4. Summary on Layout

I've covered a lot in the section on layout, including alignment, the use of HTML tables, and the design of grids. To summarize, the organization of elements on a screen is a powerful design tool and should be done with care to ensure optimal performance from the respondent. Let me reiterate some of the key points I've made in this section:

- Use a consistent layout, so respondents learn to expect where to find the question and response options.
- Change the layout only to convey a change in task, for example, numeric input versus check boxes, or the use of grids.
- Clearly associate each input field with its appropriate label and no other.
- Guide the respondent's eye from item to response options, visually distinguishing each item from the next.
- Use design to convey a sense of scale continuum for ordinal and scalar items.
- Make sure the layout works under different browser and font settings.
- Avoid the overuse of lines, shading, color, or other visual clutter.

As with the other design elements discussed in this chapter, the spatial arrangement of questions and respondents options, along with other auxiliary information, can be done to make the task appear less onerous and more visually appealing.

4.5. Screen Size and Complexity

Those designing for paper questionnaires have full control over the space available. The canvas on which they draw the questionnaire is fixed, whether it is $8\frac{1}{2}''$ × 11″ or $8\frac{1}{2}''$ × 17″ folded in booklet form (e.g., Dillman, 1978). Similarly, in computer-assisted interviewing (CAI), where the desktop or laptop computers are purchased and configured by the survey organization for its interviewers, screen layout and design (font size, color, font style, etc.) can be tightly controlled. The layout can be adjusted to fit a particular screen configuration.

This is not so on the Web. Some have tried to exercise similar control, using fixed dimensions and designing for a given screen size (e.g., 640 × 480), and I

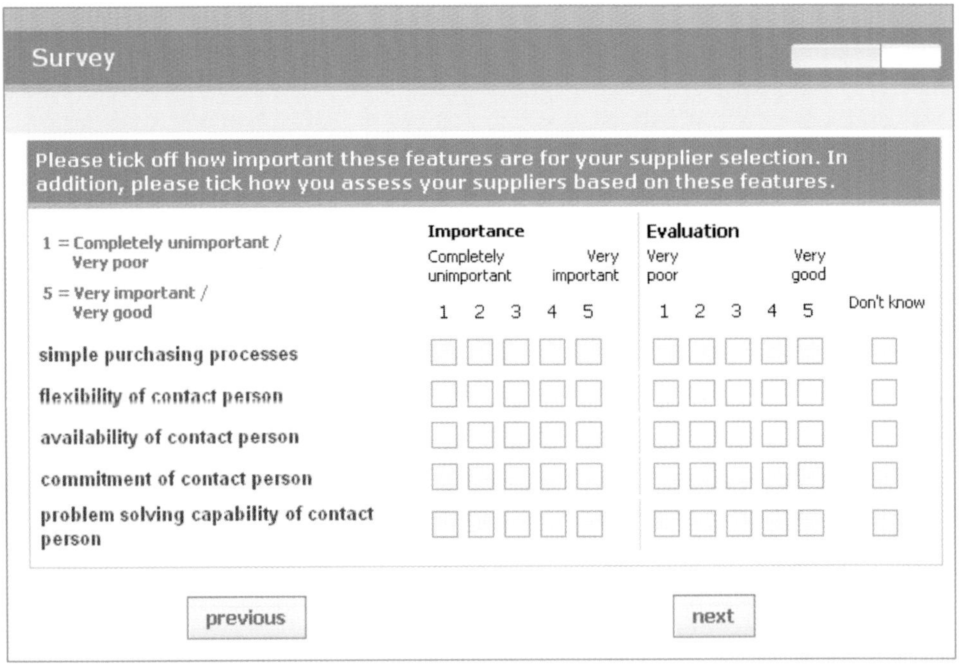

Figure 4.57 **Web Survey with Text Zoom Set at 100% (Original Size).**

continue to see examples of Web surveys designed according to this philosophy. But there are numerous ways in which respondents and the equipment available to them can mess this up. For example, changing font size can play havoc with a carefully constructed fixed-size design. Figures 4.57 and 4.58 illustrate this point. In the first figure, a table with fixed dimensions is used to present a series of items. All is well until the respondent decides to increase the text size on their browser, as shown in the second figure. At this point the survey becomes unusable.

In similar fashion, resizing the browser window can upset the carefully designed Web survey that requires a specific number of pixels for optimal viewing. Kalbach (2001) notes that there are two important things to remember when looking at screen resolution statistics:

1. Monitor size and screen resolution size are independent.
2. Screen resolution and viewable browsing area within a browser are independent.

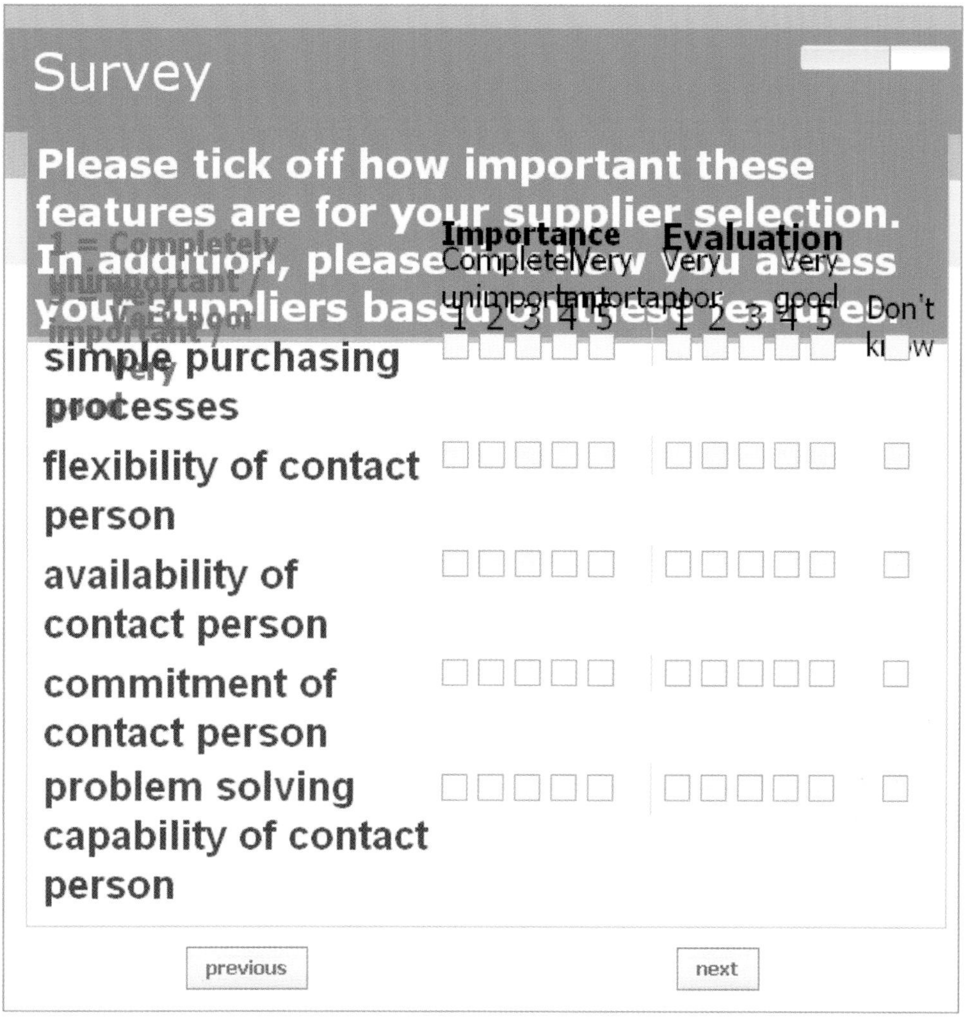

Figure 4.58 **Web Survey with Text Zoom Set at 200%.**

In fact, as monitor size increases, browser size does not increase proportionately. In other words, people buy large monitors so that they can have several different windows open simultaneously, not so that they maximize each window.

In our own studies on Web design, we capture metrics of the respondents' monitor and browser settings as they enter the survey. In one of our studies conducted

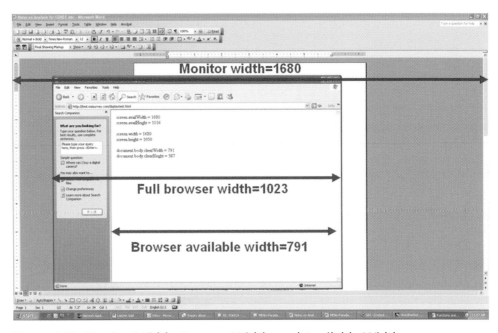

Figure 4.59 **Monitor Width, Browser Width, and Available Width.**

in late 2005, we found that 97% of respondents had a monitor at least 800 pixels wide. (I'll focus on width here, as horizontal rather than vertical scrolling is the primary concern.) Further, 54% of all respondents had a monitor width of at least 1024 pixels. Of greater interest is the *browser* width. We found that 50% of respondents had their browser set to less than 800 pixels in width. Further, we find the relationship posited by Kalbach: the wider the monitor, the less likely the browser will be maximized to the full screen. For example, when the monitor width is less than 900 pixels, the average ratio of browser width to monitor width is 96%; this declines to 93% for a monitor width of 800, 87% for a monitor width of 1024 and 84% for a monitor width of 1280 pixels.

While the size of monitors has continued to increase, these ratios have remained relatively stable. In a study using a different opt-in panel in early 2007, we found 35% of respondents with their browser width set to less than 800 pixels, although only 16% had a monitor width of less than 1024 pixels (Baker and Couper, 2007). The relationship between monitor width, browser width, and the width available to the survey designer is illustrated in Figure 4.59. On a browser that is 1680 pixels wide, the browser is not maximized to full screen, and is only 1023 pixels wide. However, a further 232 pixels are used by the search pane, leaving 791 pixels for the survey content. If the survey uses a navigation pane, this may be further reduced.

What's the implication? Just because respondents have increasingly large monitors doesn't mean that we can assume all these pixels are available to us when designing Web pages to be viewed without the need for horizontal scrolling. However, the wider a respondents' browser pane, the more spread out the text and response options will be if the survey is set to use the full browser width. This is one of the trade-offs of flexible design on the Web. We have little control over the respondent's monitor and browser settings, yet they may see (and experience) the survey differently because of these settings. In my view, fixed-width tables that require horizontal scrolling for those with constrained browser size are worse than the elongation of response options across a large monitor. Those facing the latter problem have recourse – they can make their browser smaller – while there is little that those with the former problem can do.

Kalbach (2001) argues forcefully against the notion of designing Web sites to match a particular screen resolution. Nielsen (2000, p. 174) similarly argues for the use of "liquid" or resolution-independent designs (see also his Alertbox of July 31, 2006 at http://www.useit.com/alertbox/screen_resolution.html). While he recommends optimizing for a monitor resolution of 1024 × 768, he strongly cautions against designing solely for a specific monitor size and recommends a liquid or flexible layout. Our own research (Baker and Couper, 2007) supports this. Web pages with fixed widths had higher breakoff rates, especially when those widths exceeded the pixels available on the respondents' browsers.

Cascading style sheets offer the designer more tools in controlling the various layout elements. For example, in CSS one can now define minimum and maximum widths for a table or for specific cells. This allows the designer to constrain table width to be within a certain range, that is, to give the user flexibility within certain limits.

With the previous discussion in mind, I offer the following three recommendations with regard to monitor and browser size:

1. Design for maximum flexibility – never define things in absolutes. One can optimize for the most common settings, but the survey should accommodate alternatives.
2. Test the design on a variety of platforms and using a variety of user-controlled settings to avoid egregious design errors.
3. Do research on whether the layout variations that result from flexible design matter in terms of comprehension of the question and completion of the task.

A key premise about Web design is that the user – not the survey designer – has control over the browser. The design of page layout, as with other elements of Web survey design, should accommodate this.

Another common – and related – question I am asked is, "how much information should I put on each screen in a Web survey?" Or, "how many questions are too many?" Again, there is no easy answer to this question. In the days of DOS, when a computer screen was relatively standardized, and eighty columns by twenty-five rows could be used to represent various characters, the amount of text or information on a screen was easily measurable. In this way, Tullis's early work on screen complexity could talk of the percentage of the screen that was filled with text (e.g., Tullis, 1983, 1988). In graphical user interfaces where screen dimensions are measured in pixels, and vary greatly from one computer to the next – not to mention the additional variation in browser settings – defining the amount of screen space (or window space) that contains information is difficult. Furthermore, as we've already noted, information is not binary (as in the monochrome DOS days of either being black or white). Color conveys information, even if it is uniform across the large parts of the screen. Pictures convey much greater complexity in the same space than text may do. So, given all this, the trite answer may be, as much information as is necessary, but no more. Obviously, this provides the designer with little practical guidance for designing Web surveys, so we must delve a little deeper into this issue.

The issue is not so much one of the *amount* on the Web page but about the perceived *complexity* of the page content. There are several dimensions of complexity, or ways in which the same content (the same questions and response options) can be made to appear more or less complex. These include:

1. The type and variety of input methods. A series of questions all with radio button or check box input (i.e., requiring mouse clicks) should appear less complex (and should take less time to complete) than questions where the input form varies, moving between mouse and keyboard, for example.
2. The spatial arrangement of elements. When the items are presented in an orderly, symmetrical manner (i.e., achieving the state of *Prägnanz*, see Section 4.4), the task will be perceived as less complex.
3. The number and variety of visual elements. The addition of lines, colors, patterns, images, and changes in color, typeface, font size, and so, may create a sense of increased complexity, especially if these elements do not contribute to the flow of the design.

Regarding the last of these points especially, it is not that the use of these design tools *per se* that produce a sense of complexity, but how they are employed rhetorically, that is whether they facilitate or interfere with the task. Given this, I have discussed several ways of reducing complexity in this chapter. These include such strategies as:

- Remove unnecessary content; if this is not possible, move it behind a link; if this is still not possible, move it out of the main content area of the page and use visual and spatial design to make it less prominent so it does not interfere with the task of survey completion.
- Reduce the number of different colors, restrict typographic variety (font size, typeface, emphasis, etc.), and eliminate unnecessary lines to achieve visual simplicity.
- Use consistent design throughout the instrument so that the respondent knows what to expect and where to find it.
- Don't try to put too much on one page – use blank space effectively.
- Consider breaking long or complex tasks into more manageable chunks.

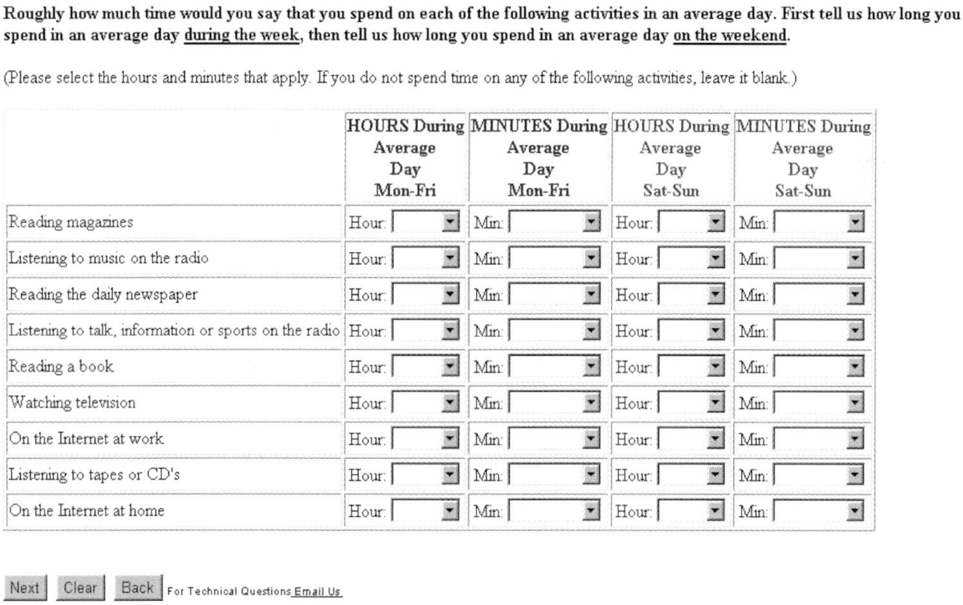

Roughly how much time would you say that you spend on each of the following activities in an average day. First tell us how long you spend in an average day <u>during the week</u>, then tell us how long you spend in an average day <u>on the weekend</u>.

(Please select the hours and minutes that apply. If you do not spend time on any of the following activities, leave it blank.)

	HOURS During Average Day Mon-Fri	MINUTES During Average Day Mon-Fri	HOURS During Average Day Sat-Sun	MINUTES During Average Day Sat-Sun
Reading magazines	Hour:	Min:	Hour:	Min:
Listening to music on the radio	Hour:	Min:	Hour:	Min:
Reading the daily newspaper	Hour:	Min:	Hour:	Min:
Listening to talk, information or sports on the radio	Hour:	Min:	Hour:	Min:
Reading a book	Hour:	Min:	Hour:	Min:
Watching television	Hour:	Min:	Hour:	Min:
On the Internet at work	Hour:	Min:	Hour:	Min:
Listening to tapes or CD's	Hour:	Min:	Hour:	Min:
On the Internet at home	Hour:	Min:	Hour:	Min:

Next   Clear   Back   For Technical Questions Email Us

Figure 4.60 **Use of Drop Boxes to Fit Many Items on One Page.**

There are strategies that some employ to make the task *look* less daunting, but may in fact have the opposite effect. One such strategy is to use drop boxes to squeeze a lot of questions onto the Web page. Figure 4.60 shows one example of this relatively common strategy. In my view, not only must the task look relatively easy, but it must also be so – if not, respondents will quickly catch on and abandon the effort.

4.6. Summary Remarks

I don't want to create the impression that I'm advocating plain, boring survey design. I have no objection to cosmetic or aesthetic enhancements to Web surveys, and believe they can have a positive experience on respondents. Given the competing attentions in the online world, we should be sure to avoid dull surveys, in terms of both content and design. However, if the design acts to the detriment of the task, it does not serve a useful purpose.

The goal of design should be to enhance the experience and facilitate the task. How does this translate into survey language? If the appeal of the design keeps respondents from abandoning the survey (thereby potentially reducing nonresponse error), it is facilitative. Similarly, if the graphical or visual enhancements do not distract from the task of answering the questions, or lead the respondent to a different answer than suggested by the question, measurement error is not affected. In other words, if no harm is done to the quality of the survey data, and the respondent exits the survey a little more satisfied, the design is supportive. If, however, the design frustrates the respondent, either through longer downloads, or increased difficulty of finding the question and figuring out what to do, the design interferes with the task.

According to the well-known dictum attributed to the architect Henry Louis Sullivan (1896), "Form ever follows function." This doesn't mean function alone. It means that the functions should be enhanced by the design (form) rather than the other way around. As Norman (2004) has so well articulated, aesthetically pleasing design can enhance performance. Similarly, Schneiderman (1992) pointed out that the notion of usability has several measurable outcomes, satisfaction being only one of them. Good Web survey design is about striking a balance.

Chapter 5

Putting the Questions Together to Make an Instrument

The whole is greater than the sum of the parts

A questionnaire is more than merely a collection of questions. We have chosen the questions we want to include in the survey instrument, we have chosen the appropriate tools to deliver those questions and accept the responses, and we have decided on an overall design or "look and feel" for the presentation of these items. Next, we want to combine the items into a single questionnaire and add the elements that make it a usable survey instrument. This chapter will cover the following topics:

- Customization, including skips or routing, randomization, and fills
- Flow and navigation, including question numbering and action buttons
- Error messages
- Help and instructions
- Progress indicators and survey length

The topics in this chapter relate to the interactive elements of Web surveys. That is, what happens when the respondent enters a value into a field, presses a button, clicks on a link, or performs some other action? They are also about progress or movement through the instrument. The way many of these tools are designed and implemented depends on whether a scrolling or paging design is employed and whether active content (such as dynamic HTML or JavaScript) is used.

I've made a distinction between verbal and visual elements (see Chapter 3), between task and style elements (see Chapter 4), and between dynamic and static elements (see Chapter 3), but there is one final distinction that can be made, namely, between visible elements and hidden elements. On a paper questionnaire, everything is visible – the questions and answer fields, the instructions, the keying or coding frame, and so on. In computerized surveys, much of the auxiliary information is hidden, potentially leaving only the questions and response options visible. The focus of this book is on what the respondent sees and does, but in this chapter, we also need to look at what the program running the survey may be doing insofar as it can affect the respondent's behavior. In the extreme, each respondent may receive a unique version of the instrument, and be completely unaware of the alternative paths and forms the survey may have taken if they had made different choices. The reason for doing so is usually to improve the "flow" of the survey – that is, increasing the relevance of each question to a particular respondent, thereby improving data quality and reducing breakoffs.

The general theme of this chapter is that of guiding respondents along the appropriate path to completion of the instrument, and providing them with the tools to complete the task. The first broad area I'll address relates to question customization, that is, presenting certain questions to some respondents and not to others (skips or routing), varying the order or form in which questions or response options are presented to respondents (randomization), and varying the content of the questions themselves to reflect answers to prior questions or other knowledge about the respondent (fills). The first of these (skips) can be accomplished with statically generated HTML pages, whereas fills usually require dynamic generation of HTML pages based on information already provided. Randomization may involve a choice of one of a set of alternative static pages, or may require the dynamic generation of a page based on some algorithm. In other words, these customization tools may be viewed as varying on a continuum from static to dynamic.

5.1. Skips or Routing

One of the powerful features of computerized instruments is that they can take the decision of what question to answer next out of the hands of the respondent. Such routing decisions can vary in complexity from simple binary choices (if A = yes, ask B, else ask C) to complex algorithms based on a series of prior responses. The more complex the routing rules, the greater the potential for programming errors, but also the greater the need to take these decisions out of the hands of respondents.

The rules that control the flow of the instrument are variously called skips, branching, filters, or routing (see Dillman, Redline, and Carley-Baxter, 1999; House, 1985; House and Nicholls, 1988; Redline and Dillman, 2002). The best way to illustrate skips is to look at an example. Figure 5.1 shows a page from the 1992 round of the National Longitudinal Survey of labor Market Experience, Youth Survey (NLS/Y). This illustrates the kinds of manual tasks interviewers had to perform before computerization of surveys. It may not be surprising that this was one of the first surveys to move to computer-assisted personal interviewing (CAPI) in the United States. Remarkably, despite the complexity of these tasks, interviewers made very few errors (see Olsen, 1992; Baker, Bradburn, and Johnson, 1995). Computer-assisted interviewing has reduced such skip errors to almost nothing – I say *almost* nothing because this assumes there are no programming errors.

The excerpt contains both conditional statements (e.g., "Ask women only") and routing instructions (e.g., "If yes, go to A"). In addition, there is preparation for fills (e.g., "Enter name...for each child listed"), which I will address later. The routing instructions in Figure 5.1 were designed to be followed by trained interviewers. Asking respondents to follow these themselves may be too much. Most skip instructions in self-administered paper surveys are much less complex. Figure 5.2 shows an example from a mailed follow-up to a Web survey, where the skips were automated in the Web version (Couper, Peytchev, Strecher, Rothert, and Anderson, 2007).

There are many different types of skips or conditional routing, and there are many ways to program these, depending on the software used. Norman (2001, p. 6) offers the following classification of skip types:

- Simple: if answer A to Q1, go to Q2.1, if answer B to Q1, go to Q2.2
- Disjunctive: if answer A OR B to Q1, go to Q2.1, if answer C or D go to Q2.2
- Conjunctive: if answer A AND B to Q1, go to Q2.1, else go to Q2.2
- Inter-question: if answer A to Q1 and A to Q2, go to Q3.1, else go to Q3.2

These types are all based on discrete choices. Skips can also be based on ranges (e.g., if $40 \leq$ age ≤ 60), Boolean (e.g., if A and not B) or other mathematical operations (e.g., if income <125% of poverty threshold, which in turns depends on household size), complex sequences of items (e.g., if at least three symptoms listed as moderate to severe), and the like. Skips may even be based on data

SECTION 10: CHILDCARE

1. ┌─────────────────────────┐
   │   **ASK WOMEN ONLY:**   │
   └─────────────────────────┘

2. <u>INTERVIEWER</u>: ARE ANY CHILDREN LISTED ON THE **CHILDREN'S RECORD FORM, <u>PART A</u>**?

   YES 1

   NO . . . . (SKIP TO Q.27, PAGE 10-138) 0   26-27/

3. <u>INTERVIEWER</u>: DO WE NEED TO ASK CHILDCARE QUESTIONS FOR ANY CHILDREN LISTED ON THE **CHILDREN'S RECORD FORM, <u>PART A</u>**? (ARE QS. 6, 13, OR 20 PREPRINTED UNDER "CHILDCARE"?)

   YES . . . . (GO TO A) 1

   NO . . . . (GO TO B) 0   28-29/

   A. <u>INTERVIEWER</u>: NOTE THE FOLLOWING INSTRUCTIONS BEFORE BEGINNING THE REST OF THE CHILDCARE QUESTIONS.

      ENTER NAME AND ID # ON TOP OF COLUMNS IN Q.4 ON PAGE 10-114 FOR EACH CHILD LISTED ON THE **CHILDREN'S RECORD FORM, PART A** FOR WHOM WE NEED TO ASK CHILDCARE QUESTIONS, THEN GO TO B.

   B. <u>INTERVIEWER</u>: WAS THERE A LIVE BIRTH SINCE DATE OF 1988 OR PRIOR INTERVIEW?

      YES . . . . (SKIP TO Q.4) 1

      NO . . . . (ASK C) 0   30-31/

   C. <u>INTERVIEWER</u>: IS Q.3 OR Q.3B CODED 1 -- "YES"?

      YES . . . . (GO TO Q.4) 1

      NO . . . . (SKIP TO Q.27, PAGE 10-138) 0   32-33/

Figure 5.1 Example of Skip Instructions from NLS/Y.

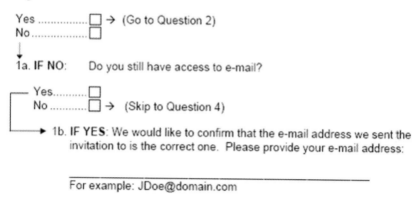

Instructions: Check a box in response to each question, or write your response on the line provided.

1. We recently sent you an e-mail request to participate in a follow-up survey to the weight management study you enrolled in. Do you recall receiving that e-mail message?

Yes .... ☐ → (Go to Question 2)
No .... ☐

1a. IF NO: Do you still have access to e-mail?

Yes........... ☐
No .... ☐ → (Skip to Question 4)

1b. IF YES: We would like to confirm that the e-mail address we sent the invitation to is the correct one. Please provide your e-mail address:

_____

For example: JDoe@domain.com

Figure 5.2 **Example of Skips in a Mail Survey.**

obtained from external sources or prior waves of the survey, in combination with answers obtained in the current wave (e.g., Hill, 1994; Jäckle, 2004; Lynn, Jäckle, Jenkins, and Sala, 2006). In theory, the complexity of computer-controlled skips is limited only by the imagination of the designer and the constraints of the software used to execute them. In practice, increased complexity comes at the expense of increased development and testing time, and the increased risk of errors.

From a programming perspective, there are two broad approaches to skips or routing logic. The first is as "go to" logic, common in linear programming. The selection of a response triggers the logic to direct the system to display the next applicable question. The CASES software system for CAI uses a "go to" approach (see http://cases.berkeley.edu). A second approach is as "if-then-else" logic, more common in object-oriented programming. In this case, each question is evaluated against a filter. If applicable, the question is displayed to the respondent; if not, it is not presented. The Blaise CAI system (see www.cbs.nl/blaise) uses the latter approach. The choice of approach is largely determined by the software one is using to deliver the Web survey.

These approaches are sometimes reflected in the design of skip logic in paper surveys or static Web survey. For example, the "go to" approach is illustrated in Figure 5.1. The selection of the "yes" response in Question 1 leads to the instruction to skip to Question 2. The "if-then-else" or filter approach is also seen in Question 1a, with the "If no" instruction – Redline and Dillman (2002) refer to this as the "detection technique."

There are many different ways to control the flow of Web questionnaires. In fact, Norman (2001) identifies eleven different ways of implementing conditional branching, depending on the type of Web survey design employed (see also Norman and Pleskac, 2002). These vary along the dimensions of client-side versus server-side scripts, passive (or static) versus dynamic approaches, and user-controlled versus computer-controlled (or automated) skips. I will focus primarily on this latter dimension, discussing flow control in scrolling designs first, before turning to paging designs.

5.1.1. User-Controlled Skips in Scrolling Designs

User-controlled skips in scrolling surveys resemble those in paper questionnaires in that they are visible to the respondent and require the respondent to take some action to comply with the instruction. The belief is that such skips should be as simple as possible – I say "belief" because I know of no studies that have examined the effect of skip complexity on compliance with the instructions. But it is good advice nonetheless. In practice, user-controlled skips are generally restricted to the simple conditionals identified earlier and illustrated in Figure 5.2.

While they resemble those in paper surveys, skips in static or scrolling Web surveys present different design challenges. Many of the visual cues available to the designer in paper surveys (such as the arrows in Figure 5.2) are harder to implement in a consistent manner on the Web.

An example from Tourangeau, Couper, Galesic, and Givens (2004) is presented in Figure 5.3. This design had to be accomplished using table elements in HTML to control the position of the brace brackets. While the braces may work on paper and under ideal testing conditions on the Web, as soon as the respondent resizes the browser or change the font size, the relationship of the elements could be disturbed. This is why trying to replicate paper skips on the Web using symbolic language (Redline and Dillman, 2002) is generally quite difficult.

An exception, shown in Figure 5.4, is from the 2001 Norwegian Census (Haraldsen, Dale, Dalheim, and Strømme, 2002). Here, the arrow symbols used, and their position relative to the response options, are unaffected by changes in the browser settings. But this works only for relatively simple skip instructions.

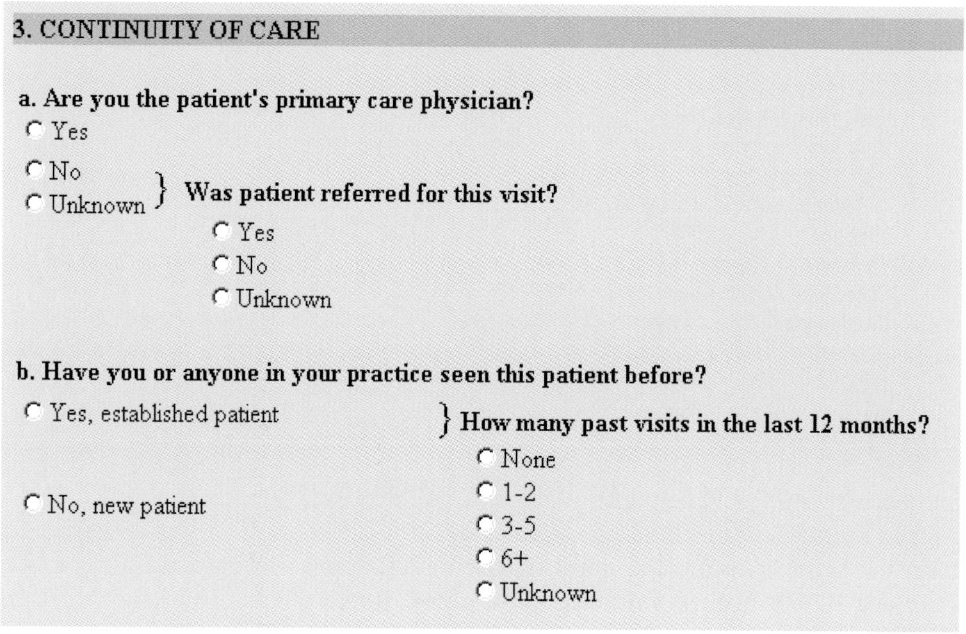

3. CONTINUITY OF CARE

a. Are you the patient's primary care physician?

◯ Yes

◯ No
◯ Unknown } **Was patient referred for this visit?**

      ◯ Yes
      ◯ No
      ◯ Unknown

b. Have you or anyone in your practice seen this patient before?

◯ Yes, established patient   } **How many past visits in the last 12 months?**
      ◯ None

◯ No, new patient
      ◯ 1-2
      ◯ 3-5
      ◯ 6+
      ◯ Unknown

Figure 5.3 **Skip Example from Scrolling Web Survey.**

The more complex the skips, the more attractive a paging design becomes. Look at the example in Figure 5.5. The skip instructions could be accomplished with brace brackets and/or arrows on a paper questionnaire, but as already noted, these are difficult to do on the Web. The result is a question that looks much more complex than it need be. Turning this into a paging design would eliminate all the skip instructions.

A more common alternative is to include a skip instruction as a hypertext link, which on being clicked, simply jumps the respondent lower down in the same

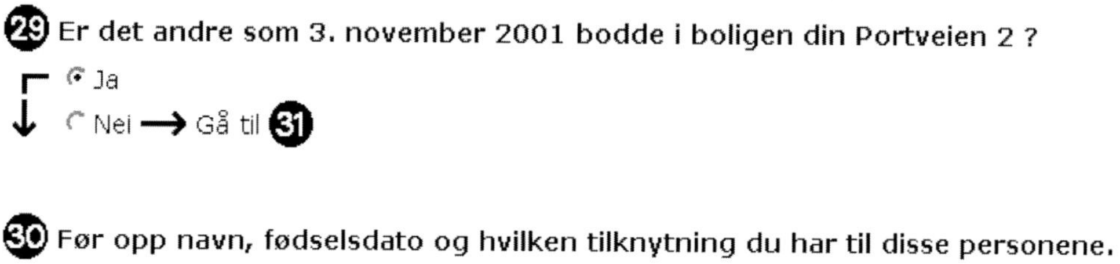

29 Er det andre som 3. november 2001 bodde i boligen din Portveien 2 ?

◉ Ja
↓ ◯ Nei → Gå til **31**

30 Før opp navn, fødselsdato og hvilken tilknytning du har til disse personene.

Figure 5.4 **Skip Example from the Norwegian Census.**

23 a. How did you usually get to work LAST WEEK? *If you usually used more than one method of transportation during the trip, check the box of the one used for most of the distance.*

○ Car, truck or van
○ Bus or trolley bus -> *Skip to 24a*
○ Streetcar or trolley car -> *Skip to 24a*
○ Subway or elevated -> *Skip to 24a*
○ Railroad -> *Skip to 24a*
○ Ferryboat -> *Skip to 24a*
○ Taxicab -> *Skip to 24a*
○ Motorcycle -> *Skip to 24a*
○ Bicycle -> *Skip to 24a*
○ Walked -> *Skip to 24a*
○ Worked at home -> *Skip to 27*
○ Other method -> *Skip to 24a*

Figure 5.5 **Example of Complex Skips in a Scrolling Survey.**

form to the next applicable question. Using hyperlinks to navigate a page is a standard HTML feature that does not require active content, and the function should be familiar to most users of the Web. This is illustrated in Figure 5.6.

The design challenge is to render the link in such a way that it is clicked *after* the respondent has selected the appropriate response. In other words, it must be visible enough that they notice it, but not too visible that they do so *before* answering the question, as Dillman (2000, p. 395) has noted. How much of a problem, if at all, is such premature skipping? I'll address the research on this issue in Section 5.1.4.

5.1.2. System-Controlled Skips in Scrolling Designs

An alternative in scrolling surveys is to use client-side scripts to gray out or deactivate the inappropriate items. This can be done using JavaScript, for

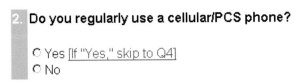

2. **Do you regularly use a cellular/PCS phone?**

○ Yes [If "Yes," skip to Q4]
○ No

Figure 5.6 **Use of Hyperlink for Skip in Scrolling Survey.**

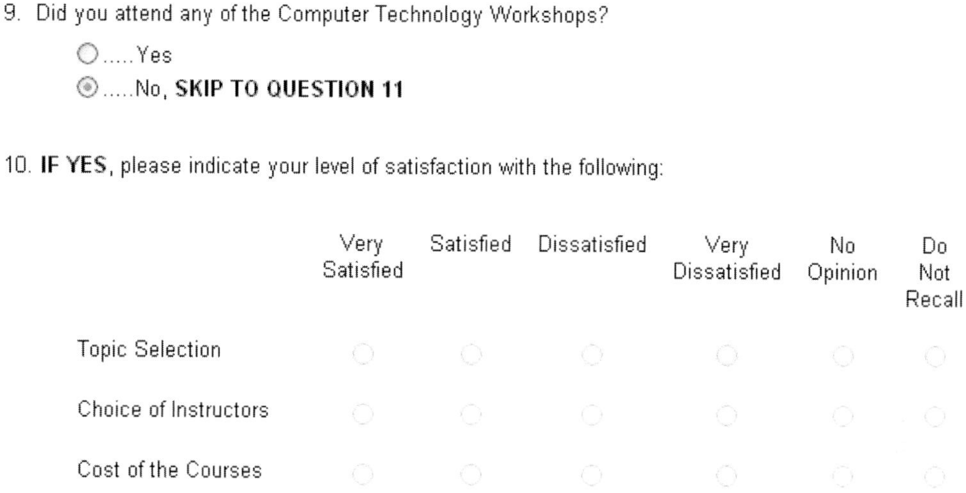

9. Did you attend any of the Computer Technology Workshops?

    ○ ..... Yes
    ◉ ..... No, **SKIP TO QUESTION 11**

10. **IF YES**, please indicate your level of satisfaction with the following:

	Very Satisfied	Satisfied	Dissatisfied	Very Dissatisfied	No Opinion	Do Not Recall
Topic Selection	○	○	○	○	○	○
Choice of Instructors	○	○	○	○	○	○
Cost of the Courses	○	○	○	○	○	○

Figure 5.7 **Use of JavaScript to Control Flow in a Scrolling Survey.**

example. While it is very difficult to change page content (i.e., the wording of questions) using client-side scripting, formatting changes such as font color are less difficult.

This feature of JavaScript is used to control the flow of the survey in Figure 5.7. Given that the "no" response was chosen in Question 9, the items in Question 10 are made inaccessible. They are still visible, but clicking on them will have no effect. If the "no" was switched to a "yes" in Question 9, the items and response options in Question 10 would change to a normal font and be active. In the only known study of this approach, Kjellström and Bälter (2003) conducted a small-scale usability study with 19 users, and found that users spent a lot of time and energy trying to read the gray text, and consequently paid less attention to the question. They recommend against this approach.

5.1.3. Skips in Paging Designs

The more complex the skip, the greater the likelihood of errors, and the more critical automation becomes. As scrolling approaches are limited to relatively simple routing rules, more complex survey designs are more likely to use a paging approach, as discussed in Chapter 1. As the logic is hidden from the respondent and (usually) executed on the server-side, very complex skips can be executed.

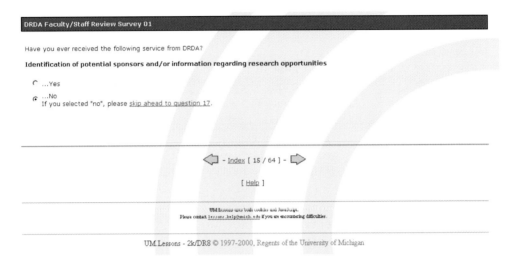

Figure 5.8 **Use of Hyperlink Skip in a Paging Design.**

Figure 5.8 shows an example of a hyperlink skip in a paging design. The hyperlink instruction should be unnecessary, other than to make visible to the respondent the routing through the instrument. The forward and backward arrows should achieve the same goal. The user's expectation here may be that the hyperlink does something different from the forward arrow. If a paging design is used, I recommend against making the skips visible to the respondent, as in this example.

The advantage of the Web is that complex logic can be applied in a self-administered survey without relying on the respondent to figure out what to do next. The disadvantage is that there is no trained interviewer present to recover from an incorrectly programmed skip, to override the system, or to explain to the respondent what to do if an unexpected problem is encountered. Given the invisibility of the logic, respondents have only two courses of action: either to abandon the survey or to answer the subsequent questions as best they can. Because of this, greater burden is placed on the designer to get the logic correct and account for all eventualities. This implies more time – and hence more money – for design and programming, and the need for more careful and thorough testing.

As far as interface design is concerned, with the branching logic hidden from the respondent, there are fewer design issues to consider than in paging designs. Four potential issues need to be considered:

1. Backing up and changing the path
2. Recovering from a routing error

3. Question numbering
4. Progress indicators

The latter two will be discussed later in this chapter, in Sections 5.5.1 and 5.8, respectively. The first two present tricky dilemmas for the designer. In interviewer-administered surveys, the interviewer is usually free to back up to earlier points in the interview and change the answer to the question that generated the skip error. But would we want to give respondents the same freedom in a Web survey? It is common in market research applications to prevent respondents from moving backward in the instrument, presumably in part to avoid these difficulties. But what if a respondent makes an honest mistake and is made aware of this by the apparent irrelevance of subsequent questions? I'll return to this issue later in Section 5.4.2. But for now, preventing backing up along with requiring a respondent to answer all questions is a bad combination. It is better to permit respondents to back up and choose a different path. At least on the Web, we can measure how often this occurs and under what conditions.

Allowing respondents to skip (not answer) questions or providing a "rather not answer" option for each question mitigates the potential problems caused by programming errors in routing. In this way, if they do go down an incorrect path, respondents are at least not forced to provide a meaningless substantive response. However, providing respondents with an "out" also means that greater care must be taken in programming the instrument. Routing decisions for these nonanswers must be explicitly made at the design phase.

5.1.4. Research on Skip Errors

Skip errors are of two types: errors of commission and errors of omission. The former occur when respondents answer questions they are not supposed to answer, while the latter are questions that should have been answered but were not. Both types of errors can occur in scrolling surveys. Further, in a scrolling survey, inadvertent omission skip errors cannot be distinguished from items that are deliberately skipped because the respondent does not want to answer them. In paging surveys, errors of commission cannot occur – if the instrument is programmed correctly – and errors of omission can usually be attributed to a respondent's deliberate choice not to answer the question.

Omissions are more critical than errors of commission. From an analytic perspective, it doesn't matter whether respondents answer every question in the questionnaire, even if some do not apply to them. It simply wastes more of the respondents' time (increases burden), but if they seem willing to do so, what's the harm? Well, one has to wonder about the veracity of answers provided by such respondents, or their commitment to the task, when they can blithely provide answers to every question, whether sensible or not. But the responses to inapplicable questions can easily be removed during postsurvey processing, so the effect of commission errors on data quality is likely to be minimal.

Yet, errors of omission can have a critical effect on the resultant data, requiring decisions about the need for imputation or some other form of analytic compensation for the missing data. A discussion of this issue is beyond the scope of this book.[1] Dealing with missing data after the fact presents challenges for the analyst, and preventing the missing data from being produced in the first place is an important part of effective design. The literature on human error suggests that while error prevention is the most effective strategy, errors are still likely to occur, and giving users the opportunity to detect and correct errors is an important element of error management (see Couper, 1999).

Automated skips are an effective way to prevent errors of commission and hopefully reduce errors of omission by presenting only those questions relevant to the respondent. But later we shall talk about "error" messages designed to further reduce errors of omission or item missing data.

What research is there on the incidence of skips errors in scrolling versus paging surveys? The evidence is limited but suggests that commission errors are less common than omission errors and that scrolling surveys tend to produce higher rates of errors of omission than paging surveys (errors of commission not being possible in the latter).

As part of a study into the feasibility of conducting the National Ambulatory Medical Care Survey online (Tourangeau et al., 2004), we experimentally compared a scrolling versus paging design of the patient record form (PRF). The PRF contains about twenty-six questions, four of which are contingent on answers to earlier questions. The scrolling version is illustrated in Figure 5.3. We found that the scrolling version produced an average of 0.36 errors of commission per PRF, while there were no such errors in the paging version, by definition. Errors of omission were also significantly larger in the scrolling version (an average of 1.13 items missed per PRF) than in the paging version (an average of 0.52 items missed).

---

[1]   See Little and Rubin (2002) for a comprehensive treatment of assumptions and statistical solutions relating to missing data. See de Leeuw (2001) for an overview of ways to reduce missing data.

In another experimental comparison of scrolling versus paging designs (Peytchev, Couper, McCabe, and Crawford, 2006), we found an overall commission error rate of 2.3% and omission error rate of 6.9% in the scrolling version containing hyperlink skips (similar to the design in Figure 5.6). Stem questions with hyperlinks did not appear to be any more susceptible to errors of omission than other questions. In other words, we found no indication that respondents were clicking on hyperlinks without first selecting a response. There were no commission errors in the paging version (as expected), and no omission errors, as an answer to each question was required to proceed through the survey.

A concern about the presence of visible skips in a scrolling survey is that they may encourage respondents to select responses that will allow them to skip large numbers of questions. There were two such questions in the survey that produced skips of four or more questions, and we found limited evidence (not significant in one case, marginally so in the other) that the presence of visible skips tempts respondents to choose a response to avoid subsequent questions.

I know of no research on the *design* of skip instructions in a Web survey. The closest is Redline and Dillman's (2002) work on branching instructions in paper questionnaires. For example, Redline, Dillman, Dajani, and Scaggs (2003) report that nearly 20% of respondents failed to follow branching instruction in Census 2000. An alternative design they tested reduced commission errors by about one-third and omission errors by about one-fourth. They found similar results in a parallel study among college students (Redline, Dillman, Carley-Baxter, and Creecy, 2005), where commission error rates of 21% on the control form were reduced to 9% and 8%, respectively, for two alternative designs. These relatively high levels of errors and the difficulty of implementing many of the graphical designs they employ on the Web suggests that using paging designs to eliminate the possibility of such errors makes sense when the questionnaire contains complex skips.

5.1.5. Summary on Skips and Branching

My preference for using a paging design to manage complex routing, rather than leaving it to the respondent, is already clear. Given this, I offer the following additional summary thoughts:

- If using skips in scrolling designs, make sure the instructions are clear and the target question well identified.

- Permit respondents to back up and change answers even if this takes them down a different path.
- Thoroughly test all paths of the instrument if complex skips are used.

Norman and Pleskac (2002) also offer a set of useful guidelines for the design of conditional branching and navigation in Web surveys.

5.2. Randomization

Randomization is another feature that exploits the computing capabilities of Web surveys. Randomization in paper questionnaires is limited to relatively simple "split-ballot" designs (see, e.g., Schuman and Presser, 1981), with different forms being printed for different versions of the instrument.[2] With the randomization capabilities of online surveys, the distinction between surveys and experiments is becoming blurred, and researchers are increasingly realizing the potential of embedded experiments. Web-based experimentation is a burgeoning field in its own right (see, e.g., Birnbaum, 2000a; Reips, 2001, 2002), but here I am concerned primarily with randomization in the survey context, and particularly with the design implications of such randomization. I'll briefly address two questions: (1) why randomize, and (2) when or how to do so?

5.2.1. Reasons for Randomization

There are several reasons one would want to use randomization in a Web survey. Some of these uses of randomization are

1. Controlling or measuring context effects
2. Methodological research
3. Matrix sampling
4. Conjoint methods

I'll discuss each of these in turn.

---

[2] With high-speed laser printers and print-on-demand capabilities, there is no reason that individually tailored paper questionnaires cannot be printed for each respondent, but this capability has not been exploited much, to my knowledge.

The first use of randomization goes back to the early days of split-ballot designs. Initially used to measure response effects, the randomization of response options within a question, the randomization of question order, or even the randomization of section order within a questionnaire, is increasingly employed in an effort to counter or control possible order effects. As we saw in Section 2.3, items near the top of a check-all-that-apply list are endorsed more often than those at the bottom. One simple way to counter this frequently employed tendency in Web surveys is to randomize the order of response options. The effect of item order goes well beyond answers to survey questions (see Miller and Krosnick, 1998). The survey literature also has many examples where the order in which questions are delivered changes the context for the respondent (e.g., Schwarz and Sudman, 1992; Tourangeau, Rips, and Rasinski, 2000). Randomizing the order of items or questions does not eliminate the order effect; it only distributes the effect across all items, thereby reducing their impact on survey estimates.

Web surveys have represented a boon for survey methodologists, given the ease with which randomization can be accomplished. Sample persons can be randomized to different incentive schemes and invitation treatments (see Chapter 6), and respondent can be routed to different versions of the questionnaire, all to test the effect of different treatments on the likelihood of response or on the answers given to survey questions. Methodological experiments embedded in surveys can range from relatively simple single-factor designs to very complex randomization schemes. In our methodological experiments on Web survey design, we are pushing the randomization capabilities of the software to the limits. For example, one of our recent surveys contained about twelve different experiments, each with several different factors, representing a $2 \times 4 \times 2 \times 8 \times 8 \times 8 \times 4 \times 3 \times 3 \times 2 \times 3 \times 2 \times 2 \times 3 \times 4 \times 3 \times 2 \times 4 \times 2 \times 5 \times 3 \times 3 \times 3 \times 2 \times 5 \times 4$ design, which would produce over 917 billion unique versions if fully crossed. Each of the experiments was independently randomized to respondents at the point of encounter, and we tested for the presence of carryover effects from one experiment to the next. Such a design would be unthinkable in a paper-based world. Many other researchers are using similarly complex randomization schemes to test a wide variety of design issues in Web surveys. Indeed, this book probably wouldn't have been possible without the number of experiments that have already been done.

Another use of randomization involves matrix sampling. The goal of matrix sampling is burden reduction. Separate modules or subsets of items are randomly assigned to different respondents, while a set of common items are used to fill in the gaps in the data matrix and estimate the covariance structure (see Raghunathan and Grizzle, 1995). Matrix sampling allows the researcher to ask more questions than would ordinarily be possible, using imputation to complete the data matrix. While practitioners do not yet appear to have fully embraced the idea, matrix sampling offers great promise for minimizing burden while maximizing the information obtained from respondents. The idea behind matrix sampling is evident in conjoint methods too.

Unlike matrix sampling, conjoint methods have gained wide acceptance, especially in marketing research. Conjoint methods grew out of the desire to have respondents consider several attributes jointly when evaluating products (hence "con" and "joint"), but with several attributes, this could result in a multidimensional trade-off matrix, a difficult task for respondents to perform, especially as the number of attributes or products being compared increases. While conjoint methods have been around since the early 1970s (see Green and Rao, 1971), their strength has really come to the fore with the advances in survey computerization, and particularly with self-administration on the Web.

Full profile conjoint (FPC) methods required representing each combination of attributes on a card (real or virtual), with respondents ranking all the cards, rating each card, or making pair-wise choices. The number of potential cards can quickly become very large (e.g., three attributes, each with three levels will require twenty-seven cards). Partial designs are possible if higher-order interactions can be ignored, in much the same way as fractional factorial designs are deployed. Further, card sorting is a difficult task to do on the Web (see Section 3.8.2), but ratings and pair-wise choices are more feasible.

Adaptive conjoint analysis (ACA) methods (see Johnson, 1987), require a computer for administration, as questions to be asked are determined at run-time. The computer is used to calculate estimates of the utilities as the survey proceeds, and these estimated utilities are then used to ask questions designed to refine the estimates further. In other words, rather than giving every respondent the full set of options, the process is refined as respondents' preferences become clearer.

In the choice-based conjoint (CBC) method, each respondent completes only a few tasks from a much larger set of possible tasks. The typical approach is to display a set of options, with a respondent choosing one (or none) from each set. Given the relatively small number of tasks needed (often around twelve), this approach is most suited for the Web (see Poynter, 2001). Recent methods include Hierarchical Bayes approaches (see Johnson, 2000; Gillbride and Allenby, 2004; Marshall and Bradlow, 2002), which allow subsets of questions to be asked of a large sample, and for a complete set of answers to be estimated later, much like the approach used in matrix sampling. These more recent adaptations of conjoint

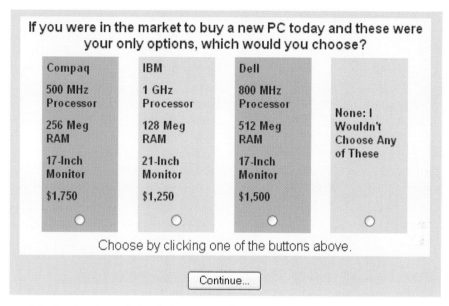

Figure 5.9 **Choice-Based Conjoint Example.**

methods are ideally suited to Web administration, and are widely used in the market research world (see Bakken and Frazier, 2006).

While randomization is hard to illustrate as it is – or should be – transparent to the respondent, I include a couple of examples here of what conjoint methods look like. The first, in Figure 5.9, is from a choice-based conjoint question from Sawtooth Software (www.sawtoothsoftware.com). Each of the five features being measured (brand, processor speed, RAM, size of monitor, and price) is varied across the successive screens displayed to the respondent, depending on the choices made on earlier screens. Figure 5.9 shows how one particular screen may look.

Of course, one can combine the dynamic elements of conjoint analysis with the visual elements made easy by the Web. Given the relative ease with which digital images can be manipulated, pictorial variations can be readily produced to illustrate the various choices in a conjoint design. Figure 5.10 shows an example of how images can be used to convey different features of vending machines in an online choice-based conjoint design. The same cautions discussed earlier (see Chapter 3) with regard to the use of images apply here.

Figure 5.10 **Use of Images in Conjoint Analysis.**

Vriens and colleagues (1998) did an early comparison of verbal versus pictorial representations of design attributes in conjoint analysis. They found that the pictorial representation produced higher ratings for 2 of 3 design attributes, as well as greater segmentation among respondents, but the verbal descriptions produced greater predictive accuracy. They suggest that the pictures improved respondents' understanding of the design attributes, while the verbal descriptions facilitated judgments (see also Sethuraman, Kerin, and Cron, 2005).

In summary, then, randomization can be used for many different purposes in Web surveys. Randomization schemes range from very simple designs (e.g., two versions of a question with random assignment to one or the other) to very complex designs such as conjoint methods or multifactor vignette studies. We are also likely to see increasing use of computerized adaptive testing (CAT) on the Web, where the probability of being assigned a particular question is conditional on the responses to one or more prior questions (e.g., van der Linden and Glas, 2000; Wainer et al., 2000). This is rapidly spreading in the education and health measurement fields and is likely to be a growth area for Web surveys.

5.2.2. Randomization Design

Given that one is using randomization, the question then turns to when and how to do so. The answer depends on the purpose of the randomization. If the focus is on a single question or series of questions, it makes sense to randomize at the point of entry to that question, to ensure equal numbers in each cell among those who get to that point. If one is examining the effect of alternative versions of a survey instrument on dropout or breakoff, randomizing respondents at the point of entry into the survey makes more sense. In this way, conditional on accessing the survey, sample persons are randomly assigned to different conditions. If one is examining overall response to the survey across different versions, randomizing at the point of, or prior to, invitation is important.

The point at which one can generate the randomization also depends on the source of the sample frame or the method of invitation. For example, if the target sample members are known, they can be assigned to different conditions prior to the invitation. If, however, this is an open access survey, preassigning sample cases is not possible, and a sequential or systematic allocation, based on the order in which respondents start the survey, may be more appropriate.

Turning to the issue of how to randomize, Reips (2002) identifies the following approaches to randomization, in order of decreasing reliability:

1. Server-side scripts (e.g., a CGI script such as Perl and PHP)
2. Client-side scripts (e.g., Java, JavaScript)
3. Respondent input

He argues that the use of server-side randomization methods may produce a delay at the point of randomization, while the script executes and delivers the appropriate set of questions. On the other hand, the client-side approaches do not work on all machines and browsers (as discussed in Chapter 3). The problem of delays in the server-side approach is becoming less of an issue as bandwidth increases and as these scripts become more efficient, so much so that respondents are not likely to notice the delay when the server is executing the randomization routine and dynamically generating the HTML code to deliver to the respondents' browsers.

Birnbaum (2001, Chapter 17) has some examples of JavaScript code for client-side generation of random numbers and assignment of respondents randomly to experimental conditions. If JavaScript is not active, he suggests having respondents enter some information (e.g., pick their month of birth) and make the random assignment based on this input (see also Birnbaum, 2000b).

A simpler approach is systematic allocation to a version of the instrument based on the order in which respondents arrive at the first page of the survey. In this way, every *n*th visitor is assigned to a different version in sequential order.

Systematic sampling and methods based on respondent input are easy to implement and useful if relatively simple randomization schemes are to be employed. For example, using month of birth gives one twelve possible assignments, which is quite sufficient for many simple factorial designs. For more complex designs, the use of a server-side script to implement the randomization makes more sense. Increasingly, Web survey software systems include tools for random assignment and random rotation schemes.

Some final cautions on the use of randomization are in order. First, be careful what the random number generator uses as a "seed." Avoid using a fixed value that is unchanged across a session (such as IP address), but rather use a variable value such as time (e.g., the seconds digits). In one early study we conducted, the same seed was used for successive randomizations within the same instrument, with the result that they were not independently generated.

Another caution in the use of randomization involves the effect of respondents backing up in the instrument. The randomization routine should be invoked only on the first path through the instrument. In other words, if a respondent backs up and then proceeds forward again, the randomization routine should not regenerate a number and assign the respondent to a different condition.

It is also important to record not only the answer provided but also the order or version in which a particular respondent saw the items. In my experience, commercial Web survey software is better at the former (generating the random order) than the latter (capturing details of the randomization). For analysis of response and question order effects in particular, it is not enough to know what the answer was; one also needs to know where the item or question appeared.

In sum, randomization is a powerful tool in the design of Web surveys but should be executed in a way that is transparent to the user and fulfills the analytic goals of the survey. Careful testing of randomization routines and an understanding

Paper version:
Now I'd like to ask you some questions about [your/PERSON'S] (current/last) (main) job. [(Are/were) you/ (Is/Was) (PERSON) self-employed, or (do/did) you (does/did) (he/she) work for someone else [at your/his/her) (current/last (main) job?]

Electronic version for a particular respondent:
Now I'd like to ask you some questions about Mary's last job. Was Mary self-employed, or did she work for someone else at her last job?

Figure 5.11 **Example of Fill from NMES.**

of how a particular tool works are necessary for effective use of this feature. As with many design features, there is a danger of overdosing on randomization. Our own experimental designs notwithstanding, too much randomization – or randomization for the sake of doing so – may add complexity to the development and testing process, and make the resulting data harder to analyze.

5.3. Fills

Fills[3] are a special type of customized question wording in that they are typically values derived from a previous response or some other source. Sometimes these are from one or more fixed response choices, sometimes they are numeric or text strings, and sometimes they are derived from several sources. Fills require dynamic generation of question content, and are generally the result of a server-side operation. In a way, fills are the extreme of the customization continuum, personalizing the survey to the extent that every questionnaire is unique to the respondent who completes it. The best way to describe fills is to illustrate their use. The example in Figure 5.11 is from the National Medical Expenditure Survey (NMES), an interviewer-administered survey. This illustrates both the potential complexity of fills and the many possible sources of information for the fills.

In the NMES example, the following information is needed to execute the fills for this question successfully:

1. Who you are talking about (the household informant or another family member)

---

[3] Fills are sometimes referred to as "piping" in the market research literature (see, for example, Smith, Smith, and Allred, 2006).

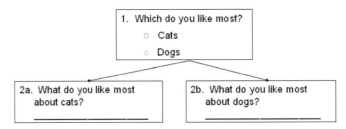

Figure 5.12 **Customization Executed Using a Skip.**

2. If another family member, their name
3. If another family member, their gender
4. Whether the person is currently or formerly employed
5. Whether they have only one or more than one job

In some of the cases, the response on which the answer is based is a text fill (e.g., "Mary"); at other times, it is based on a fixed choice response (e.g., male or female).

Basic fills can be accomplished with skips, and they can resemble skips. But the underlying logic is different and fills require dynamic generation of questions. With multiple fills, dynamic generation of pages becomes more efficient than having alternative versions of each question. This is illustrated with a simple example. Figure 5.12 shows a customized set of questions using skips. Two versions of Question 2 are created, and one or the other is delivered to the respondent depending on the answer to Question 1. The data from Questions 2a and 2b may or may not be blended together into a single variable for analysis.

Each of the items in Figure 5.12 is a static HTML page. The choice of which of Question 2a or 2b to display depends on the skip logic. As an alternative, Figure 5.13 shows the same pair of questions executed as a fill. A single version of Question 2 is created, but the particular version presented to the respondent is

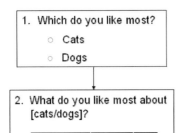

Figure 5.13 **Customization Executed Using a Fill.**

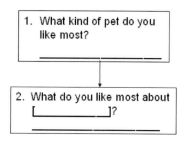

Figure 5.14 **Customization Executed as Fill Using Text String.**

generated at the time that the response to Question 1 is submitted to the server. This illustrates dynamic generation of an HTML page. This is accomplished on the server, rather than the client (or browser) side but may produce a slight delay in page delivery because of the need to generate the appropriate HTML page before transmission.

In the case of Figure 5.13, the fill is derived from a precoded response. But this need not be the case with fills. The information for fills can come from a variety of sources, as already noted. Look at the third example in Figure 5.14. Now the first question asks for information to be typed into a text field. Executing skip logic is no longer possible. The form of Question 2 depends on what the respondent typed in Question 1.

The precoded responses in Figures 5.12 and 5.13 give the designer or programmer more control than the free text responses in Figure 5.14. For example, if the respondent likes neither cats nor dogs (a possibility not accounted for by the first question), and chooses not to answer the question, the survey logic should skip over Question 2. But, if the respondent types "Neither" in Question 1 in Figure 5.14, the program will likely ask, "What do you like about Neither?", a meaningless question. This illustrates the care that needs to be taken with fills.

The information for the content of fills comes from many sources. These are illustrated in Figure 5.15. Each of the fills is presented in red. In fact, this is how we test fills in CAI instruments programmed in Blaise – by displaying them in red throughout the testing phase, then doing a global change to black for production. The source of the fill and the temporal delay between obtaining the information and using it can affect the effort required to make the fills work.

Sometimes multiple sources of information are used for a fill. For example, the age question involves input from the respondent on data of birth and a comparison to a system date (today's date minus date of birth) to generate a fill. If either the system date or the information provided by the respondent is wrong, an error in the fill will result.

Source	Examples
Text string defined at beginning of program	• your/his/her; are/were • Was Mary self-employed or did she work for someone else at her last job?
System status information, or internally derived values	• date, day, month, time • e.g., "In the last two weeks, that is since Tuesday, August 15, how many times have you seen a doctor?"
Responses to earlier items in current instrument	• e.g., Did Mary Smith work last week? • e.g., The next questions are about your relationship with John.
Results of calculations, system operations	• e.g., "Your total income from all sources amounts to $50,435. Is this correct?" • e.g., "You said you were born on January 1st, 1950. That makes you 55 years old. Is this correct?"
Data from previous waves of the survey or from an external data source	• e.g., "Last month you reported your rent as $1,000. This month you reported $3,000. Could you explain the change?"

Figure 5.15 **Sources of Information for Fills.**

Fills from fixed-choice questions (radio buttons, check boxes, or drop boxes) are under greater control than those based on open questions (text fields, text areas). Even so, in fixed-response or closed ended questions, one still must be careful to deal with missing data or nonsubstantive responses. For example, what fill (if any) should one use if the respondent answered "don't know" to the previous question or did not answer the question? Either the respondent is given a "don't know" response option, which directs the instrument around the follow-up question requiring the fill (using a skip), or code is written to parse the more obvious nonanswer types (e.g., a blank response, a "don't know"). This is not easy to do.

If the source of the open-ended fill is from a previous wave of the survey, there is at least an opportunity to edit the information or make branching decisions prior to launching the current wave of the survey. Thus, using preloaded information (Hoogendoorn, 2001) or dependent interviewing (Hill, 1994; Lynn et al., 2006) gives the designer more control over the fills than generating them directly from earlier responses in the current survey.

Given the effort involved, should one use fills at all? Some fills are easier to execute than others. Some fills may also be more important than others. Those that are key to the meaning of the question (e.g., dates, specific events, or purchases referred to) may be more valuable to include, while others may be more cosmetic (tense, pronouns, singular/plural, etc.).

Fills are widely used in CAPI and CATI surveys to make the interview flow more naturally. However, I know of no research evidence on the effect of fills on data quality or on the reduction of burden, whether actual or perceived. They take a lot of programming effort. But CAI surveys are often extremely complex, asking about a number of different family members and events, and fills may help to clarify who or what the interviewer is asking about. The types of questions often asked in Web surveys may make such high levels of customization less necessary.

While there is no evidence yet of the value of fills in terms of data quality, users of the Web may have come to expect customization and tailoring. As online shoppers, we get frustrated when merchants do not remember our preferences, asking us to provide information that we have already entered, whether earlier in the same session or in previous sessions on the same site. Will expectations of Web surveys be affected by the personalization of the general Web experience? I suspect respondents' tolerance for redundant questions – that is, ones that don't reflect what is already known about them – to be lower on the Web than on paper, and to decrease with the increasing use of customization on the Web. Therefore, whether or not it is cost-effective, we may increasingly need to tailor the survey experience to meet respondents' expectations.

This is the yin and yang of customization. The more one customizes – whether using fills, skips, or other design devices – and the more one personalizes the experience for the respondent, the more the question is directly relevant to their experience. On the other hand, the more one customizes, the greater the risk of something going wrong, and the greater the need for careful testing. We need research on the extent to which respondents notice or care about such customization.

Let's look at a few examples that show the use of fills in Web surveys. In the example in Figure 5.16, both "cat" (based on fixed input) and "Boo" (based on respondent entry) are fills. This reflects the potential advantage of fills in facilitating flow through the instrument, focusing the respondent's attention on the subject of the question.

Figure 5.17 shows the potential danger of fills. The question in Figure 5.17 is from the same survey as those in Figure 5.16. Having established that the respondent has one or more cats, this question should be about those cats. In cases like this, the question is whether the fill error is worse (i.e., produces more breakoffs or measurement error) than if a generic question about "pet(s)" was used instead. As I've noted, I know of no empirical evidence one way or the other on this issue. Intuitively, my hunch is that a failure to customize appropriately (as occurred in

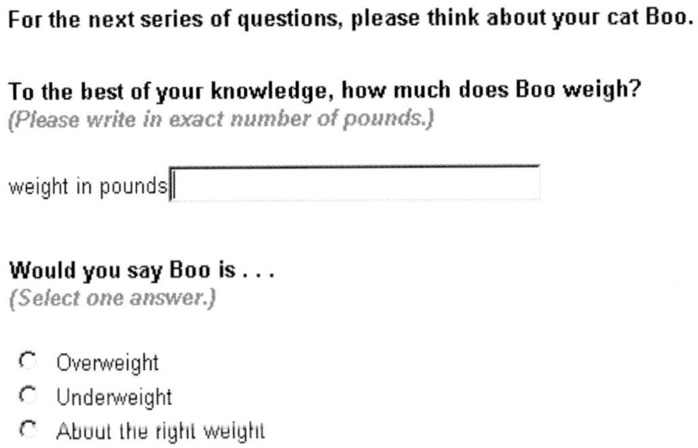

For the next series of questions, please think about your cat Boo.

To the best of your knowledge, how much does Boo weigh?
(Please write in exact number of pounds.)

weight in pounds

Would you say Boo is . . .
(Select one answer.)

- ⃝ Overweight
- ⃝ Underweight
- ⃝ About the right weight

Figure 5.16 **Use of Fills.**

Figure 5.17) is likely to be viewed as more egregious than an absence of customization. But this remains – for now – an untested hypothesis.

One more example will suffice. The question in Figure 5.18 involves partial customization. The previous question asked how many collaborations there were, the answer driving the number of rows in the current question (in this case, one). But the text of the question is designed to accommodate one or many collaborations. I'm sure respondents can deal with this without any difficulty. But the instrument

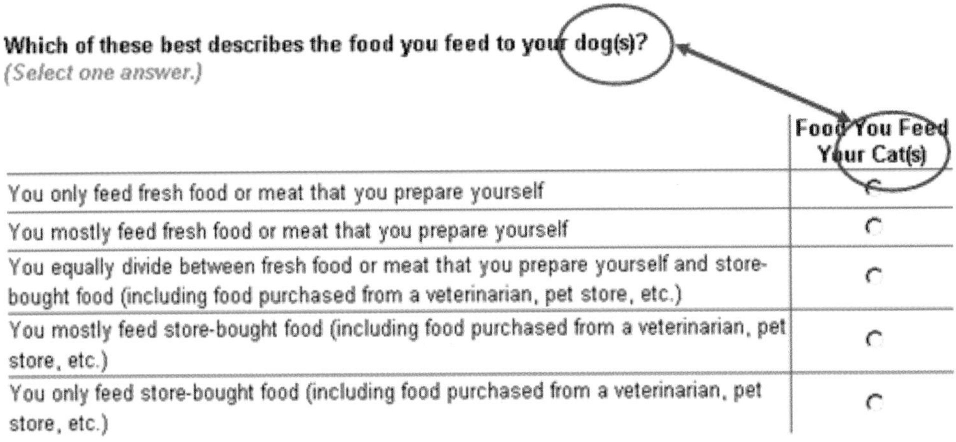

Which of these best describes the food you feed to your dog(s)?
(Select one answer.)

	Food You Feed Your Cat(s)
You only feed fresh food or meat that you prepare yourself	
You mostly feed fresh food or meat that you prepare yourself	⃝
You equally divide between fresh food or meat that you prepare yourself and store-bought food (including food purchased from a veterinarian, pet store, etc.)	⃝
You mostly feed store-bought food (including food purchased from a veterinarian, pet store, etc.)	⃝
You only feed store-bought food (including food purchased from a veterinarian, pet store, etc.)	⃝

Figure 5.17 **Fill Error.**

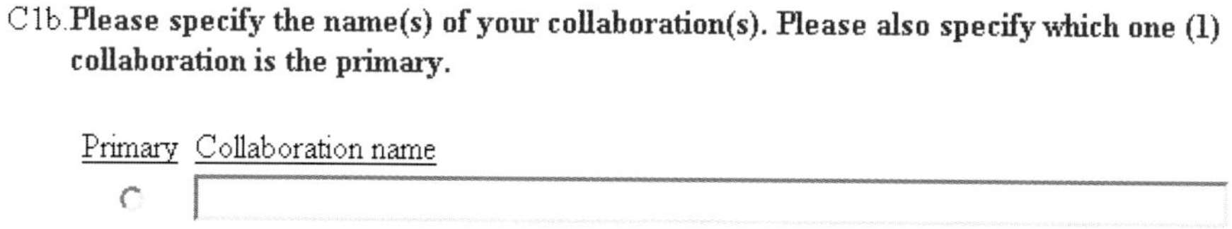

C1b. Please specify the name(s) of your collaboration(s). Please also specify which one (1) collaboration is the primary.

Primary Collaboration name

Figure 5.18 **Partial Use of Fills.**

also (unnecessarily) requires the respondent to designate the primary collabora-tion, and generates an error message if the single radio button is not selected. Having two versions of this screen – one for single collaborations and one for mul-tiple collaborations – seems a relatively simple solution to this problem. It will probably have no direct effect on data quality, but may be worth doing anyway in order to deal with the primary collaboration problem.

5.4. Summary on Customization

Skips, randomization (in part), fills, and dynamically generated HTML pages are all ways to customize or tailor the survey to individual respondents, with the (presumed) goal of producing more complete and better quality answers. However, such customization is not without costs.

The trade-off is between programming and testing effort on the part of the designer, and cognitive effort in completing the questionnaire on the part of respondents. Remember, though, when you consider this, that there are typically many thousands of respondents, and only one or two programmers or question-naire authors. A few seconds of reduction in respondent time, when multiplied over many respondents, may well outweigh a few hours of programming time. Of course, one is paying for the latter, not the former. But if one adopts a user-centered approach, efforts to reduce respondent burden or increase respondent satisfaction may have other payoffs, such as improved data quality and reduced breakoffs.

The main goal of skips is to ensure that the respondent is asked only those ques-tions that are relevant to them. Fills complement this goal by ensuring that those questions are asked in a form most relevant to the respondent's situation. Two final examples will suffice. In both cases, customization – through the dynamic genera-tion of an appropriate set of items – would have reduced burden and acknowledged information the respondent had already provided.

There are two key bits of information relevant to evaluating the first example, in Figure 5.19. The first is that the question immediately prior to this one had asked

Below is a list of seven statements. Please rate how strongly you agree or disagree with each of the following.

	Agree completely	Somewhat agree	Neither agree nor disagree	Disagree somewhat	Disagree completely
I exercise at least once a week.	○	○	○	○	○
I take vitamins and/or mineral supplements.	○	○	○	○	○
I'm willing to pay more for a beverage that is 100% juice.	○	○	○	○	○
I'm more concerned about nutritional content of beverages I give to my kids than those I give to adults.	○	○	○	○	○
I think it's important to have 5 servings of fruits and vegetables a day.	○	○	○	○	○
I'm trying to teach my kids good nutrition habits.	○	○	○	○	○
I rarely get the amount of sleep I need.	○	○	○	○	○

Figure 5.19 **Example of Lack of Customization I.**

if the respondent had any children under eighteen, and the answer was "no." The instrument is not smart enough to acknowledge this fact, and continues to ask a question irrelevant to this respondent, "I'm trying to teach my kids good nutrition habits." The second observation is that this instrument does not provide a "not applicable" option, nor does it permit the respondent to skip an item without responding (a generic error message is generated).

This leaves those without children facing a dilemma: Are they supposed to answer this question hypothetically (as if they were to have kids), or do they just choose any response knowing (hoping) than these will not be counted in the later estimates? The designer or programmer did not consider this eventuality, or was

4. Please tell us the age and gender of the following family members who are currently living in your household? (Select one answer for each household member.)

	Male	Female	Age	Does Not Apply
Self	○	○	0	○
Spouse or partner	○	○	0	○
Child 1 (oldest child)	○	○	0	○
Child 2 (second oldest child)	○	○	0	○
Child 3	○	○	0	○
Child 4	○	○	0	○
Child 5	○	○	0	○
Child 6	○	○	0	○
Other Family Member 1	○	○	0	○
Other Family Member 2	○	○	0	○

Next

Figure 5.20 **Example of Lack of Customization II.**

not aware of the constraints imposed by the software system that an answer to every question was required. Forcing a respondent to provide an answer that they cannot be expected to have is simply a bad idea.

The second example, in Figure 5.20, also needs a little explanation. On the screen before, the respondent answered a series of questions, including how many people lived in the household and the presence of any children. Given that the answer was two adults, this means that the hapless respondent must click "does not apply" eight times to avoid the nasty missing data message if a response was not provided for each row of the table. This is likely to generate a reaction of "Didn't I just tell you this?" from the respondent. When the respondent has to do more work because of poor customization, the result may be poor data quality or a breakoff. Again, the combination of required answers and irrelevant questions is likely to annoy the respondent.

We should distinguish between customization mostly for aesthetic reasons versus customization to facilitate the task of providing accurate answers. Both these examples go beyond aesthetics. Customization is worth it from the perspective of respondent satisfaction and motivation, but only if one has the time and money to test the instrument carefully. We should focus our efforts on customization that is central to question meaning and accomplishing the task, rather than on cosmetic effects. We should resist the urge to get "fill happy."

5.5. Flow and Navigation

Here we are talking about the movement from item to item or page to page in the survey. Given that the appropriate questions are delivered to the respondents in the sequence determined by the designer, how do we facilitate movement through the instrument?

The goal of instrument – as opposed to question – design is to ensure the orderly progress of the respondent from item to item. Skips or routing are one way to help ensure smooth movement through the instrument, exposing respondents to only those items that are relevant. Similarly, fills serve to contextualize the questions, and frame them better for the respondent within the larger instrument. But there are other tools and design elements that facilitate movement through the instrument. A distinction can be made between "standard" and "nonstandard" movement (e.g., see Sperry, Edwards, Dulaney, and Potter, 1998). For standard movement, the software controls the default (forward) movement through the instrument. But a respondent may need to back up and change a previous answer, access supplemental information, suspend the survey and resume at a later time, answer questions or sections of the survey out of sequence, and so on. In this section, I address a variety of issues relating to navigation and movement through the instrument, including question numbering, action buttons, and other navigation tools. Then I turn to a discussion of error messages and edit checks, which may also serve to disrupt the orderly flow of the survey. Later in this chapter, I will discuss progress indicators as a tool to convey a sense of progress to the respondent, and examine summary or review screens, which may also lead to nonstandard movement. In Chapter 6, I discuss another form of nonstandard movement – that of suspending and resuming survey completion.

5.5.1. Numbering Questions

Question numbering is common in paper surveys, and this custom is often continued in scrolling Web surveys. But is it necessary in paging designs? What function does question numbering serve? The answer differ for scrolling and paging designs.

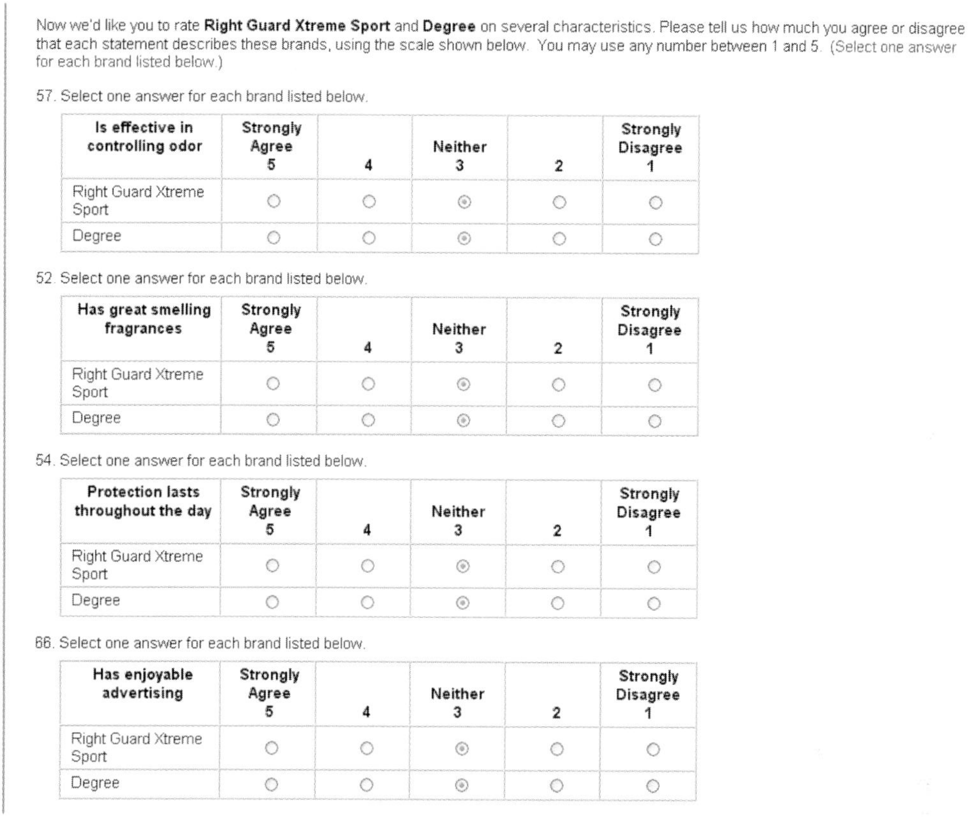

Now we'd like you to rate **Right Guard Xtreme Sport** and **Degree** on several characteristics. Please tell us how much you agree or disagree that each statement describes these brands, using the scale shown below. You may use any number between 1 and 5. (Select one answer for each brand listed below.)

57. Select one answer for each brand listed below.

Is effective in controlling odor	Strongly Agree 5	4	Neither 3	2	Strongly Disagree 1
Right Guard Xtreme Sport	○	○	◉	○	○
Degree	○	○	◉	○	○

52. Select one answer for each brand listed below.

Has great smelling fragrances	Strongly Agree 5	4	Neither 3	2	Strongly Disagree 1
Right Guard Xtreme Sport	○	○	◉	○	○
Degree	○	○	◉	○	○

54. Select one answer for each brand listed below.

Protection lasts throughout the day	Strongly Agree 5	4	Neither 3	2	Strongly Disagree 1
Right Guard Xtreme Sport	○	○	◉	○	○
Degree	○	○	◉	○	○

66. Select one answer for each brand listed below.

Has enjoyable advertising	Strongly Agree 5	4	Neither 3	2	Strongly Disagree 1
Right Guard Xtreme Sport	○	○	◉	○	○
Degree	○	○	◉	○	○

Figure 5.21 **Numbering Reveals Randomization.**

For scrolling surveys, as we have already discussed, numbering helps to distinguish one question from the next, and is important for skips and other instructions (se Figures 5.4 through 5.7 for examples). In paging designs, such numbering may be less necessary, and at times may even be distracting. This may be especially the case if the numbering doesn't follow a logical sequence, whether because of complex branching or randomization. Figure 5.21 shows an example where the randomization is revealed through the numbering of the items.

The items shown in Figure 5.21 are only a subset of the twenty statements presented on the same page in the actual survey. Respondents may well not notice the randomization. If they do, then the numbers may distract or confuse them. If they don't, then there may be no need for numbering. The only reason the

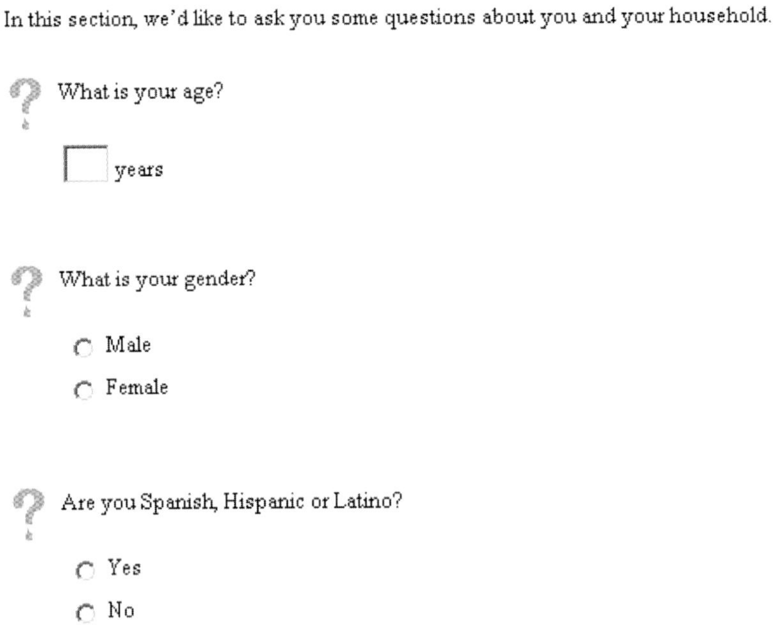

In this section, we'd like to ask you some questions about you and your household.

? What is your age?

[ ] years

? What is your gender?

○ Male
○ Female

? Are you Spanish, Hispanic or Latino?

○ Yes
○ No

Figure 5.22 **Graphical Question Identifiers.**

numbering may be helpful to respondents is if there is an error message that directs them to a particular item on the page. For example, if Q64 was not answered, an error could be generated, but in this example, it may be hard for respondents to find the unanswered Q64 unless there are other visual cues as to what as missed (see the discussion on error messages in Section 5.6).

I've focused on whether numbering is necessary for the *respondent*. Another function of numbering is to facilitate the design and analysis phases of the research. Having a short question identifier helps during instrument specification and testing, and facilitates analysis of the data. But such information as question identifiers and variable names can be part of the computerized instrument without being displayed to the respondent – these can be hidden elements in the HTML code.

Contrast the example in Figure 5.21 with that in Figure 5.22. Here there are no numbers, but the questions are still clearly identified with a graphical image. This helps to orient the respondent to the beginning of each question. The approach shown in Figure 5.22, whether using questions marks, bullets, or some other icon, is common in paging surveys where several items are placed on a single Web page.

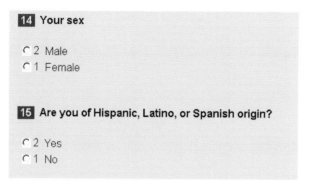

Figure 5.23 **Numbering of Items and Response Options.**

On balance, respondents need clear visual cues where each question starts and ends. In paging designs, this can be accomplished with visual cues other than numbers (e.g., icons, shading, and font changes). In scrolling surveys, numbers are likely to be more helpful, especially if the survey contains skips or error messages that refer to specific items. Other layout and design tools can be used to accomplish this end too, as discussed in Chapter 4.

While I'm on the subject of numbering, let me add a word about numbering of response options. While numbering may be popular in paper surveys, primarily to facilitate the task of keying or data entry, there is little need to include numbers in a Web survey unless they form an integral part of the response scale. Let's look at two examples. The first, in Figure 5.23, has clearly identified question numbers (this is a scrolling survey); in addition, each of the response options is numbered. But the numbering is unusual, potentially sending conflicting messages to the respondent (e.g., "yes" is listed first but numbered "2").

The second example, from the same survey, is shown in Figure 5.24. Here the question contains many sets of numbers. For example, once could click the radio button labeled "3" to indicate between five and ten written papers or reports between five and nineteen pages. At least one set of numbers – those alongside the radio buttons – could be removed, making the task at least a little easier.

Numbers are used in CATI and CAPI surveys because interviewers typically use a keyboard rather than a mouse for input. They are also common in paper surveys, to facilitate the task of data entry. But they add little in Web surveys, particularly in paging designs. Numbers convey meaning, as has been shown by Schwarz and colleagues (1991; see also Tourangeau, Couper, and Conrad, 2007). Given this, they may do more harm than good when included in Web surveys.

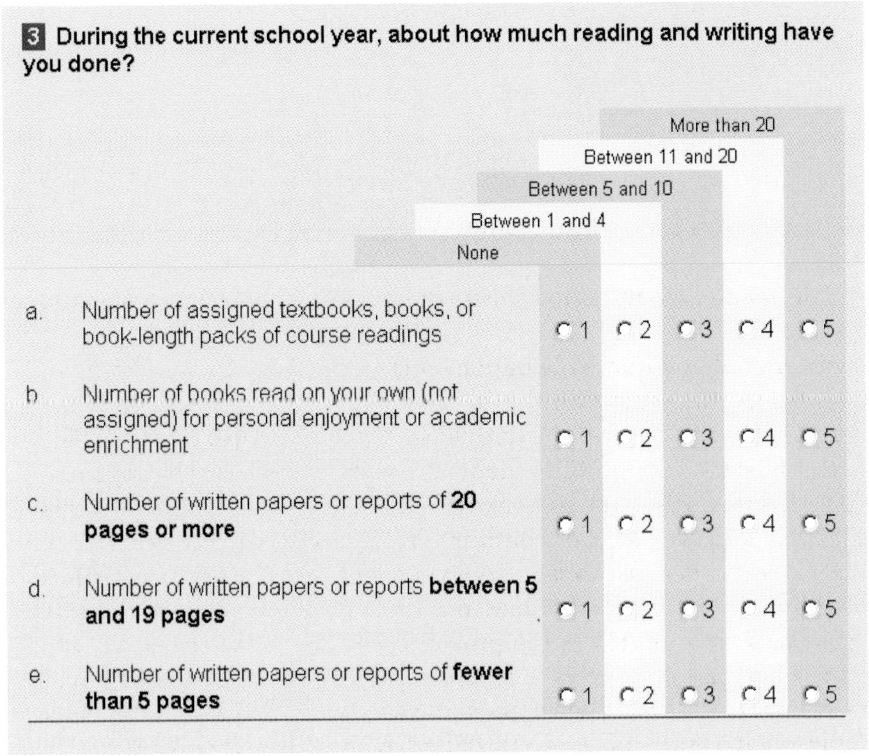

3 During the current school year, about how much reading and writing have you done?

		None	Between 1 and 4	Between 5 and 10	Between 11 and 20	More than 20
a.	Number of assigned textbooks, books, or book-length packs of course readings	○ 1	○ 2	○ 3	○ 4	○ 5
b.	Number of books read on your own (not assigned) for personal enjoyment or academic enrichment	○ 1	○ 2	○ 3	○ 4	○ 5
c.	Number of written papers or reports of **20 pages or more**	○ 1	○ 2	○ 3	○ 4	○ 5
d.	Number of written papers or reports **between 5 and 19 pages**	○ 1	○ 2	○ 3	○ 4	○ 5
e.	Number of written papers or reports of **fewer than 5 pages**	○ 1	○ 2	○ 3	○ 4	○ 5

Figure 5.24 **Numbering of Response Options.**

Unless they are necessary (such as for numbered scales), I recommend dropping such numbering of response options.

5.5.2. Action Buttons

As discussed in Chapter 2, most of the HTML widgets (radio buttons, check boxes, etc.) have no immediate effect on being clicked other than to register or accept the response. For the data to be recorded, the information needs to be transmitted to the Web server. Every Web form – as distinct from a Web page – is characterized by a "submit" button. When clicked, this button sends the content of the page to the server for further action. The only other button that takes action in a Web form is a "reset" button, which clears the page of any information entered or fields selected by the respondent. Collectively, these are referred to as push buttons. How do we

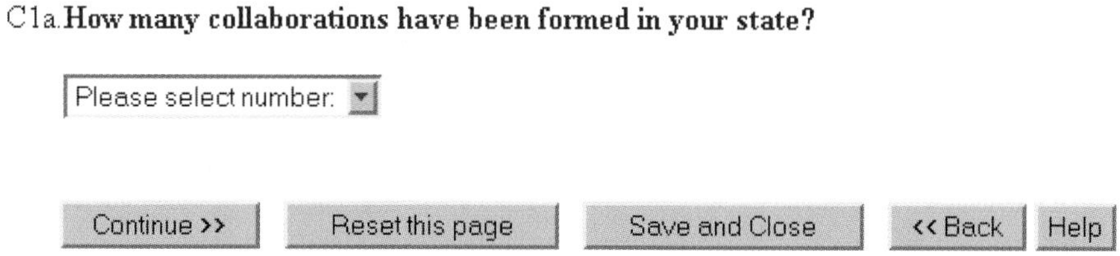

C1a. **How many collaborations have been formed in your state?**

Please select number:

Continue >> Reset this page Save and Close << Back Help

Figure 5.25 **Action Buttons in a Paging Web Survey.**

use and design these buttons to achieve the desired movement through the survey instrument?

If there are only two possible buttons, how does this explain Figure 5.25? The first point is that one has control over labeling the submit and reset buttons. The second point is that one is not limited to a single submit button. And finally, although the action in HTML is identical (the data on the Web page are sent to the server) information can be conveyed to the server that directs it to do different things. For example, the "continue" button in Figure 5.25 sends the selected response to the server, which then delivers the next applicable page to the respondent, while the "back" button does not transmit the answer to the server, but instructs the server to deliver the previous page in the sequence to the respondent. Pressing "help" delivers a different page with additional information for the respondent. This could also be achieved with a hyperlink as it requires no transmission of data to the server (I return to this issue in Section 5.7).

In other words, there are two functions, but they can perform several duties. The form of the functions in HTML is as follows:

```
<input type="submit" value="submit message">
<input type="reset" value="reset message">
```

In each case, `submit message` or `reset message` is the text that is displayed on the button. The size of the button is derived from the text in the `value` field. There is theoretically no limit to the number of submit buttons one can put on a Web form, while only one reset button is possible. In addition, the designer has control over placement of these buttons. For example, they can be arranged horizontally (as in Figure 5.25) or stacked vertically, as in Figure 5.26.

In addition, custom buttons can be designed to achieve a similar function. Many Web survey software systems provide one with a menu of different graphical buttons that can be mapped to various functions. A montage of some of the buttons that are used in Web surveys is shown in Figure 5.27. This illustrates the many different ways these buttons can be presented, both visually and verbally.

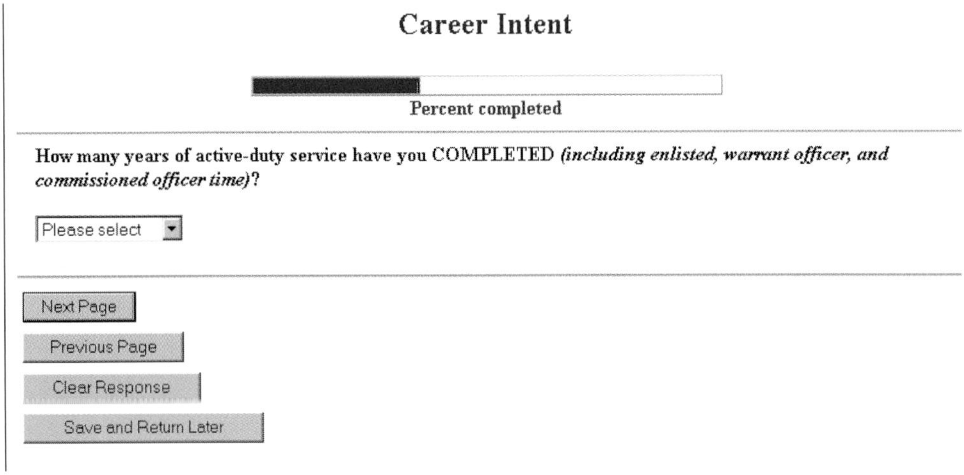

Career Intent
Percent completed
How many years of active-duty service have you COMPLETED *(including enlisted, warrant officer, and commissioned officer time)*?
Please select
Next Page
Previous Page
Clear Response
Save and Return Later

Figure 5.26 Vertically Stacked Action Buttons.

Submit
SUBMIT
Next
submit
STOP
Next Question
NEXT
Next
CONTINUE
NEXT
Back
Next
NEXT
Next Page >>
Prev
STOP
Next
BACK
CONTINUE
Next >>>
Next
<< Prev
Next >>
Next >>
Continue
NEXT
Next Question
Continue

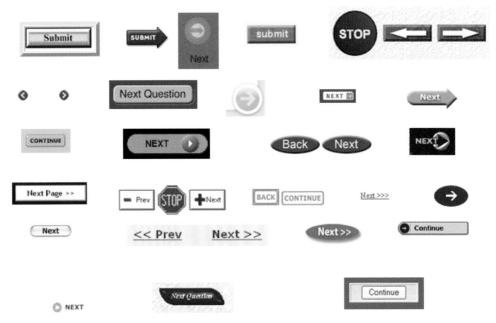

Figure 5.27 Examples of Graphical Action Buttons.

Figure 5.28 **Examples of HTML Submit Buttons.**

To do this in HTML, one simply changes the input type from submit to image as is shown below:

```
<input type="image" name="point" src="submitbutton.gif">
```

The `name = "point"` instruction specifies that the x-, y-coordinates where the mouse is located will be returned to the server when the image is clicked. This is particularly useful for a clickable map, for example, where clicking on different regions of the map may trigger different server-side actions, but the coordinate points don't add any information to the act of submission. The `src="submitbutton.gif"` identifies the name and location of the graphical image file associated with the button.

One drawback of using images for these functions is that those with assistive devices such as screen readers may have difficulty recognizing the button's function. The solution to this is to add a textual description of the button via the ALT attribute, for example `alt="submit"`. In this way, the text and function associated with the image would be clear to the respondent. A similar problem may occur when the more iconic forms of buttons are used, such as "<" and ">" (see Figure 5.28 for examples). While these visually display the notion of forward and backward movement, to those using screen readers, they would be interpreted as "less than" and "greater than," respectively, without the aid of an ALT description.

For this reason, I'm generally in favor of using the HTML buttons rather than a graphic alternative. Given this choice, one still has some design control over the appearance of the standard HTML button, using cascading style sheets (CSS).[4] For example, one can change font size and style, text and background color, and so on. And of course the text associated with the action is still under designer control. Figure 5.28 shows some of the variations that are possible within the constraints of the standard HTML buttons.

Why not use a hyperlink for navigation? This is a commonly used navigation tool in many Web sites. However, no information is transmitted to the server – clicking

---

[4] For examples of what can be done with CSS, see Lie and Bos (2005).

the hyperlink simply launches the page identified in the link. Thus, hyperlinks are useful for access to help screens, frequently asked questions (FAQs), and other auxiliary information, but not for submitting data to the Web server. At a minimum, a Web form needs a submit button.[5] The question is whether any of the other buttons are necessary. I address this question in the subsequent sections.

5.5.2.1. The Back Button

Should respondents be allowed to back up in a survey instrument? If the answer is "no," then the rest of this section is unnecessary. Several Web survey organizations do not permit respondents to back up at all. However, I believe quite strongly that the answer should be "yes." Given this answer, there are then two additional questions: (1) should there be a back button, in addition to or instead of the browser button, and (2) if so, where should it be? I address the first of these questions in this section, and the second in the context of other buttons in Section 5.5.2.3.

Why have a back button? Cockburn, McKenzie, and JasonSmith (2002) found that the browser back button accounts for "up to 42% of user actions with web browsers." They continue: "The Back button on web browsers is one of the world's most heavily used interface components, yet its behaviour is commonly misunderstood" (p. 397). Given this, we can assume that respondents are familiar with the browser back button. Then why do so many surveys instruct respondents not to use the back button? And in some cases, the survey will crash if the respondent inadvertently presses the browser back button. Let me work through an example.

Figure 5.29 shows a survey question that by itself looks innocuous. However, note the absence of a back button. Furthermore, if the browser back button is pressed – a common enough mistake given the frequency of use of this button – the survey crashes. In fact, this survey vendor as a rule does not permit respondents to go back and change answers in their surveys. When one clicks on the "help" button, one is taken to an FAQ, where the following hyperlink appears: **"A survey will not let me return to a previous question when I press the 'back' button. Is my browser broken?"** When one clicks on the link, the following is provided: "No. In

---

[5]   Some may argue that even this is unnecessary. Using JavaScript, one could advance the page automatically upon selection of a field (see Rivers, 2006). A submit button is useful because it gives respondents a chance to review and reconsider their answer before registering it. Our research (Couper, Tourangeau, Conrad, and Crawford, 2004; Couper, Singer, Tourangeau, and Conrad 2006) and that of Heerwegh (2003) suggest that changing an answer before submission is not uncommon.

6. How many air round trips have you taken for **business purposes** within the United States in the past 12 months? If you have taken more than 60 business trips in the past 12 months, please enter 60 below.

```
|                              |
```

`Next`   `Help`

Figure 5.29 **Example of Need for Back Button.**

some surveys, we disable the 'back' and 'forward' features in order to prevent a user from previewing and changing answers. This is done to protect the integrity of the data we collect." The message this conveys implies malicious intent on the part of the respondent: "we need to protect our data from the bad things you might do; we don't trust you."

The question in Figure 5.29 was followed by a sequence of questions regarding the trips one has taken. If a back button was available, two possibilities may occur. On the one hand, it is likely that detailed follow-up questions about each specific trip may bring to mind other trips that the respondent did not initially recall. Permitting a respondent to go back and change the earlier response would likely improve data quality. On the other hand, if answer A leads to a lengthy follow-up series of questions that answer B skips one out of, respondents may be more inclined to go back and change A to B. For example, if I answer "26 trips," only to discover that I'm going to have to report each trip in detail, I may be inclined to reduce the number of trips reported. As an aside, we found little evidence of this behavior in a survey of drug and alcohol use among college students (Peytchev et al., 2006).

The question is, which of these two possibilities is more likely to occur? Which is more important to us as far as data quality is concerned? What does this convey to respondents – that accuracy is not as important as data "integrity"? If the respondent is purely motivated by the reward offered for survey completion and not by the quality of responses, such control may be necessary. But why would one want such respondents to be filling out the survey, unless the survey organization's goals were similar – financial gain over quality?

In our studies, we have found that the back button is rarely used, even when it is offered. For example, in one of our experimental surveys, the back button was used an average of 0.86 times per respondent, with 59% never using it, and a further 23% using it only once throughout the survey (see also Heerwegh, 2003). This parallels the findings from interviewer-administered surveys, that nonstandard

Data Missing

This document resulted from a POST operation and has expired from the cache. If you wish you can repost the form data to recreate the document by pressing the **reload** button.

Figure 5.30 **Error Generated by Use of Browser Back Button.**

movement is an infrequent occurrence (see, e.g., Couper, Hansen, and Sadosky, 1997; Sperry et al., 1998).

In a meta-analysis of computer-administered psychological measures, Richman, Kiesler, Weisband, and Drasgow (1999) found that social desirability distortion was heightened when respondents could not backtrack to previous answers. Giving respondent the ability to go back and review – and change if necessary – the answers to previous questions is simply good practice. Having argued for the need to allow respondent to move backward, I still haven't addressed the issue of *why* we need a separate back button – why won't the browser back button suffice?

The potential risk of letting the respondent use the browser back button is that it doesn't always behave as intended. While it is quite effective for navigating Web *pages*, it can cause problems for Web *forms*. When pressed, the button loads the previously visited page from the browser's memory cache, rather than from the server. While this speeds up Web browsing, in the case of surveys in which data are transferred to a server from page to page, and new pages are delivered based on such data, it is important that the request be handled by the server rather than the browser. Some Web survey software clears the cache to prevent such problems, but this will generate the commonly seen message show in Figure 5.30 if the browser back button is pressed.

JavaScript code can be written to intercept the browser action and send the request to the server instead; JavaScript can also be used to disable the browser buttons. But I've already discussed the potential risks of relying on JavaScript. Given this, it makes sense to provide the respondent with a back button in the Web form itself. This could be coupled with a JavaScript-generated warning if the browser buttons are used, as shown in Figure 5.31.

This leaves us with a bit of a dilemma. The browser back button is commonly used, but it has unpredictable consequences. It thus makes sense to put a back button on the Web survey page, but the presence of the button may encourage its use, or its placement may get in the way of other respondent actions. This means we need careful design and placement of the button to make it available to the respondent if needed, without drawing attention to it.

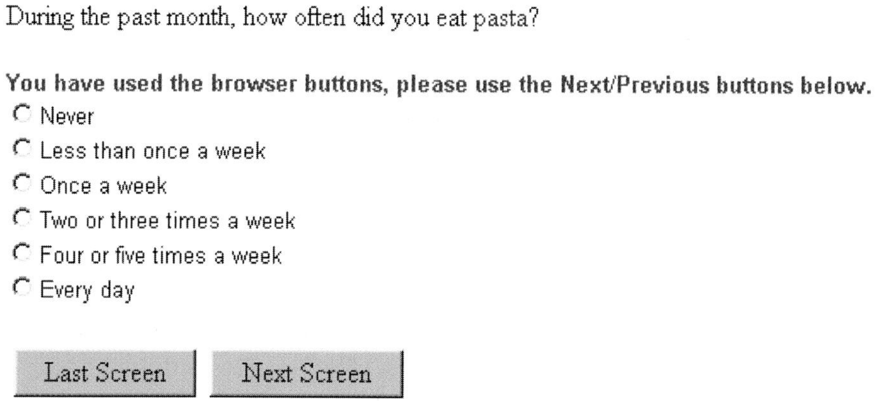

During the past month, how often did you eat pasta?

You have used the browser buttons, please use the Next/Previous buttons below.
- Never
- Less than once a week
- Once a week
- Two or three times a week
- Four or five times a week
- Every day

```
Last Screen        Next Screen
```

Figure 5.31 **Warning Generated from Use of Browser Buttons.**

5.5.2.2. The Reset Button

In contrast to the back button, the issue of a reset button is clearer. There seems to be near-universal disapprobation of the reset button in the Web design world. For example, Jarrett (2004) offered this eloquent argument against a reset button:

> How many real visitors to your website understand the term "RESET"? How many of them deliberately look for and press the RESET button so as to discard all their careful clicking and typing? I put it to you: none of them. You show me a person who has pressed RESET and I'll show you a person who is bemused, disconcerted or annoyed because their form has suddenly gone blank. They meant to press SEND and clicked on RESET by mistake. (http://www.usabilitynews.com/news/article1944.asp)

Similarly, in his Alertbox of April 16, 2000, Nielsen opined, "The Web would be a happier place if virtually all Reset buttons were removed. This button almost never helps users, but often hurts them" (http://www.useit.com/alertbox/20000416.html). Similar statements can be found throughout the literature on Web form design.

Figure 5.32 illustrates the risk of a reset button. In this example, it is placed immediately below the response options, in the logical place respondents may look for a "next" button. In a paging survey with a single question, the consequences of inadvertently pressing this button are not large. But if a similar error was made in a scrolling survey, all responses would be lost. (This example previews the discussion about placement of buttons in the next section.)

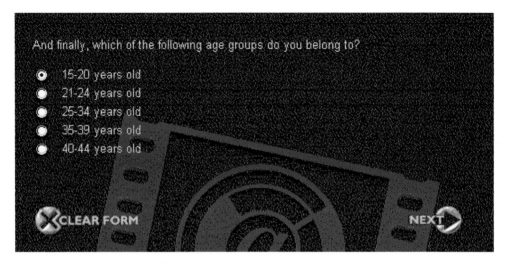

Figure 5.32 **Placement of Reset Button.**

The problem with the reset button is twofold: (1) users may click the button by mistake, and (2) it adds unnecessary clutter to the Web form. If a respondent really wants to clear all the information in a scrolling Web survey, they can press the browser refresh button or simply close the browser. In a paging survey, backing up will usually clear the current value if it hasn't yet been submitted. Again, using "refresh" or closing the browser will achieve the same effect. Of course, the latter presumes that the respondent is able to launch the survey again and continue at the point they left off (see Section 6.5.1).

5.5.2.3. Placement of Action Buttons

I've argued previously that only a "next" and "previous" button are necessary in most paging surveys. Given this, where should they be placed on the Web page? Putting the "back" or "previous" button on the left (as in Figure 5.31) may be the most logical position, and it mirrors the placement of the browser back button and the order on most other interfaces (back, forward). However, while the browser back button is used much more frequently than the forward button (and indeed, the forward button only becomes active after a back button press), it is the opposite in Web surveys. The back button is infrequently used.

There are a few drawbacks to putting the back button on the left. First, the back button will then be the first button the respondent sees after answering a question.

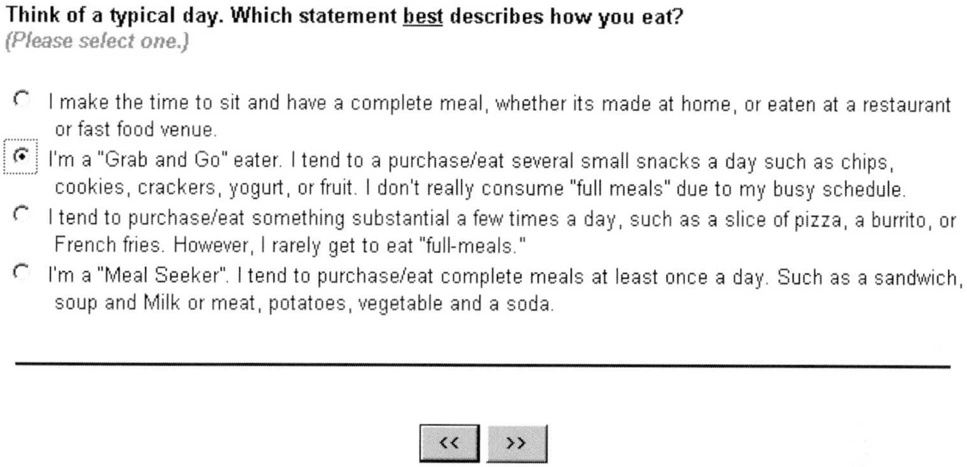

Think of a typical day. Which statement <u>best</u> describes how you eat?
(Please select one.)

   ○   I make the time to sit and have a complete meal, whether its made at home, or eaten at a restaurant
       or fast food venue.

   ◉   I'm a "Grab and Go" eater. I tend to a purchase/eat several small snacks a day such as chips,
       cookies, crackers, yogurt, or fruit. I don't really consume "full meals" due to my busy schedule.

   ○   I tend to purchase/eat something substantial a few times a day, such as a slice of pizza, a burrito, or
       French fries. However, I rarely get to eat "full-meals."

   ○   I'm a "Meal Seeker". I tend to purchase/eat complete meals at least once a day. Such as a sandwich,
       soup and Milk or meat, potatoes, vegetable and a soda.

Figure 5.33 **Activation of the Back Button.**

Second, unless the tab order is carefully controlled, it is automatically highlighted after the respondent has made a selection. This is illustrated in Figure 5.33. Note the subtle highlight around the back button (<<) after having clicked on a response option. If the respondent were to press "enter," he or she would go backward rather than forward in the instrument.

For these reasons, the U.S. Health and Human Service's Web design guidelines makes the following recommendation: "If one pushbutton in a group of pushbuttons is used more frequently than others, put that button in the first position. Also make the more frequently used button the default action, i.e., that which is activated when users press the Enter key" (U.S. Health and Human Service, 2006, p. 133).

Another reason for placing the "next" button first is that it reduces the amount of time taken to move the cursor to that point and select the item, consistent with Fitt's law (discussed in Section 2.2.2). Putting the "back" button on the right rather than the left also removes it from the main visual field, especially with response options that are vertically aligned and left justified (a common design approach).

In an unpublished study as part of our ongoing research on Web survey design, we (Baker, Couper, Conrad, and Tourangeau) explored the placement of the "next" and "previous" buttons, placing the latter on the left or the right (as in Figure 5.34).

We found that placing the "previous screen" button on the left significantly increased its use (43.9% of respondents used it at least once when on the left, compared with 38.5% when on the right). We found marginally fewer breakoffs

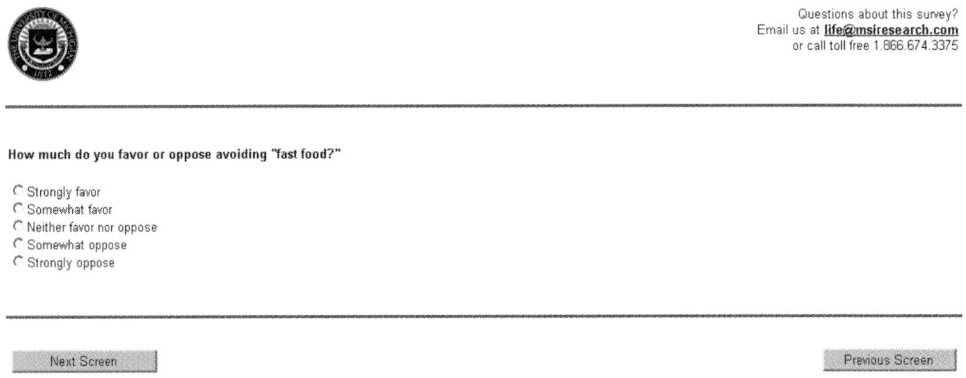

Questions about this survey?
Email us at life@msiresearch.com
or call toll free 1.866.674.3375

How much do you favor or oppose avoiding "fast food?"

- ○ Strongly favor
- ○ Somewhat favor
- ○ Neither favor nor oppose
- ○ Somewhat oppose
- ○ Strongly oppose

| Next Screen | | Previous Screen |

Figure 5.34 **Placement of "Next" and "Previous" Buttons.**

with the next button on the left, and minimally faster completion times, but neither was statistically significant. We thus found few meaningful differences between the two versions. However, the next on the left, previous on the right, approach is standard for the Web surveys we conduct with Market Strategies, Inc. (see Crawford, McCabe, and Pope, 2003).

The benefit of this button placement may depend on the orientation of response options. The approach is predicated on the assumption that most questions have the response options aligned vertically on the left side of the screen (as show in Figure 5.34), meaning that the "next" button is below the last option, potentially reducing mouse movement. But if most questions are arranged horizontally, this approach may not be so helpful.

This discussion also illustrates the potential conflict between competing design "principles." The "design consistent with expectation" principle would suggest putting the "next" button on the right. The "minimize effort" principle would suggest putting it on the left. My belief is that principles can be dangerous if blindly applied. It is better to apply thoughtful design. That is, think about the implications of a design decision, rather than simply apply a general principle. Don't blindly follow the recommendations that I or others make, but rather consider how such guidelines may apply to the particular situation.

Of course, one is not restricted to the horizontal layout used in Figure 5.34. The buttons could be arranged vertically as in Figure 5.26. One final example will suffice to illustrate the trade-offs in trying to make the back button available but get it out of the way. In Figure 5.35, the button is placed in the top right corner of the

Figure 5.35 **Placement of "Back" Button.**

page. This is likely to reduce its visibility. Unfortunately, the size and brightness of the button, especially relative to the standard HTML button used for "next," potentially has the opposite effect, drawing the respondent's eye to the button. Whatever design is chosen, use the same design consistently throughout the survey – and across surveys if the same respondents will be answering repeated surveys.

5.5.3. Other Navigation Tools

In addition to the action buttons or push buttons, what other navigation tools do respondents need and how should they be designed? Establishment surveys and household surveys (as opposed to surveys of individuals) often provide a variety of additional navigation tools. These are designed to accommodate the following types of respondent behaviors:

- Completion by multiple respondents within an establishment, organization, or family
- Completion across multiple sessions
- Completion of sections in any order

Given this, surveys aimed at these groups typically require more than a simple "submit" button each screen, and navigation menus are included, often in addition to the standard buttons permitting default forward movement.

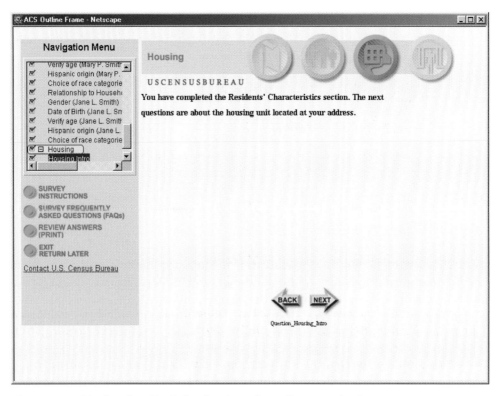

Figure 5.36 **Navigation Tools in the American Community Survey.**

An example of such a menu is shown in Figure 5.36. This is from an early test Internet version of the American Community Survey (ACS) conducted by the U.S. Census Bureau. Note the graphic-based "back" and "next" buttons in the main question area, along with the navigation menu in the left pane. In addition, there are several other buttons, including survey instructions, FAQs, a review and print option, and an option to suspend the survey and resume later.

In contrast to this example, Figure 5.37 is a screen from the 2005 National Census Test, also from the U.S. Census Bureau. This shows the use of tab-based navigation, with many of the additional buttons and links removed. This design focuses respondents more on the forward progress through the instrument, while still allowing them to back up one screen, jump to a previously completed section, access help, and the other navigation activities available in the ACS instrument, without cluttering the screen.

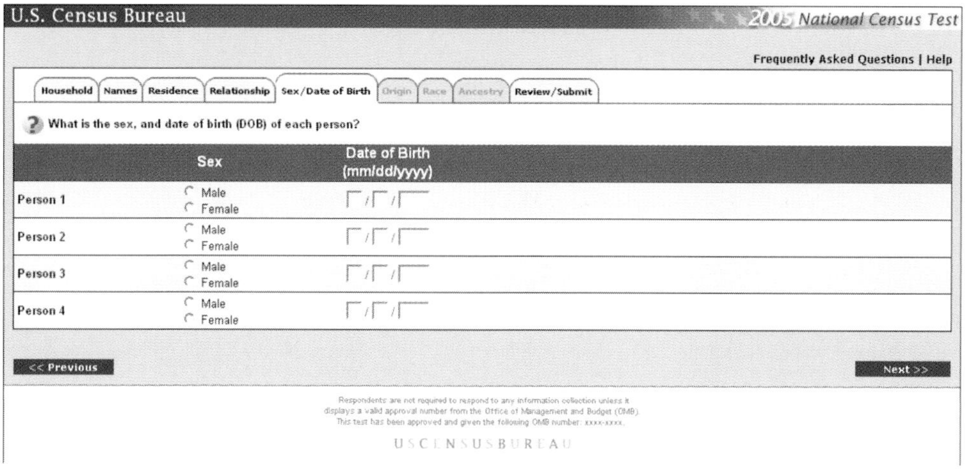

Figure 5.37 **Navigation Tools in the 2005 National Census Test.**

The next example comes from Statistics Netherlands (see Figure 5.38). Again, we see the characteristic form of an online business survey, with a navigation menu on the left, and a variety of additional buttons (send, print, save, etc.) on the bottom, in addition to the usual back and forward arrows. Again, this permits the respondent to take many actions in completing this survey.

The final example in this section comes from a survey designed using the software developed by the U.S. Government Accountability Office (GAO). The software is primarily designed for establishment surveys, but in this example, it is used for an individual survey (a conference evaluation). The main survey pane contains a "next section" action button, along with a "print" and "exit" button. The print button is a "submit" button with a prescribed function, as described in Section 5.2.2. Pressing the print button sends a request to the server to deliver a Web page suitable for printing. By contrast, pressing the browser print button will print the current Web page or form as displayed. This particular example loads the survey in a separate browser window from which the regular browser buttons are removed, so there is no browser print button or back button. The "exit" button is similarly designed to send specific instruction to the server. But, in addition to these buttons, there is a navigation menu on the left, permitting the respondent to jump around the instrument and answer sections out of order. A set of buttons at the bottom of the screen permit the respondent to jump to the beginning or end of

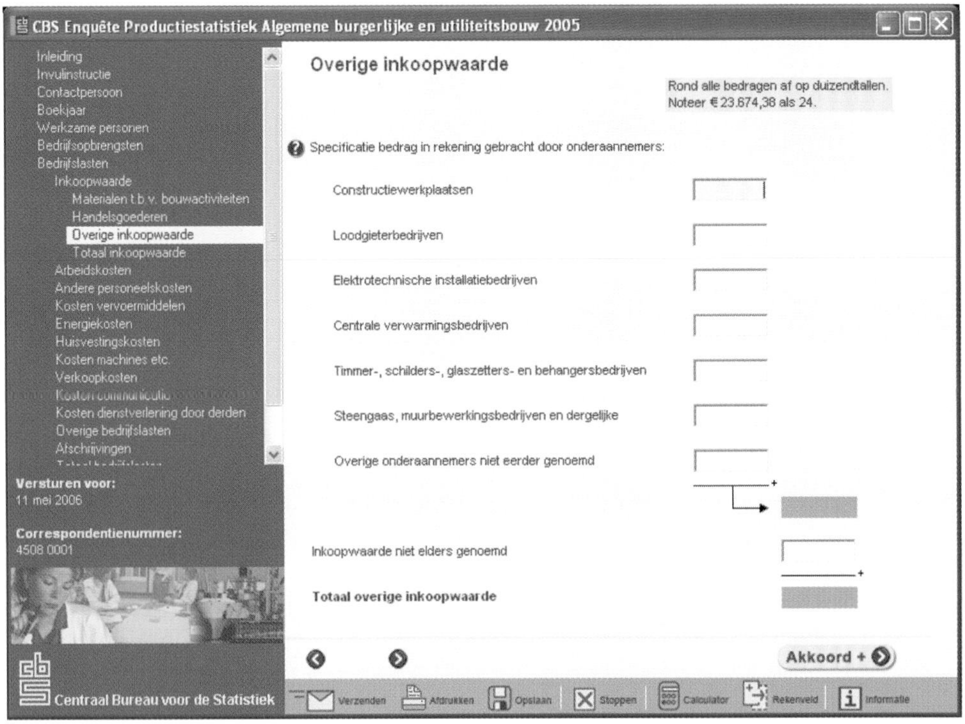

Figure 5.38 **Navigation Tools in Statistics Netherlands Survey.**

the survey, jump sections, or stop the survey. Thus, there are three different ways a respondent could navigate through the instrument.

The examples in this section are meant to illustrate that the design of more complex instruments is quite different from that of the typical survey involving linear progression through a series of questions. The latter is the primary focus of this book. This also emphasizes the risks of a one-size-fits-all approach to Web survey design. Different types of applications have different design needs, and may require different software for optimal use. The example in Figure 5.39 illustrates this, using software designed primarily for establishment surveys to administer a linear survey of individuals. While the added functions may be useful in an establishment survey, they may prove distracting or even confusing in a linear survey of individuals. Would it matter in this case? Probably not – FedCASIC is the Federal Workshop on Computer Assisted Survey Information Collection. But if the same tool was used for a survey of less technically savvy respondents, the

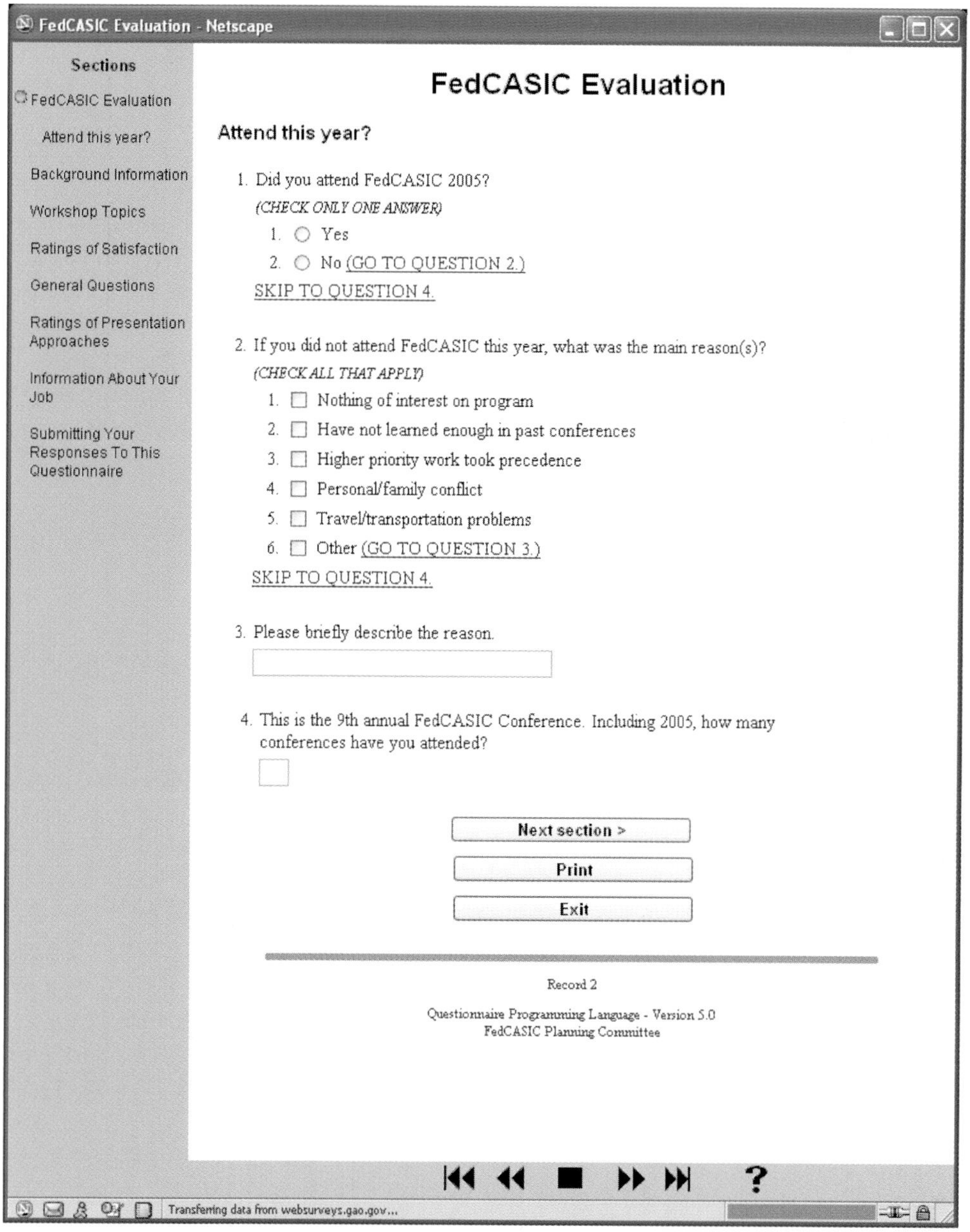

FedCASIC Evaluation - Netscape

Sections

- FedCASIC Evaluation
- Attend this year?
- Background Information
- Workshop Topics
- Ratings of Satisfaction
- General Questions
- Ratings of Presentation Approaches
- Information About Your Job
- Submitting Your Responses To This Questionnaire

FedCASIC Evaluation

Attend this year?

1. Did you attend FedCASIC 2005?
   (CHECK ONLY ONE ANSWER)
   1. ○ Yes
   2. ○ No (GO TO QUESTION 2.)
   SKIP TO QUESTION 4.

2. If you did not attend FedCASIC this year, what was the main reason(s)?
   (CHECK ALL THAT APPLY)
   1. ☐ Nothing of interest on program
   2. ☐ Have not learned enough in past conferences
   3. ☐ Higher priority work took precedence
   4. ☐ Personal/family conflict
   5. ☐ Travel/transportation problems
   6. ☐ Other (GO TO QUESTION 3.)
   SKIP TO QUESTION 4.

3. Please briefly describe the reason.

4. This is the 9th annual FedCASIC Conference. Including 2005, how many conferences have you attended?

[Next section >]

[Print]

[Exit]

Record 2

Questionnaire Programming Language - Version 5.0
FedCASIC Planning Committee

Transferring data from websurveys.gao.gov...

Figure 5.39 **Navigation Tools in GAO Survey Software Tool.**

design may well create problems. It is better to give respondents a clearly defined path through the instrument.

5.6. Error Messages

Another form of nonstandard action in Web surveys occurs when a respondent submits a response that triggers an edit check or generates a system failure. Failing to submit a response may similarly trigger a message that requires some action by the respondent before proceeding. The kinds of things we need to think about here include: (1) when and how often should such messages be delivered, (2) how should they be designed to ensure that they are noticed and acted upon, and (3) should they be treated as warnings that could be ignored by respondents, or as errors that require action in order to proceed?

I'll first review the various reasons for error messages and then review the research on error messages in Web surveys, before finally turning to a discussion of the design of such messages.

5.6.1. Item Missing Data

Item missing data is a common occurrence in Web surveys. For example, Bosnjak and Tuten (2002) reported that 35% of those who completed a Web survey left one or more items unanswered, and only 25% of respondents provided answers to every question in the survey. There are many ways to deal with item missing data, not all of which generate error messages. This issue thus deserves a different treatment than the other sources of error messages.

It is when dealing with missing data that the Web shows its versatility. A Web survey can be designed to resemble a self-administered paper survey, with or without an explicit "don't know" option, where a respondent can choose not to answer a question. It can also be designed to behave more like an interviewer-administered survey, with prompting for missing data (e.g., deRouvray and Couper, 2002).

If the designer so wished, a Web survey can be designed to require an answer to each question before proceeding to the next. This is generally a bad idea. I say this for two main reasons: (1) it violates the norms of voluntary participation, (2) it may not increase data quality at all (if this was the original intention), in that requiring *an* answer does not mean one will get the *right* answer, and it may

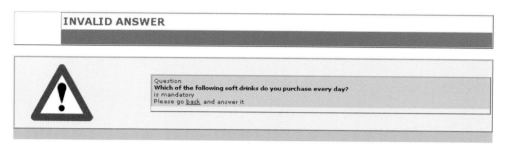

Figure 5.40 **Example of Mandatory Question.**

increase respondent frustration to the point of breakoff. Encouraging respondents to provide an answer is appropriate but forcing them to do so is not. Figure 5.40 shows an example of such a required answer. Forcing respondents to answer questions is ethically problematic and likely to result in poor quality data. Given this, how should we deal with the issue of nonanswers in Web surveys?

This is a design challenge in other modes too, and the literature on missing data or nonsubstantive responses in surveys is quite extensive (for a recent overview, see de Leeuw, 2001), but thus far there is relatively little found on Web surveys. I will not attempt to review the broader literature in this section, but rather focus on key issues relevant to Web survey design.

A common strategy in interviewer-administered surveys is to probe once for a "don't know" or "no opinion" response, but then accept that answer if offered. Many CAI systems offer special keys for these responses (e.g., Ctrl-D for "don't know" and Ctrl-R for "refused"), so that they are not routinely displayed to interviewers as viable response alternatives. Interviewers are instructed to use these only after probing. This approach can be emulated in Web surveys using automated prompting, as shown in Figure 5.41.

There are three dimensions along which the designs for addressing missing data can vary. These are

1. Whether a "don't know" (DK) or "no opinion" options is offered, or not
2. Whether an answer is required, or not
3. Whether prompting is used for missing responses, or not

I am using DK as shorthand for "Would rather not answer" or some such nonsubstantive response; for some types of questions, such as knowledge or factual questions, a DK could be considered a substantive response. The combination of

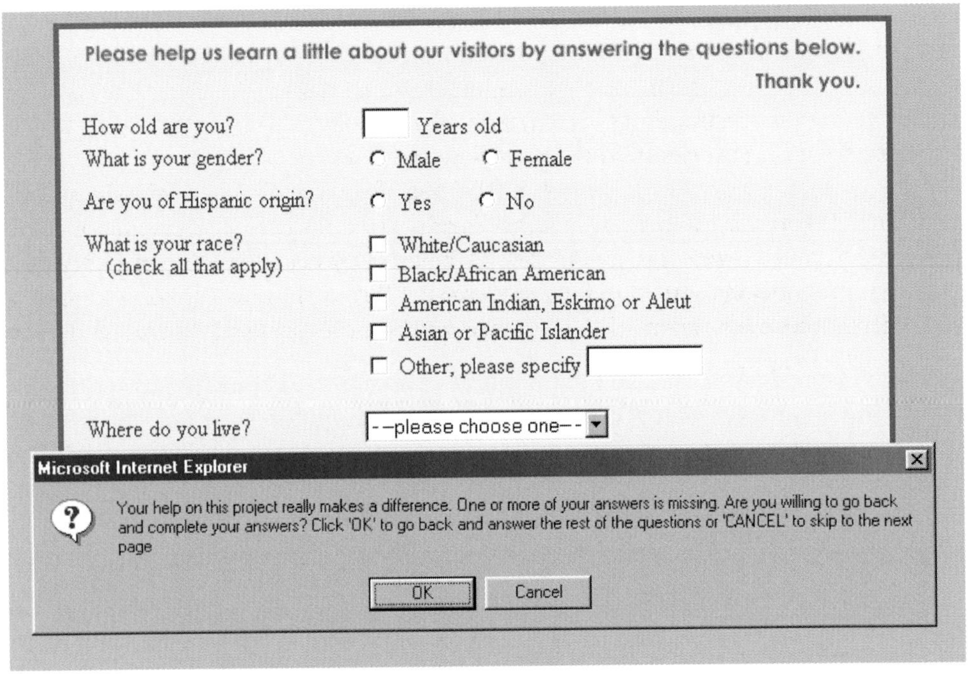

Figure 5.41 **Example of Soft Prompt for Missing Data.**

these three dimensions produces eight possible variations in design, as listed in Figure 5.42.

If we think of a required answer as generating an error message, then following such a message with an encouraging prompt (e.g., Types 3 and 7) makes little

Type	DK option	Require answer	Prompt
1	No	Yes	No
2	No	No	No
3	No	Yes	Yes
4	No	No	Yes
5	Yes	Yes	No
6	Yes	No	No
7	Yes	Yes	Yes
8	Yes	No	Yes

Figure 5.42 **Classification of Approaches to Item Missing Data.**

sense – this leaves us with six plausible approaches to missing data. In addition, this list is not exhaustive. For example, it is possible to make a DK option available only after a missing data prompt has been generated. Similarly, there can be variation in how respondents are instructed to answer. But this classification at least allows us to discuss the variety of possible options.

Type 1 is the worst and Type 4 is the best for striking the optimal balance between minimizing missing data and forcing respondents to provide answers simply to proceed through the survey. Dillman (2000, p. 394) also strongly recommends not forcing a respondent to answer. I'll return to the research evidence supporting these arguments after reviewing the other types of errors that may generate messages.

5.6.2. Edit Checks

Edit checks are broader than item missing data checks; in addition to encouraging complete responses to all questions, there can be checks for a number of additional events or conditions. Given that many Web survey questions constrain the respondents' choices by giving them a set of radio buttons or check boxes from which to choose, many single-item errors that may occur in other modes are prevented from happening on the Web. But for responses using text fields (see Section 2.5), the respondent is less constrained in what they can enter, and the need for edit checks becomes more important.

Peytchev and Crawford (2005) review the types of real-time validations that are used in Web surveys. Data type and format validations or checks are most common for fields in which alphanumeric entry is permitted. For example, if the question asks how many times one has seen a doctor in the past twelve months, the software can check for a variety of possible errors, such as whether nonnumeric values (e.g., "Many times") or ranges (e.g., "2–3") are entered. In both cases, a simple validation that only integers are entered into the field can be executed. In addition, one could run range checks to detect implausible high or low values. For example, in a survey intended for adults, values that fall below or above a certain range (e.g., 18–99) can trigger an error message.

For other types of text input in which the response has an expected format, the system can detect whether the response conforms to that format. For example, a U.S. telephone number must contain ten digits; a zip code, five digits; and so on. The check could be more or less sophisticated, for example rejecting the input

15. How much did you pay for the digital still camera? (Please enter your answer in dollars and cents, e.g., 14.25.)

$ 200

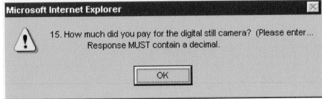

15. How much did you pay for the digital still camera? (Please enter your answer in dollars and cents, e.g., 14.25.)

$ 200|

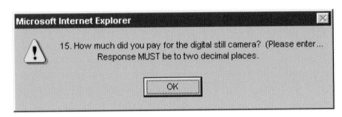

Figure 5.43 **Edit Check for Entry of Dollar Amount.**

if any nonnumeric characters (such as parentheses, hyphens, or other delimiters) are entered, or first stripping the entry of any such delimiters and seeing whether the residual numeric string is well formed.

These should be more correctly viewed as plausibility checks rather than validity checks. For example, to confirm that a valid zip code was provided, or that it corresponds to the state provided, the response must be checked against a database of active zip codes. Similarly, it is difficult to check whether a valid working telephone number or e-mail address was entered. For the latter, the validation usually involves an evaluation of the format of the entry, such as does it contain an "@" sign preceded and followed by text, is there a plausible high-level domain (.com, .edu, etc.), does the address contain any illegal characters (such as spaces), and so on. Forcing a respondent to answer such questions can lead to zip codes like 11111, telephone numbers like (123) 456-7890, and e-mail address like NoneOfYourBusiness@private.com, all of which will pass plausibility checks.

Figure 5.43 shows an example of edit checks for a dollar amount field. The first check looks for a decimal point and returns an error. The second check looks for two numbers following the decimal. Even though the respondent may not know

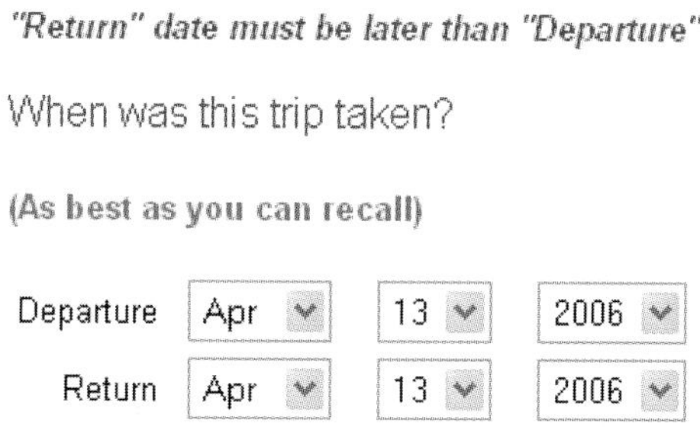

"Return" date must be later than "Departure" date

When was this trip taken?

(As best as you can recall)

| Departure | Apr ▾ | 13 ▾ | 2006 ▾ |
| Return | Apr ▾ | 13 ▾ | 2006 ▾ |

Figure 5.44 **Error Check Involving Two Dates.**

the exact amount, he or she is forced to provide the information in the required format. Another survey from the same vendor asked for an amount rounded to the nearest $10 and generated an error if a more precise number (e.g., $115) was entered (See Figure 5.50).

Edit checks can also involve two or more responses. For check-all-that-apply questions, this could involve a check of the number of responses selected (e.g., if the instruction is to select no more than three items), or whether a substantive response and a "None of the above" response were both selected. Across questions, a wide range of plausibility and consistency checks can be performed. From a technical perspective, these are limited only by the designer's ability to specify and by the software's ability to execute the specified logic. Figure 5.44 shows an example of such a logic check involving two dates. Unfortunately, only overnight trips are acceptable to the system, even though the question did not specify this.

5.6.3. System Errors

Sometimes the system, not the respondent, produces an error. Here it is even more important to be clear what happened and what the respondent should do in response to the error. There are some error messages over which the designer has little control. But others, especially those generated by the Web survey software, can be customized to communicate more clearly to the respondent what the problem is and what (if anything) can be done about it.

Figure 5.45 shows two examples from the same survey vendor, generated for similar reasons – a failure to load streaming video. Which message would one

```
Microsoft OLE DB Provider for ODBC Drivers error '80040e31'
[Microsoft][ODBC SQL Server Driver]Timeout Expired
C:\INETPUB\WWWROOT\SURVEY\..\Include/RRLib.asp, line 1936
```

Our servers are unable to process your request at this time.
Please try back later.
Thank you.

Figure 5.45 **System Error Messages.**

rather get? The first provides no useful information to the respondent, while the second takes the blame for the error, is polite, and instructs the respondent on what to do – as discussed in Section 5.6.5.

5.6.4. Research on Error Messages and Prompts

Despite the likelihood of missing data – at least until prompted or forced to respond – there is surprisingly little research on the alternative ways of dealing with missing data in Web surveys. In fact, the fully elaborated set of options outlined in Figure 5.42 is yet to be evaluated. However, some comparisons of subsets of these design options have been conducted.

In an early study using the Knowledge Networks panel, deRouvray and Couper (2002) tested alternative designs to reduce missing data in a short (fourteen-item) survey. One version had an explicit "Decline to answer" option for each question (Type 6 in Figure 5.42). A second version had the same option displayed in a lighter and smaller font – this had no effect on item missing data relative to the first version. The last two versions we tested had a prompt for missing data, one combined with the "Decline" option (Type 8) and the other not (Type 4). The latter version (Type 4) had a significantly (p < .01) lower missing data rate of just under 4%, compared with over 10% for the two versions with no prompt and 7.4% for the version with a "Decline" option and no prompt. This suggests that Type 4 may be optimal for minimizing missing data.

Heerwegh (2005a) notes the distinction between a "hard prompt" that endlessly displays the unanswered question until a response is given, and a "soft prompt" that displays the message only once before permitting a respondent to move on without answering. The former is an example of Type 1 or 5 in Figure 5.42; the latter is an example of Type 4. Heerwegh experimentally compared a no-prompt group (Type 2) with the soft and hard prompt groups in a survey of university students in Belgium. The survey was considerably longer than that of deRouvray and Couper (2002). Not all questions were followed up with a prompt.

Heerwegh found negligible differences in item missing data rates between the three versions, although in the expected direction, with the soft prompt yielding more missing data than no prompt, and both prompts (by definition) more than the hard prompt case, which did not permit missing data. Overall, respondents were rarely exposed to prompts, with 3.8% ever seeing a prompt, and the vast majority of these seeing only one prompt. Maybe more telling is that Heerwegh found a breakoff rate of 13.5% for the hard prompt group, compared to that of 10.8% for the soft prompt and 11.7% for the no prompt group (again, these differences are not statistically significant). Nonetheless, this study suggests that forcing respondents to provide an answer may come at a price in terms of break-offs.

Thomas, Lafond, and Behnke (2003) conducted an experiment in which respondents were assigned to a one of several different "out-of-range" or nonsubstantive response options. They found that a Not Applicable (NA) option had the fewest endorsements across the 10 items evaluated (8.8%), with the other alternatives being comparable in their endorsement rates: 19.6% for Don't Know (DK), 18.5% for Not Sure (NS), 17.7% for Not Familiar, and 19.0% for No Opinion. In addition to these conditions, Thomas, Lafond, and Behnke (2003) tested a forced choice approach (Type 1 in Figure 5.42) and a nonmandatory condition, with an instruction that respondents could skip an item (Type 2 in Figure 5.42). The forced response version by definition had no item nonresponse (among the completes), while the nonmandatory design had 12.2%. Their results also suggest that forcing respondents to rate aspects of a topic with which they are less familiar may lead to data that are more centrally distributed.

The design of prompts for missing data differs between paging and scrolling designs. In paging designs, the prompt can occur immediately when the respondent moves to the next page. In scrolling designs, the check of missing data only occurs after the full survey or section is submitted – unless active scripting is used to detect the error and alert the respondent when they proceed to the next item.

Kerwin, Levin, Shipp, Wang, and Campbell (2006) tested two different forms of missing data prompt in a scrolling survey with eighty-three items in seven sections. One version included the prompt at the end of the survey (after the last section had been submitted), while another included the prompt after each section, and a third version with no prompt served as a control. They found significantly (p < .05) lower proportions of surveys with any missing data for the two prompt versions (23.0% and 23.3%, respectively) than the control version with no prompts (34.8%). The mean number of missing items was also significantly (p < .01) lower for the prompt versions (0.9 for end-of-survey prompts, 1.1 for end-of-section prompts) than the control (2.2). However, Kerwin et al. (2006) also found that those who received a prompt after each section were more likely to break off than those who received one at the end (18.4% versus 8.0%, respectively). This suggests some risk of prompting respondents too often.

Together, these results suggest that hard prompts (requiring an answer) is not a good idea, and that offering an explicit opt-out response option increases the number of nonsubstantive responses. While some form of soft prompt seems effective, research remains to be done on how often such prompts should be triggered, and when (in the case of scrolling surveys). I'll discuss some of the design issues related to missing data messages in Section 5.6.5.

Aside from the studies on item missing data, the research on error messages in general, and on the design of such prompts in particular, is relatively scarce.

Mooney, Rogers, and Trunzo (2003) experimented with three different levels of error prompt in an establishment of substance abuse treatment providers. The three levels were

1. No error prompts.
2. Soft error prompts for missing, inconsistent, or out-of-range responses to critical items; the respondent could ignore the error.
3. Hard error prompts for missing, inconsistent, or out-of-range responses to critical items; the respondent could not proceed without correcting the error.

The survey contained sixty-three items, of which thirty-eight were considered critical and had prompts. They found no differences in breakoff rates or completion times across the three groups. In terms of error prompts, 68% of those in group 2 and 73% of those in group 3 encountered at least one prompt; among those that did encounter a prompt the average number of prompts encountered was 1.1 for group 2 and 1.5 for group 3. The missing data rates for the noncritical items were also similar across the three groups. Mooney, Rogers, and Trunzo (2003) conclude that the error prompts did not deter sample members from completing the survey, nor did they negatively affect respondent burden. Including the error prompts had a small but positive effect on data quality.

In another establishment survey using a scrolling design, Mockovak (2005) explored three different designs of edit messages:

1. Edit messages displayed near top of page, but only after all items had been completed and the continue button was pressed.
2. Edit messages displayed under the item triggering the edit, but only after all items had been completed and the continue button was pressed
3. Edit messages displayed under the item triggering the edit, as soon as the user moved to the next item.

While the instrument was programmed in Java, the first two designs can be viewed as server-side approaches, and the third as client-side. In each case, the edit message was presented in a text box and using a red font that was larger than the rest of the survey text.

Mockovak explored these alternatives in a laboratory-based study using scenarios, with forty-two participants each completing three scenarios, one in each design. The scenarios focused on three specific edits: (1) total hours worked (within a given range, depending on number of workers), (2) date of injury (date entered in specified format), and (3) age of worker (range of 15–85). When the edits were triggered, participants did not always notice them. The first edit (on the second item of the form) was missed 40% of the time, while the second (on item 18 of 31) was missed 21% of the time, and the third (on item 23 of 31) only 7% of the time. However, there was no consistent pattern in missing the edits across the three instrument designs. The proportion of correct actions that were taken when the users saw the edit ranged from 89% for edit 1 to 72% for edit 2 and 76% for edit 3, again with no clear pattern across the instrument designs.

While edits are generally more common in surveys of establishments than in surveys of individuals, it is not clear how much can be generalized from these two studies to either type of survey. They suggest that much work remains to be done on the design and evaluation of edit prompts in Web surveys.

5.6.5. The Design of Error Messages

How should error messages best be designed? Cooper (1995, p. 438) notes that error messages should be polite, illuminating, and helpful. The interface design literature (e.g., Galitz, 1993, Schneiderman, 1992) has recommendations on the appropriate tone and wording of error messages that are quite relevant to the Web survey setting. Similarly, the literature on human errors (see Couper, 1999, for a brief overview related to CAI) suggests that the following hierarchy is desirable in design:

Error prevention > error detection > error correction

In other words, good design should minimize the occurrence of an error in the first place. Many of the design features discussed in the book are aimed at just that – guiding the respondent to the appropriate response. But, it is inevitable that errors will still occur, and they must be easily detectable by the respondent. Feedback mechanisms such as running totals (discussed in Chapter 3) are one example of this. Finally, once an error occurs, the design of the instrument should make it easy for the respondent to correct the error. Forcing functions, such as preventing respondents from backing up to change previous answers, violate notions of error detection and correction.

Without reviewing in detail this extensive literature on error management, we can distill from this work the following recommendations on the design of error messages:

- Don't blame the user
  - Use positive nonthreatening words
  - Be polite
  - Do not punish the user for making an error
- Avoid unclear error messages
  - Show the user what the problem is
  - Suggest alternative actions
  - Avoid generic error messages

Despite these simple guidelines, there are many egregious examples of error messages in the Web survey world. I suspect this is in part because the designer never pays attention to this part of the instrument, thinking that these are system functions that cannot be modified. In fact, generic error messages are often most unhelpful, and a modicum of effort to customize the messages will pay off in better quality and more complete data. Let's look at some examples.

The first example comes from a survey with required responses (see Figure 5.46). The respondent is expected to provide an answer to every question, but the tone conveys a sense of coercion. As the designers of this survey may well have discovered, an easy option for respondents in such cases is simply to abandon the

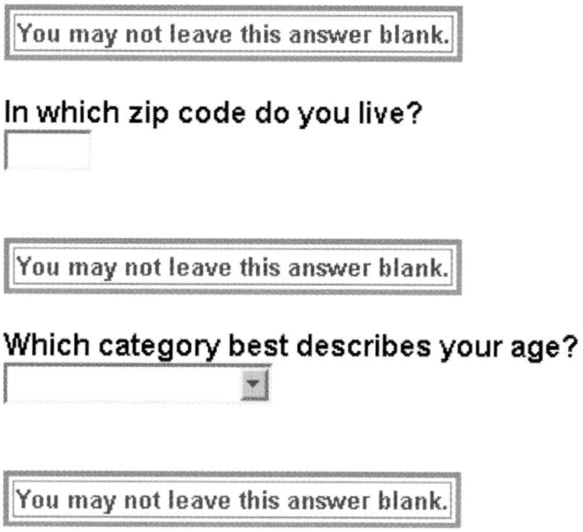

You may not leave this answer blank.

In which zip code do you live?

You may not leave this answer blank.

Which category best describes your age?

You may not leave this answer blank.

Figure 5.46 **Example of Required Answers.**

survey. In e-commerce, where the customer will directly benefit from the transaction, requiring certain information may have high compliance rates – if not, the customer is unable to complete the transaction. But in surveys, where the cost to respondents of terminating the interaction is negligible, demanding an answer is unlikely to be effective. Unfortunately, I continue to see many examples like that in Figure 5.46 in Web surveys.

The next example (see Figure 5.47) is similar, in that respondents are expected to provide an answer for every question. Here the tone of the error message is an improvement over the previous example, but the respondent is still expected to put a "00" in every field that does not apply to them. Why make the respondent do the work, when the software could quite easily take care of this, assuming that a blank is equivalent to a 0? The risks of losing respondents must be traded off against the possible loss of data quality by making such assumptions. Note too the generic message for a format error, when the respondent entered ".5" for the fourth item. The large font messages in red have the effect of shouting at the respondent.

Figure 5.48 shows another example of making the respondent do unnecessary work. Forcing a respondent to enter something in an open-ended text field simply to satisfy some requirement of the software demonstrates either the inflexibility of the software used, or the lack of thought on the part of the designer, or both.

While the examples in Figure 5.47 and 5.48 require the respondent to do unnecessary work, the example in Figure 5.49 takes it one step further. The respondent missed one row in the matrix (row 6 in question 19) when submitting the page.

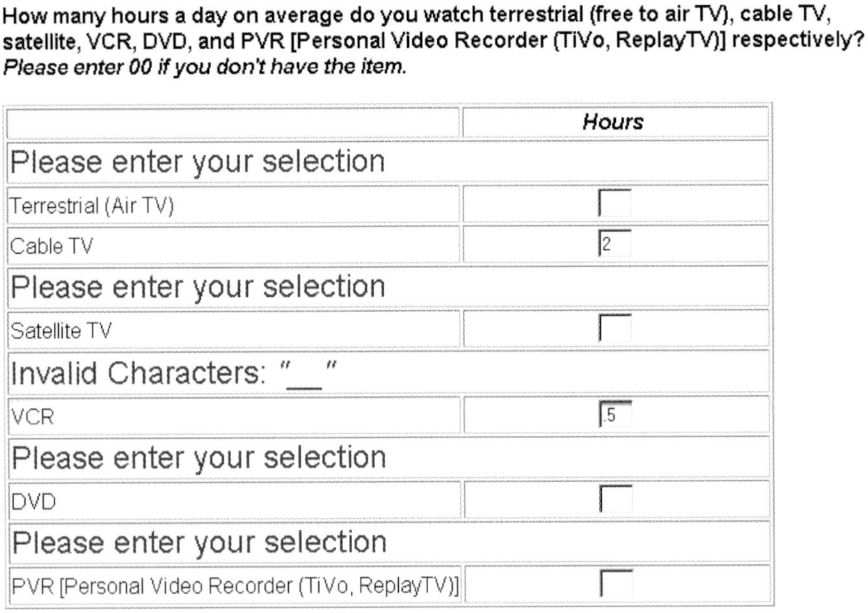
How many hours a day on average do you watch terrestrial (free to air TV), cable TV, satellite, VCR, DVD, and PVR [Personal Video Recorder (TiVo, ReplayTV)] respectively?
Please enter 00 if you don't have the item.
Hours
Please enter your selection
Terrestrial (Air TV)
Cable TV
2
Please enter your selection
Satellite TV
Invalid Characters: "__"
VCR
.5
Please enter your selection
DVD
Please enter your selection
PVR [Personal Video Recorder (TiVo, ReplayTV)]

Figure 5.47 Error Messages for Missing Data and Format.

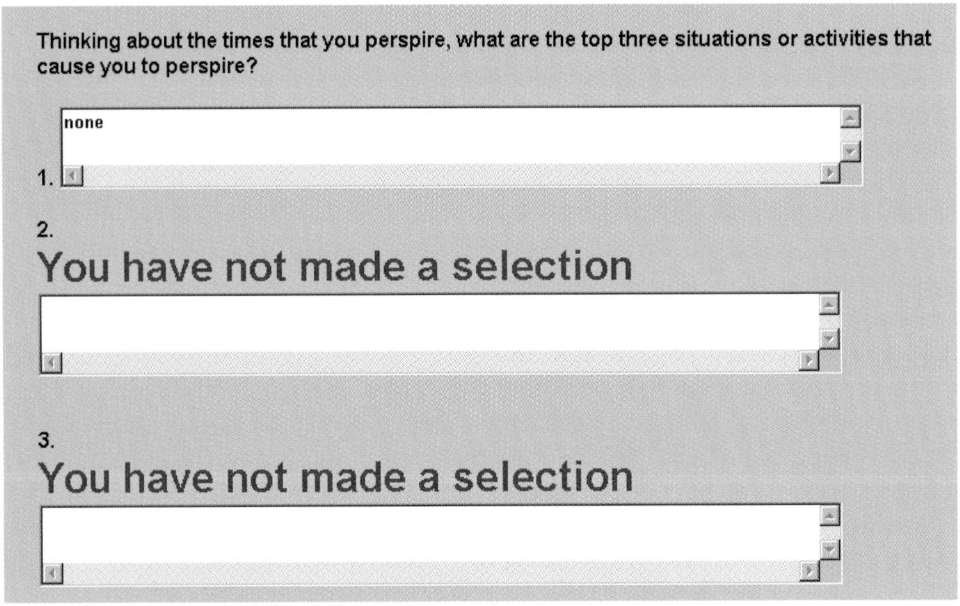
Thinking about the times that you perspire, what are the top three situations or activities that cause you to perspire?
none
1.
2.
You have not made a selection
3.
You have not made a selection

Figure 5.48 Requiring an Answer to Open-Ended Questions.

You have not selected an answer for row 6 in question 19.

18. Thinking about the groceries that are purchased for consumption in your household, which of the following statements best describes your level of involvement? (Select one answer.)

○ I am the person primarily responsible for purchasing the food consumed in my household
○ I share responsibility for purchasing the food consumed in my household
⦿ I do not have much responsibility for purchasing the food consumed in my household

19. Now we'd like you to read several statements. Please indicate how much you agree or disagree with each statement by selecting a number from "1" to "5," where "5" means you agree strongly and "1" means you disagree strongly with the statement. (Select one answer in each row.)

	Disagree Strongly 1	2	3	4	Agree Strongly 5
I like a great deal of variety in food products	○	○	○	○	○
I would trade off some taste in order to eat healthier snacks	○	○	○	○	○
I try to eat primarily fresh foods over those that have been packaged/processed	○	○	○	○	○
I make it a point to eat foods that are naturally rich sources of vitamins and minerals	○	○	○	○	○
I do not pay attention to the calories or fat in the products I eat	○	○	○	○	○
I strictly control my fat intake by counting my daily fat grams	○	○	○	○	○
I am unlikely to switch to low-fat or reduced-calorie products even if they taste as good as the original	○	○	○	○	○
I try to control the amount of salt I consume	○	○	○	○	○
I use herbal products such as teas or supplements to provide specific health benefits	○	○	○	○	○

Figure 5.49 **Requiring Answers to All Questions.**

The page was then regenerated with all the responses already provided by the respondent cleared. This is an example of punishing a respondent for what is probably a quite common error – missing one item in a large matrix of items. In Section 4.4.3, I discussed the use of dynamic shading as one way to reduce the amount of missing data in grids. Design should focus on preventing such omissions from occurring or facilitating detection of the omissions before submission of the page.

Error messages for text fields can vary in their complexity, as we have already seen. In Figure 5.48, the software merely checks whether any character has been entered into a field. For numeric or currency entry, the check can be more sophisticated. For example, in Figure 5.47, the system can accept only integers between 0 and 24. There is a danger of making these checks too inflexible, preventing respondents from providing valid, albeit sometimes unusual, responses. Figure 5.50 shows one such example. While the mask (the dollar sign preceding the text box) and instruction may serve to prevent common errors such as entering the dollar sign or decimals, an error is generated if the respondent provides a more precise amount than is desired. This seems counter-productive.

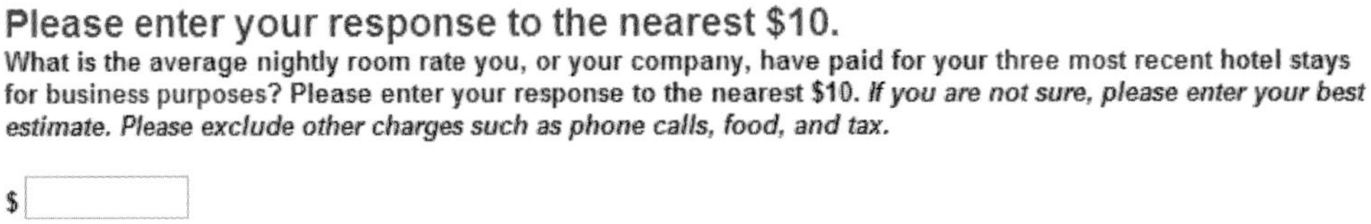

Please enter your response to the nearest $10.

What is the average nightly room rate you, or your company, have paid for your three most recent hotel stays for business purposes? Please enter your response to the nearest $10. *If you are not sure, please enter your best estimate. Please exclude other charges such as phone calls, food, and tax.*

$ [   ]

Figure 5.50 **Requiring Currency Entry in a Particular Format.**

I've seen many similar examples for currency entry. In one survey asking for annual household income, the field had no mask or instructions. Upon entering "40,000," the following error message was received: "Input invalid. Value not in range or whole number expected. 0 to 99000000." The problem was with the comma, but nothing in the generic error message made this clear to the respondent, other than through a process of elimination. In another example of this type, a question asked for the amount of money in all checking, savings, and money market accounts combined. The instruction read: "You should enter an amount in dollars. You should not use a dollar sign when entering an amount." The large text field had no masks or other instruction. Upon entering "5,000," the following error was generated: "Please enter a positive amount under 3000 and do not use commas or dots. You should not use a dollar sign when entering an amount." Here the designer or programmer had determined that $3,000 was a reasonable maximum for the sum of all such accounts, and no amount above this value could be entered.

Generic error messages are often not very helpful and should be avoided to the extent possible. It does not take a lot of effort to customize error messages to the particular issue being addressed. Figure 5.51 shows an example of such a generic message. The error was prompted by a missing item (the third in the grid). But the message reads: "Please enter a valid response. Don't know and Unanswered responses cannot be entered in combination with another valid response. For numeric responses, please use digits only. Do not use commas, dollar signs, percent signs." This message covers the waterfront, listing all the possible sources of error on a variety of question types, without clearly pointing the respondent to the source of the error.

The last two examples come from scrolling surveys in which the checks are conducted after the submission of the page containing all questions. I include these to show the contrast in design and in the message conveyed to respondents. The first of these (in Figure 5.52) is presented in bright red, while the dominant color of the rest of the survey is yellow. Red conveys a very strong message to the respondent, as do the "Warning!" and "Form is Incomplete!" messages. The tone

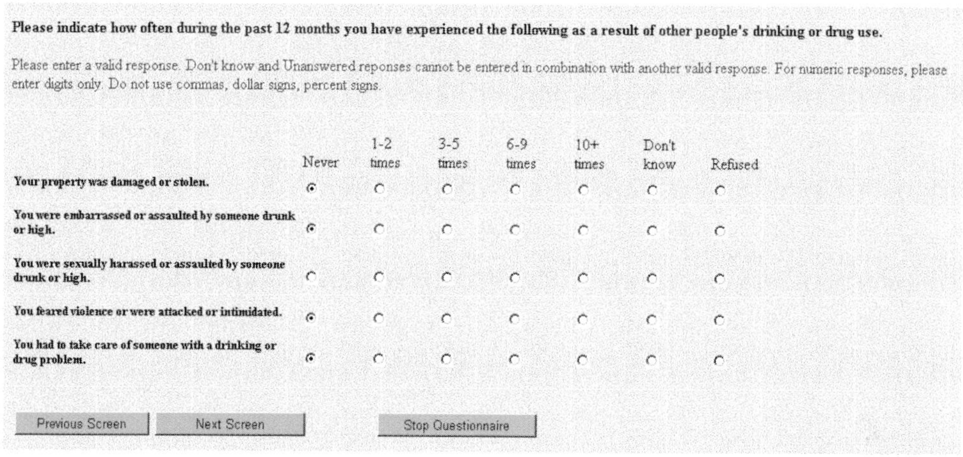

Please indicate how often during the past 12 months you have experienced the following as a result of other people's drinking or drug use.
Please enter a valid response. Don't know and Unanswered reponses cannot be entered in combination with another valid response. For numeric responses, please enter digits only. Do not use commas, dollar signs, percent signs.
Never
1-2 times
3-5 times
6-9 times
10+ times
Don't know
Refused
Your property was damaged or stolen.
You were embarrassed or assaulted by someone drunk or high.
You were sexually harassed or assaulted by someone drunk or high.
You feared violence or were attacked or intimidated.
You had to take care of someone with a drinking or drug problem.
Previous Screen
Next Screen
Stop Questionnaire

Figure 5.51 Generic Error Message.

WARNING!
FORM IS INCOMPLETE!
BACK
Please go back using the back button of your browser or click here and fill in all required fields.
FORWARD
I don't want to complete but go on
forward

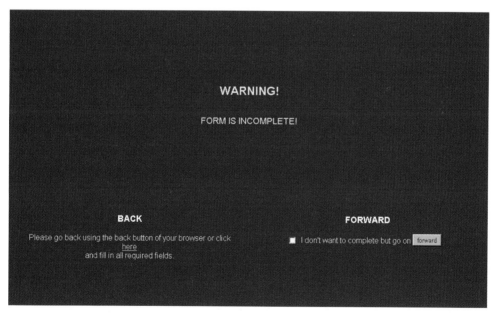

Figure 5.52 Missing Data Warning for Scrolling Survey.

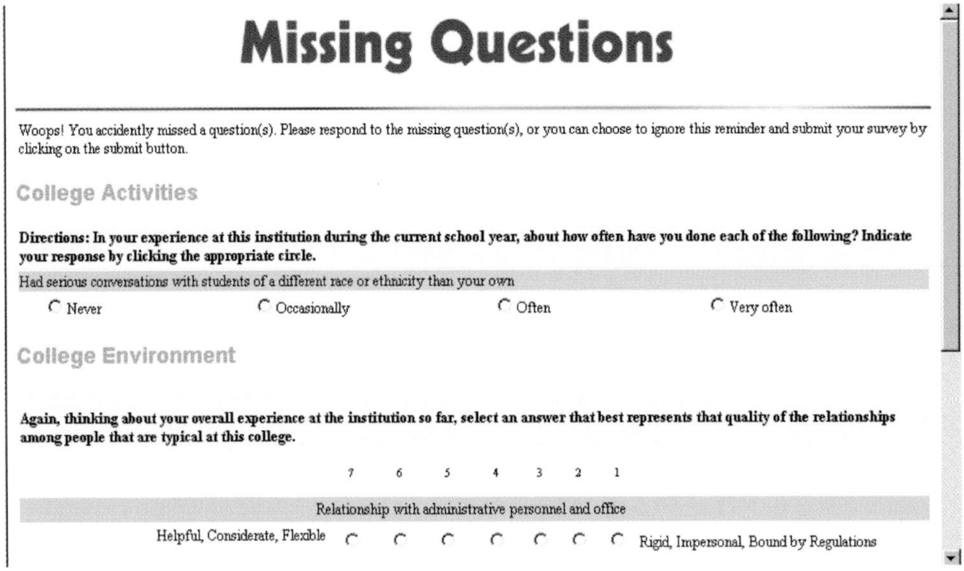

Missing Questions

Woops! You accidentally missed a question(s). Please respond to the missing question(s), or you can choose to ignore this reminder and submit your survey by clicking on the submit button.

College Activities

Directions: In your experience at this institution during the current school year, about how often have you done each of the following? Indicate your response by clicking the appropriate circle.

Had serious conversations with students of a different race or ethnicity than your own

  C Never   C Occasionally   C Often   C Very often

College Environment

Again, thinking about your overall experience at the institution so far, select an answer that best represents that quality of the relationships among people that are typical at this college.

7   6   5   4   3   2   1

Relationship with administrative personnel and office

Helpful, Considerate, Flexible C   C   C   C   C   C   C Rigid, Impersonal, Bound by Regulations

Figure 5.53 **Missing Data Approach in Scrolling Survey.**

makes it clear that it is the respondent who is at fault, undermining the text at the bottom of the screen, permitting respondents to proceed without completing the missed items.

The second example, shown in Figure 5.53, takes a very different approach. The items that the respondent skipped are presented to them again, along with the message "Woops! You accidentally missed a question(s)..." This message is less threatening, is polite, and explains to the respondent what the options are. One possible drawback of this approach is that the questions that were missed are now presented out of context. The advantage is that the respondent does not have to search through the entire instrument for the missed items. It is better to point out errors at the time they occur, rather than upon completion of the survey.

I already offered some guidelines for the design of error messages earlier in this section. It seems clear to me from most of the error messages I have encountered in Web surveys that this is an area often deemed unworthy of designer attention. I would assert that error messages, even if rarely encountered by respondents, form an important part of the overall message communicated by instrument design, and ought to be an explicit part of the design and testing process. Good design should reduce the number of error messages seen by respondents, but people inevitably make mistakes, and the instrument design should facilitate the detection and correction of errors without coercion, and in a polite and helpful manner.

5.7. Help and Assistance

A distinction can be made between three different types of assistance respondents may need as they complete a Web survey. These are

1. Procedural instructions: How to use the features of Web survey to answer the questions.
2. Help with question meaning, including definitions of terms, inclusions and exclusions, and the like.
3. General information about the survey, such as FAQs about sponsor, content, confidentiality, length, and so on.

The design issues are different for each type of assistance, so I'll address each in turn.

5.7.1. Procedural Assistance

There are differing views on whether respondents need guidance on how to complete a Web survey and, if so, how much they need. For example, Dillman (2000, p. 389) offers the following principle: "Provide specific instructions on how to take each necessary computer action for responding to the questionnaire, and give other necessary instructions at the point where they are needed." The top panel in Figure 5.54 shows an example of instructions following Dillman's principle.

How much knowledge can be presumed? The answer may depend on the population being surveyed. If those completing the Internet survey are comfortable using the Web and are familiar with Web-based form elements such as radio buttons and check boxes, specific instructions should be unnecessary. Given that Web surveys are, by definition, completed by Internet users, or those that chose Web completion over another mode in a mixed mode design, it is safe to assume that most have some such familiarity. So, as long as standard elements and consistent design are used, detailed procedural instructions should not be necessary.

There are some exceptions, however. For example, if the use of the browser buttons has unpredictable consequences (see Section 5.5.2), note this for respondents.

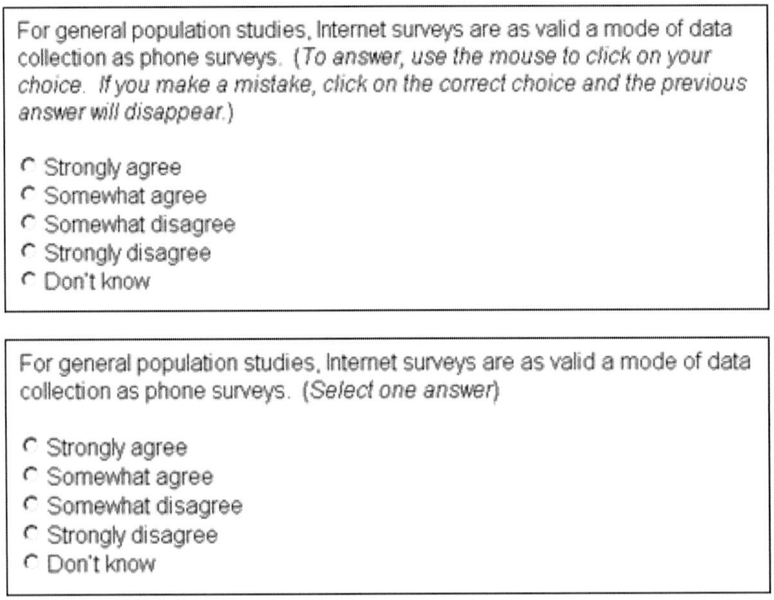

For general population studies, Internet surveys are as valid a mode of data collection as phone surveys. *(To answer, use the mouse to click on your choice. If you make a mistake, click on the correct choice and the previous answer will disappear.)*

○ Strongly agree
○ Somewhat agree
○ Somewhat disagree
○ Strongly disagree
○ Don't know

For general population studies, Internet surveys are as valid a mode of data collection as phone surveys. *(Select one answer)*

○ Strongly agree
○ Somewhat agree
○ Somewhat disagree
○ Strongly disagree
○ Don't know

Figure 5.54 **Detailed and Minimal Procedural Instructions.**

Similarly, respondents should be instructed if unfamiliar functions (e.g., visual analog scales and card sort tasks) are used or if the widgets used behave in non-standard ways.

To my knowledge, the only study that has experimentally manipulated procedural instructions was that conducted by Vehovar, Batagelj, and Lozar (1999). They varied the amount of detail provided, along the lines of the examples shown in Figure 5.54. They generally found few effects of the instruction format on responses. However, they found that slightly more people broke off the survey on later items when more detailed instructions were provided, but without replication, we cannot be sure this result will hold up in other contexts.

Given the lack of research on the topic, what design guidance can be offered with regard to procedural instructions? First, Dillman (2000) argues that the instructions should be placed at the point they are first needed, and here I agree. I have seen too many examples where detailed instructions are provided to the respondent at the outset, when they are not sure whether or when they may need the information, or whether it will be accessible to them later, when they may really need it. Figure 5.55 shows one of the two screens of instructions before the respondent began the questionnaire.

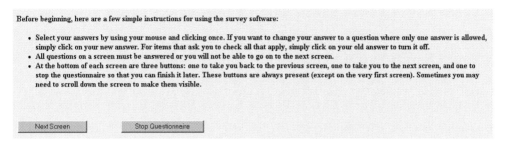

Before beginning, here are a few simple instructions for using the survey software:

- Select your answers by using your mouse and clicking once. If you want to change your answer to a question where only one answer is allowed, simply click on your new answer. For items that ask you to check all that apply, simply click on your old answer to turn it off.
- All questions on a screen must be answered or you will not be able to go on to the next screen.
- At the bottom of each screen are three buttons: one to take you back to the previous screen, one to take you to the next screen, and one to stop the questionnaire so that you can finish it later. These buttons are always present (except on the very first screen). Sometimes you may need to scroll down the screen to make them visible.

Next Screen   Stop Questionnaire

Figure 5.55 **Detailed Procedural Instructions at Start of Survey.**

The more detailed and numerous the instructions are, the more likely the respondent may be to skip them entirely. This can be especially problematic if instructions that are really needed are then ignored. For example, the second screen of instructions following those in Figure 5.55 included the following important admonition: "Do not use the BACK or FORWARD buttons on your browser during the interview; it will cause the survey software to stop responding." Embedded as it was in all the other instructions – many of them obvious to the respondent – it is likely that this instruction was missed. It is common practice in federal government surveys to include detailed initial instructions, and I would assert they are unlikely to be very useful.

Second, procedural instructions should be kept to a minimum when accompanying the question, and should be presented in such a way that they don't interfere with the task of answering the questions. While the use of italics and parentheses are one way to do this, if the instructions are long (as in the top panel in Figure 5.54), they may make it hard for the respondent to find the question. One creative alternative (see Figure 5.56) put the procedural instruction below a line below the "next question" button – in other words, out of the main field of action, but still visually accessible to the respondent. I've not seen this done anywhere else, and don't know how well it worked. Of course, one other approach – and one which appeals to me – is to remove such instructions from the Web page altogether, relegating them to a hyperlink. This presumes of course that the respondent knows how to use a hyperlink.

Finally, the need for instructions can be minimized with careful design. For example, using masks or templates for text fields will reduce the need for instructions on the correct entry format (see Section 2.5.3). Using radio buttons for a single selection question will constrain the respondents' input to only one response. Accommodating respondents' use of the browser back button (see Section 5.5) will obviate the need for detailed instructions on navigation. While good design

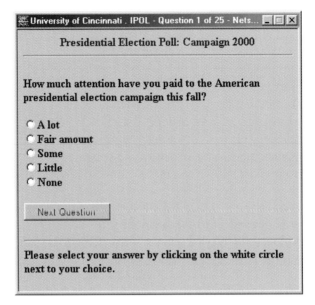

Figure 5.56 **Procedural Instructions below Action Button.**

will not completely eliminate the need for instructions, it will reduce the need for lengthy instructions that may interfere with the task of completing the survey.

5.7.2. Help With Question Meaning

The second type of assistance relates to the clarification of question meaning. Here there is quite some discussion that cuts across modes of data collection but relatively little research, with the exception of work by Conrad and Schober and their colleagues (e.g., Conrad and Schober, 2000, 2005; Conrad, Schober, and Coiner, 2007). The issue is whether all respondents should be exposed to the additional information (potentially making the questions more complex) or only those who request clarification (in which case the question stimulus may differ across respondents).

Many interviewer-administered surveys put a great deal of time and effort into developing question-by-question explanations or specifications (so-called QbyQs), with the goal of describing the purpose of the question so that the interviewer is better able to clarify meaning for the respondent or probe to get an appropriate answer. However, keystroke analyses suggest these are rarely accessed by interviewers in CATI and CAPI surveys (e.g., Couper, Horm, and Schlegel, 1997). This information is usually accessed via a function key, with an icon to indicate that additional information is available.

In paper-based surveys – especially those in the establishment survey world – the question instruction and definitions are often printed on the back of the form, which tends to convey to the respondent that such auxiliary information is not important. For example, Figure 5.57 shows the form for the Energy Information Administration's Quarterly Coal Consumption Report.[6] The instructions and definitions of key terms are on the back of the form, and are as long as the questionnaire itself.

Hyperlinks are an obvious tool in HTML for presentation of extra information such as this. They serve the purpose of moving the auxiliary information out of the main visual field while still making it easily accessible to the respondents. Using hyperlinks for clarification of question meaning is a common strategy in Web surveys.

However, our own research on question clarification in Web surveys suggests that respondents are generally disinclined to view this auxiliary information, especially when it takes a modicum of effort to do so. In our first experiment (see Conrad et al., 2006), we varied the ease of getting definitions, from a single mouse click on a hyperlink, to two mouse clicks (the first to bring up a list of terms with definitions, the second to go to the specific term), to clicking (to bring up a page with all the definitions) and scrolling (to find the relevant definition). We varied other factors too, such as the complexity of the concepts (affecting the need for definitions) and the usefulness of the definition (affecting repeated access of definitions), but I'll focus only on the ease of access here.

Overall, we found that only 13.7% of respondents accessed any of the definitions for the four items in the experiment. The amount of effort to get the definition only became apparent after the first click, so among those who requested any definition (clicked at least once), an average of 2.7 definitions were accessed in the one-click version, compared to 1.6 in the two-click and 1.5 in the click-and-scroll versions.

In a second experiment, also reported in Conrad et al. (2006), we made it even easier for respondents, contrasting the one-click and two-click versions from the first study with a rollover version in which the definition appeared as hovering text if the mouse was moved over the hyperlink. In this study, 18.3% of respondents

---

[6]   The more recent (2005) version of the form now has three pages of questions and four pages of instructions.

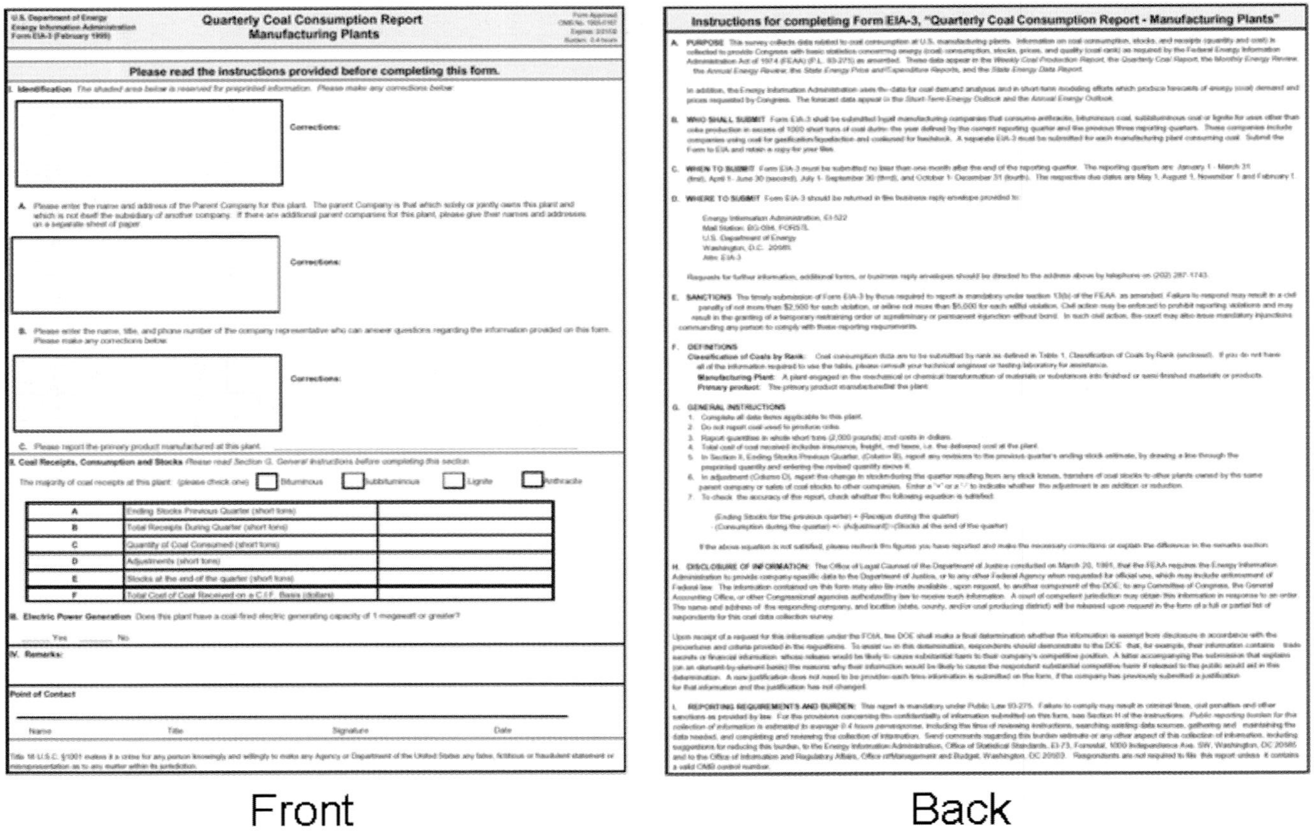

Front

Back

Figure 5.57 Instructions for EIA's Quarterly Coal Consumption Report.

obtained definitions to one or more of the eight concepts, more so in the rollover condition than in the other versions.

In general, this research suggests that even a single mouse click on a hyperlink may be sufficient to deter most respondents from seeking clarification of question meaning, even for technical terms. The addition of instructions encouraging the use of definitions (in the second experiment) did not significantly increase the proportion of respondents accessing definitions over a version with neutral instructions about accessing the definitions.

If the goal is to ensure that all respondents are using the same definition when answering a question, making it an explicit part of the item may be better than hiding it behind a hyperlink. However, this is of course still no guarantee that respondents will read it, as we have discovered in our eye-tracking research (see Galesic, Tourangeau, Couper, and Conrad, in press).

Where does this leave us? I would offer several recommendations to increase the likelihood that respondents will use definitions:

1. Consider making the definition part of the question, or change question wording so that a definition is less necessary.
2. Use definitions sparingly, so that respondents will notice when they are presented.
3. Use visual design to draw respondents' attention to the definition.
4. If appropriate, consider using images, both to draw attention to the definition and to communicate meaning.

Figure 5.58 shows one way of drawing respondents' attention to the definition. By highlighting the definition, respondents will likely notice it. By placing it between the question and response options, the respondent's eyes will likely move over the definition in the normal course of reading.

Chapter 3 has a couple of examples of the use of images to provide definitions or explanations of key concepts (see Figures 3.6 and 3.7). Another example, similar to that in Figure 5.58 but using images, is shown in Figure 5.59 (see Kypri and Gallagher, 2003; Kypri, Gallagher, and Cashell-Smith, 2004).

Much work remains to explore designs to ensure that respondents have access to definitions or clarifications when needed, without getting in the way of respondents in the normal course of answering survey questions. There is also much we don't know about how the differential access to additional question information affects the answers we obtain. But the Web offers us many visual design elements

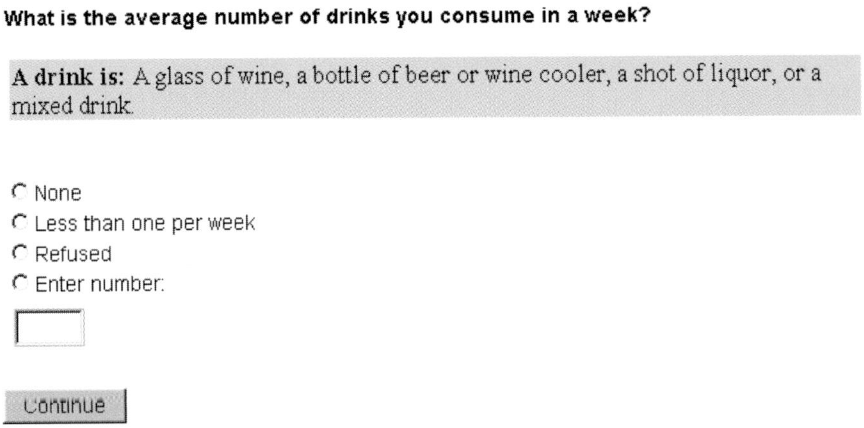

What is the average number of drinks you consume in a week?

A drink is: A glass of wine, a bottle of beer or wine cooler, a shot of liquor, or a mixed drink.

C None
C Less than one per week
C Refused
C Enter number:

[   ]

[Continue]

Figure 5.58 **Definition of Key Term.**

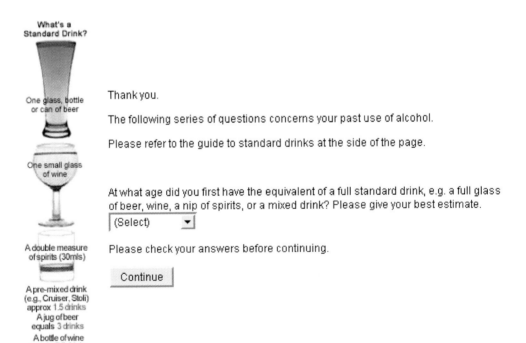

What's a
Standard Drink?

One glass, bottle
or can of beer

One small glass
of wine

A double measure
of spirits (30mls)

A pre-mixed drink
(e.g., Cruiser, Stoli)
approx 1.5 drinks
A jug of beer
equals 3 drinks
A bottle of wine
equals 7.5 drinks

Thank you.

The following series of questions concerns your past use of alcohol.

Please refer to the guide to standard drinks at the side of the page.

At what age did you first have the equivalent of a full standard drink, e.g. a full glass of beer, wine, a nip of spirits, or a mixed drink? Please give your best estimate.
[(Select)   ▼]

Please check your answers before continuing.

[Continue]

Figure 5.59 **Use of Images for Definition of Key Terms.**

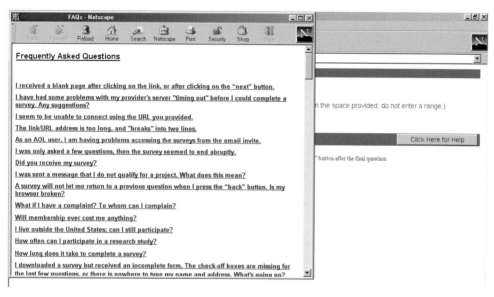

Figure 5.60 **General Information (FAQs) for an Online Panel.**

to increase the likelihood of respondents noticing definitions or other relevant information.

5.7.3. General Information

The final type of information respondents may need is background on the study. The information contained herein may not be of interest to all respondents, and should have little bearing on the survey responses, although it may affect their willingness to do the survey. Given this, it makes most sense to have this information available to respondents throughout the survey via a hyperlink. This is already common practice in many Web surveys.

Let's look at a few examples. Figure 5.60 shows an example of the kind of information that is made available to members of an online panel. This is generic information common to all surveys conducted by this vendor.

Figure 5.61 shows an example of a hyperlink with information specific to a particular survey (see Reed et al., 2004). Here a single hyperlink labeled, "Questions or comments?" on each page of the survey takes respondents to the page shown in Figure 5.61, from where they could contact someone if they have questions or

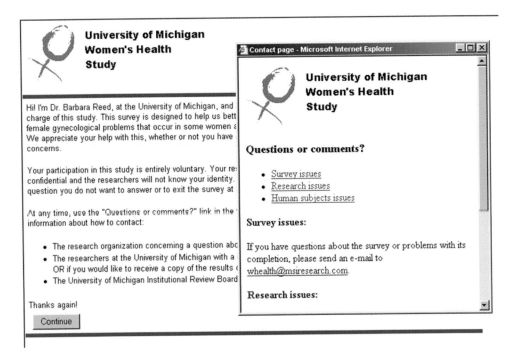

Figure 5.61 **Hyperlink for General Survey Information.**

concerns about the survey itself, or find information on the broader research topic or issues relating to human subjects.

The final example comes from the online version of the Canadian Census, conducted in 2006 (see Figure 5.62). This example contains several different types of assistance. Note the hyperlinks for help on the specific questions on the left (labeled "Help on Whom to include" and "Help on Persons that should not be included"), in addition to the more generic "Help" and "About" tabs on the top of the page. There is also a "Why we ask box" in the left pane. Note also the progress indicator, which leads us to the next topic.

5.8. Progress Indicators and Survey Length

Progress indicators have been – and remain – one of the more puzzling aspects of Web survey design I have encountered. Most survey researchers I speak with say they would want to know their progress through the instrument, and most

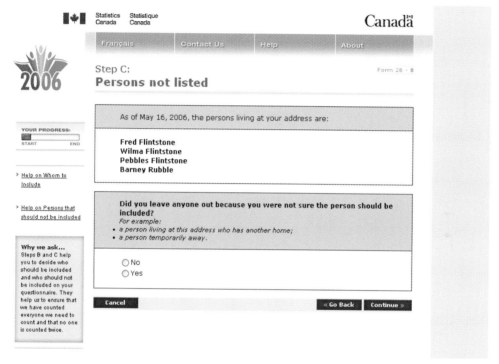

Figure 5.62 **Assistance in the 2006 Canadian Census.**

instruments I see have some form of progress indicator, yet the empirical evidence on such indicators can at best be described as mixed. Given this, I will first review various types of progress indicators and then examine the growing research literature on progress indicators, before offering some summary thoughts on the topic. But this is clearly an area of Web survey design in which the jury is still out.

Why do we need progress indicators? In scrolling Web surveys, the respondent can scroll to the bottom of the questionnaire to judge the length. Similarly, in mail surveys respondents can see how far they have to go and what type of questions remain to be answered. In interviewer-administered surveys, especially those using CAPI or CATI with no visual cues of length, the respondent can ask how much more there is to go, or the interviewer, detecting signs of respondent fatigue or impatience, can offer appropriate encouragement. In paging Web survey designs, there is no equivalent way to estimate progress through the instrument

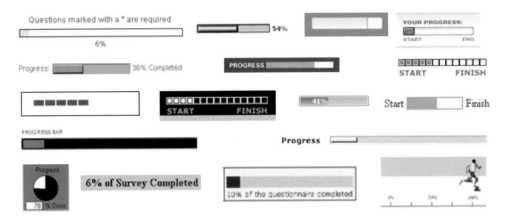

Figure 5.63 **Examples of Progress Indicators.**

or to motivate respondents to stick with the task when they don't know how close they are to finishing the survey. Given this, it seems intuitive that progress indicators would be valued by respondents and would be helpful in reducing breakoffs.

5.8.1. The Design of Progress Indicators

There are many different ways to display progress through a Web survey instrument. These can be text-based or graphical displays, as illustrated in Figure 5.63. They can be on every page, or displayed intermittently, or even displayed only upon request. Even if progress indicators were shown to be useful, there are still a number of design issues to contend with, such as:

1. How detailed should the progress be?
2. How frequently should progress be displayed?
3. How to deal with skips and contingent questions?
4. Should progress be based on number of pages, number of items/questions, or estimated time to complete each item?

Most progress indicators I have seen (such as those in Figure 5.63) show incremental movement on every page of the survey. In other words, the progress indicator is a constant presence. Further, they are typically based on the maximum number of questions, with the result that progress can jump suddenly if the respondent skips a series of questions (for an exception, see Kaczmirek, Neubarth, Bosnjak, and Bandilla, 2004, 2005). A few surveys eschew these detailed progress indicators for more intermittent feedback, but more on this later.

5.8.2. Research on Progress Indicators

Progress indicators (PIs) are designed with the intention of increasing the proportion of complete surveys among those who started, or reducing breakoffs. But do they work? In one of the first studies on PIs (Couper, Traugott, and Lamias, 2001), we used a graphical PI that showed progress as a pie chart, along with the percent completed in text (shown in the bottom left of Figure 5.63). We found a slightly (but not significantly) lower breakoff rate (10.1%) for the PI version than the no-PI version (13.6%), and surmised that downloading the graphical image may have attenuated the positive effect of the PI. This was supported by the fact that the PI version took significantly longer to complete (22.7 versus 19.8 minutes).

In a subsequent study (Crawford, Couper, and Lamias, 2001), we used a text-based PI (e.g., "17% of Survey Completed") to eliminate any differences in download time between versions. Here we found a significant difference in breakoff rates, but *higher* for the PI group (31.5%) than the no-PI group (25.3%). On closer inspection, we found that a series of open-ended questions near the beginning of the survey was to blame. On average, when respondents were about halfway through the survey (in terms of elapsed time), the PI based on the number of questions was telling them that they were only about one-fifth of the way through the survey. A follow-up study among the same respondents some six months later removed the set of open-ended questions, and found a lower but again insignificant (p=.07) breakoff rate for those getting the PI (8.2% versus 13.8% for no PI). Note how the open-ended questions increased breakoffs overall in the first study, and this is exacerbated by giving feedback that underestimated respondents' progress through the instrument.

We have subsequently conducted a series of experiments to explore the progress indicator issue further (e.g., Conrad, Couper, Tourangeau, and Peytchev, 2005; Yan, Conrad, Tourangeau, and Couper, 2007). We varied the "speed" of the PI, contrasting the standard "constant speed" approach with a "slow-to-fast" version in which the speed of progress increased over the course of the survey, and a "fast-to-slow" version in which speed decreased. Progress was presented in text form (e.g., "13% complete"). As we found before, the constant speed PI performed a little worse (p > .05) than no PI (breakoffs of 14.4% and 12.7%, respectively). The version with the good news (faster progress) early on performed significantly better (11.3% breakoffs), while the version with bad news (slower progress) at the beginning did significantly worse (21.8% breakoffs), as expected from the Crawford, Couper, and Lamias (2001) result.

In a second study, we crossed the same three PI speeds with whether the PI was always on, displayed intermittently (about every eighth page), or displayed only upon request (by clicking on a hyperlink on each page). The results for breakoff rates by PI speed matched those from the first study, with the fast-to-slow being best (11.3% breakoffs), the slow-to-fast worst (19.9%) with the constant speed PI (14.4%), and no PI (14.3%) in between. The type of PI (always on, intermittent, or on demand) had no apparent effect on breakoffs. Interestingly, in the on-demand group, only 37% of respondents ever requested the PI, and it was requested approximately 1% of the time (or 1 in every 100 pages) on average.

In a survey among students in Germany, Glauer and Schneider (2004) found a small but significant positive effect on breakoff rates for a PI (16.2%) than a no-PI (20.6%) version. Van der Horst, Snijders, and Matzat (2006) tested several different PIs in an opt-in panel. Breakoff rates were lowest for the no-PI group (8.3%) with the constant progress indicator (12.1%), a progressive PI (similar to our fast-to-slow PI, 10.3%) a degressive PI (like our slow-to-fast, 13.4%) all worse in terms of breakoffs. They also tested a descending page indicator (e.g., "3 pages to go"), which performed worst of all, with 16% breakoffs.

Finally, Heerwegh and Loosveldt (2006) experimented with giving respondents a choice at the start of the survey of displaying the PI throughout or not (77.4% chose to do so). Those who were not given a choice were assigned to a PI, the university logo, or nothing, while those who chose not to see the PI were assigned to the logo or nothing. The PI was set to behave like the fast-to-slow version used in Conrad, Couper, Tourangeau, and Peytchev (2005). Breakoff rates for those in the PI group (11.3%) were not significantly different than for those not shown a PI (12.6%). Those who were given a choice and chose the PI had a similar breakoff rate (9.5%) to those not given a choice but shown the PI (11.3%). The group with the highest breakoff rate was those offered a PI who did not choose to display it (20.7%).

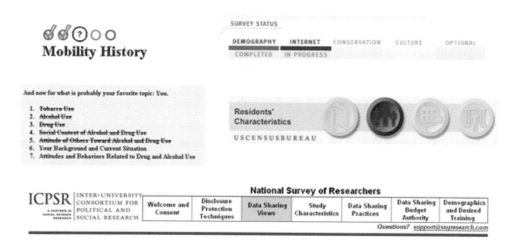

Figure 5.64 **Section-Level Progress Examples.**

So what do we make of all this? It seems clear from these studies that the typical progress indicators used in Web surveys (always on, constant speed) do not help much in reducing breakoffs, and may even hurt at times. I would thus recommend *not* using progress indicators of this type until we have a better understanding of when they do work and why.

An alternative approach – which seems intuitively appealing, but has not been empirically tested, to my knowledge – is to give respondents a general sense of where they are in the instrument, rather than page-by-page or item-by-item feedback on their progress. Examples of this kind of progress feedback are shown in Figure 5.64.

The top two examples are from the 2000 and 2001 *National Geographic* surveys, respectively (May, 1999; Witte, Amoroso, and Howard, 2000). Each section of the survey is color-coded, providing respondents additional visual cues of location in the survey. The example in the middle row is from a survey of University of Michigan students (McCabe et al., 2002), where each section has a lead-in page with completed sections crossed out. The ACS example on the middle right (see also Figure 5.36) uses color and images for the same purpose as the *National Geographic* surveys. Finally, the bottom example highlights the section the respondent is currently in. These kinds of approaches to conveying progress and location seem worthy of further testing.

5.8.3. Survey Length

While it is a truism to say that "shorter is better" in Web surveys, as in other modes of data collection, tolerable length depends on many factors, such as the sample, and the topic. As Bradburn (1978) has noted, respondent burden is more than just elapsed time (see also Bogen, 1996).

There have been many prescriptive statements about Web survey length or, more specifically, time to complete a survey. For example, Farmer (2000), on the basis of several unspecified experiments, noted that Web surveys longer than fifteen minutes have a very high probability of item nonresponse or breakoff. Rivers (2000) similarly noted that if Web surveys are kept under ten minutes, very few (if any) breakoffs are experienced. Terhanian (2000) stated that ten to twelve minutes is the optimal length for a Web survey, with abandonment (breakoff) rates increasing by 3–4% for each additional 2 minutes in length. MacElroy (2000) reported on an informal meta-analysis of 19 studies, finding that length of survey is strongly predictive of breakoff, with a correlation of 0.89. Stenbjerre and Laugesen (2005) examined the relationship between survey length and response rate in a Nordic access panel. They found a small decrease in response rate for surveys up to about twenty-five minutes in length, after which the decline is steeper, despite higher incentives for longer surveys.

A few studies have experimented with survey length. For example, Hogg and Miller (2003; see also Baker-Prewitt, 2003) report on a study in which panel members were first asked how much time they had to do a survey. Those who said fifteen minutes were assigned to a short (7.5 minute) or long (19 minute) survey, while those who said they had up to thirty minutes were assigned to the long survey. Breakoff rates were 13% for those in the short survey, 29% for those who said they had less time but were given the long survey, and 16% for those who said they had more time and were given the long survey. In other words, those who allocated more time up front were significantly less likely to breakoff than those were willing to commit to less time.

In one of our studies (Crawford, Couper, and Lamias, 2001) we varied the announced length of the survey in the invitation, with some being told it would take eight to ten minutes and others twenty minutes. The median completion time of the actual survey was just under twenty minutes. Those who got the shorter announced time were significantly more likely to start the survey (36.6% versus 32.5%). However, they were also more likely to break off during the survey, resulting in comparable completion rates (25.2% for the eight-to-ten-minute group and 23.5% for the twenty-minute group).

In a test of the effect of announced length, Galesic (2006) randomly assigned visitors to a banner-advertised survey in Croatia to one of three conditions, following a ten-question screening survey to determine their eligibility. The main part of the survey consisted of twenty blocks. One-third of those eligible were told the survey would last about ten minutes, another third twenty minutes and the final third thirty minutes. The order of the blocks was randomized. After four blocks (about one-third of the survey), respondents in the ten-minute group were told that the main part of the survey was completed but they could continue if they wished. The same message was given after eight blocks to the twenty-minute group. Using a proportional hazard model predicting the risk of dropout, Galesic found that, compared with respondents in the ten-minute group, the risk of dropout was about 20% higher for those in the twenty-minute group and 40% higher for those in the thirty-minute group. She also measured interest and perceived burden at the end of each block, and found both to have strong effects on dropout (negative for interest and positive for burden, as expected).

5.8.4. Summary on Progress Indicators and Length

The evidence suggests that constant progress indicators – those that appear on every page of the survey – seem not to have the desired effect of reducing breakoffs. In fact, a constant progress indicator may have the paradoxical effect of making the survey appear to take longer. While more research is needed on alternative ways to keep respondents informed of where they are in the survey and encourage them to complete it, progress indicators do not appear to be effective, other than possibly in the case of short surveys where they are less necessary.

What might be more important that the progress indicator is what we tell respondents up front. If it's clear at the outset what is expected of them, respondents may be more likely to set aside the appropriate amount of time to do the survey and worry less about incremental progress. In addition, if the survey is well designed and the questions are of relevance and interest to the respondents and easy to answer, the issue of tracking progress through the instrument may become less of a concern.

Given this, a key to maximizing survey completion is careful design of the survey, creating the appearance of a pleasant and easy-to-complete instrument. To the extent that "flow" (see Czikszentmihalyi, 1990) is enhanced, and perceived burden or effort is reduced, breakoffs or abandonments may be minimized.

Figure 5.65 **Confirmation Screen in Canadian Census.**

5.9. Review or Summary Screens

A final topic in constructing the Web questionnaire relates to the use of review or summary screens. These are often used in establishment or business surveys, where respondents can review the information they provided, correct it if necessary, and print it for their records, before finally submitting it to the survey organization. Review screens are also used in census data collection and other household surveys where a large amount of complex information is collected, often about several different household members. These screens are a form of customization, in that fills and skips are used to generate the information presented, and nonstandard navigation is used to make any changes that the respondent deems necessary. Figure 5.65 shows such as example from the 2006 Canadian Census. In addition to various error detection and correction strategies, these review

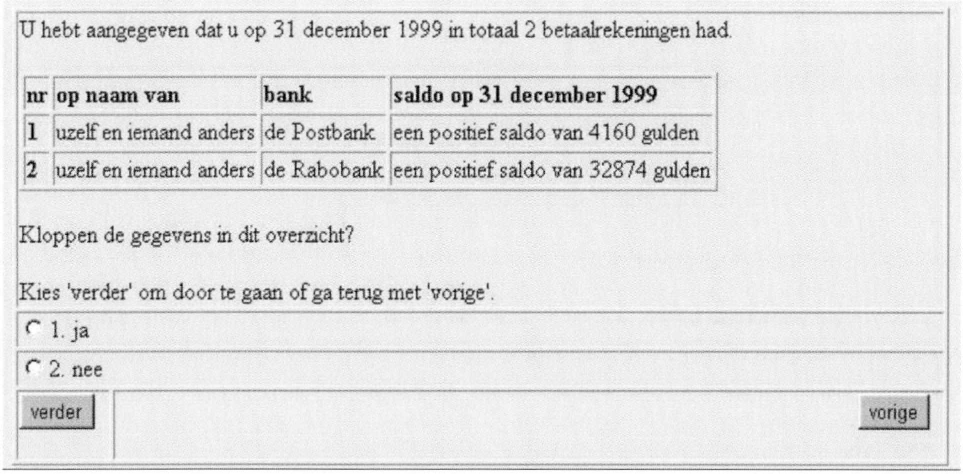

Figure 5.66 **Summary Screen from Hoogendoorn (2001).**

screens serve to feed back summary information to the respondent for verification and correction. The summary screen also uses fills based on responses to earlier questions.

Another example comes from Hoogendoorn (2001) and is shown in Figure 5.66. The translation is as follows: "You stated that you had 2 checking accounts on 31st December 1999. [Table with information about the holder, the bank, and the balance of each account] Is the information in the table correct? Choose 'next' to go on or 'previous' to go back" (Hoogendoorn, 2001, p. 2). Here the input into the table is a combination of date fills, numbers, text fields (name of bank), and numeric entry (account balance). In this survey on assets and liabilities, 1,583 respondents were presented with 6,541 review screens. Of these, 593 or 9% of the screens resulted in changes to previous answers, suggesting that the review screen improved survey accuracy (Hoogendoorn, 2001, p. 8).

Aside from this study, I know of no research on the utility of such summary screens in Web surveys. Do respondents take the time to review the information? This may depend in part on the level of error trapping included earlier in the survey. The more respondents are asked to verify or correct information along the way, the more likely they are to trust the summary to be correct. In other words, with overediting the responsibility for getting it right may shift from respondent to instrument.

Furthermore, my belief is that the value of such summary screens depends on the importance – to the respondent, not to the survey organization – of providing accurate information. For most surveys, the consequences are negligible. Summary and review screens are quite important in online travel reservations, e-commerce, tax preparation, and other examples of online interactions where the respondent is directly affected by the submission of incorrect information. In some such settings, users are even encouraged to explore the site more, with the reassurance that they can always change things before making the final purchase. In such cases, review screens take on greater importance for the users. But in most surveys the cost may be too low to encourage widespread use of such summaries, unless respondents can be convinced in other ways to provide accurate information along the way. This should be done at the outset, rather than waiting until the end of the survey. However, if there are more immediate consequences for the respondent – for example, in terms of the number and type of follow-up questions they will get – summary screens may well be used more. For example, in interviewer-administered household surveys, it is common to verify the household listing before asking detailed questions about members of the household.

In establishment surveys, where the submission of erroneous information may have consequences for the responding organization (such as generating a follow-up call to clarify inconsistencies or edit failures), such screens are likely to be used more heavily by respondents.

5.10. Summary

Creating carefully crafted and well-designed Web survey questions is only part of the task of successful design. The questions should be put together into an instrument that optimizes the sense of flow for the respondent (see Czikszentmihalyi, 1990). The questionnaire should not be a set of disjointed questions, but a coherent sequence of related topics. In this chapter, I have discussed the many ways such coherence can be achieved, ranging from the appropriate use of skips and fills, to the choice and placement of action buttons and the careful design of messages and supporting material such as help and definitions. The goal of all this is to facilitate the respondent's task of moving through the questionnaire in a linear fashion and making progress toward the goal of completing the survey, providing accurate and complete answers along the way. Unexpected, inappropriate, or overly complex questions, demanding error messages, unclear instructions and the like, may all serve to disturb the respondent's orderly progress through the instrument and interrupt the sense of flow. Good design achieves the goal of encouraging and focusing respondents on the task at hand, and leaves them with a sense of accomplishment. When this is achieved, progress indicators may be less necessary, breakoffs and item missing data may be minimized, and the respondent may feel more positive about the survey experience. Overall, it is this design philosophy – rather than any single design detail – that leads to successful Web surveys.

Chapter 6

Implementing the Design

There's many a slip 'twixt the cup and the lip.

So, we have a well-designed and carefully tested Web survey ready to go. How do we actually implement the survey to collect the data in which we are so interested? This chapter deals with a variety of design issues related to the process of data collection. I do not address technical issues such as Web hosting, database management, CGI (Common Gateway Interface) scripts to execute the survey, and so on. Rather, I focus on issues of design such as the invitation to participate, the use of incentives or other inducements to do so, the login and authentication process, the follow-up of nonrespondents and partial respondents, and so on. The focus in many of the preceding chapters was on reducing measurement error. In this chapter, the attention is more on reducing nonresponse or increasing the number of sample persons who start – and finish – the survey. No matter how well the instrument is designed, if it is poorly executed, the desired respondents may not even get to the questions that were so carefully developed.

This chapter is organized around the sequence of events that typically occur in a Web survey, from the initial invitation to the completion of the survey and then any follow-up that may be necessary. Following this, I discuss the use of incentives in Web surveys. I then end with a few general observations about a variety of topics, such as the use of paradata, the importance of pretesting, and mixed-mode surveys.

Most of the other chapters in this book apply to the design of Web surveys, no matter how participants come to the survey. For this chapter, I need to be more

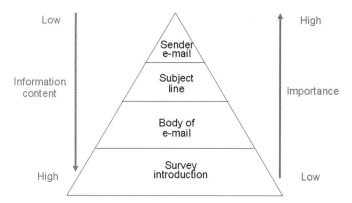

Figure 6.1 **Information Content and Importance of the Information.**

specific about the types of Web surveys I have in mind. Here, I'm thinking of surveys using list-based samples, no matter how these lists are compiled. In other words, it could be an opt-in list of volunteers who provided their e-mail addresses, as used by many commercial vendors of Web surveys. It could be a list created by some probability-based method, such as RDD (random digit dial) recruitment. Or, the list could already exist for some other purpose, such as members of a professional association, students at a particular college, registrants of a software product or online service, and so on. To put it another way, Web surveys using pop-ups, banner advertising, or other types of anonymous recruiting are *not* the focus of this chapter.

The information available on the list is crucial in determining which methods can be used to invite subjects to participate. For example, if the only information available for a sample person is an e-mail address, that pretty much narrows down the choice of recruitment options to e-mail. If, however, the list also contains a mailing address or telephone number for each person, the range of recruitment and follow-up methods become broader. Of course, the cost advantages of e-mail may outweigh other considerations, even if alternative contact information is available on the list. For now, we will consider primary recruitment by e-mail, while considering other modes as supplementary.

The task of recruiting or inviting subjects to participate in Web surveys is a challenging one. As illustrated in Figure 6.1, if the invitation is sent by e-mail, the first task is to get the recipient to open the message – assuming of course that the e-mail has made it through spam filters and has arrived at the recipient's inbox.

The only thing the recipient has to go on at this point is the sender's identity (e-mail address and/or name) and the subject of the message. As the figure suggests, the amount of information that can be conveyed with these two fields is quite limited; yet, this is an important step in the sequence of events or decisions that lead eventually to the recipient of the invitation starting the survey.

Once the recipient opens the e-mail message, significantly more information can be conveyed in the body of the message. As each successive step is taken by the recipient, the options available to the survey designer increase, but the relative importance of the information in terms of encouraging response may decline as fewer and fewer recipients make it to each succeeding step.

With this perspective in mind, let's take a step back and look at the ways we can increase the likelihood of a sample person clicking through to the URL and completing the survey. We'll start with a step before the invitation.

6.1. Prenotification

Prenotification is an often-employed strategy in interviewer-administered surveys. For example, it is common in RDD telephone surveys to precede the calling efforts with an address lookup step, followed by the mailing of an advance letter to those addresses found. The literature suggests this is a cost-effective way of increasing response rates (e.g., Hembroff, Rusz, Rafferty, McGee, and Ehrlich 2005; de Leeuw, Callegaro, Hox, Korendijk, and Lensvelt-Mulders, 2007). Advance letters are hypothesized to be effective in interviewer-administered surveys because of the ability to use official stationery and personalized signature to legitimize the request, giving recipients a chance to review the benefits of participation, invoking norms of reciprocation, and including gifts or incentives (see Groves and Couper, 1998). Dillman (2000, p. 156) notes that advance letters improve response rates to mail surveys but wonders whether the effect is because it is simply one more contact or whether it is a unique type of contact.

Given this, is prenotification effective in Web surveys? If so, what type of prenotification should be employed? The reason that prenotification may work in RDD surveys is that it is not simply one more contact attempt but that it is in a medium that differs from the other contact attempts, potentially compensating for the limitations of cold-call RDD attempts. If this is so, the *type* of prenotice should be important for Web surveys too. An e-mail prenotice, for example, is likely to be less effective than a contact using another mode.

There have been a few scattered studies on Web survey prenotification. Crawford and colleagues (2004) randomly assigned a sample of college students to a mail or e-mail prenotice. All got an e-mail invitation to the survey one week later. The mail prenotice produced a significantly higher response rate (52.5%) than the e-mail prenotice (44.9%).

Kaplowitz, Hadlock, and Levine (2004) tested a postcard prenotice versus no prenotification, also in a college student sample. The group sent the postcard prenotice yielded a 29.7% response rate, significantly higher than the 20.7% for the no-prenotice group. (A third group received a standard mail treatment, producing a 31.5% response rate.)

Harmon, Westin, and Levin (2005) compared three different types of prenotification in a sample of applicants to a government grants program. One group received an e-mail prenotice with an attached letter from the sponsoring agency in PDF format, the second received an e-mail with an attached letter from the data collection organization, and the third received a paper letter from the sponsoring agency in the mail. The third group produced the highest response rate (69.9%), followed by the first (64.4% and then the second (63.6%). Only the comparison between the first and third groups reached statistical significance ($p < .05$), but the results support those of Crawford and colleagues (2004) in suggesting that a mailed prenotice is more effective than an e-mail prenotice.

In another experiment on prenotice among college students, this time in Germany, Bosnjak, Neubarth, Couper, Bandilla, and Kaczmirek (in press) explored the effect of an SMS (short message system or text message on a mobile phone) prenotice versus and e-mail prenotice versus none. They also varied the invitation mode (SMS versus e-mail). Focusing only on the e-mail invitation group, the SMS prenotice achieved a response rate of 84% to the first wave of the survey, significantly higher than either the e-mail prenotice (71%) or no prenotice (72%).

In an early e-mail (not Web) survey of college faculty, Schaefer and Dillman (1998) also tested an e-mail versus a mail prenotice. The former achieved a 58.0% response rate, while the paper prenotice group produced a 48.2% response rate, significantly lower than that for e-mail ($p < .05$). They speculate that one reason for this reversal may be that recipients did not associate the prenotice letter with the e-mail invitation, and thus viewed the latter as unsolicited. Whatever the reason, this remains a puzzling finding that has not been replicated in subsequent studies.

While it may be too early to summarize the scant literature on this issue, these findings suggest that an e-mail prenotice may not offer many advantages over no prenotice, but a prenotice in another mode (letter or postcard) may be effective in boosting response to a Web survey. As noted earlier, mail prenotification has a number of potential advantages, especially when used in combination with an e-mail invitation to deliver the URL. But, it may also be more costly and time-consuming than a fully electronic process. In addition, both mail and e-mail addresses are needed on the frame. For certain types of populations, the extra time and effort may well be worth it. In fact, Kaplowitz, Hadlock, and Levine (2004) found that a postcard prenotice was not significantly more expensive than no prenotice, given the improvement in response rate. They report a cost per response of $1.32 for the e-mail only group, and $1.31 for the postcard prenotice plus e-mail group. By way of contrast, the mail survey group in their study cost $10.97 per complete.

While further research on this topic is warranted, the use of a mail prenotice (whether a letter or a postcard) may be advantageous if the circumstances permit. As I will discuss later, mail is also an effective way of delivering prepaid incentives, which have their own positive influence on response rates.

6.2. The Invitation

Assuming that the invitation is delivered by e-mail, several elements of the invitation are subject to the designer's influence to varying degrees. These are:

- The e-mail header:
  - The sender's name and/or e-mail address
  - The addressee's name and/or e-mail address
  - The subject line
- The e-mail body:
  - The salutation
  - The signature
  - Contact information
  - The URL
  - The content of the message

The last of these, the message content, covers various details about the survey, including length, topic, sponsor, confidentiality, and the like. Given the dearth of research on the content of the e-mail invitation, I focus on the other items and then offer some broad considerations for the content of the e-mail message.

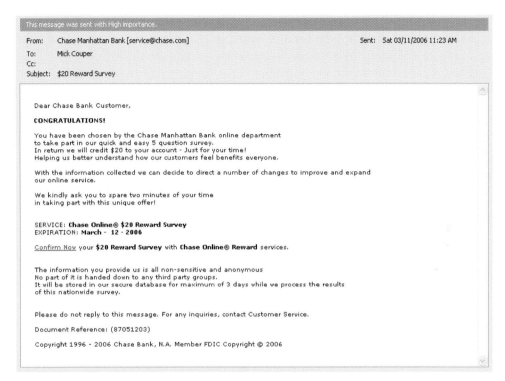

This message was sent with High importance.

From: Chase Manhattan Bank [service@chase.com]   Sent: Sat 03/11/2006 11:23 AM
To: Mick Couper
Cc:
Subject: $20 Reward Survey

Dear Chase Bank Customer,

CONGRATULATIONS!

You have been chosen by the Chase Manhattan Bank online department
to take part in our quick and easy 5 question survey.
In return we will credit $20 to your account - Just for your time!
Helping us better understand how our customers feel benefits everyone.

With the information collected we can decide to direct a number of changes to improve and expand
our online service.

We kindly ask you to spare two minutes of your time
in taking part with this unique offer!

SERVICE: **Chase Online® $20 Reward Survey**
EXPIRATION: **March - 12 - 2006**

Confirm Now your **$20 Reward Survey** with **Chase Online® Reward** services.

The information you provide us is all non-sensitive and anonymous
No part of it is handed down to any third party groups.
It will be stored in our secure database for maximum of 3 days while we process the results
of this nationwide survey.

Please do not reply to this message. For any inquiries, contact Customer Service.

Document Reference: (87051203)

Copyright 1996 - 2006 Chase Bank, N.A. Member FDIC Copyright © 2006

Figure 6.2 **Elements of an E-Mail Invitation.**

I illustrate the various parts of the e-mail invitation in Figure 6.2, using a phishing scam disguised as a survey request. If one holds the mouse over the "Confirm Now" link, the URL is revealed as http://chase-online.surveydatabase.us, which should be a giveaway to the careful reader that this is not a legitimate request (I'll return to this issue later). The key elements of the invitation e-mail header I discuss here include the sender's name and e-mail address (Chase Manhattan Bank [service@chase.com]), the addressee's name and/or e-mail address (Mick Couper), and the subject ($20 Reward Survey). Key elements in the body of the e-mail message include the salutation ("Dear Chase Bank Customer"), the signature and contact information (none, in this case), the link or URL ("Confirm Now"), and the balance of the message body.

Figure 6.2 illustrates one of the challenges of doing online research. E-mail users are inundated with messages from strangers, many of them phishing or spam messages. Separating the legitimate survey requests from the dross is difficult.

For this reason, e-mail invitations are largely a permission-based endeavor in the market research world, where the recipient has an existing relationship with the sender or has given prior permission to be contacted (see ESOMAR, 2005). The "cold call" e-mail invitation is likely to get little traction in these days of junk mail and spam.

6.2.1. The E-Mail Header

The header information is that shown on the cream background in Figure 6.2. In many e-mail systems, this information is viewable in the inbox before opening the message. I'll focus on the "From," "To," and "Subject" lines.

6.2.1.1. The Sender

This can be described in various ways, depending on how the respondent's e-mail client is configured, but think of this as the "From:" part of the e-mail invitation. Not much can be done with this, as a valid e-mail address should be used. But one question is whether this should come from a person (e.g., JoeBlow@surveysforall. com), or from a generic mailbox (e.g., healthsurvey@surveysforall.com)? Should they come from the sponsor or from the data collection agent? Do recipients (or their spam filters) pay attention to the domain (e.g., .com, .edu, or .gov)? As with many topics in this chapter, this is a little-explored area, although there are constraints on what one can do.

In the only study on this issue I'm aware of, Smith and Kiniorski (2003) tested four different "From" lines in e-mail invitations to members of the Harris Interactive panel. The standard sender e-mail is Harris_Poll@hpol.gsbc.com, and they tested the following four alternatives:

- Research@hpol.gsbc.com
- HIPoints@hpol@gsbc.com
- Jesse@hpol.gsbc.com
- Terri@hpol.gsbc.com

HIPoints is the Harris Interactive rewards program for survey participation. Response rates for the standard approach varied from 5.0% to 13.8%, reflecting variation in the topic, length, and other elements of the survey. None of the four experimental conditions improved response rates significantly over the standard approach.

My guess – consistent with Smith and Kiniosrki's (2003) finding – is that the e-mail address of the sender has minimal impact on the outcome of the invitation, at least to the extent that one can manipulate this information. In other words, if you are a dot.com, obtaining a dot.gov address is not only difficult, but may also backfire if the topic suggests contradictory information. On the other hand, if the survey sponsor is a government agency, having the e-mail come from a dot.gov domain may garner more attention but may also add logistical difficulties.

Another consideration is that the sender's e-mail should be a real e-mail address. Recipients may well reply directly to the sender – even if an alternative address is provided in the body of the e-mail – and undeliverable e-mails will be returned to that address. If, for example, Joe Blow is the principal investigator for the study, or the sponsor, having all returned e-mail messages go to his mailbox may not a good idea. If this is a one-time survey and the volume of such mail is likely to be low, this may not be a problem. But for ongoing studies, most organizations have either a generic mailbox or an e-mail address specific to each survey.

6.2.1.2. The Addressee

This is what appears in the "To:" field of the e-mail message. Little can be done with the addressee, and there is little or no research on the issue, so let me just offer a few brief observations.

A key point is that the e-mail should be sent to each individual addressee – as in the example in Figure 6.2 – rather than a group e-mail or alias. Here are two examples of survey invitations I received from my own institution:

"Michigan Students, Staff, and Faculty@umich.edu"

"The random sample of 2,400 faculty@umich.edu"

The first is a group e-mail created to communicate with the entire campus community. It clearly signals that this is a generic message, not an individually addressed one. The second one is obvious, and was created in the same way. These immediately reveal that the recipient in each case is one of many thousands who received the invitation, and there is nothing unique about their contribution to the study. Even worse is an e-mail invitation where the entire list of recipients' e-mail addresses appears in the "To:" field. Not only does this violate the privacy of individual addresses but it also conveys a lack of thought on the part of the designer. I've also received invitations where to "To:" field is blank, also suggesting some alias address or listserv.

Almost all Web survey software systems designed for individualized invitations have the capability to generate individual e-mail invitations from a database of e-mail addresses, using mail-merge procedures. It should appear to the respondent that they are the only addressee. This conveys personalization but also permits individualized salutations and the credible delivery of login and authentication information (see Section 6.3). While I know of no survey findings to support this, Chesney (2006) found that 25% of those invited by an individualized e-mail to participate in an experiment did so, compared to only 1% of those sent a group e-mail message.

The accuracy of e-mail addresses should also be underscored. Relative to invitations by mail, e-mail invitations will not be effective if the quality of the list is poor. For example, minor errors in the e-mail address will render the message undeliverable. For example, an e-mail sent to mcooper@umich.edu will never reach me, whereas one sent to mcouper@umich.edu will. The postal service is more tolerant of errors in mailing addresses – a letter addressed to "Mick Cooper" at my address will reach me. Furthermore, e-mail suffers from a great deal more "churn" than mailing addresses. E-mail addresses can change with changes in employer, ISP (Internet service provider), and the like. Many people now have several different e-mail addresses, some more temporary than others. Furthermore, e-mail doesn't enjoy the same forwarding facilities as the postal service provides for mail, and undelivered e-mail is not returned with any degree of reliability. If the accuracy of the list is in question, consider using mail, either in addition to, or instead of, e-mail. Vendors of opt-in panels are constantly managing the panel to cull nonworking e-mail addresses or inactive panel members, and update or change contact information. One of the measures of the quality of such panels is the degree of active panel maintenance that is performed.

6.2.1.3. The Subject Line

What to put in the subject line may depend on whether one is making a single survey request or one of many requests to existing panel members. There is even wide variation in how opt-in panel vendors identify each survey. Figure 6.3 shows a snapshot of subject lines from three different vendors over a two-week period. Given the frequency of invitations opt-in panel members are likely to get, clearly differentiating one invitation from the next may be important. From a nonresponse bias perspective (Groves, 2006), however, revealing the subject of the

Vendor A	Vendor B	Vendor C
Take our latest survey	We want your thoughts on	Your opinion counts! (72312)
Guaranteed One Dollar for	income protection decisions!	Your opinion counts! (72272)
completing this survey	Talk to us about you and your	Your opinion counts! (71217)
Calling All Men for a New	home!	New Survey from
Survey	Voice your opinion on a	OnlinePanel! (16540)
Your Opinion Counts – Take	variety of topics!	Survey for you... (68538)
this New Survey	Tell us about your shopping	Interactive OnlinePanel
Clinical Research Study for	habits!	Survey (68901)
Frequent Migraine Headaches	Brief survey on hotels and	OnlinePanel Survey Invite!
Guaranteed Ten Dollars for	travel!	(68602)
completing this survey	Tell us what you think about	Your feedback counts!
Guaranteed Two Dollars for	technology products!	(68740)
completing this survey	We want your opinion on a	
	collection of topics!	

Figure 6.3 **Example Subject Lines from Three Panel Vendors.**

survey at the outset may encourage only those who are interested in the particular topic to proceed. I suspect that each of these vendors – and others that maintain large opt-in panels – is constantly tinkering with ways to entice their members to open the e-mail and click on the URL. However, this is likely viewed as proprietary research by the vendors, so we know little about what may work and what may not.

In any case, I'd be uncomfortable generalizing from such opt-in or access panels to other types of online research, given the preexisting relationship with panel members. Therefore, we should look at research done with other types of samples.

Porter and Whitcomb (2005) conducted an experiment on the subject line in two samples, one of high school students who had requested information about the university but did not apply for admission (low involvement), and the other of undergraduates currently enrolled at the university (high involvement). They varied three elements of the subject line in a factorial design: the reason for the e-mail (yes/no), the survey sponsor (yes/no), and a request for assistance (yes/no).

Click-through rates for the low involvement sample ranged from 16.9% to 24.2%, and for the high involvement sample from 54.0% to 58.9%. They found no significant effects of the manipulations on click-through rates for the high-involvement subjects. However, for the low involvement subjects, main effects were found for both the reason for the e-mail ($p < .05$) and for the survey sponsor ($p < .05$), while the request for assistance had no effect. Regarding the former, mentioning the purpose of the e-mail ("Survey") yielded a lower click-through rate; the highest rate was obtained for the blank subject line. Similarly, the click-through rate was lower when the survey sponsor (i.e., a university) was identified. Porter and Whitcomb (2005) speculate that curiosity may have driven the recipients to open the e-mail with the blank subject line. When the purpose of the e-mail is revealed (that it is a survey), recipients no longer have to open the message and access the survey to determine what the e-mail is about.

For students at the university (the high involvement group), any e-mail from the institution may be regarded as important and needing to be opened. For the low involvement group, the sender is less important, and thus the subject line may convey additional information to determine the purpose and value of the e-mail. In other words, the effect of the subject line may well depend on other aspects of the e-mail, and the relationship the recipient has with the sender.

In an unpublished study, Damschroder and colleagues at the University of Michigan's Center for Behavioral and Decision Sciences in Medicine (www. cbdsm.org) tested two alternative subject lines in the e-mail invitation. Half of the members invited from an opt-in panel were exposed to a subject line that read, "Participate in an important study on health issues," while the balance saw a subject line that read "University of Michigan Health Study." They found no difference in the response to the invitation (16% versus 17%). This provides some support for the notion that in this case the recipients have a relationship with the sender (the opt-in panel vendor) that trumps the subject line in determining whether the e-mail is opened, read, and acted upon.

Trouteaud (2004) tested two different subject lines – a "plea" versus an "offer" – in a survey request sent to 7,600 subscribers to an online newsletter. The "plea" version was worded "Please help [Name of Company] with your advice and opinions," while the "offer" version read, "Share your advice and opinions now with [Name of Company]." With overall response rates around 24%, Trouteaud reported a five-percentage point advantage for the plea version.

Kent and Brandal (2003) found that a prize subject line ("Win a weekend for two in Nice") produced a significantly lower response rate than a subject line that simply stated the e-mail was about a survey (52% versus 68%) in a survey invitation to members of a customer loyalty program in Norway. Smith and Kiniorski (2003) asked respondents to a Web survey how they would react to a variety of different subject lines – whether they would open the e-mail immediately, delete it immediately, or something else. They report that respondents generally preferred subject lines with consumer products as the topic (e.g., "Share your thoughts on emerging consumer products") rather than those that mentioned the survey (e.g., "Take part in an important survey").

My guess is that the decision to open an e-mail message, especially from a known or recognized sender, is not a deeply processed one. Beyond some minimal threshold to verify that the sender is a known entity, and thus the e-mail is not spam, the subject line may receive relatively little attention.

Spammers are adept at creating innocuous-sounding topics to entice people to open and peruse the e-mail message. Even survey invitations are being used for spam, much like telemarketers use SUGGING (selling under the guise of interviewing). At the time I received the e-mail in Figure 6.2, I received a slew of other e-mails ostensibly from Chase Manhattan Bank with subject lines like "$20 Reward Survey," "Customer Survey – Get $20 Reward," "Win $20 with our question survey [sic]," and the like. The problem of distinguishing legitimate survey requests from these phishing activities has its parallel in separating cold-call RDD survey requests from telemarketing and mail surveys from direct marketing campaigns in the minds of potential respondents.

In summary, I recommend that if the survey is about a specific event the recipient attended or activity they engaged in, make this explicit in the subject line, so they understand why they are receiving the message. Otherwise, make sure the subject line reinforces the nature of the relationship between sender and recipient, so that it is again clear why the message is being sent to them, and from whom. For opt-in panels, where panel members are receiving regular requests from the vendor, the sender e-mail should suffice to trigger recognition and a reaction. Trying to come up with creative variations for several survey invitations a week is a challenge, and there is an increasing risk of the message resembling spam (e.g., "Last few days – $10 reward survey!" Or take another look at Figure 6.3). I'd avoid specific mention of the topic of the survey in the subject line, as this could lead to selective completion of the survey, potentially producing nonresponse bias. Of course, if one is only interested in a self-selected group of whiskey drinkers, for example, use the subject, "Whiskey drinkers – we have a survey for you!" But then please don't claim this is a "representative" sample – not even of whiskey-drinking Internet users.

6.2.1.4. Summary on the E-Mail Header

Given that the three header elements (sender, recipient, and subject) are often visible without opening the e-mail message, they should convey the importance

1.
From:	David Harris
To:	Mick Couper
CC:	
Subject:	UM Professor Needs Your Help

2.
From:	The Eureka Group, Inc. (A Market Research Consulting Company) [support7@markettools.com]
To:	mcouper@umich.edu
CC:	
Subject:	We need your opinion on a NEW Auto Service

3.
From:	Mk832mn57@yahoo.com
To:	
CC:	
Subject:	.

Figure 6.4 **Example E-Mail Headers.**

and legitimacy of the request. While there is not much that one can do with these elements, they should be congruent. The three examples in Figure 6.4 are all real e-mail messages I received. Each conveys quite a different message.

The first example in Figure 6.4 is from a survey conducted by a former colleague (Harris, 2002) intended for undergraduate students. The second is from a market research company. The difference in the address information indicates whether this is an internal message (Mick Couper) or one from outside the university (mcouper@umich.edu). In both cases, it is already clear who this is from, to whom it was sent and what the message is about. Contrast this with the third example. The e-mail address provides little clue as to the identity of the sender. The blank "To:" field suggests this was sent to an alias or listserv, rather than being individually addressed. Combine this with the blank subject line, and the e-mail almost screams spam, which indeed it was. Enough information needs to be conveyed in the header to reassure the recipient, and encourage the opening and reading of the e-mail message. If that is done, more information can be conveyed in the body of the message.

6.2.2. The E-Mail Body

As far as the content of the e-mail invitation to a Web survey is concerned, the number of studies is much more limited, and indeed, this is an area ripe for further research. I will first discuss some key elements of the content for which there is research evidence, before offering some general observations about other aspects of the e-mail invitation.

6.2.2.1. The Salutation

How should one address the recipient (if at all) in the body of the e-mail message? One answer depends of course on what information is available on the list, and how confident one is of the accuracy of that information. The more information is available (e.g., first name, last name, title, gender), the more options one has in addressing the respondent. Given that the way the recipient is addressed is under greater design control than, say, the sender's e-mail address, it is not surprising that several studies have been done on this topic.

Porter and Whitcomb (2003) describe an experiment on various aspects of the e-mail message. In one manipulation, they varied four elements of the e-mail invitation:

1. Salutation: personal (e.g., Dear Jane) or impersonal (Dear Student).
2. Sender's e-mail address: personal (e.g., jsmith@institution.edu) or impersonal (surveyresearch@institution.edu).
3. Authority of the e-mail signatory: high (director) or low (administrative assistant).
4. Profile of the requesting office: high (Office of Admission) or low (Office of Institutional Research).

The sample comprised high school students who contacted the university for information but did not apply for admission. The sample of more than 12,000 was randomly assigned to the eight conditions. Click-through rates ranged from 15.6% to 22.5% but none of the factors they tested reached statistical significance.

Pearson and Levine (2003) varied the level of personalization of the salutation in an e-mail invitation sent to alumni of Stanford University. The sample of 3,200 alumni was randomly assigned to one of four conditions:

1. Generic: "Dear Stanford Alum"
2. Familiar personalized: "Dear James"
3. Familiar personalized name only: "James"
4. Formal personalized: "Dear Mr. Bond"

They found that the personalized versions (regardless of type) yielded slightly higher, but not significantly different, response rates. In addition, they report on some intriguing (although again not statistically significant) effects of different salutations for different subgroups, such as age, membership in the alumni association, and school. But, the results generally support those of Porter and Whitcomb (2003), suggesting that the form of salutation does not matter. Kent and Brandal also found little effect of a personalized invitation versus an impersonal "Dear Customer" salutation (52% versus 50%, respectively).

Heerwegh and colleagues (2005) conducted two experiments on salutations among students. In the first, a sample of 2,000 first-year college students was randomly assigned to two groups, one receiving an impersonal salutation ("Dear student") and the other personal ("Dear [First name] [Last name]"). The survey was about attitudes toward marriage and divorce and attitudes and behavior concerning sexuality. The login rate was significantly ($p < .001$) higher for the group receiving the personalized salutation (64.3% versus 54.5%). Interestingly, they found some hint that the personal condition may have led to more impression management (i.e., more socially desirable reporting) than the impersonal condition. A replication a year later among 2,520 first-year students at the university yielded similar significant effects for the personalization manipulation, with login rates of 68.1% for the personal and 61.2% for the impersonal condition (Heerwegh, 2005b). In this second study, no evidence of socially desirable reporting was found, although in response to a debriefing question, the impersonal group reported feeling significantly more at ease answering honestly and sincerely.

Joinson and colleagues have conducted a similar series of experiments on salutations, also looking at disclosure of sensitive information. Joinson and Reips (2007) report on a study in which 10,000 Open University students were invited to join a student Web survey panel. Invitees were randomly assigned to one of four salutations:

1. "Dear Student"
2. "Dear Open University Student"
3. "Dear [First name]" (e.g., "Dear John")
4. "Dear [First name] [Last name]" (e.g., "Dear John Doe")

The response rates (percentage agreeing to join the panel) ranged from 13.4% for the first group and 13.5% for the second, to 15.7% for the fourth group and 17.9% for the third. The "Dear John" version was significantly higher ($p < .001$) than both the impersonal conditions, while the "Dear John Doe" was marginally so ($p < .05$).

Joinson and Reips (2007) followed this up with an e-mail to panel members to leave the panel, using the same four salutations conditions. Those in the personalized conditions were less likely to do so, suggesting that the effect of personalization condition is not due to the higher likelihood of a message being read or actively attended to, but rather due to greater social desirability, or the desire to please the high status requestor.

In a subsequent study, Joinson and Reips (2007) manipulated both personalization ("Dear Student," "Dear John Doe," and "Dear John") and the status of the source of the e-mail ("From [Name] versus "From Professor [Name], Pro-vice chancellor") in a survey invitation to members of the panel. The size of the effect of the salutation was larger when the source was of high power than when it was of neutral power (see also Guéguen and Jacob, 2002b). The highest response rate (53.4%) was obtained from the high-power personalized (Dear John) condition, and the lowest (40.1%) from the neutral power "Dear Student" condition.

Joinson, Woodley, and Reips (2007) conducted an experiment among members of the panel. Both personalization ("Dear John" versus "Dear PRESTO panel member") and status of the sender (high versus neutral, as in the Joinson and Reips study) were manipulated in a 2 × 2 design. The highest response rate (48.8%) was obtained for the high power and personalized salutation condition, compared to 45.3% for the high power impersonal condition, 44.1% for the neutral power personalized condition, and 44.4% for the neutral power impersonal condition. They also found slight evidence that the personalized salutation led to reduced disclosure of a sensitive personal question (on salary), but the effect was not statistically significant. Finally, Joinson (2005) reports on a staff survey among a sample of over 4,700 in which a "Dear John" condition achieved an 82% response rate while a "Dear colleague" condition achieved 66%.

The Joinson and Reips (2007) and Joinson, Woodley, and Reips (2007) studies suggest that personalization only works when the sender is of high status. They also note that personalization increases response rates, but reduces anonymity, and hence may decrease disclosure. Heerwegh (2005b) similarly suggests that personalization may be less effective if the sender and recipient do not have an existing relationship. He also finds some suggestion of an effect of reduced anonymity on disclosure, but the effect is also modest. Thus, while personalized salutations appear to be effective in increasing click-through rates in Web surveys, they may not do so under all conditions, and may affect the answers to sensitive questions in the subsequent survey.

On balance, it is beneficial to personalize the salutation. If one does so, I also believe one should use a level of informality appropriate to the relationship between sender and recipient.

6.2.2.2. The Signature

Details about the sender are conveyed in two ways, first by the e-mail address in the "From:" field of the e-mail message, and secondly, by the signature appearing at the bottom of the e-mail message. I addressed the former briefly in Section 6.2.1.1, and return to the issue here while focusing on the signature.

In terms of research on the issue, I've already reviewed the findings of Joinson and Reips (2007) and Joinson, Woodley, and Reips (2007) that the status of the sender has an effect on response rates. Crawford and colleagues (2004) varied the description of the sender in a study of University of Michigan students. They randomly assigned the sample to one of the following four conditions, with about 5,320 students in each condition:

1. No name
2. Carol J. Boyd
3. Professor Carol J. Boyd
4. Substance Abuse Research Center

In all cases, the actual e-mail address used was umsl@msiresearch.com. They report response rates ranging from 40.1% for version 4, to 41.1% for version 1, 42.1% for version 2, and 43.0% for version 3. The response rate for version 3 was significantly higher than that for version 1 or version 2 ($p < .05$) or version 4 ($p < .01$), but these effects are modest at best. With the sender's information typically appearing at the bottom of the e-mail message, below the URL, it may well be that the decision to participate or not is made before this point is even reached.

Guéguen and Jacob (2002a) went further to draw attention to the sender of the invitation, by including a digital photograph of a male or female requester in an HTML e-mail invitation to a Web survey sent to students (n = 160) at a university in France. When a photograph was included, subjects were more likely to comply with the request (83.8%) than when no photograph was included (57.5%). There was also a main effect of the gender of the requester, and an interaction of the inclusion of the photograph and the gender of the requester, such that the female requester was helped more of the time than the male requester when a photograph was included, but there was no difference when no photograph was included.

While this small-scale study suggests that photographs may help, this may not be a good idea for a number of reasons. Not all e-mail clients will download images, and not all will do so automatically. For example, the default setting in Microsoft

Outlook 2003 is to block images. The user has to click on the hidden image to reveal it, or change the Outlook settings to permit all images, which raises virus and security concerns. A related concern is that phishers and spammers often use images to avoid the text-detection algorithms used by spam filters. This may raise concerns of guilt by association.

Should a real signature be used? As with digital photographs, a digital signature could be included. The mail survey literature (e.g., Dillman, 1978) suggests that a signature helps. But, in an e-mail invitation, this is achieved through a graphical image, which some may not be able to view, and others may be reluctant to open, depending on the preference settings of the e-mail client.

The graphical enhancements – and this would include logos and other potentially legitimizing devices – are best left to the Web page welcoming the respondent to the survey (see Section 6.4). An e-mail invitation that can be read and acted upon by someone using a plain-text e-mail client maximizes the chances of all recipients being able to view the message and reduces the likelihood of interception by spam filters.

6.2.2.3 Contact Information

In addition to the sender e-mail and the signature, other information can be communicated to give recipients a way to verify the veracity of the request or to obtain additional information about the survey or the task. At a minimum, an e-mail address should be provided for such queries. This may be the same as the sender e-mail, it may be the e-mail address of the person whose signature appears in the e-mail, it may be a generic e-mail address such as support@surveysforall.com, or one created specifically for each survey project (e.g., healthsurvey@surveysforall.com or travel@surveysforall.com). It is valuable to also include a phone number and mailing address in the e-mail invitation. This helps establish the legitimacy of the request, and gives those who may fear that all hyperlinks are questionable, an alternative route to find out more about the request. What needs to be included here may depend on a variety of factors, such as the nature and topic of the survey, the sponsor, requirements of institutional review boards (IRBs), and the like. But, more information – that is, more ways for potential respondents to get additional information if they so desire – is better than less. What message does a researcher hiding behind a generic e-mail address or hyperlink convey to potential respondents who may be asked to provide information on the intimate details of their lives? The norm of reciprocity and openness should trump any concerns about being overwhelmed by queries about the study.

6.2.2.4. The URL

The uniform resource locator (or URL) is the Web address or location of the survey. Arguably, this is the most important part of the invitation. The major advantage of an e-mail invitation is that it can deliver a URL to permit easy access to the survey. There is no break in the media or technology – the respondent is already at a computer, with access to the Internet – and clicking on the URL should launch the survey directly from the e-mail client.

As with the recipient's e-mail address, getting the URL correct is critical to the success of the survey. But, while each incorrect e-mail address may lose one potential respondent, an incorrect URL could potentially lose them all.

The same advice about URLs in general should apply to URLs in Web survey invitations: They should be short, understandable, and easy to transcribe or retype. This is for three reasons. First, long URLs may wrap over two or more lines in the e-mail message. While this is not a challenge for most modern e-mail clients, some still have problems dealing with long URLs. This seems to be especially true of text-based e-mail clients (i.e., those that do not accommodate rich text or HTML), and messages delivered from many listservs (which also tend to be text-based to control viruses). The success of services such as www.tinyurl.com provides evidence for the demand for short and easy URLs.

Second, not everyone will want to access the Web survey directly by clicking on the URL. Some may want to write down the address and access the survey from another computer. Some may need to cut and paste the URL into their browser, rather than clicking on the link in the e-mail. Others may simply be suspicious of hyperlinks.

Third, invitations to Web surveys are not always delivered by e-mail. For many samples an e-mail address may not be available, and the login information needs to be communicated by mail or other means, necessitating typing the URL in the browser.

Here's an example of a URL from an e-mail invitation I received, slightly altered to mask the identity of the company:

    http://sms.surveysforall.com/stm/VerifyPage.aspx?enparams=VLG%3d485%26ZLG%
    3d478%26FHLG%3d5%26SLG%3d175149%26LLG%3d4309%26TLG%
    3d4384&InviteID=2832&utcoffset=5

In actuality, this monstrosity was hidden behind a graphical "launch survey" button in the e-mail invitation. But if the recipient had graphics disabled (a default option in Microsoft Outlook), they would not be able to get to the survey.

Holding the mouse over the button revealed the URL, and it was also displayed in the address bar of the browser. Typing the URL is simply not an option. Contrast this with http://surveysforall.com/survey456/start.asp?S=3423 where the "survey456" identifies the specific survey and "S=3423" passes an authentication parameter directly to the server (see Section 6.3), or even "Go to http://surveysforall.com/survey456 and enter the passcode found in the invitation."

For another example, some years ago, I received a postcard inviting me to complete a Web-based survey for National Academies Travel. The message said, "to complete the survey, simply go to:

http://www8.nationalacademies.org/survey/2003travelsurvey.htm

Leaving out the "8" after www resulted in one of those unpleasant "404 file not found" errors. Similarly, inadvertently typing "html" instead of "htm" at the end resulted in a "page not found" message. Stopping after the first "/survey/" yielded a "directory listing denied" message. In other words, the URL has to be typed exactly as it appears on the postcard. Is this all necessary? There were no access controls on this survey, so at least the URL contained no embedded unique code. Given that the National Academies owns the domain www.nas.edu, why not simply http://www.nas.edu/travelsurvey? If the invitation was sent via e-mail, allowing the respondent to simply click on the URL, the long URL may be less of a problem.

In addition to having a short and clear URL, I suggest that it be placed "above the fold" in the e-mail message, to use newspaper parlance. In other words, respondents should not need to scroll down in the e-mail message to see the link and/or password. While there may be other information in the message (see Section 6.2.2.5), the most important elements are those that get them to the Web site to start the survey, and these should be prominently and clearly displayed. The goal should be to make it as easy as possible for the invitee to start the survey.

6.2.2.5. Content of the E-Mail Invitation

Aside from the topics discussed separately earlier, I know of no published research on the content of the e-mail invitation. Several questions could be asked:

- How long should the message be, and how much detail should it contain?
- In what order should the information be presented?
- What should be in the invitation e-mail versus on the welcome page?

The answers may depend on the nature of the sample and the inviting organization. For example, members of opt-in panels know who the e-mail is from and generally what it is about, and most likely focus on the elements that change from one invitation to the next – the survey length, the topic, the size of the payment or reward, and so on. For those with no prior relationship with the sender, additional information may be necessary. Some organizations (e.g., government agencies, or those governed by IRBs) may have different requirements for what the invitation must contain.

While there is some advice on how to craft invitation or cover letters for mail surveys (e.g., Dillman, 1978, 2000), the question remains whether these guidelines translate to the Web. The culture of the Internet is different. People do not like to read much online (see Nielson, 2000, Chapter 3). Shorter may be better. In addition, many of the useful legitimizing tools used in mail surveys (such as personally addressed envelopes, stamps, letterhead, signatures, etc.), while increasingly technically possible in e-mail, may raise red flags for the recipient.

My speculation is that, having made the decision to open the message, few potential respondents read the entire contents. Rather, they scan the message for key elements. If this is the case, the following implications follow:

- Make sure that the URL is clearly visible and near the top of the message.
- Make sure that other critical information needed to proceed to the survey itself (e.g., password, login instructions) is visually accessible.
- Provide only the critical elements in the invitation, leaving details to the Web survey welcome page or to links accessible from the survey.

As with many of the issues discussed so far in this chapter, I hope to see more research on the content of the invitation. However, my guess is that – as with the other elements of the e-mail discussed previously – manipulations of e-mail content may have little effect because potential respondents aren't paying much attention to the messages, if they read them at all.

6.2.3. Combining Mail and E-Mail

As I've already noted, getting sample persons to open and read the e-mail invitation is often the most challenging part of the process. Furthermore, we know little or nothing about what is done, or not done, at this stage. We don't know whether the message got lost in cyberspace, was intercepted by a spam filter, was discarded by the recipient before opening the message, or was opened and then ignored, deleted, or forgotten. Once the recipient visits the survey's welcome page, we can measure what happens, so we have greater purchase on the latter parts of the survey participation process.

As we have seen in the previous sections, relatively little can be done with the e-mail invitation to ensure it is opened, read, and acted on. This remains our biggest challenge as Web survey designers. However, one possible solution is to use the power of the different media. Where feasible – depending on the information available on the sampling frame, the resources available, and the importance of higher response rates – a combination of a mailed letter and an e-mail invitation may be most effective. Mail is best for gaining attention, legitimizing the survey, providing reassurances about the nature of the request, delivering an incentive, and so on. E-mail is best for delivering the URL, providing a password, and getting people to the Web site in an efficient manner. As with advance letters in telephone surveys (e.g., Link and Mokdad, 2005; Hembroff et al., 2005), an advance letter, followed shortly by an e-mail invitation, should increase the likelihood of the invitation being acted upon.

While e-mail is a cheap and easy way to get in touch with sample members, this very convenience may be its downfall for surveys. I fear that what telemarketers did to telephone surveys, spammers and phishers[1] may do to Web surveys. More and more people are using spam filters, and more and more people are deleting e-mails without opening them. Add to this the increasing numbers of e-mails people receive, and the odds of a recipient receiving, noticing, and acting upon an e-mail invitation are only likely to go down. Given this, the use of mailed prenotification in combination with an e-mail invitation may become increasingly important.

6.2.4. Summary on Invitations

We should view the e-mail invitation as a Gestalt. In other words, the tone of the salutation should match that conveyed by the identity of the sender and the topic, and appropriate to that expected by the recipient. Overly familiar salutations may come across as insincere if used incorrectly. Mismatches between different

[1] Spammers use e-mail to send unsolicited bulk messages with the goal of selling some product or service. Phishers use bulk e-mail in an attempt to acquire sensitive information (password, credit card number, social security number, etc.) with the goal of committing fraud.

elements of the invitation e-mail may raise red flags for the recipient, or, even worse, for their spam filter. All elements of the e-mail invitation should convey a consistent message to engender credibility and get a fair reading from the recipient. Similarly, the transition from the e-mail to the Web site should be a fluid one from the recipient's perspective. Careful design of these steps, as with other elements of the online survey, can convey the attributes – such as legitimacy, importance, trustworthiness, urgency, and so on – needed to encourage recipients of the e-mail to login to the survey and proceed with the task of answering the questions, and to do so in as honest and considered a manner as possible.

6.3. Login and Authentication

For an open-access survey with no restriction on who may complete the survey or how many times they may do so, this is not an issue. But for those who want to control access to the survey, the login and authentication process is an important filter that should let legitimate users in with ease, but keep unwanted people or software agents out. In addition to controlling access, the login may influence potential respondents' perceptions of confidentiality, and hence affect their willingness to provide honest answers, if indeed they choose to participate. There have been several studies of the login process, and I review these briefly before offering some summary observations.

There are several different ways to control access to a Web survey. Some are more passive, requiring little or no work on the part of the respondent, while others require some action by the respondent to access the survey.

Passive authentication methods include the use of IP (Internet protocol) addresses or cookies as a way to limit ballot stuffing. Both these approaches have their limitations. An IP address is a series of numbers (e.g., 141.122.53.12) that identifies a device connected to the Internet. IP addresses can be permanent or temporary. For many dial-up users or those who access the Internet by means of an ISP, the IP address identifies whatever modem or device they are connected to at the time, not the specific machine they are using. Even with a fixed IP address, I can complete the same survey on several different machines at work and home, and can go to an Internet café or library and do it even more times. Using IP addresses may screen out gross violations (e.g., scores of submissions from the same IP address) but does not prevent multiple completions. Cookies are even more specific – they are associated with a particular browser on a particular machine. I use Internet Explorer, Netscape, and Firefox to browse the Internet, and each has its own set of cookies. Furthermore, I can easily delete the cookies placed by a Web site or survey, and start all over again. Privacy settings can also be used to block cookies. In one Web software system, if cookies are disabled, the system repeatedly regenerates the same page, no matter how many times one tries to answer the question.

A third passive or automatic authentication approach uses a unique ID and or password embedded in the URL. For list-based samples, most survey software can handle this process, essentially generating a unique URL for each respondent that links them to their survey and no other.

The active or manual approaches to authentication represent variations on this theme. One could include an ID in the URL but have the respondent manually enter a password. One could require them to enter both ID and password to gain access to the survey. One could have them enter their e-mail address as a way to log in.

Some form of unique ID and password, whether embedded in the URL or entered by the respondent, is the most effective way of controlling access for a survey involving individual invitations. The choice of particular approach may depend on the security requirements and the sensitivity of the topic.

Let's look at the research. In a study on affirmative action among University of Michigan students, we randomly assigned sample persons to an active (manual) authentication where they had to enter a username and password provided in the e-mail address, or a passive (automatic) authentication in which the username and password were embedded in the URL (Crawford, Couper, and Lamias, 2001). Figure 6.5 illustrates the two versions. We achieved response rates (completes+partials) of 36.8% for the automated group and 32.2% for the manual group, this difference being statistically significant (p < .01). We found no differences in data quality between the two login versions.

In a survey of University of Michigan faculty on diversity initiatives, Crawford (personal communication, 2001) embedded an experiment on manual versus automatic authentication, crossed with a short (four-digit) versus long (nine-digit) PIN. Those in the manual version were further split between single entry (PIN) versus double entry (ID plus PIN) treatments. With over 4,000 faculty randomized to these different treatments, none of the effects were statistically significant. For example, response rates were 28.0% for the automatic and 26.8% for the manual, and 28.1% for the single entry and 25.4% for the double entry authentication, suggesting some advantage of requiring less effort, but these differences were not large.

Heerwegh and Loosveldt (2002a) conducted a similar experiment among students at the University of Leuven, in a study on environment attitudes. Students were randomly assigned to an automatic authentication, in which the PIN was

Manual Authentication:

```
To participate, please click on this link (or cut and paste it into a web browser):
http://projects.isr.umich.edu/aaos/start.cfm
```

```
Username: 9879
Password: 26830
```

```
Please enter the username and password below when prompted at the beginning of the survey.
This password ensures that you and only you can enter this survey.
```

Automatic Authentication:

```
To participate, please click on this link (or cut and paste it into a web browser):
http://projects.isr.umich.edu/aaos/start.cfm?er=9764&sw=60256
```

```
The address is encoded with a unique identifier to insure that you and only you can enter
this survey.
```

Figure 6.5 **Examples of Manual and Automatic Authentication.**

embedded in the URL, or a manual authentication requiring entry of a four-digit PIN. They obtained response rates (completes+partials) of 52% for the automatic and 54% for the manual group. While not statistically significant, the trend is in the opposite direction to ours, suggesting the manual login is more effective. In addition, they found that those in the manual authentication group were slightly more likely to complete the entire survey (i.e., not drop out), and they found fewer nonsubstantive answers (less missing data) in the manual login condition.

In a second study, again with University of Leuven students and on the same topic, Heerwegh and Loosveldt (2003) tested a semiautomatic login, in addition to the manual and automatic conditions. Those in the manual login condition entered a four-digit PIN and five-digit user name, while those in the semiautomatic condition entered just the PIN, while the user name was embedded in the URL. In the automatic condition, the user name and PIN were embedded in the URL. The manual login achieved a response rate of 57.3%, compared to 65.7% for the semiautomatic and 60.3% for the automatic login. While these differences don't reach statistical significance, they do suggest that some combination of automatic (passive) and manual (active) login methods may be most effective. We can summarize the conclusions from the three studies with respect to response rates as follows:

1. Crawford, Couper, and Lamias (2001): automatic > manual
2. Heerwegh and Loosveldt (2002a): semiautomatic > automatic
3. Heerwegh and Loosveldt (2003): semiautomatic > automatic > manual

In addition, Heerwegh and Loosveldt (2003) found the manual version to produce high ratings of perceived confidentiality among respondents, followed by the semiautomatic version. The semiautomatic version also produced the lowest rates of nonsubstantive answers. While more research is needed to see if these results hold for different populations[2] and for different survey topics (varying on sensitivity), I concur with Heerwegh and Loosveldt's (2003) conclusion that the semiautomatic authentication approach is the most effective. This allows the password to be kept relatively short, making entry a little easier.

Given that one might require respondents to enter an ID or password, it is important that this be free of any ambiguities. In one of our early Web surveys (Couper, Traugott, and Lamias, 2001) we included an alphanumeric password. Several telephone calls and e-mail messages from sample persons complaining about problems accessing the survey led us to investigate further. Those passwords that included ambiguous characters (e.g., 1, l, O, 0) produced significantly fewer successful logins (43.7%) than those that did not (50.4%). If respondents are to type in the ID and/or password, make sure it is relatively easy to do. Of course, we're all warned that longer passwords, and those containing a mix of upper and lower case letters and numbers are more secure, but what good does it do if one cannot get into the survey?

On the other hand, the ID should be sufficiently long to prevent accidental access to someone else's survey. For example, a four-digit ID gives one only 9,999 unique codes. With a sample size of 1,000, this means that 1 in 5 of the possible numbers are assigned. If the sample size increased to 5,000, one in every two IDs is an active ID, and the likelihood of entering another survey through deliberate or accidental mistyping is increased. Partly for this reason, the U.S. Decennial Census uses a fourteen-digit ID and the Canadian census a fifteen-digit ID. This is another reason why the semiautomatic approach – the combination of an embedded ID and a manually entered numeric password – may strike the best balance between security and ease of access.

Finally, while none of the studies have examined the use of e-mail addresses as an authentication method, it is an approach used by some vendors of opt-in panels. I'm not a big fan of this approach. Respondents may be reluctant to provide an e-mail address for confidentiality and security reasons. Entering an e-mail address serves to highlight the identifiability of the responses relative to entering a string of numbers provided by the survey organization. In terms of security, entry of

---

[2] For example, in opt-in panels, trust is built up over several successive surveys, and the convenience of an automatic login may trump other considerations.

information in a recognizable format such as an e-mail address runs the risk of interception by spambots, spiders, or other programs trolling the Web to harvest such information, unless a secure site is used. On the other hand, using an e-mail address as a login is easy for respondents to remember, and is a common practice in e-commerce in combination with a user-generated password.

In summary, the login and authentication process should strike a balance between making it easy for respondents to get to the survey, and providing appropriate levels of security to reassure respondents that one takes issues of confidentiality seriously. The particular approach one uses may then depend on the nature of the relationship with the potential respondent and the sensitivity of the information being collected.

6.4. The Welcome or Splash Page

Depending on the authentication approach used, this may be the same page as the login. For surveys using automatic authentication or those with no access restrictions, this is the first page the potential respondent sees when they click on or type in the URL. If the invitee has gotten this far, they have shown at least some inclination to proceed, or are at least interested or curious enough to read further. The splash page plays an important role in sealing the deal – in turning the invitee into a respondent.

In our research on breakoffs, by far the largest number of those who drop out do so on this initial page. With each succeeding page of the survey, the likelihood of dropout declines. But at this initial stage, the Web survey still has little "stickiness" – little to attract and keep the respondent committed to continuing. Even though they have come this far, our work is far from over.

Unlike the previous steps I have discussed thus far, once invitees reach the splash page, we have the full power of the Web at our disposal to encourage them to proceed. Despite its potential importance and design potential, the welcome page has received surprisingly little research attention – in fact, none, to my knowledge.

What function should the welcome page serve? Aside from the login process, it should serve to reassure the potential respondent that they have arrived at the right place and encourage them to proceed to the questionnaire itself. Here is where many of the legitimizing tools that are difficult to include in e-mail messages can be used – logos, signatures, pictures of the researcher or research organization, contact numbers and e-mail addresses, links to company or organization home pages, descriptions of the research, links to FAQs on the study, statements about confidentiality, and so on.

The splash page should be seen as a permeable membrane, permitting the respondent to pass through to the survey with ease, but providing additional information if needed. Many designs I have seen – especially those for government surveys – treat this page instead as a barrier, putting up so many hurdles that only the most deeply committed respondent makes it through to the first question. This is not very welcoming.

For example, one survey I was shown had not one but several introductory pages before the start of the questions proper. These included:

1. A welcome page, with little other information other than the logo of the agency and the name of the survey.
2. An introduction outlining the ten parts of the survey; each of these was a push button for additional information on each part.
3. If one clicked on one of the buttons, a description of that part of the questionnaire was displayed on a separate page.
4. A page of instructions, including instructions on how to log in, that required scrolling to access the "next" button.
5. A page of definitions of key terms, again requiring scrolling.
6. The Privacy Act statement, addressing confidentiality issues.
7. The login page, on which the ID and password were to be entered, with different buttons for first-time and returning respondent.

Finally, after these seven steps, the first page of the questionnaire was reached. Even if respondents had already started the survey and were returning to complete it, they would still need to proceed through these steps before getting to the point they were before. This process could be considerably shortened.

Some introductory material may be required by law (such as the Privacy Act statement or Paper Reduction Act statement for U.S. federal surveys); others may be required by IRBs. In the commercial world, there are sometimes nondisclosure agreements, for example, if the respondents are going to be shown proprietary information.

In addition, academic disciplines differ in their approach to informed consent (see Kraut et al., 2004). For example, the tradition in psychological experimentation is that of signed consent. In survey research, given that respondents can drop out without prejudice at any point in the process, and given that many surveys do not involve direct contact with respondents, the tradition has been more

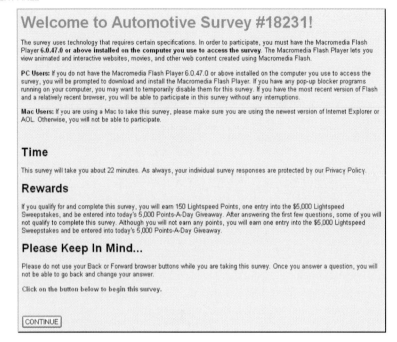

Figure 6.6 **Welcome Page from Lightspeed Consumer Panel Survey.**

that of implicit consent. The normative pressures to continue a Web survey once started are much less than the pressures to see a laboratory experiment to its conclusion once one has begun participation. These traditions are reflected in the online world, with most online experiments including a consent page with an "I agree" check box in order to proceed to the experiment. Online surveys typically presume that continued participation in the survey implies consent, and simply take the respondent from the welcome page to the first question.

Let's look at a few examples of welcome pages. The first, in Figure 6.6, contains the key information needed for the respondent to proceed with the survey, including topic, length, special technical requirements, instructions for completion, and the rewards for participation. Given that this is a consumer panel, the latter is probably of some importance to the panel member. The welcome page has a statement about the company's privacy policy, but no link on this page to that policy.

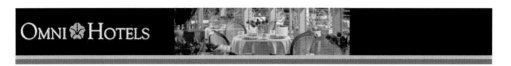

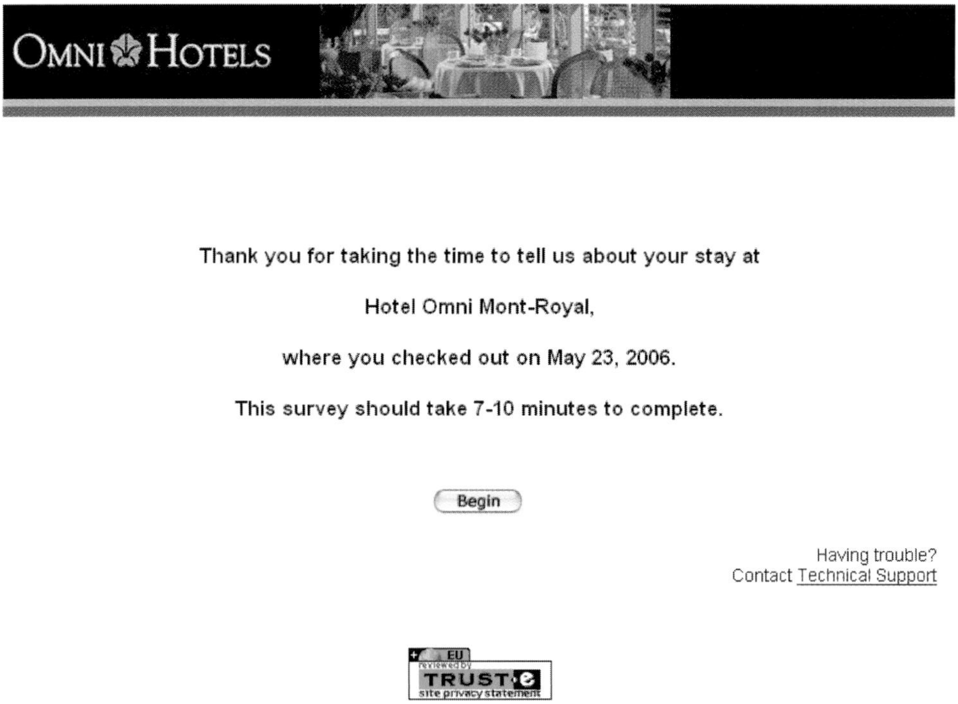

OMNI HOTELS
Thank you for taking the time to tell us about your stay at
Hotel Omni Mont-Royal,
where you checked out on May 23, 2006.
This survey should take 7-10 minutes to complete.
Begin
Having trouble?
Contact Technical Support
EU
reviewed by
TRUSTe
site privacy statement

Figure 6.7 Welcome Page for Omni Hotels Satisfaction Survey.

Contrast the example in Figure 6.6 with the next example in Figure 6.7. Here the survey is about a specific event, and there is no expectation of an ongoing interaction with the survey organization. There are no special technical requirements, and the welcome page is designed to get the respondent quickly to the short one-time survey.

The next example comes from one of our own surveys (Singer, Couper, Conrad, and Groves, in press), conducted in collaboration with Market Strategies, Inc. (see Figure 6.8). In similar fashion to the Lightspeed and Omni Hotels examples, topic and length are mentioned, as is the voluntary nature of the survey. A link to the privacy policy is provided, and, in accordance with university regulations, the IRB statement and contact information is provided. Both an e-mail address and telephone number are provided in case the respondent needs more information about the survey. No mention is made of any incentives, as these are delivered separately from the panel vendor who provided the sample.

Study on Survey Participation

Welcome to the University of Michigan Study on Survey Participation

We appreciate your cooperation. This study will provide valuable information to researchers at the University of Michigan. This survey will take about 10 minutes.

Your participation is voluntary and you may skip any questions you prefer not to answer. All of your responses will be kept completely confidential. There are no risks to taking part. We hope you enjoy it.

If you have any questions or experience difficulty with the survey you may contact us via e-mail at participation@msisurvey.com or call toll free 1-866-674-3375.

Should you have questions regarding your rights as a participant in research, please contact:

Institutional Review Board – Behavioral Sciences
540 East Liberty Street, Suite 202
Ann Arbor, MI 48104-2210
734-936-0933
e-mail: irbhsbs@umich.edu

As you move through the survey, please use only the Next or Back buttons at the bottom of the screen. Do not use the Back or Forward buttons on your browser. Should your survey session be interrupted for any reason simply wait at least five minutes and then repeat the steps for accessing the survey. You will be returned to the point in the survey where you left off.

Click here to view our Privacy Policy.

Click the "Next" button to begin the survey.

Next

Email: participation@msisurvey.com | Phone: 1-866-674-3375 | FAQ

Figure 6.8 **Welcome Page for University of Michigan Study on Survey Participation.**

The final example (in Figure 6.9) comes from a federally funded establishment survey in the United States. Given the sensitivity of the topic, a brief introduction to the survey is given on the welcome page, but additional information on the survey is available through tabs at the top of the page. The survey has its own branding and home page, in addition to that of the sponsoring agency and data collection organization. The user name and login is required to enter the survey – given that several persons within the responding organization may be required to provide information, an automatic authentication process is probably not appropriate for a survey of this type.

As shown in these examples, at a minimum the welcome page should contain the following elements:

• Branding or identifying information, to confirm that the respondent is at the right place.
• A brief statement of what the survey is about, and what is required of the respondent.
• An estimate of the time to complete the survey.
• Mention of any special requirements for completing the survey.
• Links to additional information on privacy, confidentiality, and so on.

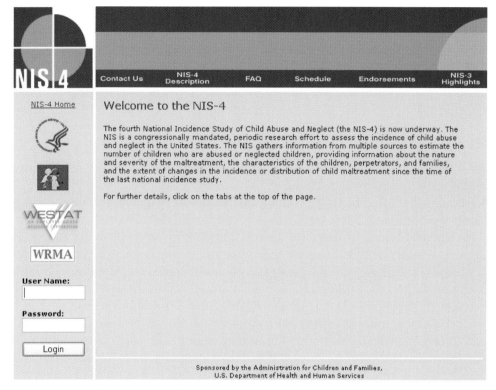

Figure 6.9 **Welcome Page for National Incidence Study of Child Abuse and Neglect.**

- If manual authentication is used, clear instructions on how to log in.
- A clearly identified action to start the survey.

The goal of the welcome page should be to get respondents to the task as fast as they would want, but permit them to access auxiliary information if they so desire and when they want to do so. In other words, don't force them to proceed through a series of required pages, because the likelihood that they will read them is low. A welcome page should be just that – welcoming.

6.5. Follow-Up

If the respondent has successfully passed through all the steps outlined earlier, they are at the first question of the survey. Whether they stick with the task until the very last question and the "Thank you" and logout screen is a matter of design – the topics of the preceding chapters in this book. Two last topics in this sequence remain – that of following up with respondents who abandoned the survey before they reached the end, and that of following up with those who failed to start the survey. I'll discuss these two related issues in turn.

6.5.1. Suspending and Resuming

Breakoffs – also called incompletes, partials, or abandonments – are undesirable in that incomplete data are obtained. Good survey design can help reduce their occurrence in the first place. The importance of following up breakoffs may depend on the type of survey being conducted.

For surveys among online access panels, there may be less need to follow up those who break off. Incentives are usually contingent upon completion. The pool of potential respondents may be seen as sufficiently large that the initial invitation is sent to a larger group to account for both potential nonrespondents and breakoffs. For Web surveys conducted on probability samples, the number of sample units is generally finite, and concerns about the inferential threats from nonresponse and breakoffs usually leads to efforts to minimize such loss. In such cases, additional steps can be taken to bring the partial respondents or breakoffs back into the fold. In establishment surveys, having the ability to suspend and resume the survey at a later time or by another respondent in the organization may be a critical element of successful survey design and implementation. Finally, scrolling surveys present different challenges for those wishing to suspend the survey and resume at a later time. In paging surveys, the data are saved up to the point of breakoff, but in scrolling surveys, a special function is needed to save the data entered up to that point. If breakoffs are likely to occur, and if respondents should be able to resume where they left off, a paging design is preferred.

Breakoffs can occur for a variety of different reasons, some of which are as follows:

- The respondent is tired, bored, or annoyed with the survey and does not want to continue.
- The respondent might be called away by another task or wants to take a break.
- The respondent may decide to link to some other site to check some information and return to the survey.

- The respondent may inadvertently press the browser back button when not allowed, which may generate a suspension (see Section 5.5.2.1).
- The survey may time out after a period of inactivity for security reasons.
- The Internet connection may go down.

The first reason – a deliberate breakoff on the part of the respondent – is unlikely to yield great returns with follow-up efforts. But for many of the other reasons, the respondent may well want to complete the survey, and the design should make it easy for them to do so. Paper surveys are more easily set aside for completion in later sittings. In Web surveys, special efforts are needed to permit respondents to suspend and resume if necessary, and to encourage them to complete the survey if they do break off before the end.

How often do such interrupted sessions occur? In one of our Web experiments, among 3,195 persons who started the survey, 534 broke off. Of these, 94 returned, with 56 of them completing the survey and the remaining 38 breaking off a second time. These 56 suspend-and-resume cases account for 2.1% of all completes. The likelihood of breaking off and resuming may well depend on the length of the survey. In a three-month follow-up survey to an online health intervention with an average length of thirteen minutes, 95.6% of respondents completed the survey in a single session. The twelve-month follow-up survey averaged 30 minutes in length, and 83.2% of respondents completed it in a single session.

Given that a nontrivial number of respondents suspend and resume completion of a Web survey, such behavior should be accommodated. There are three elements to the design of this process:

1. Allowing respondents to breakoff without encouraging them to do so.
2. Giving respondents easy access to the point of breakoff to resume the survey.
3. Sending respondents reminders to complete the survey if they fail to do so within a specified time frame.

Few studies have addressed these issues and few researchers on Web survey design even mention the problem of recovery from a breakoff.

In an unpublished experiment as part of one of our studies (Crawford, Couper, and Lamias, 2001), we randomly assigned sample persons to versions of the instrument with and without a continue button (see Figure 6.10). The design of the continue button and its placement had the unintended consequence of encouraging respondents to click it, with the effect of slightly (but not significantly) decreasing

Question #1				3% of Survey Completed	

Please evaluate to what extent you believe the University of Michigan has done a good job in each of the following areas:

The overall job the University of Michigan is doing with regard to affirmative action admission policies can be best described…	very bad job	bad job	neither bad nor good job	good job	very good job
for Asian Americans, as a	1 ○	2 ○	3 ○	4 ○	5 ○
for Black or African Americans, as a	1 ○	2 ○	3 ○	4 ○	5 ○
for Hispanic, Mexican, Puerto Rican, or Spanish speaking Americans, as a	1 ○	2 ○	3 ○	4 ○	5 ○
for Native Americans, a	1 ○	2 ○	3 ○	4 ○	5 ○
for White or Euro Americans, as a	1 ○	2 ○	3 ○	4 ○	5 ○

Next Question | Continue Later

Figure 6.10 **Use of "Continue Later" Button.**

the percentage of those completing the survey, among those who started it (from 85.6% to 82.5%).

The idea should be to permit respondents to return to a suspended survey, but not encourage them to suspend in the first place. Figure 6.11 shows an example of a survey that makes it hard for people to complete the survey in more than one sitting. The approach in Figure 6.11 assumes that the decision to leave the survey is a deliberate one. The effort required to save the URL for later completion is likely to deter many respondents from doing so. Simply having the respondent use the initial URL provided in the invitation should be sufficient. There should be no need for an explicit "suspend" or "continue later" button – closing the browser should have the same effect.

Figure 6.12 shows an example from the Harris Poll Online. The top pane shows the "Resume later" button, and the bottom pane the page displayed when this is pressed. In contrast to our early study (shown in Figure 6.10), this makes the option available without encouraging its use. Returning to the survey is also made easy.

If security concerns warrant it (see Section 6.7.1), an additional password could be required to permit reentry to a partially completed survey. This is the approach adopted by Statistics Canada for the 2006 Census. In this case, an explicit "Stop and Finish Later" button took respondents to the screen shown in Figure 6.13. In addition to entering the fifteen-digit Internet access code required to begin completing an empty questionnaire, an additional password is needed to return to a survey containing information. However, for most paging surveys, reusing the same URL and authentication process as was used to start the survey should be sufficient.

If you want to leave the survey and continue later, please copy and save this url and use it to reenter:

http://survey7.surveys-are-fun.com/wix/p21137377.aspx?r=284137&s=THTMTVJT&l=9

Figure 6.11 **Provision of URL for Reentry to a Survey.**

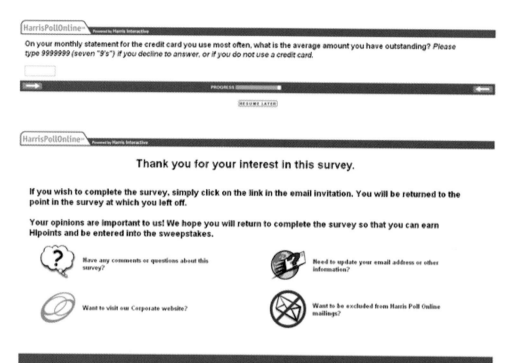

Figure 6.12 "Resume Later" Button and Message from Harris Interactive.

For scrolling surveys, given that closing the browser will mean that all information entered to that point is lost, a special button for explicitly saving the answers is needed. When a respondent returns to the survey, the entire page – along with the information already entered – needs to be regenerated by the system. In a paging survey, taking respondents directly to the last unanswered question is an easy process, well within the capability of most Web survey software systems.

The final issue on suspensions is whether reminders to those sample persons are efficacious. Although I know of no research on this issue, reminders are likely to yield a positive return.

6.5.2. Reminders

While there is no research on the effectiveness of reminders for those who started but did not complete the survey, several studies have addressed the issue of reminders for nonrespondents, or those who did not start the survey. There seems

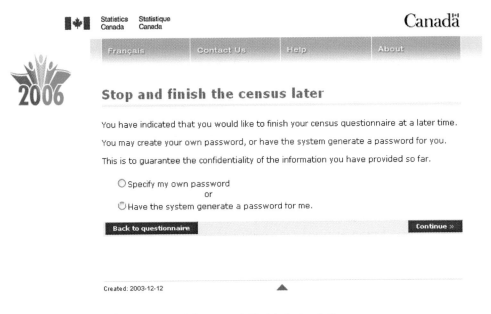

Figure 6.13 **Canadian Census "Stop and Finish Later" Page.**

to be consensus that sending e-mail reminders increases response rates to Web surveys, contributing up to one-third of the sample size (Vehovar, Batagelj, Lozar Manfreda, and Zaletel, 2002). To give one example, Tuten (2005) reported an 18.2% initial response rate, and a 26.7% final response rate, following e-mail reminders sent after 8 days. Similar results are reported by Trouteaud (2004) and by Harmon, Westin, and Levin (2005).

The key question here is not so much whether to send reminders, but when to do so. Vehovar et al. (2002) note that, in comparison to traditional mail surveys, the time interval between follow-up strategies should be shortened. Crawford, Couper, and Lamias (2001) conducted a study on the timing of reminders, with half of the sample who had not yet responded getting a reminder after two days, and the other half after five days. The two-day reminder group had a significantly ($p < .05$) higher response rate (26.2%) than the five-day reminder (21.7%). However, this study was conducted on a student sample, which may have different expectations and tolerances for e-mail reminders than other populations. Deutskens, de Ruyter, Wetzels, and Oosterveld (2004) experimented with an early (one-week) versus late (two-week) reminder in a market research survey of a general population. The early reminder achieved a slightly (but not significantly) higher response rate (21.2%

versus 19.5%). The timing of reminders may well depend on the population being studied. For example, if people are expected to complete the survey from home, waiting until after a weekend may make sense. The timing of reminders in mail surveys is well-studied, and Dillman (2000, p. 179) recommends the first reminder be mailed seven days after the questionnaire mailing. Given the near instantaneous delivery of e-mail, one need not wait that long to send e-mail reminders.

A second question is how many reminders should be sent. While there is little experimental work focused on this issue, our experience in a variety of Web surveys as part of online interventions (see, e.g., Couper, Peytchev, Strecher, Rothert, and Anderson, 2007) suggests that there are diminishing returns on additional e-mail messages beyond the first or second reminder. While it is certainly possible to continue to get completed surveys with additional reminders, the low returns and annoyance factor mitigate against continued e-mail reminders. Instead of continuing to send e-mail messages to nonresponding sampling units, one should consider switching to a different approach (see Section 6.5.3).

Finally, while I know of no research on this issue, I would assert that reminders – whether to those who have not reacted to the invitation at all, or to those who started but did not complete the survey – should be targeted. In other words, generic messages to the entire sample, regardless of their completion status, are likely to be less effective and an annoyance to those who have already complied. This assumes a survey design in which sample persons are identifiable. In anonymous surveys, where it is not known who has responded and who has not, such targeted reminders are not possible. Most Web survey software can easily handle targeted reminders.

6.5.3. Switching Modes for Follow-Up

E-mail messages are not the only form of follow-up. After a certain point, continuing to send e-mail reminders is ineffective and may even be counterproductive. Just because it is cheap to send repeated e-mail reminders doesn't mean it is a good idea to do so. One study I was involved in sent up to twenty-one reminders. If the goal is to maximize response rates and minimize the possibility of nonresponse error, one should consider switching to an alternative mode of data collection. Several studies have explored this issue, demonstrating the benefits of a mode switch.

Kaplowitz, Hadlock, and Levine (2004) tested a postcard follow-up to an e-mail survey of college students, along with a postcard prenotice (see Section 6.1). The reminder was sent ten days after the initial e-mail invitation, and was targeted

342 • Designing Effective Web Surveys

only to those who had not yet responded. When there was no postcard prenotice, the postcard reminder increased response rates from 20.7% to 25.4%. However, when a postcard prenotice was used, those who were sent the postcard reminder achieved a lower response rate (28.6%) than those who were not sent a reminder postcard (29.7%), although this difference is not significant. Their results suggest that the positive effect of the reminder postcard was limited to those who were not sent a prenotice postcard.

Tarnai and Allen (2002) sent a letter to 12,562 students, inviting them to complete a Web survey. A total of 1,228 responded to the Web survey, for a response rate of 9.8%. They followed this with a mail questionnaire to the nonrespondents. Of these, 927 returned the questionnaire, and 554 completed the survey on the Web, increasing the response rate to 21.6%.

As part of an online weight management intervention, we followed up the nonrespondents to the twelve-month online survey, randomly assigning cases to mail or telephone follow-up (see Couper et al., 2007). The telephone follow-up survey achieved a 58.6% response rate, while the mail survey achieved a 55.0% rate. In addition, the telephone follow-up survey cost about $34 per sampled case ($54 per completed survey), compared to $15 per sampled case and $28 per complete for the mail survey, which included a $5 prepaid incentive. The mail survey response distributions were also found to be closer to the Web survey responses, especially for questions subject to social desirability bias, like weight and satisfaction with the program. In a subsequent mail-only follow-up to another online weight management intervention, a response rate of 63.2% was obtained from a sample of the Web survey nonrespondents.

These results suggest that switching modes can be quite effective in increasing response rates to Web survey (see also Ekman, Dickman, Klint, Weiderpass, and Litton, 2006; Schonlau, Asch, and Du, 2003). Of course, doing so requires that both an e-mail and regular mail address (or telephone number) are available, which limits this approach to certain sample frames. In addition, mail or telephone follow-up may add considerably to the costs of data collection over a Web-only approach. Nonetheless, these approaches are useful when circumstances warrant. I return to this issue in Section 6.7.4.

6.5.5. Summary on Follow-Up

This is a relatively little-studied area in Web surveys, in part possibly because of the dominance of nonprobability surveys, where nonresponse is more an issue of operational efficiency than of inferential limitations. While there remain several unanswered questions with respect of follow-up strategies for Web surveys, it seems that enough is known to make the following generalizations:

1. E-mail follow-up to nonrespondents is effective; it is also cheap and should be easy to do.
2. Such reminders should be targeted only to those who have not yet responded (or not completed the survey).
3. One, or at most two, e-mail reminders are likely sufficient; additional reminders yield diminishing returns and may increase respondent annoyance.
4. The optimal timing of reminder messages is not fully known, but the research suggests that they should be sent sooner than reminders in mail surveys, that is, three to four days rather than seven to ten days.
5. Switching modes (especially to mail) is an effective way of increasing the number of survey completes.

Much of the work on reducing nonresponse in Web surveys has focused on the front end – the invitation, incentive, and so on. The discussion in this section suggests that much can be gained by focusing also on follow-up strategies.

6.6. Incentives

A discussion of incentives doesn't fit well in the sequence of events described previously, as the mention of incentives – and indeed their payment – can occur at various points in the sequence, from the prenotification to following completion of the survey. Hence, I deal with incentives separately here.

The general survey literature on incentives is well established (see, e.g., Church, 1993; Edwards, Cooper, Roberts, and Frost, 2005; Singer, 2002). A large number of studies of incentive use in various modes of data collection lead to the following general conclusions:

- Some form of incentive is better than no incentive.
- Prepaid incentives are better than promised (conditional) incentives.
- Cash is better than an in-kind incentive.
- Giving everyone a small incentive is better than giving everyone a chance at winning a larger amount (lottery or sweepstakes).

The questions for Web surveys are (1) do these findings translate to the online world and (2) how should incentive schemes best be implemented, given the electronic medium? I address these two questions together.

A growing body of research on incentives in Web surveys exists, leading to a meta-analysis (Göritz, 2006). It is not my intention to review all this work here; rather I will highlight a few key findings and focus on the design challenges. The way incentives are used will differ depending on the sample selection process. For example, members of opt-in panels may have very different views on, and responses to, incentives than those invited to one-time surveys from a list or those responding to intercept-based approaches. Whether one can deliver incentives, how one can do so, and what type of incentive can be offered, depends in large part on the nature of the sample and the richness of the sampling frame. We need to keep this in mind when thinking about how to use incentives effectively to encourage participation.

Despite the finding in the general survey literature that lotteries (often called prize draws or sweepstakes for legal reasons) are less effective than other forms of incentive, their use is widespread in Web surveys, especially in the opt-in panel world. This is largely driven by the two considerations. First, the cost of delivering a small incentive to each (potential) respondent in a fully electronic survey setting may exceed that of the incentive payment itself. Second, with the relatively low response rates common in many Web surveys – especially those among opt-in panel members, where some form of compensation is common – offering everyone a prepaid incentive to yield a response rate in the single digits is hardly a good use of resources.

Overall, Göritz's (2006) meta-analysis suggests that material incentives have a positive effect on response rates in Web surveys, with a predicted odds ratio of 1.19 (with a 95% confidence interval of 1.13 to 1.25). In other words, material incentives increase the odds of responding by 19% over the odds without incentives. However, none of the study characteristics she explored (including list-based sample versus other; lottery versus no lottery; prepaid versus promised, and other features of the survey) correlated significantly with the incentive effect. This may be explained by the relatively small number of studies manipulating each of these features.

Let's look at some specific studies on incentives before summarizing the research. Bosnjak and Tuten (2002) tested four incentive types in a survey of members of a local professional sales association. The sample was randomly assigned to a $2 prepaid incentive (via PayPal), a $2 promised incentive (also via PayPal), entry into a prize draw upon completion (one $50 prize and four $25 prizes, for a sample of roughly 330), or a no-incentive control group. The prize draw performed best, with 36% accessing the survey welcome page, and 23% completing the survey. The prepaid (26% access and 14% complete) and promised (27% accessed and 16% complete) incentive groups did no better than the group receiving no incentive (27% accessed and 13% complete). One post hoc explanation is that the $2 delivered via PayPal has less value than $2 cash, as it requires an online purchase and additional money in the account to make it useful.

This is supported by Birnholtz, Horn, Finholt, and Bae's (2004) study. They conducted an experiment among earthquake engineering faculty and students, with 145 subjects assigned to each of three incentive groups: a mail invitation containing $5 cash, a mail invitation containing a $5 Amazon.com gift certificate, and an e-mail invitation with a $5 Amazon.com e-certificate. While all incentive conditions were prepaid and of equal face value, the cash incentive significantly outperformed the paper certificate incentive and the electronic certificate, with response rates of 57%, 40%, and 32%, respectively.

These two studies demonstrate the dilemma of incentive delivery in an electronic world. Given the temptation to use lottery incentives, we'll look at a few more studies. Porter and Whitcomb (2003) embedded an incentive experiment in a survey of prospective college students who had sought information. There were four lottery conditions, with prize draws for Amazon.com gift certificates valued at $50, $100, $150, and $200, and a no-incentive control group. They found no overall effect of incentive, with the four incentive groups averaging a 15.2% response rate, compared to 13.9% for the control group. For some populations at least, lotteries may have little effect.

Göritz (2004) tested thirteen different incentive conditions in a survey among members of a commercial opt-in panel. This included eight different money lotteries with prize draws ranging from 100 DM (about €50 in 2000) to 700 DM, four different bonus point options, ranging from three to eight bonus points guaranteed upon completion (1 BP was valued at about .5 DM), and finally a gift lottery prize draw (for prizes ranging from watches to key-ring flashlights). The value of the money offered in the lottery had no significant effect on the response rate, with rates ranging from 75.9% for the 2×50 DM lottery to 79.6% for the 10×50 DM lottery. The number of bonus points similarly had no linear effect on response rates, but overall the bonus points yielded a significantly higher response rate (82.4% on average) than the money lottery (78.0% on average), with the gift lottery at 78.6%. The cost per complete of the bonus point options was higher (2.63 DM on average) than for the cash lotteries (0.96 DM on average). While these differences are modest, they suggest that a guaranteed payment of bonus points may be preferable to the chance of winning a larger amount, a finding consistent with the general literature on incentives (see also van Heesen, 2005).

Exploring the lottery idea further, Tuten, Galesic, and Bosnjak (2004) compared an immediately versus delayed notification of prize draw results in a banner-advertised Web survey in Croatia. The group notified immediately following the survey if they had won or not produced a 76.6% response rate compared to 70.6% for the delayed group and 62.3% for the control group receiving no incentive. Similar results were found for a European access panel (Bosnjak and Wenzel, 2005).

Given this quick review of some of the many studies on incentives, it seems fair to conclude that their effect may be different for one-time Web surveys based on list samples and for repeated surveys of members of opt-in panels. The reaction to the request, the expectation of the potential respondent, the long-term relationship with the survey organization, and the expected response rates, all differ. I would argue that prepaid monetary incentives are likely to be more effective for list-based samples where the goal is to obtain a high response rate. If these can be delivered in cash form by mail, they have the added potential advantage of a mailed-based prenotification (see Section 6.1). For opt-in panels, some form of promised payment seems best, with some suggestion that small guaranteed payments outperform prize draws in terms of response rates, although the costs may be higher. However, this presumes a long-term relationship with the panel member in which they can accumulate a meaningful number of points or cash over an extended period of time. Göritz (2005) also offers useful advice on the use of incentives in Web surveys.

While incentives have a positive effect on response rates and on data quality, as research by Göritz (2004) and others suggest, I am concerned about the over-reliance on monetary rewards for participation, especially in the case of opt-in panels. My fear is that we are creating a group of professional respondents, who mindlessly click through the surveys for the anticipated reward. Several consolidator sites (e.g., http://money4surveys.com) have already sprung up, encouraging respondents to sign up to many different online panels. Some of these even charge users for the privilege of signing up for Web surveys (e.g., http://cash4surveys.com; http://surveyscout.com), implying large financial rewards for doing so. One even offers to include "special software that will help you fill out your surveys up to 3 times faster – so you can make more money in less time." This has led some to question the quality of data from opt-in panels, and others to develop methods to detect such professional respondents and remove them from analysis

The Africa-American Voice Survey Panel!!!

E-Poll - Take Daily Survey Polls For Rewards!!!

Take Surveys For A Chance To Win A Trip to Hawaii!!!

Take Surveys And Get Up To A $1,000 Hotel Gift Card!!!

Give Your Opinion For A Chance To Win A Flat Screen Television!!!

Give Your Opinion For A Chance To Win A Lexus Plus A Year's Supply Of Gas!!!

Join This Interactive Survey Panel For A Chance To Win A $500.00 Shopping Spree!!!

Home Business Match-Up Service - Take The Free Business Interest Survey To Find The Perfect Business!!!

Join The Nielson/NetRatings Panel And Help Shape The Future Of The Internet Plus Win Some Cool Prizes!!!

Figure 6.14 **Links to Reward-Based Online Surveys.**

(e.g., Downes-Le Guin, Mechling, and Baker, 2006). If respondents are doing Web surveys solely for the extrinsic rewards offered, one wonders about the veracity of their answers. Figure 6.14 shows an example of the types of surveys available through one of these consolidator sites.

6.7. Other Topics

In this final section, I offer a few observations about a set of topics that each deserve fuller coverage in their own right. However, these are not the major focus of this book, and this section is not meant to be exhaustive. There are still other topics of great interest to those interested in designing or implementing Web surveys that I do not cover at all. For example, the question of what software should be used for Web surveys is one that I am asked frequently. A discussion of this issue is likely to date very quickly, and is beyond the scope of this book. Similarly, I have not addressed the very important issue of pretesting Web surveys, nor have I discussed the *process* of developing an instrument. I also leave a fuller discussion of accessibility and designing for respondents with disabilities or limitations to others. And I could go on. For further information on these topics, and many more, I direct the reader to http://websm.org/. This valuable site is a comprehensive source of information on Web survey design and implementation. The interested reader can find much more there. This section is intended as a light touch of some of these additional topics.

6.7.1. Security and Confidentiality Issues

This is certainly not my area of expertise and I will leave a detailed discussion of security issues to the experts. However, I do want to make a few observations, relevant to survey design, and particularly to the tradeoff between maximizing security to ensure confidentiality versus maximizing the ease of completion of the survey.

The biggest threat to security in Web surveys is not during the transmission of the data over the Internet, but rather through unauthorized access to the database on the survey organization's server. Yet much of the focus of the discussion about security is on the former rather than the latter. In fact, the transmission of paper questionnaires via the mail may be more risky because both the questions and the answers – and sometimes identifying information such as a name or address – are transmitted together "in the clear." In Web surveys, each submitted page only need contain the encoded answers to the questions, along with an ID number that contains no identifying information. Objections to Web surveys on security grounds are misplaced.

However, several things can de done to minimize the risk of any harm from an intrusion during data transmission and storage. First, be careful about including fields with an identifiable format, such as a social security number, telephone number, e-mail address, and so on. Even without the accompanying metadata (description of the question or data field), such data are recognizable. Consider if it is really necessary to collect this kind of information. If so, using some form of encryption is advisable. For most surveys, using Secure Sockets Layer (SSL) or, more currently, Transport Layer Security (TLS), for basic encryption should be sufficient. The same level of security as used for e-commerce should be more than enough for most survey applications. The Census Bureau and other federal agencies in the United States have required 128-bit encryption for a number of years.

Another simple way to reduce the risk from a security breach is to avoid transmitting meaningful variable names along with the data. Consider the following two alternatives:

- Marijuana use? Yes
- Q27: 1

The former may reveal sensitive information to an intruder, while the latter is meaningless without the accompanying metadata. The question text and variable labels do not need to be transmitted to and from each respondent.

Another potential security risk can come from respondents (or others) inadvertently entering someone else's ID. For this reason, both an ID and a password are recommended, especially for surveys eliciting sensitive information. The ID should be sufficiently long that consecutive numbers are not used. For example, the online version of the 2000 U.S. Decennial Census required entry of a fourteen-digit ID, with several of these likely being check digits. This is more than sufficient to prevent accidental entry of another active ID. Similarly, the 2006 Canadian census required entry of a fifteen-digit ID to access the online version. The Canadian census went one step further to prevent unauthorized access to census responses. If one wished to suspend and resume completion of the online form, one was required to create a unique password to regain access to the partially completed form (see Figure 6.13). In other words, an additional level of authentication was required to see information already entered on a form. This strikes me as a reasonable and measured approach to security, given the context.

On the other hand, if it is too difficult for respondents to remember or enter their authentication codes, they may be deterred from completing the survey. For example, Harrell, Rosen, Gomes, Chute, and Yu (2006) found that Web responses to the Current Employment Statistics (CES) program were declining, and attributed this in part to the procedures required for Web reporting. Respondents were provided with a temporary account number and password and were required to set up either a permanent account number and password or a digital certificate. They found that 20% of respondents failed to create an account, and many who did would forget the information. They created an alternative data entry system, Web-Lite, which permitted access to the site using the CES report number printed on the form. They added a Completely Automated Public Turing Test to Tell Computers and Humans Apart (CAPTCHA; see http://www.captcha.net/; von Ahn, Blum, and Langford, 2004) to prevent automated attempts to access the site. However, given the reduced security required for access, the Bureau's security rules required that access to contact information and previously submitted data be eliminated. Harrell and colleagues (2006) report a twelve-percentage-point improvement in response rate from the old to the new Web reporting system. This illustrates the trade-off between security and ease of use.

Another source of security concern may be those using public terminals (e.g., at a library or Internet café) to complete Web surveys. Here it is important to clear cache (the temporary memory used to store Web pages to reduce bandwidth usage and server load) at the end of a session, so subsequent users cannot access these pages. Similarly, if cookies are used to control the process of survey completion, use transient rather than persistent cookies. This means that the cookies are not retained after the browser is closed. These steps help ensure that someone else cannot revisit the pages submitted by the respondent.

The approach to security should be measured. Consider the trade-off from the respondent's perspective. Consider the risks and benefits relative to the kinds of information being collected, and from whom. If the information is not particularly sensitive, and the consequences of any disclosure are minimal, this should be reflected in the degree of security and confidentiality implemented. Provide an appropriate level of security, enough to reassure respondents but not frighten them away from doing the survey. Strike a balance between making it easy for respondents to get to the survey, and providing appropriate levels of security to reassure respondents that one takes issues of confidentiality seriously.

6.7.2. Paradata

I've alluded to paradata at various points throughout the book. In this section, I collect these scattered thoughts together. I coined the term "paradata" in 1998 to refer to process data that are often generated as a byproduct of the computerized data collection process (see Couper and Lyberg, 2005). Web surveys provide a variety of paradata that can provide us with insights into the effect of different designs on users and their responses.

For example, browser characteristics or user metrics are routinely captured by many Web sites, to gather information on visitors. These include such information as browser type and version, operating system, IP address and domain, screen and browser dimensions, whether the browser has JavaScript, Java, Flash, or other active scripting enabled, and so on. These can be captured at the point of login to a Web survey, either to enhance the respondents' experience or to understand more about our respondents and how they interact with the survey instruments. For example, in one of our studies we detected whether respondents had Java enabled. Those who did were assigned to one of the visual analog scale versions we were testing, while those who did not were assigned to a non-Java version of the questions (Couper et al., 2006). We also track screen and browser dimensions over time and across samples to guide the optimal layout of Web survey pages (see Baker and Couper, 2007). We examine whether breakoffs occur differentially across various characteristics of the respondents' systems to provide an indirect indicator whether the survey is working well across all platforms.

In addition to session-level paradata, a variety of information can be collected on a page-by-page basis, providing rich detail on the process of survey completion. A distinction can be made between server-side paradata and client-side paradata (see Heerwegh, 2003). Server-side paradata capture information about each page submitted, and require no active scripting. All information transmitted to the server can be used. Of particular interest here is the time taken to complete and transmit the page to the server. Client-side paradata can also be used to record events that occur within a page. This can include the time taken from the loading of the page to the first click, the order of clicks, activation of hyperlinks, scrolling, and the like.

Client-side paradata require placing JavaScript code in the page to record the information as the respondent interacts with the Web page and transmit the information to the server along with the survey responses when the respondent submits the page. If the respondent does not have JavaScript enabled, such paradata will not be captured, although the respondent will still be able to complete the survey. Client-side paradata have been used to examine a variety of response behaviors, include response latencies, change of answers, access of supplementary material, use of slider bars, and so on (see Couper et al., 2004, 2006; Conrad et al., 2006; Haraldsen, Kleven, and Stålnacke, 2006; Heerwegh, 2003). We use both server-side and client-side paradata routinely in our experimental studies on Web survey design, and find the data to be a valuable adjunct to the experimental outcomes. Heerwegh's JavaScript code for capturing client-side paradata is available at http://perswww.kuleuven.be/~u0034437/public/csp.htm.

Yan and Tourangeau (2008) examined both client-side and server-side response times. They found that the server-side times are on average three to four seconds longer than the client-side times, which exclude download time and time to click on the "next" button after selecting a response. However, the correlations between the two times ranged from 0.91 to 0.99 across the sixteen items they examined, with an average correlation of 0.96. This suggests that the server-side response times may be sufficient for most purposes.

My point is that these data are cheap and easy to collect, and have little or no impact on the response process. Analyzing the paradata that are collected provides us with valuable insights into what the respondent may be doing, which allows us to focus our (more expensive) research attention on why they are doing so and what can be done about it.

6.7.3. Pretesting

Again, a quick word or two about pretesting. Given the speed with which Web surveys can be developed and deployed, it seems that pretesting the instrument is given short shrift. Of course, if the survey will be completed in three days, it doesn't make sense to devote three months to pretesting. Similarly, if the survey will cost less than $20,000, spending more than that on pretesting makes little sense. However, I have seen many Web surveys where a modicum of testing would have revealed some of the more egregious errors that make the data suspect and the survey not worth the effort. Striking a balance is important.

Many things can be done to minimize the deployment of poorly designed Web surveys. Careful pretesting is one of them. But, given that instrument design can largely be separated from content – for example, using CSS or design templates – the testing of the design can be amortized over many different Web surveys, leaving the focus of testing on individual surveys to issues of question content. This is where a set of design standards can be most helpful. Such standards can reflect the research evidence on alternative design, such as presented in this book. But they also reflect the organization's identity and the type of surveys conducted. Furthermore, they can and should be adapted and updated as experience grows and new information is obtained. Standards or guidelines require ongoing maintenance. Examples of such standards to guide design can be found in Crawford, McCabe, and Pope (2003) and Baker, Crawford, and Swinehart (2004). I'm not advocating that survey organizations adopt these standards whole cloth. I'm suggesting that each survey organization should develop its own set of standards or guidelines for Web survey design, based on what is known about what works and what does not, but adapted to each organization's "look and feel" for purposes of branding, and reflecting the types of surveys the organization conducts.

Standards help to reduce the likelihood of poor design. Other forms of testing have benefits beyond a single survey implementation, and should be conducted on an ongoing basis by those who do many Web surveys. These include technical testing and user testing. Technical testing involves testing the design template and common functions under a variety of real-world conditions. Instruments are often developed under ideal conditions – the programmer has a large monitor, fast processor, high-speed Internet connection, the latest browser, and all the plugins. This is not the case for all users. A design that works under optimal conditions may not work as well for a user accessing the survey over a dial-up connection, using an older version of Netscape Navigator, and a 640 × 480 monitor. Monitoring of these kinds of statistics, using paradata, can help one decide what range of users to accommodate. But technical testing to ensure the instrument works under a variety of settings is a critical part of the ongoing development process.

User testing is also something that can be an ongoing process. Valuable insights can be gained from watching real users interact with the survey instrument. One of the drawbacks of the distributed nature of Web surveys is that we generally do not see how respondents react to the survey. We gain indirect insight into the process from examining the paradata or asking some debriefing questions at the end of the survey. But there is no substitute for actually watching respondents struggle through a design that we thought was perfect. A general discussion of usability testing for surveys can be found in Hansen and Couper (2004), and examples of testing of Web survey instruments can be found in Bates and Nichols (1998), Murphy and Ciochetto (2006), and Fox, Mockovak, Fisher, and Rho (2003). For testing of look-and-feel issues (as opposed to content), many survey organizations have developed a generic instrument that contains a variety of different question types. This allows testing of design issues to be separated from the content of a particular survey.

This brief discussion has focused more on general testing, as opposed to survey-specific testing. In addition to the testing already discussed, individual instruments need to be tested both for technical integrity and for content. For a broad review of questionnaire testing issues, see Presser et al. (2004). Baker, Crawford, and Swinehart (2004), in that volume, provide a good review of the various steps and procedures used in testing Web questionnaires.

6.7.4. Web Surveys in a Mixed-Mode Environment

The main focus of this book is on standalone Web surveys, where the strengths of the medium can be fully exploited to maximize data quality. Developing Web surveys for use in a mixed-mode environment presents different design challenges. By "mixed-mode," I'm referring to surveys completed using more than one mode, ignoring different methods of recruitment and reminder. In this section, I offer a few brief observations about the implications of mixed-mode approaches for Web survey design.

The main reasons for mixing modes are reductions in costs, noncoverage and nonresponse. Costs are reduced by increasing the proportion of respondents using the Web than the more costly alternatives such as mail or telephone. For example, in the 2006 Canadian Census, nearly one in five households (18.5%) completed their Census forms on the Web, potentially saving a lot of money in terms of mailing, scanning, and keying operations related to paper forms (see www.statcan.ca/english/census06/reference/info/). In terms of noncoverage, Web data collection is often supplemented with another mode (typically mail) for those without Internet access or who cannot be reached by e-mail. Similarly, alternative modes (again mostly mail and telephone) are used to follow up nonrespondents to a Web survey, with the goal of maximizing response rates. In establishment surveys, timeliness is also given as a reason for using the Web in a mixed-mode survey (e.g., Clayton and Werking, 1998). For a good review of the various types of mixed-mode designs and their benefits and drawbacks, see de Leeuw (2005). Dillman (2000) devotes a chapter to mixed-mode design and offers a number of suggestions for minimizing mode differences.

In general, the focus of mixed-mode survey designs has not been on measurement error. It is argued (or assumed) that the improvements in coverage or response, or the financial benefits of mixing modes, come with no corresponding loss of data quality, and that the data obtained from the different modes are at least comparable. However, increasingly research is focusing on potential differences in responses between Web and mail (e.g., McCabe et al., 2002; McCabe, Diez, Boyd, Nelson, and Weitzman, 2006) and between Web and telephone (e.g., Dillman and Christian, 2005; Dillman and Smyth, 2007), and on how to compensate for these differences. Martin et al. (2007) show some of the complexities inherent in designing for multiple survey modes.

Designing for a single mode – Web, in our case – means one can optimize the design for that mode, using all the tools and techniques available to enhance data quality. Designing for more than one mode inevitable involves compromise of some sort. Striving to eliminate any measurement differences between the modes may lead to lowest common denominator approaches and nonoptimal design. For example, because interactive features such as edit checks, skips, and fills cannot be implemented in paper surveys, some argue they should not be used in the Web version either. Similarly, I have heard some argue that because a paper survey cannot restrict a respondent to the selection of only one response (e.g., "yes or "no") as radio buttons can do on the Web, the Web version of the survey should use check boxes, permitting multiple responses (e.g., both "yes" and "no"). This strikes me as a suboptimal solution. Rather than aiming for the lowest common denominator, I would argue for maximizing the quality in each mode, using the strengths of the technology. This approach requires an understanding of how the design differences may affect the answers, so that appropriate adjustments can be made when combining the data from both modes. Comparable data are more important than identical data. For example, if missing data or the need for edits can be reduced in the Web mode using interactive features, why not use them?

Many design decisions need to be made when considering mixed-mode designs. For example, the choice of a scrolling or paging Web survey design may depend on the other mode being used. A scrolling design more closely resembles a mail questionnaire, in that respondents can answer questions in any order and see subsequent questions. Similar context effects are likely when the organization of items on a Web page is similar to that on the paper questionnaire. On the other hand, if Web is being combined with telephone, a paging design with a single question per screen most closely parallels the way survey items are presented and answered in telephone surveys. Thus, the choice of scrolling versus paging design may be influenced by mixed-mode considerations.

In terms of response order effects, primacy effects – in which earlier options are selected more often than later items – are common to both visual modes of survey administration (mail and Web). However, recency effects – in which the later options are endorsed more often – are more likely in telephone surveys. If so, response order effects are likely to produce larger differences between Web and telephone responses than between Web and mail. One design advantage available to both the Web and telephone survey designer (assuming CATI) is to randomize response options where appropriate, thereby distributing the order effects across the items. This is harder to do on paper.

Another challenge facing the mixed-mode designer is how to discourage non-substantive responses such as "don't know" (DK) or refusal. As I discussed in Chapter 1, Section 1.2), a paging Web instrument can be designed to be similar to the telephone mode, in terms of no initially offering of a DK option, but then giving that option to respondents after prompting. If explicit DK options are offered on paper, offering them on the Web version too will likely produce similar levels of nonsubstantive responses. Another option is to exclude such response options from the instrument but instruct respondents to leave the item blank if they do not wish to answer. Again, the design of the Web instrument may be dictated in part by the constraints of the other mode.

The complex routing, edit checking, and other features available in interactive or paging designs are similarly available to the telephone survey designer, but not the paper questionnaire designer. The use of these features will be influenced by comparability considerations in mixed-mode designs.

While there are many similarities between paper and Web questionnaires – for example, both are self-administered, both are visual – the two instruments can never be made identical. Some design elements such as layout, font, spacing, alignment, and the like (all things discussed in Chapter 4) can be made similar, but the dynamic and interactive tools unique to the Web cannot. For example, drop boxes have no functional equivalent in paper surveys, and there are no input constraints such as those discussed in Chapter 2.

Similarly, dynamic Web designs and CAI have much in common, and in fact, many survey software vendors have products that do both; other features of the modes make equivalence of measurement difficult. For example, interviewer effects such as social desirability are more of an issue in telephone surveys than on the Web, and the aural versus visual presentation of questions and answers is likely to make identical measurement a challenge. Dillman (2000, Chapter 6) and Tourangeau, Rips, and Rasinski (2000, Chapter 10) provide fuller discussions of how mode may affect responses.

I mentioned earlier that context effects are likely to be the same in the two modes when the layout of items on the Web is similar to that of the paper questionnaire. On the other hand, the design of paper questionnaires is often constrained to minimize the amount of paper used, and no such constraint exists on the Web. Striving for identical design in terms of layout and visual presentation of items is likely to be less than optimal for either mode. The question then is to understand which features matter in terms of response differences between modes, and to find ways to focus on minimizing those differences while still exploiting the design features available in each mode.

The broad goal for mixed-mode design involving Web surveys is to figure out which design elements matter and in what way. This information will then help guide the design, whether striving for optimal equivalence or exploiting the design features of each mode. These decisions will in part also be influenced by consideration of the primary mode. For example, if most respondents are expected to complete the survey online, with a few using mail or telephone, optimizing design for the Web may make most sense. Alternatively, if the dominant mode is likely to be paper (as in the Canadian Census example), the design choices may well be different, especially if it is likely that the respondents may have the paper questionnaire in front of them, or even already filled in, when they complete the Web version.

6.7.5. Web Design for Establishment Surveys

This book is focused primarily on personal surveys – those completed by individuals, reporting their own attitudes, opinions, behaviors, intentions, behaviors, and other attributes. Establishment surveys – those completed by one or more individuals, reporting on behalf of an organization, business, or other enterprise, and providing information about the establishment – present different design challenges for Web surveys. While many of the design elements discussed in this book apply to establishment surveys, a number of additional design considerations have not been addressed. To provide a thorough overview of these issues is beyond the scope of this work. Furthermore, it is fair to say that research on Web survey design for establishments lags behind that of surveys of individuals (for some exceptions, see Fox et al., 2003; Haraldsen, 2004).

For this reason, I offer a brief and incomplete list of some of the design issues facing such surveys (borrowing heavily from Burnside, 2000), in the hope that it will encourage further research on these issues:

- Respondents are often unlikely to "know" the answer but are expected to be able to have access to the information needed to produce an answer.
- Data are assembled over a period of time from different data sources and areas of the business.
- Surveys generally include a smaller number of questions, with a higher proportion of these being applicable to all respondents.
- Items are more likely to contain definitions.
- "Correct" responses are often more important than in surveys of individuals.
- Surveys often involve repeated measures from the same units, with relatively short gaps (weeks or months) between waves.
- Respondents need the ability to print completed questionnaires for record purposes (especially for mandatory surveys).

These and other characteristic features of establishment surveys present different design challenges for Web surveys. Some of the implications of these features relevant to the design issues discussed in this book are briefly mentioned next.

The way in which establishment surveys are completed – often in nonsequential order and by different people or at different times – means that the design should accommodate this approach. Many establishment surveys use scrolling designs that permit respondents to save incomplete surveys, or paging designs that permit nonstandard movement using tabs or other navigation devices. This in turn has implications for designing edit checks and missing data messages. For example, should they be triggered at the point they occur, or only when the respondent is ready to submit the instrument? How should they be designed to attract the respondent's attention at the appropriate time? Research by Mockovak (2005) points to some of the challenges of designing such edits, while some guidance is offered by Anderson, Murphy, Nichols, Sigman, and Willimack (2004). However they are implemented, edits are a common feature of establishment surveys. Such surveys often involve the collection of numeric data, whether counts or currency amounts. Running tallies are thus a common feature of such surveys, helping respondents prevent errors in data entry. Given the nonstandard movement, embedded edits, and the like, the use of JavaScript is probably more common in establishment surveys than in individual surveys.

Complex routing may be less of an issue for establishment surveys, which may reduce the complexities inherent in nonstandard movement. But the respondent may need to refer to definitions more frequently than in personal surveys, and the definitions may have greater potential effect on the responses provided. The design and placement of such definitions in establishment surveys is an area ripe for research.

The repeated nature of many establishment surveys is a potential advantage in terms of training respondents over time, and having them become familiar with the way the instrument works. Initial respondent effort in mastering more complex designs may pay off over time. In addition, data from prior waves are often used to evaluate current-wave responses, and so the preloading of data is a more common characteristic of establishment surveys. This brings with it design challenges with respect to balancing confidentiality of the data with ease of access (see Harrell et al., 2006). But it also makes edit checks more complex, potentially permitting respondents to change both prior values and current values.

Together these features mean that the look and feel of establishment surveys on the Web is often quite different from that of personal surveys. The example in Figure 6.15 serves to illustrate this point. This is from a construction survey conducted by Statistics Netherlands.

Several things can be briefly noted about this example. First, a detailed navigation bar on the left permits the respondent to skip around the instrument. Second, the main question area shows an example of a running tally, with both a subtotal and total. The question mark icon provides a link to additional instructions on the question. Respondents can move forward and backward in the instrument without triggering edit checks, while the "Akkoord" button serves to indicate confirmation of the values entered. The icons at the bottom of the page allow respondents to transmit the completed survey, print the questionnaire, save the responses, and so on. Designs such as this can be contrasted with the relatively straightforward design of personal surveys seen throughout this book.

My expectation is that we will increasingly see research on design issues related to establishment surveys. In addition, these are often mixed-mode surveys, bringing in some of the additional design challenges raised in the previous section.

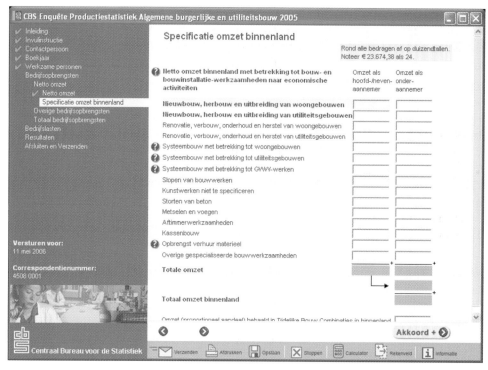

Figure 6.15 **Establishment Survey Example from Statistics Netherlands.**

6.7.6. Research on Web Survey Design

As a careful reader will notice, many issues related to Web survey design have not been fully explored, and the Web is constantly changing, presenting new design challenges and opportunities, and new methods and techniques to evaluate. It is premature to presume that we know what we need to know about designing Web surveys, as the brief reviews of mixed-mode and establishment surveys suggest. Ongoing research and evaluation should be part of the Web survey culture, and indeed part of the survey culture more broadly.

One of the advantages of Web surveys is the relative easy with which experiments can be conducted. In large face-to-face or telephone surveys, the types of methodological experiments that can be conducted are somewhat limited. Given the involvement of interviewers, many of the design features one may want to test are difficult to control or expensive to implement.

Many of the studies needed on effective Web survey design can be embedded in ongoing surveys. Given the fully automated and computerized nature of the Web, it is a superb medium for the control of experimental designs in ongoing surveys. The marginal cost of such embedded experiments is small relative to other modes of data collection and, given the relative newness of the medium, most such studies will add to our body of knowledge. Almost every Web survey should be seen as an opportunity to test some element of design, whether it be the wording of the e-mail invitation, the timing of reminders, the layout or typeface used, and so on. This is not to say that the answers to all the design questions can be obtained this way, nor to say that all design decisions require empirical testing. Many research questions need special studies, and many of the experiments we have done would not be possible without dedicated funding to support exploration of these methodological issues. But every time we do a Web survey, we should be thinking of ways to increase our knowledge about how best to design such surveys. This may take the form of small embedded experiments. But it may also take the form of careful analysis of the paradata, examining the frequency and location of breakoffs, the speed of returns, item completion times, and a variety of other indirect indicators of potential difficulties with the instrument. Other work needs to be done in a laboratory setting, including usability studies, eye-tracking research, and the like. Still other insights can be gained from observations of users in the field or debriefing questionnaires. The prevailing perspective should be one of continuous quality improvement, based if possible on empirical evidence.

6.8. Summary Remarks

I've tried to communicate throughout this book that design is a deliberate choice in Web surveys, as in other modes of data collection. Design should be considered an integral part of the process of developing and deploying a Web survey. The time and effort expended in improving the design of Web surveys will pay off in terms of producing better-quality data and more complete data and will leave respondents with a more positive feeling about the experience – in short, good design can be effective. It is not so much the specific details and recommendations I have offered here that are important – these are likely to change over time as the Web evolves and as our research knowledge expands. What is more important is the design philosophy – the perspective that design *does* matter, along with an understanding of why certain design features affect the answers that respondents provide. Poor design communicates a simple message to respondents: if you didn't put time and effort into designing the survey, why should they devote time and effort to answering the survey?

This book should not be viewed as the last word on the topic. There remain many unanswered questions about optimal Web design. The Web is constantly changing (see Couper, 2007), and new tools and techniques are being developed. Research on design is going on as this is being read. I look forward to seeing how our knowledge and use of this valuable and powerful survey tool evolves.

This is not the end. This is the beginning.[3]

---

[3]   J. R. R. Tolkien, *The Lord of the Rings: The Two Towers.*

References

Knowledge is of two kinds. We know a subject ourselves, or we know where we can find information upon it.

Samuel Johnson (1709–1784), British author, lexicographer

Anderson, A. E., Murphy, E. D., Nichols, E. M., Sigman, R. S., and Willimack, D. K. (2004), "Designing Edits for Electronic Economic Surveys and Censuses: Issues and Guidelines." *Proceedings of the Joint Statistical Meetings of the American Statistical Association.* Alexandria, VA, pp. 4912–4919.

Athale, N., Sturley, A., Skoczen, S., Kavanaugh, A., and Lenert, L. (2004), "A Web-Compatible Instrument for Measuring Self-Reported Disease Activity in Arthritis." *Journal of Rheumatology*, 31 (2): 223–228.

Baker, R. P., Bradburn, N. M., and Johnson, R. A. (1995), "Computer-Assisted Personal Interviewing: An Experimental Evaluation of Data Quality and Costs." *Journal of Official Statistics*, 11 (4): 415–431.

Baker, R. P., and Couper, M. P. (2007), "The Impact of Screen Size and Background Color on Response in Web Surveys." Paper presented at the General Online Research Conference (GOR'07), Leipzig, March.

Baker, R. P., Couper, M. P., Conrad, F. G., and Tourangeau, R. (2004), "Don't Know and No Opinion Responses in Web Surveys." Paper presented at the RC33 International Conference on Social Science Methodology, Amsterdam, August.

Baker, R. P., Crawford, S. D., and Swinehart, J. (2004), "Development and Testing of Web Questionnaires." In S. Presser, J. Rothgeb, M. P. Couper, J. Lessler, E. A. Martin, J. Martin, and E. Singer (eds.), *Methods for Testing and Evaluating Survey Questionnaires.* New York: Wiley, pp. 361–384.

Baker-Prewitt, J. (2003), "All Web Surveys are not Created Equal: Your Design Choices Can Impact Results." Presentation at the SumIT03 Global Market Research Symposium, Montreal, October. www.burke.com.

Bakken, D., and Frazier, C. L. (2006), "Conjoint Analysis: Understanding Consumer Decision Making." In R. Grover and M. Vriens (eds.), *The Handbook of Marketing Research*. Thousand Oaks, CA: Sage, pp. 288–311.

Bälter, O., and Bälter, K. A. (2005), "Demands on Web Survey Tools for Epidemiological Research." *European Journal of Epidemiology*, 20: 137–139.

Bartlett, J. (1919), *Familiar Quotations* (10th ed.). Boston: Little, Brown.

Bartram, D. (1982), "The Perception of Semantic Quality in Type: Differences Between Designers and Non-Designers." *Information Design Journal*, 3 (1): 38–50.

Bates, N., and Nichols, E. (1998), "The Census Bureau WWW Hiring Questionnaire: A Case Study of Usability Testing." Paper presented at the Joint Statistical Meetings of the American Statistical Association, Dallas, TX, August.

Bayer, L. R., and Thomas, R. K. (2004), "A Comparison of Sliding Scales with Other Scale Types in Online Surveys." Paper presented at the RC33 International Conference on Social Science Methodology, Amsterdam, August.

Bell, D. S., Mangione, C. M., and Kahn, C. E. (2001), "Randomized Testing of Alternative Survey Formats Using Anonymous Volunteers on the World Wide Web." *Journal of the American Medical Informatics Association*, 8 (6): 616–620.

Bentley, M., and Tancreto, J. G. (2006), "Analysis of Self-Response Options and Respondent-Friendly Design from the 2005 National Census Test." *Proceedings of the American Statistical Association, Survey Research Methods Section*. Alexandria, VA: ASA, pp. 2755–2762 [CD].

Benway, J. P. (1998), "Banner Blindness: The Irony of Attention Grabbing on the World Wide Web." *Proceedings of the Human Factors and Ergonomics Society 42nd Annual Meeting*, pp. 463–467.

Benway, J. P., and Lane, D. M. (1998), "Banner Blindness: Web Searchers Often Miss 'Obvious' Links." *ITG Newsletter*, 1 (3). http://www.internettg.org/newsletter/dec98/banner_blindness.html.

Bergman, L. R., Kristiansson, K.-E., Olofsson, A., and Säfström, M. (1994), "Decentralized CATI versus Paper and Pencil Interviewing: Effects on the Results in the Swedish Labor Force Surveys." *Journal of Official Statistics*, 10 (2): 181–195.

Bernard, M., and Mills, M. (2000), "So, What Size and Type of Font Should I Use on My Website?" *Usability News*, 2.2 http://psychology.wichita.edu/surl/usabilitynews/2S/font.htm.

Bernard, M., Mills, M., Peterson, M., and Storrer, K. (2001), "A Comparison of Popular Online Fonts: Which Is Best and When?" *Usability News*, 3.2 http://psychology.wichita.edu/surl/usabilitynews/3S/font.htm. Accessed March 14, 2008.

Billiet, J., and Loosveldt, G. (1988), "Improvement of the Quality of Responses to Factual Survey Questions by Interviewer Training." *Public Opinion Quarterly*, 52 (2): 190–211.

Birnbaum, M. H. (ed.) (2000a), *Psychological Experiments on the Internet*. San Diego: Academic Press.

Birnbaum, M. H. (2000b), "SurveyWiz and FactorWiz: JavaScript Web Pages That Make HTML Forms for Research on the Internet." *Behavior Research Methods, Instruments, and Computers*, 32 (2): 339–346.

Birnbaum, M. H. (2001), *Introduction to Behavioral Research on the Internet*. Upper Saddle River, NJ: Prentice-Hall.

Birnholtz, J. P., Horn, D. B., Finholt, T. A, and Bae, S. J. (2004), "The Effects of Cash, Electronic, and Paper Gift Certificates as Respondent Incentives for a Web-based Survey of Technologically Sophisticated Respondents." *Social Science Computer Review*, 22 (3): 355–362.

Bischoping, K., and Schuman, H. (1992), "Pens and Polls in Nicaragua: An Analysis of the 1990 Preelection Surveys." *American Journal of Political Science*, 36 (2): 331–350.

Blackwell, A. F. (2001), "Pictorial Representation and Metaphor in Visual Language Design." *Journal of Visual Languages and Computing*, 12: 223–252.

Bogen, K. (1996), "The Effect of Questionnaire Length on Response Rates – a Review of the Literature." *Proceedings of the American Statistical Association, Survey Research Methods Section*. Alexandria, VA: American Statistical Association, pp. 1020–1025.

Bosnjak, M., Neubarth, W., Couper, M. P., Bandilla, W., and Kaczmirek, L. (in press), "Prenotification in Web Surveys: The Influence of Mobile Text Messaging versus E-Mail on Response Rates and Sample Composition." *Social Science Computer Review.*

Bosnjak, M., and Tuten, T. L. (2001), "Classifying Response Behaviors in Web-Based Surveys." *Journal of Computer-Mediated Communication*, 6 (3), http://jcmc.indiana. edu/vol6/issue3/boznjak.html.

Bosnjak, M., and Tuten, T. L. (2002), "Prepaid and Promised Incentives in Web Surveys – An Experiment." *Social Science Computer Review*, 21 (2): 208–217.

Bosnjak, M., and Wenzel, O. (2005), "Effects of Two Innovative Techniques to Apply Incentives in Online Access Panels." Paper presented at the German Online Research Conference, Zurich, March.

Bowker, D., and Dillman, D. A. (2000), "An Experimental Evaluation of Left and Right Oriented Screens for Web Questionnaires" Paper presented at the annual meeting of the American Association for Public Opinion Research, Portland, OR, May.

Boyarski, D., Neuwirth, C., Forlizzi, J., and Regli, S. H. (1998), "A Study of Fonts Designed for Screen Display." *Proceedings of CHI 98*. New York: ACM, pp. 87–94.

Bradburn, N. M. (1978), "Respondent Burden." *Proceedings of the American Statistical Association, Survey Research Methods Section*. Alexandria, VA: American Statistical Association, pp. 35–40.

Brenner, M. (1982), "Response-Effects of 'Role-Restricted' Characteristics of the Interviewer." In W. Dijkstra and J. van der Zouwen (eds.), *Response Behaviour in the Survey-Interview*. London: Academic Press, pp. 131–165.

Brinck, T., Gergle, D., and Wood, S. D. (2002), *Usability for the Web: Designing Web Sites that Work*. San Francisco: Morgan Kaufmann.

Brophy, S., Hunniford, T., Taylor, G., Menon, A., Roussou, T., and Callin, A. (2004), "Assessment of Disease Severity (in Terms of Function) Using the Internet." *Journal of Rheumatology*, 31 (9): 1819–1822.

Brosius, H.-B., Donsbach, W., and Birk, M. (1996), "How Do Text-Picture Relations Affect the Informational Effectiveness of Television Newscasts?" *Journal of Broadcasting & Electronic Media*, 40: 180–195.

Brown, C. M. (1988), *Human-Computer Interface Design Guidelines*. Norwood, NJ: Ablex.

Burnside, R. (2000), "Towards Best Practice for Design of Electronic Data Capture Instruments (Methodology Advisory Committee)." Belconnen, ACT: Australian Bureau of Statistics, Research Paper 1352.0.55.036.

Burris, J., Chen, J., Graf, I., Johnson, T., and Owens, L. (2001), "An Experiment in Web Survey Design." Paper presented at the annual meeting of the American Association for Public Opinion Research, Montreal, Quebec, May.

Carney, R. N., and Levin, J. R. (2002), "Pictorial Illustrations *Still* Improve Students' Learning From Text." *Educational Psychology Review*, 14 (1): 5–26.

Castro, E. (2003), *HTML for the World Wide Web, Fifth Edition, with XHTML and CSS.* Berkeley, CA: Peachpit Press.

Chesney, T. (2006), "The Effect of Communication Medium on Research Participation Decisions." *Journal of Computer-Mediated Communication*, 11 (3): article 10 http://jcmc. indiana.edu/vol11/issue3/chesney.html.

Childers, T. L., and Jass, J. (2002), "All Dressed Up with Something to Say: Effects of Typeface Semantic Associations on Brand Perceptions and Consumer Memory." *Journal of Consumer Psychology*, 12 (2): 93–106.

Christian, L. M. (2003), "The Influence of Visual Layout on Scalar Questions in Web Surveys." Unpublished Master's Thesis. Pullman: Washington State University.

Christian, L. M., and Dillman, D. A. (2004), "The Influence of Graphical and Symbolic Language Manipulations on Responses to Self-Administered Questions." *Public Opinion Quarterly*, 68 (1): 57–80.

Christian, L. M., Dillman, D. A., and Smyth, J. D. (2007), "Helping Respondents Get It Right the First Time: The Influence of Words, Symbols, and Graphics in Web Surveys." *Public Opinion Quarterly*, 71 (1): 113–125.

Church, A. H. (1993), "Estimating the Effect of Incentives on Mail Survey Response Rates: A Meta-Analysis." *Public Opinion Quarterly*, 57 (1): 62–79.

Clark, R. L., and Nyiri, Z. (2001), "Web Survey Design: Comparing a Multi-Screen to a Single Screen Survey." Paper presented at the annual meeting of the American Association for Public Opinion Research, Montreal, Quebec, May.

Clayton, R. L., and Werking, G. S. (1998), "Business Surveys of the Future: The World Wide Web as a Data Collection Methodology." In M. P. Couper, R. P. Baker, J. Bethlehem, C. Z. F. Clark, J. Martin, W. L. Nicholls II, and J. O'Reilly. (eds.), *Computer Assisted Survey Information Collection.* New York: Wiley, pp. 543–562.

Cockburn, A., McKenzie, B., and JasonSmith, M. (2002), "Pushing Back: Evaluating a New Behaviour for the Back and Forward Buttons in Web Browsers." *International Journal of Human-Computer Studies*, 57: 397–414.

Coles, P., and Foster, J. J. (1975), "Typographic Cues as an Aid to Learning from Typewritten Text." *Programmed Learning and Educational Technology*, 12: 102–108.

Conrad, F. G., Couper, M. P., Tourangeau, R., and Galesic, M. (2005), "Interactive Feedback Can Improve Quality of Responses in Web Surveys." Paper presented at the annual meeting of the American Association for Public Opinion Research, Miami Beach, May.

Conrad, F. G., Couper, M. P., Tourangeau, R., and Peytchev, A. (2005), "Impact of Progress Indicators on Task Completion: First Impressions Matter." *Proceedings of CHI (Computer Human Interaction) '05*, Portland, OR. New York: Association for Computing Machinery.

Conrad, F. G., Couper, M. P., Tourangeau, R., and Peytchev, A. (2006), "Use and Non-Use of Clarification Features in Web Surveys." *Journal of Official Statistics*, 22 (2): 245–269.

Conrad, F. G., and Schober, M. F. (2000), "Clarifying Question Meaning in a Household Telephone Survey." *Public Opinion Quarterly*, 64 (1): 1–28.

Conrad, F. G., and Schober, M. F. (2005), "Promoting Uniform Question Understanding in Today's and Tomorrow's Surveys." *Journal of Official Statistics*, 21 (2): 215–231.

Conrad, F. G., Schober, M. F., and Coiner, T. (2007), "Bringing Features of Human Dialogue to Web Surveys." *Applied Cognitive Psychology*, 21: 165–187.

Cook, C., Heath, F., and Thompson, R. L. (2001), "Score Reliability in Web- or Internet-Based Surveys: Unnumbered Graphic Rating Scales Versus Likert-Type Scales." *Educational and Psychological Measurement*, 61 (4): 697–706.

Coon, D. (2002), "Challenges to Creating Accessible Web and Internet Surveys." Paper presented at the Federal CASIC Workshops, Washington, DC, February.

Cooper, A. (1995), *About Face: The Essentials of User Interface Design*. Foster City, CA: IDG Books.

Couper, M. P. (1994), "Discussion: What Can CAI Learn from HCI?" In *Proceedings of the Seminar on New Directions in Statistical Methodology*. Washington, DC: Statistical Policy Office, Office of Management and Budget (Statistical Policy Working Paper No. 23, pp. 363–377. http://www.fcsm.gov/working-papers/spwp23index.html.

Couper, M. P. (1999), "The Application of Cognitive Science to Computer Assisted Interviewing." In M. G. Sirken, D. J. Hermann, S. Schechter, N. Schwarz, J. M. Tanur, and R. Tourangeau (eds.), *Cognition and Survey Research*. New York: Wiley, pp. 277–300.

Couper, M. P. (2000), "Web Surveys: A Review of Issues and Approaches." *Public Opinion Quarterly*, 64 (4), 464–494.

Couper, M. P. (2005), "Technology Trends in Survey Data Collection." *Social Science Computer Review*, 23 (4): 486–501.

Couper, M. P. (2007a), "Whither the Web: Web 2.0 and the Changing World of Web Surveys." in M. Trotman et al. (eds.), *The Challenges of a Changing World: Proceedings of the Fifth International Conference of the Association for Survey Computing*. Berkeley, UK: ASC, pp.7–16.

Couper, M. P. (2007b), "Technology and the Survey Interview/Questionnaire." In M. F. Schober and F. G. Conrad (eds.), *Envisioning the Survey Interview of the Future*. New York: Wiley, pp. 58–76.

Couper, M. P., Blair, J., and Triplett, T. (1999), "A Comparison of Mail and E-Mail for a Survey of Employees in Federal Statistical Agencies." *Journal of Official Statistics*, 15 (1): 39–56.

Couper, M. P., Conrad, F. G., and Tourangeau, R. (2003), "The Effect of Images on Web Survey Responses." In R. Banks et al. (eds.), *Survey and Statistical Computing IV: The Impact of Technology on the Survey Process*, pp. 343–350.

Couper, M. P., Conrad, F. G., and Tourangeau, R. (2007), "Visual Context Effects in Web Surveys." *Public Opinion Quarterly*, 71 (4): 623–634.

Couper, M. P., Hansen, S. E., and Sadosky, S. A. (1997), "Evaluating Interviewer Performance in a CAPI Survey." In L. Lyberg, P. Biemer, M. Collins, E. de Leeuw, C. Dippo,

N. Schwarz, and D. Trewin (eds.), *Survey Measurement and Process Quality*. New York: Wiley, pp. 267–285.

Couper, M. P., Horm, J., and Schlegel, J. (1997), "Using Trace Files to Evaluate the National Health Interview Survey CAPI Instrument." *Proceedings of the Section on Survey Research Methods, American Statistical Association*. Alexandria: ASA, pp. 825–829.

Couper, M. P., Kapteyn, A., Schonlau, M., and Winter, J. (2007), "Noncoverage and Nonresponse in an Internet Survey." *Social Science Research*, 36 (1): 131–148.

Couper, M. P., Kenyon, K., and Tourangeau, R. (2004), "Picture This! An Analysis of Visual Effects in Web Surveys." *Public Opinion Quarterly*, 68 (2): 255–266.

Couper, M. P., and Lyberg, L. E. (2005), "The Use of Paradata in Survey Research." Paper presented at the International Statistical Institute, Sydney, Australia, April.

Couper, M. P., and Nicholls, W. L., II (1998), "The History and Development of Computer Assisted Survey Information Collection." In M. P. Couper, R. P. Baker, J. Bethlehem, C. Z. F. Clark, J. Martin, W. L. Nicholls II, and J. O'Reilly (eds.), *Computer Assisted Survey Information Collection*. New York: Wiley, pp. 1–21.

Couper, M. P., Peytchev, A., Little, R. J. A., and Rothert, K. (2005), "Combining Information from Multiple Modes to Evaluate and Reduce Nonresponse Bias." Alexandria, VA: Proceedings of the Survey Research Methods Section, American Statistical Association [CD].

Couper, M. P., Peytchev, A., Strecher, V. J., Rothert, K., and Anderson, J. (2007), "Following Up Nonrespondents to an Online Weight Management Intervention: Randomized Trial Comparing Mail versus Telephone." *Journal of Medical Internet Research*, 9 (2): e16.

Couper, M. P., Singer, E., and Tourangeau, R. (2004), "Does Voice Matter? An Interactive Voice Response (IVR) Experiment." *Journal of Official Statistics*, 20 (3): 551–570.

Couper, M. P., Singer, E., Tourangeau, R., and Conrad, F. G. (2006), "Evaluating the Effectiveness of Visual Analog Scales: A Web Experiment." *Social Science Computer Review*, 24 (2): 227–245.

Couper, M. P., and Tourangeau, R. (2006), "Taking the Audio out of Audio-CASI?" Paper presented at the European Conference on Quality in Survey Statistics, Cardiff, Wales, April.

Couper, M. P., Tourangeau, R., and Conrad, F. G. (2007), "How the Shape and Format of Input Fields Affect Answers." Paper presented at the Internet Survey Methodology workshop, Lillehammer, Norway, September.

Couper, M. P., Tourangeau, R., Conrad, F. G., and Crawford, S. D. (2004), "What They See Is What We Get: Response Options for Web Surveys." *Social Science Computer Review*, 22 (1): 111–127.

Couper, M. P., Traugott, M., and Lamias, M. (2001), "Web Survey Design and Administration." *Public Opinion Quarterly*, 65 (2): 230–253.

Crawford, S. D. (1999), "The Web Survey Choice in a Mixed Mode Data Collection." Unpublished Paper. Ann Arbor: University of Michigan.

Crawford, S. D., Couper, M. P., and Lamias, M. (2001), "Web Surveys: Perceptions of Burden." *Social Science Computer Review*, 19 (2): 146–162.

Crawford, S. D., McCabe, S. E., and Pope, D. (2003), "Applying Web-Based Survey Design Standards." *Journal of Prevention and Intervention in the Community*, 29 (1/2): 43–66.

Crawford, S. D., McCabe, S. E., Saltz, B., Boyd, C. J., Freisthler, B., and Paschall, M. J. (2004), "Gaining Respondent Cooperation in College Web-Based Alcohol Surveys: Findings from Experiments at Two Universities." Paper presented at the annual meeting of the American Association for Public Opinion Research, Phoenix, AZ, May.

Curry, J. (2003), "Complementary Capabilities for Conjoint, Choice, and Perceptual Mapping Web Data Collection." Paper presented at the Tenth Sawtooth Software Conference, April.

Czikszentmihalyi, M. (1990), *Flow: The Psychology of Optimal Experience.* New York: Harper & Row.

Dahan, E., and Hauser, J. R. (2002), "The Virtual Customer." *Journal of Product Innovation Management*, 19: 332–353.

Dahan, E., and Srinivasan, V. (2000), "The Predictive Power of Internet-Based Product Concept Testing Using Visual Depiction and Animation." *Journal of Product Innovation Management*, 17: 99–109.

David, P. (1998), "News Concreteness and Visual-Verbal Association: Do News Pictures Narrow the Recall Gap Between Concrete and Abstract News?" *Human Communication Research*, 25 (2): 180–201.

De Leeuw, E. D. (2001), "Reducing Missing Data in Surveys: an Overview of Methods." *Quality & Quantity*, 35: 147–160.

De Leeuw, E. D. (2005), "To Mix or Not to Mix Data Collection Modes in Surveys." *Journal of Official Statistics*, 21 (2): 233–255.

De Leeuw, E. D., Callegaro, M., Hox, J. J., Korendijk, E., and Lensvelt-Mulders, G. (2007), "The Influence of Advance Letters on Response in Telephone Surveys: A Meta-Analysis." *Public Opinion Quarterly*, 71 (3): 413–444.

DeMay, C. C., Kurlander, J. L., Lundby, K. M., and Fenlason, K. J. (2002), "Web Survey Comments: Does Length Impact 'Quality'?" Paper presented at the International Conference on Questionnaire Development, Evaluation and Testing Method, Charleston, SC, November.

Dennis, M., deRouvray, C., and Couper, M. P. (2000), "Questionnaire Design for Probability-Based Web Surveys." Paper presented at the annual meeting of the American Association for Public Opinion Research, Portland, OR, May.

DeRouvray, C., and Couper, M. P. (2002), "Designing a Strategy for Capturing 'Respondent Uncertainty' in Web-Based Surveys." *Social Science Computer Review*, 20 (1): 3–9.

Deutskens, E., de Ruyter, K., Wetzels, M., and Oosterveld, P. (2004), "Response Rate and Response Quality of Internet-Based Surveys: An Experimental Study." *Marketing Letters*, 15 (1): 21–36.

DeVoto, J. A. E. (1998), "Seven Mortal Sins of Professional Web Designers." http://www.jaedworks.com/shoebox/no-cookie/mortal-sins.html.

Dillman, D. A. (1978), *Mail and Telephone Surveys: The Total Design Method.* New York: Wiley.

Dillman, D. A. (2000), *Mail and Internet Surveys: The Tailored Design Method.* New York: Wiley.

Dillman, D. A., and Christian, L. M. (2005), "Survey Mode as a Source of Instability in Responses across Surveys." *Field Methods*, 17 (1): 30–52.

Dillman, D. A., Redline, C. D., and Carley-Baxter, L. R. (1999), "Influence of Type of Question on Skip Pattern Compliance in Self-Administered Questionnaires." *Proceedings of the American Statistical Association, Survey Research Methods Section.* Alexandria, VA: American Statistical Association, pp. 979–984.

Dillman, D. A., and Smyth, J. D. (2007), "Design Effects in the Transition to Web-Based Surveys." *American Journal of Preventive Medicine*, 32 (5S): S90–S96.

Dillman, D. A., Smyth, J. D., Christian, L. M., and Stern, M. J. (2003), "Multiple Answer Questions in Self-Administered Surveys: the Use of Check-All-That-Apply and Forced-Choice Question Formats." Paper presented at the Joint Statistical Meetings of the American Statistical Association, San Francisco, August.

Dondis, D. A. (1973), *A Primer of Visual Literacy.* Cambridge, MA: MIT Press.

Downes-Le Guin, T., Mechling, J., and Baker, R. P. (2006), "Great Results from Ambiguous Sources." Paper presented at the ESOMAR Conference on Panel Research '06, Barcelona, Spain.

Duchastel, P. C. (1978), "Illustrating Instructional Texts." *Educational Technology*, 18 (11): 36–39.

Duchastel, P. C. (1980), "Research on Illustrations in Text: Issues and Perspectives." *Educational Communication and Technology Journal*, 28 (4): 283–287.

Duchastel, P. C., and Waller, R. (1979), "Pictorial Illustration in Instructional Texts." *Educational Technology*, 19 (11): 20–25.

Dyson, M. C. (2004), "How Physical Text Layout Affects Reading from Screen." *Behaviour and information technology*, 23 (6): 377–393.

Edwards, P., Cooper, R., Roberts, I., and Frost, C. (2005), "Meta-Analysis of Randomised Trials of Monetary Incentives and Response to Mailed Questionnaires." *Journal of Epidemiology and Community Health*, 59 (11): 987–999.

Ekman, A., Dickman, P. W., Klint, A., Weiderpass, E., and Litton, J.-E. (2006), "Feasibility of Using Web-Based Questionnaires in Large Population-Based Epidemiological Studies." *European Journal of Epidemiology*, 21: 103–111.

Elig, T., and Waller, V. (2001), "Internet versus Paper Survey Administration: Impact on Qualitative Responses." Unpublished Paper. Arlington, VA: Defense Manpower Data Center.

ESOMAR (2005), *ESOMAR Guideline on Conducting Market and Opinion Research Using the Internet*, updated August 2005, http://www.esomar.org.

Etter, J.-F., Cucherat, M., and Perneger, T. V. (2002), "Questionnaire Color and Response Rates to Mailed Surveys: A Randomized Trial and a Meta-Analysis." *Evaluation and the Health Professions*, 25 (2): 185–199.

Fagerlin, A., Wang, C., and Ubel, P. A. (2005), "Reducing the Influence of Anecdotal Reasoning on People's Health Care Decisions: Is a Picture Worth a Thousand Statistics? *Medical Decision Making*, 25 (4): 398–405.

Farmer, T. (2000), "Using the Internet for Primary Research Data Collection." InfoTek Research Group, Inc. http://www.researchinfo.com/library/infotek/index.shtml.

Faubert, J. (1994), "Seeing Depth in Color – More than Just what Meets the Eyes." *Vision Research*, 34 (9): 1165–1186.

Fitts, P. M. (1954), "The Information Capacity of the Human Motor System in Controlling the Amplitude of Movement." *Journal of Experimental Psychology*, 47: 381–391.

Forsman, G., and Varedian, M. (2002), "Mail and Web Surveys: A Cost and Response Rate Comparison in a Study of Students Housing Conditions." Paper presented at the International Conference on Improving Surveys, Copenhagen, August.

Fox, J. E., Mockovak, W., Fisher, S., and Rho, C. (2003), "Usability Issues Associated with Converting Establishment Surveys to Web-Based Data Collection." Paper presented at the FCSM Conference, Arlington, VA, November.

Fox, S. (2005), *Digital Divisions*. Washington, D.C.: Pew Internet and American Life Project. http://www.pewinternet.org.

Freyd, M. (1923), "The Graphic Rating Scale." *Journal of Educational Psychology*, 14: 83–102.

Fricker, R. D., and Schonlau, M. (2002), "Advantages and Disadvantages of Internet Research Surveys: Evidence from the Literature." *Field Methods*, 14 (4): 347–365.

Fuchs, M. (2007), "Asking for Numbers and Quantities: Visual Design Effects in Web Surveys and Paper & Pencil Surveys." Paper presented at the annual meeting of the American Association for Public Opinion Research, Anaheim, CA, May.

Fuchs, M., and Couper, M. P. (2001), "Length of Input Field and the Responses Provided in a Self-Administered Survey: A Comparison of Paper and Pencil and a Web Survey." Paper presented at the International Conference on Methodology and Statistics, Ljubljana, Slovenia, September.

Funke, F. (2005), "Visual Analogue Scales in Online Surveys." Paper presented at the General Online Research (GOR '05) conference, Zurich, March.

Funke, F., and Reips, U.-D. (2007), "Dynamic Forms: Online Surveys 2.0." Paper presented at the General Online Research Conference (GOR'07), Leipzig, March.

Gadeib, A., and Kunath, J. (2006), "Virtual Research Worlds – Simulate the Difference! Efficient Concept Testing with in Virtual Market Simulations Online." Paper presented at the General Online Research Conference (GOR '06), Bielefeld, Germany, March.

Galesic, M. (2006), "Dropouts on the Web: Effects of Interest and Burden Experienced During an Online Survey." *Journal of Official Statistics*, 22 (2): 313–328.

Galesic, M., Tourangeau, R., Couper, M. P., and Conrad, F. G. (in press), "Eye-Tracking Data: New Insights on Response Order Effects and Other Signs of Cognitive Shortcuts in Survey Responding." *Public Opinion Quarterly*.

Galesic, M., Tourangeau, R., Couper, M. P., and Conrad, F. G. (2007), "Using Change to Improve Navigation in Grid Questions." Paper presented at the General Online Research Conference (GOR'07), Leipzig, March.

Galitz, W. O. (1993), *User-Interface Screen Design*. Boston: QED.

Garrett, J. J. (2005), "Ajax: A New Approach to Web Applications." http://www.adaptivepath.com/publications/essays/archives/00385.php.

Gaskell, G. D., O'Muircheartaigh, C. A., and Wright, D. B. (1994), "Survey Questions about the Frequency of Vaguely Defined Events: the Effects of Response Alternatives." *Public Opinion Quarterly*, 58 (2): 241–254.

Gillbride, T. J., and Allenby, G. M. (2004), "A Choice Model with Conjunctive, Disjunctive, and Compensatory Screening Rules." *Marketing Science*, 23 (3): 391–406.

Giner-Sorolla, R., Garcia, M. T., and Bargh, J. A. (1999), "The Automatic Evaluation of Pictures." *Social Cognition*, 17 (1): 76–96.

Glauer, R., and Schneider, D. (2004), "Online-Surveys: Effects of Different Display Formats, Response Orders as Well as Progress Indicators in a Non-Experimental Environment." Paper presented at the 6th German Online Research Conference, Duisburg-Essen, Germany, March.

Godar, S. H. (2000), "Use of Color and Responses to Computer-Based Surveys." *Perceptual and Motor Skills*, 91: 767–770.

Göritz, A. S. (2004), "The Impact of Material Incentives on Response Quantity, Response Quality, Sample Composition, Survey Outcome, and Cost in Online Access Panels." *International Journal of Market Research*, 46 (3): 327–345.

Göritz, A. S. (2005), "Incentives in Web-Based Studies: What to Consider and How to Decide." WebSM Guide No. 2. www.websm.org.

Göritz, A. S. (2006), "Incentives in Web Studies: Methodological Issues and a Review." *International Journal of Internet Science*, 1 (1): 58–70.

Gorn, G. J., Chattopadhyay, A., Sengupta, J., and Tripathi, S. (2004), "Waiting for the Web: How Screen Color Affects Time Perception." *Journal of Marketing Research*, XLI (May): 215–225.

Gorn, G. J., Chattopadhyay, A., Yi, T., and Dahl, D. W. (1997), "Effects of Color as an Executional Cue in Advertising: They're in the Shade." *Management Science*, 43 (10): 1387–1400.

Graber, D. A. (1996), "Say it with Pictures." *Annals of the American Academy of Political and Social Science*, 546: 85–96.

Grabinger, R. S., and Osman-Jouchoux, R. (1996), "Designing Screens for Learning." In H. van Oostendorp and S. de Mul (eds.), *Cognitive Aspects of Electronic Text Processing*. Norwood, NJ: Ablex, pp. 181–212.

Gräf, L. (2002), "Optimierung von WWW-Umfragen: Three Years After." Paper presented at the German Online Research conference, Göttingen, May.

Gräf, L. (2005), "Befragung mit neuer Kommunikationstechnik: Online-Umfragen." Unpublished Paper. Köln, Germany: GlobalPark.

Grandjean, E. (1987), *Ergonomics in Computerized Offices*. New York: Taylor & Francis.

Green, P. E., and Rao, V. (1971), "Conjoint measurement: A New Approach to Quantify Judgmental Data." *Journal of Marketing Research*, 8 (3): 355–363.

Grice, P. (1967), "Utterer's Meaning and Intentions." In P. Grice (ed.), *Studies in the Way of Words*. Cambridge, MA: Harvard University Press, 1989, pp. 86–116.

Groves, R. M. (1989), *Survey Errors and Survey Costs*. New York: Wiley.

Groves, R. M. (2006), "Nonresponse Rates and Nonresponse Error in Household Surveys." *Public Opinion Quarterly*, 70 (5): 646–675.

Groves, R. M., and Couper, M. P. (1998), *Nonresponse in Household Interview Surveys*. New York: Wiley.

Guéguen, N., and Jacob, C. (2002a), "Social Presence Reinforcement and Computer-Mediated Communication: The Effect of the Solicitor's Photograph on Compliance to a Survey Request Made by E-Mail." *CyberPsychology and Behavior*, 5 (2): 139–142.

Guéguen, N., and Jacob, C. (2002b), "Solicitations by E-Mail and Solicitor's Status: A Field Study of Social Influence on the Web." *CyberPsychology and Behavior*, 5 (4): 377–383.

Hagenaars, J. A., and Heinen, T. G. (1982), "Effects of Role-Independent Interviewer Characteristics on Responses." In W. Dijkstra and J. van der Zouwen (eds.), *Response Behaviour in the Survey-Interview*. London: Academic Press, pp. 91–130.

Hall, R. H., and Hanna, P. (2004), "The Impact of Web Page Text-Background Colour Combinations on Readability, Retention, Aesthetics, and Behavioural Intent." *Behaviour and Information Technology*, 23 (3): 183–195.

Hansen, S. E., and Couper, M. P. (2004), "Usability Testing as a Means of Evaluating Computer Assisted Survey Instruments." In S. Presser, J. Rothgeb, M. P. Couper, J. Lessler, E. A. Martin, J. Martin, and E. Singer (eds.), *Methods for Testing and Evaluating Survey Questionnaires*. New York: Wiley, pp. 337–360.

Hansen, S. E., Couper, M. P., and Fuchs, M. (1998), "Usability Evaluation of the NHIS Instrument." Paper presented at the Annual Meeting of the American Association for Public Opinion Research, St. Louis, May.

Haraldsen, G. (2004), "Identifying and Reducing Response Burdens in Internet Business Surveys." *Journal of Official Statistics*, 20 (2): 393–410.

Haraldsen, G., Dale, T., Dalheim, E., and Strømme, H. (2002), "Mode Effects in a Mail plus Internet Designed Census." Paper presented at the International Conference on Improving Surveys, Copenhagen, August.

Haraldsen, G., Kleven, Ø., and Stålnacke, M. (2006), "Paradata Indications of Problems in Web Surveys." Paper presented at the European Conference on Quality in Survey Statistics, Cardiff, Wales, April.

Harmon, M. A., Westin, E. C., and Levin, K. Y. (2005), "Does Type of Pre-Notification Affect Web Survey Response Rates?" Paper presented at the annual conference of the American Association for Public Opinion Research, Miami Beach, May.

Harrell, L., Rosen, R., Gomes, A., Chute, J., and Yu, H. (2006), "Web Versus Email Data Collection: Experience in the Current Employment Statistics Program." *Proceedings of the Joint Statistical Meetings of the American Statistical Association*, Seattle, August. Alexandria, VA: ASA, pp. 3104–3108 [CD].

Harris, D. R. (2002), "In the Eye of the Beholder: Observed Race and Observer Characteristics." Ann Arbor: University of Michigan, Population Studies Center Research Report 02-522.

Hartley, J., Davies, L., and Burnhill, P. (1977), "Alternatives in the Typographic Design of Questionnaires." *Journal of Occupational Psychology*, 50: 299–304.

Hayes, M. H., and Patterson, D. G. (1921), "Experimental Development of the Graphic Rating Method." *Psychological Bulletin*, 18: 98–99.

Heerwegh, D. (2003), "Explaining Response Latencies and Changing Answers Using Client-Side Paradata from a Web Survey." *Social Science Computer Review*, 21 (3): 360–373.

Heerwegh, D. (2005a), *Web Surveys: Explaining and Reducing Unit Nonresponse, Item Nonresponse and Partial Nonresponse*. Unpublished Ph.D. thesis. Leuven, Belgium: Katholieke Universiteit Leuven, Faculteit Sociale Wetenschappen.

Heerwegh, D. (2005b), "Effects of Personal Salutations in E-Mail Invitations to Participate in a Web Survey." *Public Opinion Quarterly*, 69 (1): 588–598.

Heerwegh, D., and Loosveldt, G. (2002a), "Web Surveys: The Effect of Controlling Survey Access Using PIN Numbers." *Social Science Computer Review*, 20 (1): 10–21.

Heerwegh, D., and Loosveldt, G. (2002b), "An Evaluation of the Effect of Response Formats on Data Quality in Web Surveys." *Social Science Computer Review*, 20 (4): 471–484.

Heerwegh, D., and Loosveldt, G. (2003), "An Evaluation of the Semiautomatic Login Procedure to Control Web Survey Access." *Social Science Computer Review*, 21 (2): 223–234.

Heerwegh, D., and Loosveldt, G. (2006), "An Experimental Study on the Effects of Personalization, Survey Length Statements, Progress Indicators, and Survey Sponsor Logos in Web Surveys" *Journal of Official Statistics*, 22 (2): 191–210.

Heerwegh, D., Vanhove, T., Matthijs, K., and Loosveldt, G. (2005), "The Effect of Personalization on Response Rates and Data Quality in Web Surveys." *International Journal of Social Research Methodology*, 8 (2): 85–99.

Hembroff, L. A., Rusz, D., Rafferty, A., McGee, H., and Ehrlich, N. (2005), "The Cost-Effectiveness of Alternative Advance Mailings in a Telephone Survey." *Public Opinion Quarterly*, 69 (2): 232–245.

Hemsing, W., and Hollwig, J. O. (2006), "The Impact of Visualization of Question Types and Screen Pages on the Answering Behavior in Online Surveys." Paper presented at the General Online Research Conference (GOR '06), Bielefeld, Germany, March.

Hennessy, D. G. (2002), "An Evaluation of Methods for Testing Internet Survey Questions." Unpublished Honors Thesis. Wollongong, Australia: University of Wollongong, Department of Psychology.

Hill, D. H. (1994), "The Relative Empirical Validity of Dependent and Independent Data Collection in a Panel Survey." *Journal of Official Statistics*, 10: 359–380.

Hogg, A., and Masztal, J. J. (2002), "Drop-Down Boxes, Radio Buttons or Fill-in-the-Blank?" *CASRO Journal 2002*, pp. 53–55.

Hogg, A., and Miller, J. (2003), "Watch out for Dropouts: Study Shows Impact of Online Survey Length on Research Findings." *Quirk's Marketing Research Review*, July/August, article 1137. www.quirks.com.

Hoogendoorn, A. (2001), "Some Techniques for Internet Interviewing." *Proceedings of the Seventh International Blaise Users Conference*, Washington D.C., September.

Hoogendoorn, A. (2004), "A Questionnaire Design for Dependent Interviewing that Addresses the Problem of Cognitive Satisficing." *Journal of Official Statistics*, 20 (2): 219–232.

Hoogendoorn, A., and Sikkel, D. (2002), "Feedback in Web Surveys." Paper presented at the International Conference on Improving Surveys, Copenhagen, August.

Horn, R. E. (1998), *Visual Language: Global Communication for the 21st Century*. Bainbridge Island, WA: MacroVU.

Horrigan, J. B. (2006), *Home Broadband Adoption 2006*. Washington, D.C.: Pew Internet and American Life Project. http://www.pewinternet.org.

Horrigan, J. B., and Smith, A. (2007), *Home Broadband Adoption 2007*. Washington, D.C.: Pew, press release June 3, 2007. http://www.pewinternet.org.

Horton, S. (2006), *Access by Design: A Guide to Universal Usability for Web Designers*. Berkeley, CA: New Riders.

Horton, W. (1991), "Overcoming Chromophobia: A Guide to the Confident and Appropriate Use of Color." *IEEE Transactions on Professional Communication*, 34 (3): 160–171.

House, C. C. (1985), "Questionnaire Design with Computer Assisted Telephone Interviewing." *Journal of Official Statistics*, 1 (2): 209–219.

House, C. C., and Nicholls, W. L., II (1988), "Questionnaire Design for CATI: Design Objectives and Methods." In R. M. Groves, P. P. Biemer, L. E. Lyberg, J. T. Massey, W. L. Nicholls II, and J. Waksberg (eds.), *Telephone Survey Methodology*. New York: Wiley, pp. 421–436.

Howlett, V. (1996), *Visual Interface Design for Windows*. New York: Wiley.

Iglesias, C. P., Birks, Y. F., and Torgerson, D. J. (2001), "Improving the Measurement of Quality of Life in Older People: The York SF-12." *Quarterly Journal of Medicine*, 94: 695–698.

Inside Research (2007), "U.S. Online MR Continues Strong." January. www.MarketResearch.com.

Itten, J. (2003), *The Elements of Color*. New York: Wiley.

Jäckle, A. (2004), "Does Dependent Interviewing Really Increase Efficiency and Reduce Respondent Burden?" Colchester: University of Essex (Working Papers of the Institute for Social and Economic Research, paper 2005–11).

Jansen, B. J., Spink, A., and Saracevic, T. (2000), "Real Life, Real Users, and Real Needs: A Study and Analysis of User Queries on the Web." *Information Processing and Management*, 36: 207–227.

Jeavons, A. (1998), "Ethology and the Web: Observing Respondent Behaviour in Web Surveys." *Proceedings of the Worldwide Internet Conference*, London, February. ESOMAR.

Jenkins, C. R., and Dillman, D. A. (1997), "Towards a Theory of Self-Administered Questionnaire Design." In L. Lyberg, P. Biemer, M. Collins, E. de Leeuw, C. Dippo, N. Schwarz, and D. Trewin (eds.), *Survey Measurement and Process Quality*. New York: Wiley, pp. 165–196.

Johnson, R. M. (1987), "Adaptive Conjoint Analysis." *Sawtooth Software Conference on Perceptual Mapping, Conjoint Analysis, and Computer Interviewing*. Ketchum, ID: Sawtooth Software, pp. 253–265. http://www.sawtoothsoftware.com.

Johnson, R. M. (2000), "Understanding HB: An Intuitive Approach." Proceedings of the *Sawtooth Software Conference*. Ketchum, ID: Sawtooth Software, pp. 195–205. http://www.sawtoothsoftware.com.

Joinson, A. N. (2005), "Audience Power, Personalized Salutation and Responses to Web Surveys." Paper presented at the ESF Workshop on Internet Survey Methodology, Dubrovnik, Croatia, September.

Joinson, A. N., and Reips, U.-D. (2007), "Personalized Salutation, Power of Sender and Response Rates to Web-Based Surveys." *Computers in Human Behavior*, 23 (3): 1372–1383.

Joinson, A. N., Woodley, A., and Reips, U.-D. (2007), "Personalization, Authentication and Self-Disclosure in Self-Administered Internet Surveys." *Computers in Human Behavior*, 23: 275–285.

Juran, J. M. (1979), 'Basic Concepts', in Juran, J. M., Gryna, F. M., and Bingham, R. S. (eds.), *Quality Control Handbook*, third edition. McGraw-Hill: New York, pp. 1–24.

Kaczmirek, L., Neubarth, W., Bosnjak, M., and Bandilla, W. (2004), "Progress Indicators in Filter Based Surveys: Computing Methods and their Impact on Drop Out." Paper presented at the RC33 International Conference on Social Science Methodology, Amsterdam, August.

Kaczmirek, L., Neubarth, W., Bosnjak, M., and Bandilla, W. (2005), "Progress Indicators in Filter Based Surveys: Individual and Dynamic Calculation Methods." Paper presented at the General Online Research Conference (GOR05), Zurich, March.

Kaczmirek, L., and Thiele, O. (2006), "Flash, JavaScript, or PHP? Comparing the Availability of Technical Equipment among University Applicants." Paper presented at the 8th International General Online Research Conference (GOR06), Bielefeld, Germany, March.

Kalbach, J. (2001), "The Myth of 800x600." *Dr. Dobbs Journal*, March 16, 2001. http://www.ddj.com/documents/s=2684/nam1012432092/index.html.

Kane, E. W., and Macauley, L. J. (1993), "Interviewer Gender and Gender Attitudes." *Public Opinion Quarterly*, 57 (1): 1–28.

Kaplowitz, M. D., Hadlock, T. D., and Levine, R. (2004), "A Comparison of Web and Mail Survey Response Rates." *Public Opinion Quarterly*, 68 (1): 94–101.

Karlgren, J., and Franzén, K. (1997), "Verbosity and Interface Design in Information Retrieval." SICS Technical Report T2000:04. Swedish Institute for Computer Science, Stockholm. http://www.sics.se/~jussi/Artiklar/2000_TR_irinterface/irinterface.html.

Kent, R., and Brandal, H. (2003), "Improving Email Response in a Permission Marketing Context." *International Journal of Market Research*, 45 (1): 489–506.

Kenyon, K., Couper, M. P., and Tourangeau, R. (2001), "Picture This! An Analysis of Visual Effects in Web Surveys." Paper presented at the annual conference of the American Association for Public Opinion Research, Montreal, Canada, May.

Kerwin, J., Levin, K., Shipp, S., Wang, A., and Campbell, S. (2006), "A Comparison of Strategies for Reducing Item Nonresponse in Web Surveys." Paper presented at the Joint Statistical Meetings of the American Statistical Association, Seattle, August.

Kiesler, S., and Sproull, L. S. (1986), "Response Effects in the Electronic Survey." *Public Opinion Quarterly*, 50: 402–413.

Kiousis, S. (2002), "Interactivity: A Concept Explication." *New Media and Society*, 4 (3): 355–383.

Kjellström, O., and Bälter, O. (2003), "Design of Follow-up Questions in Web Surveys." Paper presented at the 25th International Conference on Information Technology Interfaces, Cavtat, Croatia, June.

Koffka, K. (1935), *Principles of Gestalt Psychology*. New York: Harcourt, Brace, and World.

Kostelnick, C., and Roberts, D. D. (1998), *Designing Visual Language*. Boston: Allyn and Bacon.

Kraut, R. M., Olson, J., Banaji, M., Bruckman, A., Cohen, J., and Couper, M. P. (2004), "Psychological Research Online: Report of Board of Scientific Affairs' Advisory Group on the Conduct of Research on the Internet." *American Psychologist*, 59 (2): 106–117.

Krosnick, J. A. (1991), "Response Strategies for Coping with the Cognitive Demands of Attitude Measures in Surveys." *Applied Cognitive Psychology*, 5: 213–236.

Krosnick, J. A., and Alwin, D. F. (1987), "An Evaluation of a Cognitive Theory of Response-Order Effects in Survey Measurement." *Public Opinion Quarterly*, 51 (2): 201–219.

Krosnick, J. A., and Fabrigar, L. R. (1997), "Designing Rating Scales for Effective Measurement in Surveys." In L. Lyberg, P. Biemer, M. Collins, E. de Leeuw, C. Dippo, N. Schwarz, and D. Trewin (eds.), *Survey Measurement and Process Quality*. New York: Wiley, pp. 141–164.

Krysan, M., and Couper, M. P. (2003), "Race in the Live and Virtual Interview: Racial Deference, Social Desirability, and Activation Effects in Attitude Surveys." *Social Psychology Quarterly*, 66 (4): 364–383.

Krysan, M., and Couper, M. P. (2005), "Race-of-Interviewer Effects: What Happens on the Web?" *International Journal of Internet Science*, 1 (1): 5–16.

Květon, P., Jelínek, M., Vobořil, and Klimusová, H. (2007), "Computer-Based Tests: the Impact of Test Design and Problem of Equivalency." *Computers in Human Behavior*, 23 (1): 32–51.

Kypri, K., and Gallagher, S. J. (2003), "Incentives to Increase Participation in an Internet Survey of Alcohol Use: A Controlled Experiment." *Alcohol & Alcoholism*, 38 (5): 437–441.

Kypri, K., Gallagher, S. J., and Cashell-Smith, M. L. (2004), "An Internet-Based Survey Method for College Student Drinking Research." *Drug and Alcohol Dependence*, 76 (1): 45–53.

Lenert, L. A., Sturley, A., and Watson, M. E. (2002), "iMPACT3: Internet-Based Development and Administration of Utility Elicitation Protocols." *Medical Decision Making*, November–December: 464–474.

Lie, H. W., and Bos, B. (2005), *Cascading Style Sheets: Designing for the Web, Third Edition*. Upper Saddle River, NJ: Addison-Wesley.

Link, M. W., and Mokdad, A. (2005), "Advance Letters as a Means of Improving Respondent Cooperation in Random Digit Dial Studies: A Multistate Experiment." *Public Opinion Quarterly*, 69 (4): 572–587.

Little, R. J. A., and Rubin, D. A. (2002), *Statistical Analysis with Missing Data* (2nd ed.). New York: Wiley.

Lowney, G. (1998), "But Can They Read It?" *MDSN News*, July/August. http://www.microsoft.com/mdsn/news/julaug98/access7.htm.

Lozar Manfreda, K., and Vehovar, V. (2002), "Design of Web Survey Questionnaires: Three Basic Experiments." *Journal of Computer Mediated Communication*, 7 (3). http://jcmc.indiana.edu/vol7/issue3/vehovar.html.

Lütters, H., Westphal, D., and Heublein, F. (2007), "SniperScale: Graphical Scaling in Data Collection and its Effect on the Response Behaviour of Participants in Online Studies." Paper presented at the General Online Research Conference (GOR '07), Leipzig, March.

Lynch, P. J., and Horton, S. (1997), *Yale Center for Advanced Media WWW Style Manual*, 1st ed. http://info.med.yale.edu/caim/manual/.

Lynch, P. J., and Horton, S. (2001), *Web Style Guide: Basic Design Principles for Creating Web Sites* (2nd ed.). New Haven, CT: Yale University Press.

Lynn, P., Jäckle, A., Jenkins, S. P., and Sala, E. (2006), "The Effects of Dependent Interviewing on Responses to Questions on Income Sources." *Journal of Official Statistics*, 22 (3): 357–384.

MacElroy, B. (2000), "Variables Influencing Dropout Rates in Web-Based Surveys." *Quirk's Marketing Research Review*, July/August. www.modalis.com.

MacElroy, B., Mikucki, J., and McDowell, P. (2002), "A Comparison of Quality in Open-Ended Responses and Response Rates Between Web-Based and Paper and Pencil Survey Modes." *Journal of Online Research*, 1 (1). http://www.ijor.org/.

Magee, C. G., Straight, R. L., and Schwartz, L. (2001), "Conducting Web-Based Surveys: Keys to Success." *The Public Manager*, Summer: 47–50.

Marsh, E. E., and White, M. D. (2003), "A Taxonomy of Relationships between Images and Text." *Journal of Documentation*, 59 (6): 647–672.

Marshall, P., and Bradlow, E. T. (2002), "A Unified Approach to Conjoint Analysis Methods." *Journal of the American Statistical Association*, 97 (459): 674–682.

Martin, E. A., Childs, J. H., DeMaio, T., Hill, J., Reiser, C., Gerber, E., Styles, K., and Dillman, D. A. (2007), *Guidelines for Designing Questionnaires for Administration in Different Modes*. Washington, D.C.: U.S. Census Bureau.

May, V. A. (1999), "Survey 2000: Charting Communities and Change." *National Geographic*, 196 (6): 130–133.

Maynard, D. W., Houtkoop-Steenstra, H., Schaeffer, N. C., and van der Zouwen, J. (eds.) (2002), *Standardization and Tacit Knowledge: Interaction and Practice in the Survey Interview*. New York: Wiley.

McCabe, S., Boyd, C., Couper, M. P., Crawford, S. D., d'Arcy, E., Boyd, C., Couper, M. P., Crawford, S. D., and d'Arcy, H. (2002), "Mode Effects for Collecting Alcohol and Other Drug Use Data: Web and US Mail." *Journal of Studies on Alcohol*, 63 (6): 755–761.

McCabe, S. E., Diez, A., Boyd, C. J., Nelson, T. F., and Weitzman, E. R. (2006), "Comparing Web and Mail Responses in a Mixed Mode Survey in College Alcohol Use Research." *Addictive Behaviors*, 31: 1619–1627.

McCarthy, M. S., and Mothersbaugh, D. L. (2002), "Effects of Typographic Factors in Advertising-Based Persuasion: A General Model and Initial Empirical Tests." *Psychology & Marketing*, 19 (7–8): 663–691.

McCloud, S. (1993), *Understanding Comics: The Invisible Art*. New York: HarperCollins.

McMillan, S. J., and Hwang, J.-S. (2002), "Measures of Perceived Interactivity: An Exploration of the Role of Direction of Communication, User Control, and Time in Shaping Perceptions of Interactivity." *Journal of Advertising*, 31 (3): 29–42.

Meadows, K. A., Greene, T., Foster, L., and Beer, S. (2000), "The Impact of Different Response Alternatives on Responders' Reporting of Health-Related Behaviour in a Postal Survey." *Quality of Life Research*, 9: 385–391.

Mehta, R., and Sivadas, E. (1995), "Comparing Response Rates and Response Content in Mail Versus Electronic Mail Surveys." *Journal of the Market Research Society*, 37 (4): 429–439.

Miller, J. M., and Krosnick, J. A. (1998), "The Impact of Candidate Name Order on Election Outcomes." *Public Opinion Quarterly*, 62 (3): 291–330.

Miller, S., and Jarrett, C. (2001), "Should I Use a Drop-down? Four Steps for Choosing Form Elements on the Web." Unpublished Paper. Leighton Buzzard, England: Effortmark.

Mockovak, W. (2005), "An Evaluation of Different Design Options for Presenting Edit Messages in Web Forms." Paper presented at the FedCASIC Workshop, Washington, D.C., March.

Mooney, G. M., Rogers, B., and Trunzo, D. (2003), "Examining the Effect of Error Prompting on Item Nonresponse and Survey Nonresponse in Web Surveys." Paper presented at the annual conference of the American Association for Public Opinion Research, Nashville, TN, May.

Moore, P., and Fitz, C. (1993a), "Gestalt Theory and Instructional Design." *Journal of Technical Writing and Communication*, 23 (2): 137–157.

Moore, P., and Fitz, C. (1993b), "Using Gestalt Theory to Teach Document Design and Graphics." *Technical Communication Quarterly*, 2 (4): 389–410.

Moreno, R., and Mayer, R. E. (1999), "Cognitive Principles of Multimedia Learning: The Role of Modality and Contiguity." *Journal of Experimental Psychology*, 91 (2): 358–368.

Murphy, E., and Ciochetto, S. (2006), "Usability Testing of Alternative Design Features for Web-Based Data Collection: Selected Issues, Results, and Recommendations." Paper presented at FedCASIC, Washington, D.C., March.

Nass, C., Isbister, K., and Lee, E.-J. (2001), "Truth Is Beauty: Researching Embodied Conversational Agents." In J. Cassell, J. Sullivan, S. Prevost, and E. Churchill (eds.), *Embodied Conversational Agents*. Cambridge, MA: MIT Press, pp. 374–402.

Nass, C., Moon, Y., and Carney, P. (1999), "Are People Polite to Computers? Responses to Computer-Based Interviewing Systems." *Journal of Applied Social Psychology*, 29 (5): 1093–1110.

Nass, C., Moon, Y., and Green, N. (1997), "Are Machines Gender Neutral? Gender-Stereotypic Responses to Computers with Voices." *Journal of Applied Social Psychology*, 27 (10): 864–876.

Nass, C., Robles, E., Bienenstock, H., Treinen, M., and Heenan, C. (2003), "Speech-Based Disclosure Systems: Effects of Modality, Gender of Prompt, and Gender of User." *International Journal of Speech Technology*, 6: 113–121.

Neubarth, W. (2006), "Ranking vs. Rating in an Online Environment." Paper presented at the General Online Research Conference (GOR '06), Bielefeld, Germany, March.

Nielsen, J. (2000), *Designing Web Usability*. Berkeley, CA: New Riders.

Nielsen, J., and Loranger, H. (2005), *Fundamental Guidelines for Web Usability*. London: Nielsen Norman Group (Usability Week Tutorial Materials).

Norman, D. A. (1988), *The Design of Everyday Things*. New York: Doubleday.

Norman, D. A. (2004), *Emotional Design: Why We Love (or Hate) Everyday Things*. New York: Basic Books.

Norman, K. L. (2001), "Implementation of Conditional Branching in Computerized Self-Administered Questionnaires." Unpublished Report. College Park: University of Maryland, Institute for Advanced Computer Studies.

Norman, K. L., Friedman, Z., Norman, K., and Stevenson, R. (2001), "Navigational Issues in the Design of Online Self-Administered Questionnaires." *Behaviour and Information Technology*, 20 (1): 37–45.

Norman, K. L., and Pleskac, T. (2002), "Conditional Branching in Computerized Self-Administered Questionnaires: An Empirical Study." Unpublished Paper. College Park: University of Maryland, Institute for Advanced Computer Studies.

Novemsky, N., Dhar, R., Schwarz, N., and Simonson, I. (2007), "Preference Fluency in Choice." Journal of Marketing Research, 44 (3): 347–356

Nugent, G. C. (1992), "Pictures, Audio, and Print: Symbolic Representation and Effect on Learning." *Educational Communication and Technology Journal*, 30: 163–174.

Nyiri, Z., and Clark, R. L. (2003), "Web Survey Design: Comparing Static and Dynamic Survey Instruments." Paper presented at the annual conference of the American Association for Public Opinion Research, Nashville, TN, May.

Olsen, R. J. (1992), "The Effects of Computer-Assisted Interviewing on Data Quality." Working Papers of the European Scientific Network on Household Panel Studies, Paper 36. Colchester, England: University of Essex.

O'Muircheartaigh, C. A. (1997), "Measurement Error in Surveys: A Historical Perspective." In L. Lyberg, P. Biemer, M. Collins, E. de Leeuw, C. Dippo, N. Schwarz, and D. Trewin (eds.), Survey Measurement and Process Quality. New York: Wiley, pp. 1–25.

Pagendarm, M., and Schaumburg, H. (2001), "Why Are Users Banner-Blind? The Impact of Navigation Style on the Perception of Web Banners." Journal of Digital Information, 2 (1). http://journals.tdl.org/jodi/article/view/jodi-37/38.

Paivio, A. (1979), Imagery and Verbal Processes. Hillsdale, NJ: Lawrence Erlbaum.

Pearson, J., and Levine, R. A. (2003), "Salutations and Response Rates to Online Surveys." Paper presented at the Association for Survey Computing Fourth International Conference on the Impact of Technology on the Survey Process, Warwick, England, September.

Peytchev, A. (2005), "How Questionnaire Layout Induces Measurement Error." Paper presented at the annual meeting of the American Association for Public Opinion Research, Miami Beach, FL, May.

Peytchev, A. (2006), "Participation Decisions and Measurement Error in Web Surveys." Unpublished PhD Dissertation. Ann Arbor: University of Michigan.

Peytchev, A., Couper, M. P., McCabe, S. E., and Crawford, S. (2006), "Web Survey Design: Paging Versus Scrolling." Public Opinion Quarterly, 70 (4): 596–607.

Peytchev, A., and Crawford, S. (2005), "A Typology of Real-Time Validations in Web-Based Surveys." Social Science Computer Review, 23 (2): 235–249.

Piazza, T., and Sniderman, P. M. (1998), "Incorporating Experiments into Computer Assisted Surveys." In M. P. Couper, R. P. Baker, J. Bethlehem, C. Z. F. Clark, J. Martin, W. L. Nicholls II, and J. O'Reilly (eds.), Computer Assisted Survey Information Collection. New York: Wiley, pp. 167–184.

Pope, D., and Baker, R. P. (2005), "Experiments in Color for Web-Based Surveys." Paper presented at the FedCASIC Workshops, Washington, D.C., March.

Porter, S. R., and Whitcomb, M. E. (2003), "The Impact of Lottery Incentives on Student Survey Response Rates." Research in Higher Education, 44 (4): 389–407.

Porter, S. R., and Whitcomb, M. E. (2005), "E-Mail Subject Lines and Their Effect on Web Survey Viewing and Response." Social Science Computer Review, 23 (3): 380–387.

Poynter, R. (2001), "A Guide to Best Practice in Online Quantitative Research." In A. Westlake, W. Sykes, T. Manners, and M. Rigg (eds.), The Challenge of the Internet: Proceedings of the ASC International Conference on Survey Research Methods. London: Association for Survey Computing, pp. 3–19.

Presser, S., Rothgeb, J., Couper, M. P., Lessler, J., Martin, E. A., Martin, J., and Singer, E. (eds.) (2004), Methods for Testing and Evaluating Survey Questionnaires. New York: Wiley.

Prior, M. (2002), "More Than a Thousand Words? Visual Cues and Visual Knowledge." Paper presented at the annual meeting of the American Political Science Association, Boston, August.

Raghunathan, T. E., and Grizzle, J. E. (1995), "A Split Questionnaire Survey Design." Journal of the American Statistical Association, 90 (429): 54–63.

Ramirez, C., Sharp, K., and Foster, L. (2000), "Mode Effects in an Internet/Paper Survey of Employees." Paper presented at the annual conference of the American Association for Public Opinion Research, Portland, OR, May.

Rasinski, K. A., Mingay, D., and Bradburn, N. M. (1994), "Do Respondents Really 'Mark All That Apply' on Self-Administered Questions?" *Public Opinion Quarterly*, 58: 400–408.

Reber, R., and Schwarz, N. (1999), "Effects of Perceptual Fluency on Judgments of Truth." *Consciousness and Cognition*, 8: 338–342.

Redline, C. D., and Dillman, D. A. (2002), "The Influence of Alternative Visual Designs on Respondents' Performance with Branching Instructions in Self-Administered Question-naires." In R. M. Groves, D. A. Dillman, J. A. Eltinge, and R. J. A. Little (eds.), *Survey Nonresponse*. New York: Wiley, pp. 179–193.

Redline, C., Dillman, D. A., Dajani, A., and Scaggs, M. A. (2003), "Improving Navigational Performance in U.S. Census 2000 by Altering the Visually Administered Languages of Branching Instructions." *Journal of Official Statistics*, 19 (4): 403–419.

Redline, C. D., Dillman, D. A., Carley-Baxter, L., and Creecy, R. (2005), "Factors that Influence Reading and Comprehension of Branching Instructions in Self-Administered Ques-tionnaires." *Allgemeines Statistisches Archiv*, 89 (1); 29–38.

Reed, B. D., Crawford, S., Couper, M. P., Cave, C., and Haefner, H. K. (2004), "Pain at the Vulvar Vestibule – A Web-Survey." *Journal of Lower Genital Tract Disease*, 8 (1): 48–57.

Reips, U.-D. (2001), "The Web Experimental Psychology Lab: Five Years of Data Collection on the Internet." *Behavior Research Methods, Instruments, and Computers*, 33 (2): 201–211.

Reips, U.-D. (2002), "Internet-Based Psychological Experimenting; Five Dos and Five Don'ts." *Social Science Computer Review*, 20 (3): 241–249.

Reips, U.-D., and Funke, F. (in press), "Interval Level Measurement with Visual Analogue Scales in Internet Based Research: VAS Generator." *Behavior Research Methods*.

Reja, U., Lozar Manfreda, K., Hlebec, V., and Vehovar, V. (2002), "Open vs. Closed Questions in Web Surveys." Paper presented at the International Conference on Methodology and Statistics, Ljubljana, Slovenia, September.

Richman, W. L., Kiesler, S., Weisband, S., and Drasgow, F. (1999), "A Meta-Analytic Study of Social Desirability Distortion in Computer-Administered Questionnaires, Traditional Questionnaires, and Interviews." *Journal of Applied Psychology*, 84 (5): 754–775.

Rigden, C. (1999), "'The Eye of the Beholder' – Designing for Colour-Blind Users." *British Telecommunications Engineering*, 17: 2–6.

Rivers, D. (2000), "Fulfilling the Promise of the Web." *Quirk's Marketing Research Review*, February 2000. Online: article 0562. www.quirks.com.

Rivers, D. (2006), "Web Surveys for Health Measurement." Paper presented at Building Tomorrow's Patient-Reported Outcome Measures: The Inaugural PROMIS Conference, Gaithersburg, MD, September 11–13, 2006.

Robinson, J. P., Neustadtl, A., and Kestnbaum, M. (2002), "Why Public Opinion Polls are Inherently Biased: Public Opinion Differences among Internet Users and Non-Users." Paper presented at the annual meeting of the American Association for Public Opinion Research, St. Petersburg, FL, May.

Rossett, B. (2006), "The Basics of Section 508." Paper presented at the Federal Workshop on Computer Assisted Survey Information Collection (FedCASIC), Washington, DC, March.

Rowe, C. L. (1982), "The Connotative Dimensions of Selected Display Typefaces." *Information Design Journal*, 1: 30–37.

Schaefer, D. R., and Dillman, D. A. (1998), "Development of a Standard E-Mail Methodology: Results of an Experiment." *Public Opinion Quarterly*, 62 (3): 378–397.

Schafer, J. L., and Graham, J. W. (2002), "Missing Data: Our View of the State of the Art." *Psychological Methods*, 7 (2): 147–177.

Schneiderman, B. (1992), *Designing the Use Interface: Strategies for Effective Human-Computer Interaction, Second Edition*. Reading, MA: Addison-Wesley.

Schober, M. F., and Conrad, F. G. (eds.) (2007), *Envisioning Survey Interviews of the Future*. New York: Wiley.

Schober, M. F., Conrad, F. G., Ehlen, P., and Fricker, S. S. (2003), "How Web Surveys Differ from Other Kinds of User Interfaces." *Proceedings of the Joint Statistical Meetings of the American Statistical Association*. Alexandria: ASA, pp. 190–195 [CD].

Schonlau, M., Asch, B. J., and Du, C. (2003), "Web Surveys as Part of a Mixed-Mode Strategy for Populations That Cannot Be Contacted by E-Mail." *Social Science Computer Review*, 21 (2): 218–222.

Schonlau, M., Fricker, R. D., and Elliott, M. N. (2002), *Conducting Research Surveys via E-Mail and the Web*. Santa Monica, CA: RAND.

Schonlau, M., Zapert, K., Simon, L. P., Sanstad, K. H., Marcus, S. M., Adams, J., Spranca, M., Kan, H.-J., Turner, R., and Berry, S. H. (2004), "A Comparison between Responses from a Propensity-Weighted Web Survey and an Identical RDD Survey." *Social Science Computer Review*, 22 (1): 128–138.

Schriver, K. A. (1997), *Dynamics of Document Design*. New York: Wiley.

Schuman, H., and Presser, S. (1979), "The Open and Closed Question." *American Sociological Review*, 44: 692–712.

Schuman, H., and Presser, S. (1981), *Questions and Answers in Attitude Surveys*. New York: Academic Press.

Schwarz, N. (1996), *Cognition and Communication: Judgmental Biases, Research Methods and the Logic of Conversation*. Hillsdale, NJ: Lawrence Erlbaum.

Schwarz, N., Grayson, C. E., and Knäuper, B. (1998), "Formal Features of Rating Scales and the Interpretation of Question Meaning." *International Journal of Public Opinion Research*, 10 (2): 177–183.

Schwarz, N., Knäuper, B., Hippler, H.-J., Noelle-Neumann, E., and Clark, F. (1991), "Rating Scales: Numeric Values May Change the Meaning of Scale Labels." *Public Opinion Quarterly*, 55: 618–630.

Schwarz, N., and Sudman, S. (Eds.) (1992), *Context Effects in Social and Psychological Research*. New York: Springer-Verlag.

Schwarz, S., and Reips, U.-D. (2001), "CGI Versus JavaScript: A Web Experiment on the Reversed Hindsight Bias." In U.-D. Reips and M. Bosnjak (eds.), *Dimensions of Internet Science*. Lengerich, Germany: Pabst Science Publishers, pp. 75–90.

Sethuraman, R., Kerin, R. A., and Cron, W. L. (2005), "A Field Study Comparing Online and Offline Data Collection Methods for Identifying Product Attribute Preferences Using Conjoint Analysis." *Journal of Business Research*, 58: 602–610.

Sikkel, D. (1998), "The Individualized Interview." In M. P. Couper, R. P. Baker, J. Bethlehem, C. Z. F. Clark, J. Martin, W. L. Nicholls II, and J. O'Reilly (eds.), *Computer Assisted Survey Information Collection*. New York: Wiley, pp. 147–165.

Silverstein, C., Marais, H., Henzinger, M., and Moricz, M. (1999), "Analysis of a Very Large Web Search Engine Query Log." *SIGIR Forum*, 33 (1): 6–12.

Singer, E. (2002), "The Use of Incentives to Reduce Nonresponse in Household Surveys." In R. M. Groves, D. A. Dillman, J. L. Eltinge, and R. J. A. Little (eds), *Survey Nonresponse*. New York: Wiley, pp. 163–177.

Singer, E., Couper, M. P., Conrad, F. G., and Groves, R. M. (in press), "Risk of Disclosure, Perceptions of Risk, and Concerns about Privacy and Confidentiality as Factors in Survey Participation." *Journal of Official Statistics*.

Sinibaldi, J., Crawford, S. D., Saltz, R., and Showen, S. (2006), "Using Interactive Web-Based Maps to Collect Geographical Data in a Student Survey." Paper presented at the annual meeting of the American Association for Public Opinion Research, Montreal, Canada, May.

Smith, R. M., and Kiniorski, K. (2003), "Participation in Online Surveys: Results from a Series of Experiments." Paper presented at the annual meeting of the American Association for Public Opinion Research, Nashville, TN, May.

Smith, S. M., Smith, J., and Allred, C. R. (2006), "Advanced Techniques and Technologies in Online Research." In R. Grover and M. Vriens (eds.), *The Handbook of Marketing Research*. Thousand Oaks, CA: Sage, pp. 132–158.

Smyth, J. D., Dillman, D. A., Christian, L. M., and Stern, M. J. (2004), "How Visual Grouping Influences Answers to Internet Surveys." Paper presented at the annual meeting of the American Association for Public Opinion Research, Nashville, May.

Smyth, J. D., Dillman, D. A., Christian, L. M., and Stern, M. J. (2005), "Comparing Check-All and Forced-Choice Question Formats in Web Surveys: The Role of Satisficing, Depth of Processing, and Acquiescence in Explaining Differences." Paper presented at the annual meeting of the American Association for Public Opinion Research, Miami Beach, FL, May.

Sperry, S., Edwards, B., Dulaney, R., and Potter, D. E. B. (1998), "Evaluating Interviewer Use of CAPI Navigation Features." In M. P. Couper, R. P. Baker, J. Bethlehem, C. Z. F. Clark, J. Martin, W. L. Nicholls II, and J. O'Reilly (eds.), *Computer Assisted Survey Information Collection*. New York: Wiley, pp. 351–365.

Stanley, N., and Jenkins, S. (2007), "Watch What I Do! Using Graphic Input Controls in Web Surveys." In M. Trotman et al. (eds.), *The Challenges of a Changing World; Proceedings of the Fifth International Conference of the Association for Survey Computing*. Berkeley, England: ASC, pp.81–92.

Staples, L. (2000), "Typography and the Screen: A Technical Chronology of Digital Typography, 1984–1997." *Design Issues*, 16 (3): 19–34.

Statistics Netherlands (1996), *Blaise Developer's Guide (Blaise III)*. Heerlen, The Netherlands: Statistics Netherlands, Department of Statistical Informatics.

Statistics Netherlands (2002), *Blaise 4.5 Developer's Guide*. Heerlen, The Netherlands: Statistics Netherlands, Methods and Informatics Department.

Stenbjerre, M., and Laugesen, J. N. (2005), "Conducting Representative Online Research." *Proceedings of ESOMAR Conference on Worldwide Panel Research; Developments and Progress*, Budapest, Hungary. Amsterdam: ESOMAR, pp. 369–391 [CD].

Sudman, S., and Bradburn, N. M. (1982), *Asking Questions: A Practical Guide to Questionnaire Design*. San Francisco: Jossey-Bass.

Szabó, Z. G. (2006), "The Distinction between Semantics and Pragmatics." In E. Lepore and B. Smith (eds.), *The Oxford Handbook of Philosophy and Language*. Oxford: Oxford University Press.

Tarnai, J., and Allen, T. (2002), "Characteristics of Respondents to a Web Survey of the General Public." Paper resented at the annual meeting of the American Association for Public Opinion Research, St. Petersburg Beach, FL, May.

Terhanian, G. (2000), "How To Produce Credible, Trustworthy Information through Internet-Based Survey Research." Paper presented at the annual conference of the American Association for Public Opinion Research, Portland, OR, May.

Thomas, R. K., Bayer, L. R., Johnson, A., and Behnke, S. (2005), "A Comparison of an Online Card Sorting Task to a Rating Task." Paper presented at the annual meeting of the American Association for Public Opinion Research, Miami Beach, FL, May.

Thomas, R. K., and Couper, M. P. (2007), "A Comparison of Visual Analog and Graphic Rating Scales." Paper presented at the General Online Research Conference (GOR'07), Leipzig, March.

Thomas, R. K., Lafond, R. C., and Behnke, S. (2003), "Can What We Don't' Know (About "Don't Know") Hurt Us? Effects of Item Non-Response." Paper presented at the annual conference of the American Association for Public Opinion Research, Nashville, May.

Toepoel, V., Das, M., and van Soest, A. (2005), "Design of Web Questionnaires: A Test for Number of Items per Screen." Tilburg University: CentERdata Discussion Paper No. 2005-114.

Toepoel, V., Das, M., and van Soest, A. (2006), "Design of Web Questionnaires: The Effect of Layout in Rating Scales." Tilburg University: CentERdata Discussion Paper No. 2006-30.

Tourangeau, R., Couper, M. P., and Conrad, F. G. (2004), "Spacing, Position, and Order: Interpretive Heuristics for Visual Features of Survey Questions." *Public Opinion Quarterly*, 68 (3): 368–393.

Tourangeau, R., Couper, M. P., and Conrad, F. G. (2007), "Color, Labels, and Interpretive Heuristics for Response Scales." *Public Opinion Quarterly*, 71 (1): 91–112.

Tourangeau, R., Couper, M. P., Galesic, M., and Givens, J. (2004), "A Comparison of Two Web-Based Surveys: Static vs Dynamic Versions of the NAMCS Questionnaire." Paper presented at the RC33 International Conference on Social Science Methodology, Amsterdam, August.

Tourangeau, R., Couper, M. P., and Steiger, D. M. (2003), "Humanizing Self-Administered Surveys: Experiments on Social Presence in Web and IVR Surveys." *Computers in Human Behavior*, 19: 1–24.

Tourangeau, R., Rips, L., and Rasinski, K. (2000), *The Psychology of Survey Response*. Cambridge, England: Cambridge University Press.

Tourangeau, R., and Smith, T. W. (1996), "Asking Sensitive Questions: The Impact of Data Collection Mode, Question Format, and Questions Context." *Public Opinion Quarterly*, 60 (2): 275–304.

Trollip, S., and Sales, G. (1986), "Readability of Computer-Generated Fill-Justified Text." *Human Factors*, 28: 159–164.

Trouteaud, A. R. (2004), "How You Ask Counts: A Test of Internet-Related Components of Response Rates to a Web-Based Survey." *Social Science Computer Review*, 22 (3): 385–392.

Tufte, E. R. (1990), *Envisioning Information*. Cheshire, CT: Graphics Press.

Tufte, E. R. (2001), *The Visual Display of Quantitative Information* (2nd ed.). Cheshire, CT: Graphics Press.

Tullis, T. S. (1983), "The Formatting of Alphanumeric Displays: A Review and Analysis." *Human Factors*, 25 (6): 657–682.

Tullis, T. S. (1988), "A System for Evaluating Screen Formats: Research and Application." In H. R. Hartson and D. Hix (eds.), *Advances in Human-Computer Interaction* (Vol. 2). Norwood: Ablex, pp. 214–286.

Turner, C. F., Forsyth, B. H., O'Reilly, J. M., Cooley, P. C., Smith, T. K., Rogers, S. M., and Miller, H. G. (1998), "Automated Self-Interviewing and the Survey Measurement of Sensitive Behaviors." In M. P. Couper, R. P. Baker, J. Bethlehem, C. Z. F. Clark, J. Martin, W. L. Nicholls II, and J. O'Reilly (eds.), *Computer Assisted Survey Information Collection*. New York: Wiley, pp. 455–473.

Tuten, T. L. (2005), "Do Reminders Encourage Response but Affect Response Behaviors? Reminders in Web-Based Surveys." Paper presented at the ESF Workshop on Internet Survey Methodology, Dubrovnik, Croatia, September.

Tuten, T. L., Galesic, M., and Bosnjak, M. (2004), "Effects of Immediate Versus Delayed Notification of Prize Draw Results on Response Behavior in Web Surveys." *Social Science Computer Review*, 22 (3): 377–384.

U.S. Department of Health and Human Services (HHS) (2006), *Research-Based Web Design & Usability Guidelines*. Washington, D.C.: Government Printing Office.

Valdez, P., and Mehrabian, A. (1994), "Effect of Color on Emotions." *Journal of Experimental Psychology: General*, 123 (4): 394–409.

Van Der Horst, W., Snijders, C., and Matzat, U. (2006), "The Effect of Progress Indicators in Online Survey Compliance." Paper presented at the General Online Research Conference (GOR '06), Bielefeld, Germany, March.

Van der Linden, W. J., and Glas, C. A. W. (eds.) (2000), *Computerized Adaptive Testing: Theory and Practice*. Boston: Kluwer Academic.

Van der Molen, W. J. H. (2001), "Assessing Text-Picture Correspondence in Television News: The Development of a New Coding Scheme." *Journal of Broadcasting and Electronic Media*, 43 (3): 483–498.

Van Heesen, B. (2005), "Online Access Panels and Effects on Response Rates with Different Types of Incentives." *Proceedings of ESOMAR Conference on Worldwide Panel Research; Developments and Progress*, Budapest, Hungary. Amsterdam: ESOMAR, pp. 393–408 [CD].

Vartabedian, A. G. (1971), "The Effect of Letter Size, Case and Generation Method on CRT Display Search Time." *Human Factors*, 13 (4): 363–368.

Vehovar, V., Lozar Manfreda, K., and Batagelj, Z. (1999), "Design Issues in WWW Surveys." Paper presented at the annual meeting of the American Association for Public Opinion Research, Portland, OR, May.

Vehovar, V., Batagelj, Z., Lozar Manfreda, K., and Zaletel, M. (2002), "Nonresponse in Web Surveys." In R. M. Groves, D. A. Dillman, J. L. Eltinge, and R. J. A. Little (eds.), Survey Nonresponse. New York: Wiley, pp. 229–242.

Vehovar, V., Manfreda, K. L., and Batagelj, Z. (2000), "Design Issues in Web Surveys." Proceedings of the Survey Research Methods Section of the American Statistical Association, pp. 983–988.

Von Ahn, L., Blum, M., and Langford, J. (2004), "Telling Humans and Computers Apart Automatically." *Communications of the ACM*, 47 (2): 57–60.

Vriens, M., Loosschilder, G. H., Rosbergen, E., and Wittink, D. R. (1998), "Verbal versus Realistic Pictorial Representations in Conjoint Analysis with Design Attributes." *Journal of Product Innovation Management*, 15 (5): 455–467.

Wainer, H., Dorans, N. J., Flaugher, R., Green, B. F., Mislevy, R. J., Steinberg, L., and Thissen, D. (2000), *Computerized Adaptive Testing; A Primer* (2nd ed.). Mahwah: Lawrence Erlbaum.

Ware, C. (2000), *Information Visualization: Perception for Design*. San Francisco: Morgan Kaufman.

Weinman, L. (1996), *Designing Web Graphics*. Berkeley, CA: New Riders.

Weller, L., and Livingston, R. (1988), "Effects of Color of Questionnaire on Emotional Responses." *Journal of General Psychology*, 115 (4): 433–440.

Wertheimer, M. (1938a), "Gestalt Theory." In W. D. Ellis (ed.), *A Source Book of Gestalt Psychology*. New York: Humanities Press, pp. 1–11.

Wertheimer, M. (1938b), "Laws of Organization in Perceptual Forms." In W. D. Ellis (ed.), *A Source Book of Gestalt Psychology*. New York: Humanities Press, pp. 71–88.

Wertheimer, M. (1958), *Principles of Perceptual Organization*. New York: Van Nostrand.

Wherrett, J. R. (1999), "Issues in Using the Internet as a Medium for Landscape Preference Research." *Landscape and Urban Planning*, 45: 209–217.

Wherrett, J. R. (2000), "Creating Landscape Preference Models Using Internet Survey Techniques." *Landscape Research*, 25 (1): 79–96.

White, J. V. (1990), *Color for the Electronic Age*. New York: Watson-Guptill Publications.

Williams, J. R. (1988), "The Effects of Case and Spacing on Menu Option Search Time." *Proceedings of the Human Factors Society 32nd Annual Meeting*, pp. 341–343.

Witte, J. C., Amoroso, L. M., and Howard, P. E. N. (2000), "Method and Representation in Internet-Based Survey Tools – Mobility, Community, and Cultural Identity in Survey2000." *Social Science Computer Review*, 18 (2): 179–195.

Witte, J. C., Pargas, R. P., Mobley, C., and Hawdon, J. (2004), "Instrument Effects of Images in Web Surveys: A Research Note." *Social Science Computer Review*, 22 (3): 363–369.

Wojtowicz, T. (2001), "Designing Lengthy Internet Questionnaires: Suggestions and Solutions." In A. Westlake, W. Sykes, T. Manners, and M. Rigg (eds.), *The Challenge of the Internet; Proceedings of the ASC International Conference on Survey Research Methods*. London: Association for Survey Computing, pp. 25–32.

Yan, T. (2005a), "What They See Is Not What We Intend – Gricean Effects in Web Surveys." Paper presented at the annual meeting of the American Association for Public Opinion Research, Miami Beach, FL, May.

Yan, T. (2005b), *Gricean Effects in Self-Administered Surveys*. Unpublished Doctoral Dissertation. College Park: University of Maryland.

Yan, T., Conrad, F. G., Tourangeau, R., and Couper, M. P. (2007), "Should I Stay or Should I Go? The Effects of Progress Indicators, Promised Duration, and Questionnaire Length on Completing Web Surveys." Paper presented at the annual meeting of the American Association for Public Opinion Research, Anaheim, CA, May.

Yan, T., and Tourangeau, R. (2008), "Fast Times and Easy Questions: The Effects of Age, Experience and Question Complexity on Web Survey Response Times." *Applied Cognitive Psychology*, 22 (1): 51–68.

Yost, P. R., and Homer, L. E. (1998), "Electronic Versus Paper Surveys: Does the Medium Affect the Response?" Paper presented at the annual meeting of the Society for Industrial/Organizational Psychology, Dallas, TX, April.

Zetie, C. (1995), *Practical User Interface Design: Making GUIs Work*. New York: McGraw-Hill.

Author Index

Subject Index